Oral-Scribal Dimensions of Scripture, Piety, and Practice

Oral-Scribal Dimensions of Scripture, Piety, and Practice

Judaism, Christianity, Islam

EDITED BY

Werner H. Kelber and Paula A. Sanders

CASCADE *Books* • Eugene, Oregon

ORAL-SCRIBAL DIMENSIONS OF SCRIPTURE, PIETY, AND PRACTICE
Judaism, Christianity, Islam

Cascade Books
An Imprint of Wipf and Stock Publishers
199 W. 8th Ave., Suite 3
Eugene, OR 97401

www.wipfandstock.com

ISBN 13: 978-1-4982-3669-0

Cataloging-in-Publication data:

Names: Kelber, Werner H. | Sanders, Paula.

Title: Oral-scribal dimensions of scripture, piety, and practice : Judaism, Christianity, Islam / edited by Werner H. Kelber and Paula A. Sanders.

Description: Eugene, OR: Cascade Books. | Includes bibliographical references and indexes.

Identifiers: ISBN 13: 978-1-4982-3669-0 (paperback). | ISBN 13: 978-1-4982-3671-3 (hardcover). | ISBN 13: 978-1-4982-3670-6 (ebook).

Subjects: LCSH: Judaism. | Christiantiy. | Isalm. | Oral tradition—Congresses. | Oral tradition—Mediterranean Region—History. | Written communication—Mediterranean Region—History.

Classification: BL221 O85 2016 (PRINT). | BL221 (ebook).

Manufactured in the U.S.A.

In Memory of

John Miles Foley

(1947–2012)

One of the Foremost Experts
in Oral Comparative Traditions

Contents

List of Contributors | *ix*

Preface | Werner H. Kelber | *xiii*

Acknowledgments | *xxvii*

1. Ancient and Modern Democracies: Orality, Texts, and Electronic Media | *John Miles Foley* | 1

2. Torah on the Heart: Literary Jewish Textuality within Its Ancient Near Eastern Context | *David Carr* | 21

3. Guarding Oral Transmission: Within and between Cultures | *Talya Fishman* | 49

4. The Interplay between Written and Spoken Word in the Second Testament as Background to the Emergence of Written Gospels | *Holly E. Hearon* | 67

5. Oral and Written Communication and Transmission of Knowledge in Ancient Judaism and Christianity | *Catherine Hezser* | 89

6. Oral and Written Aspects of the Emergence of the Gospel of Mark as Scripture | *Richard A. Horsley* | 110

7. The History of the Closure of Biblical Texts | *Werner H. Kelber* | 137

8. Two Faces of the Qur'an: Qur'ān and Muṣḥaf | *Angelika Neuwirth* | 170

9. Biblical Performance Criticism: Performance as Research | *David Rhoads* | 188

10. The Constitution of the Qur'an as a Codified Work: Paradigm for Codifying Hadith and the Islamic Sciences? | *Gregor Schoeler* | 240

11. From *Jāhiliyyah* to *Badīʿiyyah*: Orality, Literacy, and the Transformations of Rhetoric in Arabic Poetry | *Suzanne Pinckney Stetkevych* | 255

12. Response from an Africanist Scholar | *Ruth Finnegan* | 280

13. Summation | *William A. Graham* | 292

Scripture Index | 303

Subject Index | 310

Contributors

David M. Carr is Professor of Old Testament/Hebrew Bible at Union Theological Seminary in New York. Among his publications on textuality, orality, and literacy is *Writing on the Tablet of the Heart: Origins of Scripture and Literature* (2005). He recently published a work on trauma, memory, and the Bible titled *Holy Resilience: The Bible's Traumatic Origins* (2014).

Ruth Finnegan is Professor Emerita at the Open University. A social anthropologist and Africanist, her books include *Oral Literature in Africa* (1970/2012), *Modes of Thought* (joint ed., 1973), *Oral Poetry* (1977/1992), *Literacy and Orality* (1988), *The Hidden Musicians* (1989/2007), *Oral Traditions and the Verbal Arts* (1992), *South Pacific Oral Traditions* (joint ed., 1995), Communicating (2002/2013), *The Oral and Beyond: Doing Things with Words in Africa* (2007), *Entrancement, Integrating Consciousness in Dreams, Death and Music* (ed., 2016) and (forthcoming) *Shared Minds: Living in Dream, Experience, and Knowledge*. Her first novel, *The Black-Inked Pearl*, will be published in summer 2015.

Talya Fishman is Associate Professor of Medieval Middle Eastern Religion, Department of Near Eastern Languages and Civilizations, and Director of the Jewish Studies Program at the University of Pennsylvania. She has held Guggenheim, American Council of Learned Societies, and National Endowment for the Humanities fellowships. Among her publications are *Shaking the Pillars of Exile: "Voice of a Fool"'s Early Modern Jewish Critique of Rabbinic Culture* (1997) and *Becoming the People of the Talmud: Oral Torah as Written Tradition in Medieval Jewish Cultures* (2011), which won the Nahum M. Sarna Award for Scholarship of the Jewish Book Council in 2012.

John Miles Foley was the Curator's Professor of Classical Studies and English, and the W. H. Byler Distinguished Chair in the Humanities, University of Missouri. He was the founder of the journal of *Oral Tradition* (1968), founding director of the the *Center for Studies in Oral Tradition* (1986), and founding editor of the *Center for eResearch* (2005). His publications include *Traditional Oral Epic: The Odyssey, Beowulf, and the Serbo-Croatian Epics* (1990), *Immanent Art: From Structure to Meaning in Traditional Oral Epic* (1991), *How to Read an Oral Poem* (2002), and *Oral Tradition and the Internet: Pathways of the Mind* (2012). He served as the editor of *Festschriften* in honor of Albert Lord (*Oral Traditional Literature*, 1981) and in memory of Milman Parry (*Comparative Research on Oral Traditions*, 1987).

William A. Graham is Albertson Professor of Middle Eastern Studies, Faculty of Arts and Sciences, and University Distinguished Service Professor, Harvard University. He has held Guggenheim and von Humboldt fellowships and is a Fellow of the American Academy of Arts and Sciences. Among his writings are *Divine Word and Prophetic Word in Early Islam* (1977, ACLS History of Religions Prize), *Beyond the Written Word: Oral Aspects of Scripture in the History of Religion* (1987), and *Islamic and Comparative Religious Studies* (2010).

Holly E. Hearon is the T. J. and Virginia Liggett Professor of Christian Traditions Emerita at Christian Theological Seminary. She has published numerous articles on the written and spoken word in the first-century CE Mediterranean world. She is the author of *The Mary Magdalene Tradition: Witness and Counter-witness in Early Christian Communities* (2004), the co-editor of *The Bible and Ancient and Modern Media: Story and Performance* (2009), and a series editor of Biblical Performance Criticism Series.

Catherine Hezser is Professor of Jewish Studies at the School of Oriental and African Studies (SOAS) of the University of London. Having received doctoral degrees in both Biblical Studies (University of Heidelberg, Germany), and Jewish Studies (Jewish Theological Seminary, New York), she has held academic posts at the Free University Berlin, The Hebrew University Jerusalem, and Trinity College, Dublin. Hezser's particular research interests are rabbinic literature, the social history and daily life of Jews in Roman Palestine, literacy and orality, and non-verbal communication. Her publications include *The Social Structure of the Rabbinic Movement in Roman Palestine* (1997), *Jewish Literacy in Roman Palestine* (2001), and *Jewish Travel in Antiquity* (2011).

Richard A. Horsley, Distinguished Professor of Liberal Arts and the Study of Religion at the University of Massachusetts, Boston, is the author of many books, including *"Whoever Hears You Hears Me": Prophets, Performance, and Tradition in Q* (with Jonathan Draper, 1999), *Hearing the Whole Story: The Politics of Plot in Mark's Gospel* (2001), *Jesus in Context: Power, People, Performance* (2008), *Text and Tradition in Performance and Writing* (2013), and edited many others, including *Christian Origins* (A People's History of Christianity, 2010).

Werner H. Kelber is the Isla Carroll and Percy E. Turner Professor Emeritus of Biblical Studies at Rice University. His work has focused on gospel narrativity, oral tradition, biblical hermeneutics, the historical Jesus, media studies, memory, rhetoric, text criticism,and the history of biblical scholarship. Among his publications are *The Oral and the Written Gospel: The Hermeneutics of Speaking and Writing in the Synoptic Tradition, Mark, Paul, and Q* (1983; 1997), and *Imprints, Voiceprints, and Footprints of Memory* (2013).

Angelika Neuwirth is Professor of Arabic Studies at the Freie Universität Berlin. She studied Persian and Arabic languages and literature at the Universities of Teheran, Göttingen, Jerusalem, and Munich, and served as guest professor at the University of Jordan (1977–83). Since 1991 she has been Chair of Arabic studies at Berlin, and from 1994–2000 she was Director of the German Orient Institute in Beirut and Istanbul. Presently she is Director of the *Corpus Coranicum*, a research program dedicated to the historical-critical study of the Qu'ran. Among her numerous publications is *Der Koran als Text der Spätantike: Ein Europäischer Zugang* (2010). She is Honorary Member of the *American Academy of Arts and Sciences* (2011), and recipient of the *Sigmund-Freud-Preis for Scientific Prose* (2013).

David Rhoads is Emeritus Professor of New Testament at the Lutheran School of Theology, Chicago. He is the author of *Mark as Story: An Introduction to the Narrative of a Gospel* (with Joanna Dewey and Donald Michie, 3rd ed., 2012), *Reading Mark, Engaging the Gospel* (2004), and editor of *From Every People and Nation: The Book of Revelation in Intercultural Context* (2005). He also published "Performance Criticism: An Emerging Discipline in Second Testament Studies" (Parts One and Two), *Biblical Theology Bulletin* (2006), along with other articles on performance criticism. He performs several New Testament writings, co-hosts *www.biblicalperformaancecriticism.org*, and serves as series editor of the Biblical Performance Criticism Series (Cascade Books).

Paula A. Sanders is Professor of History and Vice Provost for Academic Affairs at Rice University, where she teaches courses in the medieval Mediterranean, pre-modern Islamic world, and the history of Jewish communities in the lands of Islam. Her areas of research are medieval Islam and Egyptian history, with a focus on Ismaili Shiism and the history of Cairo. Her publications include *Ritual, Politics, and the City in Fatimid Cairo* (1994, *Choice* Outstanding Academic Book Award) and *Creating Medieval Cairo: Empire, Religion, and Architectural Preservation in Nineteenth Century Egypt* (2008).

Gregor Schoeler has been the chair of Islamic Studies at the University of Basel, Switzerland, from 1982 to 2009. In 2000 he lectured at the École Pratique des Hautes Études at the Sorbonne in Paris, and in 2010 he delivered a series of lectures at Cornell University. He has collaborated on both the Abū Nuwas project (edition of the 4th vol. of *Diwan*) and the Cataloging of Oriental Manuscripts in Germany. His recent publications include *The Oral and the Written in Early Islam* (2006), *The Genesis of Literature in Islam: From the Aural to the Written* (2009), and the edition and translation of Abu-l-ʿAlāʾ al-Maʿārri's *The Epistle of Forgiveness* with G. J. van Gelder (2 vols., 2013–14).

Suzanne Pinckney Stetkevych is Sultan Qaboos bin Said Professor of Arabic & Islamic Studies at Georgetown University and Ruth N. Halls Emerita Professor of Near Eastern Languages and Cultures at Indiana University. A specialist in ritual, myth, and performance in classical Arabic poetry, her books include *The Mute Immortals Speak: Pre-Islamic Poetry and the Poetics of Ritual* (1993), *The Poetics of Islamic Legitimacy: Myth, Gender, and Ceremony in the Classical Arabic Ode* (2002), and *The Mantle of Odes: Arabic Praise Poems to the Prophet Muhammad* (2010).

Preface

Werner H. Kelber

ORALITY-SCRIBALITY IN THE CONTEXT OF SCHOLARSHIP

THE STUDY OF RELIGIONS is no stranger to the oral factor in Scripture, piety, and practice of the three monotheistic faiths. There has been a recognition, especially in Scandinavian scholarship,[1] that the composition of many texts of the Hebrew Bible was variously informed by oral dynamics, and that long after their textual solidification the principal means of transmission continued to be oral. As for the New Testament, an early period of active oral processing of the Jesus tradition, massive oral footprints in the gospels, and the intensely rhetorical nature of the Pauline epistles are by now well-recognized features. In Second Temple Judaism, the oral-rhetorical quality of the rabbinic tradition and its identification with Oral Torah have been standard issues in the scholarly discussion. It is likewise well known that from the earliest existence of the Qur'an its vocal character was a subject central to the Muslim perception of Scripture. In a general sense, those are all accepted data in the study of the three monotheistic religions.

In spite of this general knowledge of oral tradition, there has been an observable emphasis in the academic study of Judaism, Christianity, and Islam to reduce their concept of Scripture to a narrowly conceived textual authority. Two discernible factors have contributed to this limited, text-centric perspective. There was firstly the obvious fact that sacred Scripture in the three faiths acquired canonical status. The written medium was thereby empowered and the textual identity of Scriptures privileged to a

1. Nyberg, *Hoseabuch*; Engnell, *Isaiah*; Ringgren, "Transmission"; Nielsen, *Oral Tradition*.

degree entirely unprecedented in the Greco-Roman and Hellenistic culture of antiquity and late antiquity. There is secondly the fact that the religiously grounded textual identity of the three faiths was reinforced through what Ruth Finnegan in her summarizing piece aptly refers to as "the pervading influence of philological textual models in the study of the monotheistic religions." Western scholarship has pursued and processed the study of religions (as most other humanistic issues) via the two dominant media of chirography and typography. Mindful of the impact of communications technology on epistemology, it stands to reason that the organizing principles, formatting techniques, editorial processes, and cognitive conventions associated with the two media shaped and reinforced a distinctly textual identity of religions. While the modern history of the study of religions has increasingly proved open-minded in taking account of cultural complexities and entering into constructive conversation with sociology, psychology, history, literary criticism, and so forth, the unmistakable tendency was to define the scholarly objective, in the words of Wikipedia, as the study of "the written record of human religious experiences and ideas." The oral factor was thereby at best relegated to the status of an epiphenomenon, acknowledged yet considered secondary to the texts, while the print versions of the sacred texts were taken to be the most important and nearly sufficient mode of representation and interpretation. It is, therefore, entirely consequential that the modern history of the academic study of religions wound up with an understanding of the three monotheistic faiths as quintessential religions of the book.

In the modern era a number of individuals, academic developments, and a technical revolution converged in raising the issue of media and communication in a novel and unprecedented way. There was first the academic conceptualization of oral style, composition, and structure of thought which is associated with the French scholar Marcel Jousse (1886–1961) and the North American classicist Milman Parry (1902–1935). Jousse's publication of *Le Style oral rhythmique et mnémotechnique chez les Verbo-moteurs* launched his career and earned him a number of prestigious academic positions in Paris.[2] Enjoying immense popularity for a quarter of a century in French academia, he delivered over 1,000 lectures, mostly without the assistance of a script, at the Sorbonne, the École des Hautes Études, and the École d'Anthropologie. Today we are inclined to dismiss Jousse as architect of the *Great Divide*, a concept that has fallen into disrepute for driving too crude and unrealistic a distinction between oral and written. But within the larger context of humanistic scholarship, Jousse's work assumes a

2. Jousse, "Le Style Orale."

noteworthy position. Irrespective of the correctness of all his premises, the conceptualization of a comprehensive *Oral Theory* marked a groundbreaking innovation in Western intellectual history. His *ethnography of speaking* took serious account of roughly ninety-five percent of human communication and reawakened sensibilities long eclipsed by a dominantly textual and philological intellectualism.

The academic standing of Milman Parry, the second founding figure of what came to be the modern discipline of *Oral Tradition*, is closely associated with his advancement of the *Oral-Formulaic Hypothesis*, his celebrated litmus test of Homeric orality.[3] Combining the fruits of an exacting philological analysis of the Iliad and the Odyssey with extensive fieldwork in the Western Balkans, Parry concluded that close to ninety percent of Homeric language was constructed on a formulaic diction of the kind he had identified in his fieldwork. The contemporary South Slavic *guslari*, he concluded, had practiced a technology of word processing that must have been similar to the ancient Homeric bards: both employed pre-formulated elements handed down by predecessors, while exercising a degree of freedom in shaping the received tradition into their respective performances. In short, both the ancient Homeric epics and those performed in remote areas of the former Yugoslavia were not merely traditional, but specifically oral. They had both been constructed under the pressures of oral performances. The challenge Parry posed was enormous. In effect, he confronted Western cultural self-consciousness to come to terms with the two monumental Homeric epics not as the first in a long and impressive line of "great books" but as the fossilized remnants of a once living performance tradition.

Alongside the founding figures of Jousse and Parry, Albert Lord (1912–1991) ranks as co-founder of the modern discipline of *Oral Tradition*. In his classic study of *The Singer of Tales* (1960) and a follow-up volume, *Epic Singers and Oral Tradition* (1991),[4] he expanded both Parry's concept of formula and the cultural range of oral, traditional literature. Soon the *Oral-Formulaic Hypothesis* came to be designated as the *Parry-Lord Thesis*. While the Parry-Lord Thesis met with little success in classical philology, it was to inaugurate what Foley has described as "one of the most far-reaching research programs in the humanities over the last century."[5] Over time, scholarship inspired by Parry-Lord affected over one hundred language areas, extending from Sumerian to ancient Greek, and Old English

3. Parry, "Studies in the Epic Technique: I"; and Parry, "Studies in the Epic Technique: II."

4. Lord, *Singer of Tales*; Lord, *Epic Singers*.

5. Foley, *How to Read*, 109–10.

to medieval Spanish, including languages from the Indian subcontinent and the South Pacific, and from the Americas as well as Africa. Perhaps most importantly, the sheer volume of new data and insights encouraged a growing realization of "a wholesale shift in perception and awareness"[6] that was different from the conventional apprehension of literacy as the medium through which all human communication was processed and interpreted.

A second development which brought oral traditions and their textualization to the foreground of media and communication were the three overlapping disciplines of ethnopoetics, folkloristics, and a branch of anthropology. They converged in creating an intellectual climate that was favorably disposed toward orality studies. Over the past fifty years the work of Dennis Tedlock, Dell Hymes, and Jerome Rothenberg among others was instrumental in founding the discipline of ethnopoetics (and its subdiscipline of the ethnography of speaking). Along with folkloristics, the new field of knowledge concerned itself with the recording and examining of indigenous traditions in their authentic social contexts. As a result of their studies, numerous syntactical structures, poetic patterns, and aesthetic qualities of a vast amount of ethnopoetic, folkloric materials came to be identified as performance features which required special appreciation and treatment. Keenly attuned both to the oral quality of the materials and to the typographic medium employed in scholarly representations, ethnopoetics endeavored to come to grips with the problem of media transposition: how to capture the manifestly oral poetics on the uniformly linearized, meticulously formatted, and voiceless page of the printed editions.

In the discipline of anthropology it was Africanists who made the most significant contributions to our understanding of *Oral Tradition*. Among them the work of Jan Vansina and Ruth Finnegan stands out as being of seminal importance. Drawing on fieldwork in the Central African countries of the Congo, Rwanda, and Burundi, Vansina's *Oral Tradition: A Study in Historical Methodology* (1965; French original 1961) designed a comprehensive theory of speaking culture.[7] Not since Jousse's *Le Style oral et mnémotechnique* had there been a study of similar empirical concreteness and theoretical sophistication. Vansina's achievement is all the more noteworthy since it was written at a time when Western historiography was ill-equipped to deal with the history of a people who predominantly communicated via unwritten traditions, and which regarded African verbal art frequently as "primitive literature." It was the author's express aim to explore whether, and to what extent, the unwritten traditions, which heavily relied

6. Foley, "Reading the Oral Traditional Text," 189.

7. Vansina, *Oral Tradition.*

on memory, were dependable sources for the reconstruction of a people's history. The issue, as Vansina saw it, was, therefore, to test the reliability of *Oral Tradition* so as to make it safe for history. It is worth noting that by no means all Africanists share Vansina's position. Many do not aim at the recovery of *Oral Tradition*, purified from historical errors, as an aid in the work of historiography, but regard the unqualified integrity of *Oral Tradition* itself as an essential component of a people's history (Jeff Opland, Liz Gunner, Annekie Joubert, and numerous others).

With Finnegan's *Oral Literature in Africa* (1970) and *Oral Poetry* (1977/1992), two classics in oral scholarship, a new level of global outreach and comparative perspective was achieved.[8] An Africanist by training, her work covers an unprecedented and dazzling array of traditions, genres, and topics from across the world, ranging from Tibet to Oceanea, and from the Fiji islands to Uzbekistan, including praise songs and Muslim poetry, chanted sermons and Texas prison tunes, and treating love, heroic deeds, mourning, political elections, and many more. Increasingly, her approach challenged *Oral Tradition's* assumed purity, untrammelled by scribal interference. Growing skeptical of the *Great Divide,* she made the interfacing of oral and written a principal theme of her scholarship. More than that, she distanced herself from a purely linguistic conceptualization of *Oral Tradition*, and sought to capture its intrinsic multisensory and paralinguistic features. Many of these concerns are addressed in Finnegan's summarizing piece. On the whole, her work exhibits a trajectory from the linguistic turn to intermediality and on to the multi-sensory qualities of oral performance.

There was a third feature which specifically affected scholarly sensibilities in the study of world religions: the work of William Graham, the author of *Beyond the Written Word: Oral Aspects of Scripture in the History of Religion* (1987),[9] who has summarized the proceedings of the Rice Conference. The book appeared like an arbitrary intrusion into the established, heavily text-oriented scholarship of world religions. Although written some thirty years ago, it has lost nothing of its significance. In fact, it is only in the present scholarly environment that its intellectual incisiveness and relevance are becoming more fully apparent. Graham's principal objective was the study of Sacred Scripture in the major religious traditions, and in the popular and academic practices of Western modernity. While highlighting the function of the Qur'an in Muslim society, he also examined the archaic Vedic corpus and sacred Scripture in Hinduism, Judaism, Buddhism, Christianity, and other religions. *Beyond the Written Word* is an exceptionally

8. Finnegan, *Oral Literature*; Finnegan, *Oral Poetry.*

9. Graham, *Beyond the Written Word.*

rewarding example of comparative studies which yields a deeper and richer understanding of the role of sacred Scripture than most focused studies on a single religion could provide.

Whereas in Jewish-Christian modernity the relatively recent paradigm for Scripture is the tangible print Bible, in most religious traditions, both ancient and contemporary, piety and practice are characterized by a high degree of what Graham called *scriptural orality*. The latter, a key concept in Graham's study, acknowledges the textual materiality of Scripture, but pays close attention to its functional orality which entailed a process of vocal readings, recitative dynamics, and memorial interiorization. "The authority of being written down," Graham explained in his summarizing piece, "takes nothing away from the authority of the living oral word that is inscribed in the heart/memory as well as on the page/tablet." *Scriptural orality* is a concept which has not received the attention it deserves, not only because of the ephemeral quality of speech but also because Western modernity has—until recently—made the printed text the yardstick of civilized communication. The point Graham made is that the strictly textual hermeneutics of Scripture, when viewed in global perspectives, may be narrowly culture-bound, aberrant even.

There is fourthly the contemporary electronic revolution which manifests itself most palpably in the Internet, the system of global computer networking. It has forced the issue of media with unprecedented relevancy upon us. The Web vastly extends the conventional oral, scribal, and typographic means of communication, facilitates new modes of expression and perception, and introduces a hitherto unacknowledged dimension to hermeneutics, while at the same time it retains via Microsoft Word the facility of conventional linear textuality. Not unlike the print technology of the fifteenth and sixteenth centuries, so does the high tech of the twentieth and twenty-first centuries impact virtually every aspect of the human lifeworld.

Especially noteworthy is the effect the electronic medium has on our perception of communications history itself. The novel set of scribal-visual-aural configurations generated by the digital medium allows, and indeed compels, us to come to terms with all previous media in the newly emerging historical communications context. As we are trying to assimilate the new medium in its multiple ramifications, the established media are beginning to present themselves in a different light, and appear to be in the process of being relativized. By way of example, our everyday experience with digital technology generates sufficient cognitive distance from our conventional modes of communication to enable us see more clearly, and perhaps for the first time, the distinct characteristics as well as limitations of our Western literary, textual vision. Specifically, navigating the Internet's pathways can have the effect of raising consciousness about the linear, fixed, and static nature of "the brick-and-mortar book" (Foley) which has made us distrust, and even forget, an oral tradition that is all around us and forever in the making, and has seduced us to identifying oral tradition with illiteracy. In short, the limited perspectives of text-centrism begin to dawn upon us as we learn "to think outside the most restrictive box of all: the book."[10]

Most startlingly, the new medium helps us discover unexpected analogies between the Internet and oral tradition, both of them forestalling finality, exercising radical democracy, speaking with a multitude of voices, facilitating open-access, inviting near-universal participation, providing oral-digital immediacy, and approaching the ideal of global communication. All of this can generate a newly acquired sensitivity toward oral tradition, enabling us to appreciate "oral performance as a shared Internet," as something that happens as we proceed, and not as a product fully formed and derived from the textual medium. These are all developments discussed by John M. Foley in his keynote address, and they encourage us to take another look at the excessively textual interpretation of religions, and to aspire to a much fuller grasp of Scripture, piety, and practice in the three faiths.

ORALITY-SCRIBALITY IN THE CONTEXT OF WORLD RELIGIONS

In discussing the communicative aspects of Judaism, Christianity, and Islam, the authors of this volume distance themselves from the limiting perspectives of text-centrism and move beyond the textual paradigm as the sole path to understanding sacred Scripture. Whether explicitly or by implication, all rise above the supremacy of print literacy, and all break away from the strictly textual approach to Scripture, tradition, and poetic writings. To the extent that historians of religion have been in the habit of focusing on the documentary, literary authority and interpretation of Scripture, this book seeks to break new ground. Particulars notwithstanding, the authors are agreed as well that Scripture is frequently conceived in terms of a dual mediality, implemented and experienced in the interplay of oral-written dynamics. They either challenge or simply move beyond the so-called *Great Divide* in favor of Scripture's oral-scribal identity and social entanglements. Variously addressed by all authors, dual mediality is a feature most thoroughly developed by Hearon. It suggests degrees of fluidity in media technologies, with oral and writing interpenetrating and mutually influencing each other in myriad ways, a phenomenon which implies that

10. Foley, *Oral Tradition*, 124.

the media boundaries were porous in ways quite unimaginable in the print medium, even though the two media are perfectly capable of functioning independently.

Implied in Scripture's dual medium authority is an attribute more central to the book than any other: the notion of Scripture as living voice. Although existing as written word, Scripture is predominantly appropriated and encountered as spoken word. As recognized by all contributors, and most intimately described by Horsley and Rhoads, this is a concept shared by all three faiths, and applicable to numerous other religious and non-religious traditions as well. Across ancient Near Eastern and Mediterranean cultures, extending from Mesopotamia to Egypt, and including ancient Israel and Greece, *long-duration literature* (such as represented for example by the Hebrew Bible) served the educational project of *enculturation*. It entailed frequent rewritings, reception via oral transmission and memorization, with the objective of achieving interiorization in people's hearts and minds. This is the principal thesis of Carr's contribution. As far as early Christianity is concerned, most, if not all, New Testament texts reflect the sound patterns and rhetorical strategies of performance literature, a notion most thoroughly developed by Rhoads. On the subject of relations between text and performance, he observes, the logic of the ancients runs directly counter to our own understanding. Whereas we seek to recover performative features from the transcribed text, the early Christians, "who were not people of the book," composed and performed orally before they committed their compositions to writing. The gospel of Mark, Horsley writes, was not only performed orally, but it was rooted in traditions "long cultivated among the people." In rabbinic Judaism, the fitting mode of transmission and interpretation of Mishnah, Midrash, Tosefta, and Talmud was the oral medium. For centuries the oral implementation was, and continues to be, both highly desirable and religiously meaningful, even though the distinction between oral and written, we shall see below, was firmly maintained. The Qur'an, "unframed by any narrative scenario," is and was perceived to be speech throughout, and in fact "often a meta-discourse, a speech about speech" (Neuwirth). Displaying "unmatchable rhetorical beauty" (Stetkevych), it was destined to be transmitted "through oral recitation" (Schoeler). Its vocal presence dominates the public sphere of Muslim societies via recitation and cantillation, educational memorization, and enactments at religious festivals. Medieval Western Christendom encountered the Bible less as a text contained between two covers, and more frequently as an oral authority implemented in homiletical instruction, liturgical celebration, and worship (Kelber).

The concept of Scripture as living voice may seem plain, commonsensical, or trivial even. And yet, it merits sustained reflection. For whereas in Western modernity the dominantly influential model for Scripture continues to be the printed text, with philology as the standard approach and literary, textual interpretation as the central act of hermeneutics, the view introduced here is that of the living voice of Scripture, recited, aurally received, and internalized. It follows that textual interpretation by no means provides the sole key to understanding. In bringing the performance dimension of Scripture to the fore, some authors are beginning to explore more fully the receptionist implications of their approach. Receptionalism suggests a reorientation from texts themselves to their recipients, or, perhaps more precisely, it grants hearers and readers full partnership through the processes of textual recitation and interiorization. Either way, Scripture as living voice implies that meaning does not reside in texts alone, but arises from the interplay of text and recipients. Rhoads and Carr come closest to developing the fuller implications of the perception of Scripture as *vox intexta*, with the former postulating that "the text is still fluid in its diverse performative incarnations"—although canonical texts in particular are trying to set limits to textual variance, as we shall see below—and the latter affirming "the absolutely central role of the mind" in the process of internalization.

Of all contributions, Finnegan's *Response* draws the most consistent conclusion from the prevalence of *scriptural orality*. Such is the pervasive presence of the interfacing of speech with writing, she suggests, that it challenges the very premise of a separate and discrete status of orality versus literacy. To such an extent do oral and written modes of communication overlap, that meaningful distinctions seem unworkable. Furthermore, orality, just like literacy, is itself multiform and transacted through a variety of channels. Audiences and individuals can experience Scripture via dictation and recitation, homiletical and catechetical instruction, prayer and liturgical chanting. Hence Finnegan's recommendation that we should more appropriately acknowledge "multi-literacies" and "multi-oralities." Moreover, orality itself, she explains, is not confined to purely verbal or even linguistic features. It can embody multimodal performance qualities, be they gestural, musical, or tactile. Last not least, an apperception of the full reality of Scripture also entails the visual sense. Scripture as physical object appeals to viewers' sense of aesthetics and can open up worlds of ravishing visual beauty, veneration of meticulously copied Torah scrolls, awe of illuminated Bible manuscripts, and reverential treatment of aesthetically designed

Qur'an volumes.[11] Many chapters in this volume are taking account of the multisensory character and function of Scripture, and promote appreciation of a fuller identity of Scripture.

ORALITY–SCRIBALITY IN THE MEDIA CONTEXT

There is, however, some difference in emphasis among the contributors between those who are thinking of orality and scribality more strictly in media terms, and others who emphasize the enmeshment of media in the context of history. The difference is between giving weight to media universals versus the environmental entaglements of media. Both viewpoints merit readers' attention, and ideally both are taken into consideration. Some chapters thematize media and media history, conceptualize media trajectories, and identify media assets and liabilities. It is in that vein that Foley's keynote address formulates a macro-historical vision consisting of the three technologies (*agoras*) of orality, textuality, and the electronic medium, each setting a series of conditions, facilitating networks of options, and positing a number of cognitive advantages and disadvantages. My own contribution develops a sweeping perspective of the history of biblical traditions that run from oral, memorial sensibilities and scribal multiformity toward an increasingly chirographic control over biblical texts, and culminates in the modern and postmodern closure of the print Bible.

As far as the performance of biblical texts is concerned, Rhoads describes the performer who experiences words off the page initially as sound and eventually as imaginable scenes by way of interior visualization. Schoeler observes analogous codification processes both for the Qur'an and for its tradition, which proceeded from disparate written fragments to deliberate collections all the way to a recension or systematic compilations. Using categories devised by Parry, Lord, Havelock, and Ong, Stetkevych explains a transition from pre-Islamic to Arabic-Islamic intellectual history from a "poetics of orality" to literacy, associated with abstraction and scientific thought, and a "retooling of rhetoric" relieved from mnemonic imperatives and formulaic diction. All of the above authors are keenly aware that each medium technology constitutes a complex cultural phenomenon, interacting with other media and with the contingencies of history as well. Yet their

11. Neuwirth, *Text der Spätantike*, 35, has described how the "Multimedialität" of the Qur'an became apportioned among three separate academic disciplines: visual aesthetics and calligraphy were relegated to art history, the oral, acoustic dimension became the special domain of ethnomusicology, and the textual manifestation was consigned to philology.

studies show that media thinking, broadly conceived, illuminates aspects of history that have previously remained closed to us.

This volume further demonstrates that the concepts of orality versus literacy are not extraneous impositions on the three religious faiths. Rabbinic Judaism, Fishman explains, endorsed a media classification that "distinguished sharply between two types of transmission." Moving beyond oral-scribal interfaces, it took the historic step of *conceptualizing* Oral Tradition apart from written Scripture. The impetus for this distinction arose from tension between the teachings of the sages and the Mosaic revelation of Scripture. At stake was the locus and status of rabbinic tradition which forced the question of the *raison d'etre* of the oral performative tradition vis-à-vis the written Torah. To affirm the additional authority of tradition and yet to ward off risks of splitting Judaism into two separate sources of revelation, Oral Torah emerged as the designation suitable for securing extra-biblical traditions' "equal billing with Scripture" (Fishman). Both Scripture and tradition were validated as Torah, and both were perceived to have been revealed at Sinai, while all along both retained their separate identities by way of media distinctions. At the same time, however, the principle of *scriptural orality* was preserved: Scripture continued to be implemented *viva voce*, and the massive body of written tradition remained culturally significant and religiously meaningful by way of memorization and oral transmission.

Islam, not unlike Judaism, had to contend with oral versus written communication, but the media dynamics and interfaces are still more intricate. As pointed out above, the Qur'an, more so than the Bible, presented itself as a rhetorical authority, whose recitation of its melodic cadences formed an essential part of Muslim life. Nonetheless, in the post-canonical era, following the death of the Prophet, Qur'anic texts acquired the status of a reified literary artifact which was eventually shaped into something akin to a critical edition. However, this new scriptural identity had to affirm itself in competition with Jewish and Christian rival forms of canonical authority. To reinforce the scriptural authority of the Qur'an, Islam postulated a transcendental origin for Scripture in the form of "the archetypal, celestial book" (Neuwirth). Yet in spite of the elevation of Qur'an's scriptural profile as "'the book' par excellence" (Schoeler), Islam held on to the fundamental conviction that the Word of God was inaccessible to humans except through oral communication. The principle of *scriptural orality*, therefore, continued to be operative. This already complex relationship of oral versus written authority was compounded when the issue of tradition was taken into consideration. It was the tradition's modus of communication that aroused "a vehement discussion," whether it should be committed to writing or exist entirely in oral discourse (Schoeler). Islamic scholarship resolved the issue by mandating the oral transmission and teaching of tradition, even though with the passing of time the scriptural codification of tradition became a practical reality. Thus, while thematizing the concept of *scriptural orality*, this volume likewise demonstrates that distinctions between the oral and the scribal medium are historically justifiable because they proved religiously relevant.

A number of chapters illustrate the point that media, far from operating in isolation and solely driven by their own communicative dynamics, are inexorably involved in the human habitat, variously conditioned by social life and in turn impacting it. This applies above all to oral verbalization which, more than written words, directly engages hearers in the particularities of social life. Spoken words are inevitably bound up with lived human existence. So are manuscripts, but due to their material existence they are a step removed from the human lifeworld, and over time still grow further apart from it. By comparison with oral discourse, therefore, texts represent a form of indirection and noninvolvement, a stand-alone, seemingly stable existence aloof from direct speaker-audience interaction.

The texts of Sacred Scriptures, however, this volume makes abundantly clear, do not come into their own except via re-oralization and in relation to hearers.[12] Among performance contexts for *scriptural orality* distinct places such as synagogues and Temple, marketplaces and villages, private homes and families are singled out (Hearon). As if by instinctual reflex, performers and reciters were inclined to tune in to their venue, and to take account of the beliefs, customs, and sentiments of the assembled spectators and listeners so as to shape their message by way of audience adjustments. In many instances context mattered, and response to it was crucial for effective performances.

An ubiquitous venue for Scripture's vocal presence were devotional piety and liturgical practices that marked the daily lives of the faithful in houses of worship. To the extent that prayers and scriptural citations were authoritatively prescribed and memorized, their performance tended to be habitual, attentive to verbal minutiae, and therefore largely context-free. And yet, much depended on the existence and impact of a normative texts. As long as scriptural orality was implemented in the absence of widely acknowledged canonical norms, diverse performative incarnations and so-called variants abounded (Horsley, Kelber, Neuwirth, Schoeler), and social context exercised a noticeable effect. In that pre-canonical period, for example, the verbal stability of recitations such as the Shema, the Lord's Prayer, or the five daily Muslim prayers was not likely to be absolute. But

12. The concept of "reoralization" was coined by Margaret A. Mills, "Domains."

once the canonical edition took control, fixedness prevailed, and memorization exerted an overriding influence over social venue. Yet even if the words spoken are exactly the same, performers and reciters could shape their memorized texts by way of sound, emotional impact, rhetorical emphases, and numerous paralinguistic features.

Among numerous examples of the interaction between communication and social history, Hezser focuses on a very basic, yet little acknowledged mode of transmission. Her network theory links communication with a culture of traveling and mobility. Living in an age of electronic hyperconnectivity, we need reminding that in ancient history and late antiquity the physical mobility that comes with traveling was critical for the transmission of information. In early Christian history and in rabbinic Judaism, Hezser explains, traveling served as a material prerequisite for the exchange of letters and face-to-face communication among Christians and halakhic and exegetical knowledge between rabbis living at spatially separate places. The ancient road system and "the late Roman 'culture of mobility'" can, therefore, be considered a social basis for the transmission, and eventual collection and editing of Christian and rabbinic traditions.

The readers of this volume are being treated to an array of scriptural enactments, involvements, performances, and implementations. Scripture in Judaism, Christianity, and Islam manifests itself in many faces: source for devotional practices, conversation with other texts, textual redaction of antecedent traditions, echo of diverse voices, factor in polemical and competitive environments, resource for doctrinal affirmations, vocal, visual, and aesthetic factor, social force in cultural, political history, a textual, canonical authority, and, above all a *scriptural orality* projecting a vocal presence or living voice in performance. When all scriptural attributes are being considered—form and content, affective role and contextual impact, relational quality and functional capability—it follows that the full reality of Scripture in the three monotheistic religions is not exclusively knowable as a literary genre and textual authority committed to the printed page, subject to literary and theological interpretation, and read in silence. And therein may in fact lie the very significance and purpose of the book: to convey a sense of the immense complexity of Sacred Scripture and by implication of the phenomenon of religion itself.

BIBLIOGRAPHY

Engnell, Ivan. *The Call of Isaiah: An Exegetical and Comparative Study*. Uppsala Universitets Arksskrift 4. Uppsala: Lundequistska, 1949.

Finnegan, Ruth. *Oral Literature in Africa*. Oxford: Oxford University Press, 1970.

———. *Oral Poetry: Its Nature, Significance and Social Context*. Cambridge: Cambridge University Press, 1977.

Foley, John Miles. *How to Read an Oral Poem*. Urbana: University of Illinois Press, 2002.

———. *Oral Tradition and the Internet. Pathways of the Mind*. Urbana: University of Illinois Press, 2012.

———. "Reading the Oral Traditional Text: Aesthetics of Creation and Response." In *Comparative Research on Oral Traditions: A Memorial for Milman Parry*, edited by John Miles Foley, 185–212. Columbus, OH: Slavica, 1987.

Graham, William A. *Beyond the Written Word: Oral Aspects of Scripture in the History of Religion*. Cambridge: Cambridge University Press, 1987.

Jousse, Marcel. *Le Style oral rhythmique et mnémotechnique chez les Verbo-moteurs*. Paris: Beauchesne, 1925.

Lord, Albert B. *The Singer of Tales*. Harvard Studies in Classical Philology 24. 1960. Reprinted New York: Atheneum, 1968.

———. *Epic Singers and Oral Tradition*. Ithaca, NY: Cornell University Press, 1991.

Mills, Margaret A. "Domains of Folkloristic Concerns: Interpretation of Scriptures." In *Text and Tradition: The Hebrew Bible and Folklore*, edited by Susan Niditch, 231–41. Semeia Studies 32. Atlanta: Scholars, 1990.

Neuwirth, Angelika. *Der Koran als Text der Spätantike: Ein europäischer Zugang*. Berlin: Verlag der Weltreligionen, 2010.

Nielsen, Eduard. *Oral Tradition: A Modern Problem in Old Testament Introduction*. Studies in Biblical Theology 11. Translated by Asta Lange. London: SCM, 1954.

Nyberg, H. S. *Studien zum Hoseabuch: Zugleich ein Beitrag zur Klärung des Problems der Alttestamentlichen Textkritik*. Uppsala Universitets Arksskrift 6. Uppsala: Lundequistska, 1935.

Parry, Milman. "Studies in the Epic Technique of Oral Verse-Making: I. Homer and Homeric Style." *Harvard Studies in Classical Philology* 41 (1930) 73–148.

———. "Studies in the Epic Technique of Oral Verse-Making: II: The Homeric Language as the Language of Oral Poetry. *Harvard Studies in Classical Philology* 43 (1932) 1–50.

Ringgren, Helmer. "Oral and Written Transmission in the O. T.: Some Observations." *Studia Theologica* 3 (1949) 34–59.

Vansina, Jan. *Oral Tradition: A Study in Historical Methodology*. Translated by H. M. Wright. London: Routledge & Kegan Paul, 1965.

Acknowledgments

The present volume has grown out of a conference initiated and convened by Werner Kelber and Paula Sanders at Rice University on April 12–14, 2008. The conference papers, initially published in an online version of the journal *Oral Tradition* 25/1 (2010), are republished here in print as *Oral-Scribal Dimensions of Scripture, Piety, and Practice: Judaism, Christianity, Islam*. The Rice conference was the seventh in a series of Orality-Literacy conferences that was inaugurated in 2001 at the University of Natal, Pietermaritzburg, South Africa, and over the years was convened in Europe, North America, and again in Africa. The series has focused on the topics of colonialism, the world of the Spirits, memory, diversity, ritual, and tradition—always under the heading of Orality-Scribality.

A distinct feature of this volume is the participation of experts in Judaism, Christianity, and Islam. The aim is not to unify oral-scribal aspects of the three faiths into a single paradigm—if such one existed at all. Rather, the readers are treated to a sizable repertoire of communicative strategies, themes, and sensibilities. Consultation of the authors' respective bibliographies will reveal an even fuller range of oral, scribal, and memorial potentialities. But the focus on the communicative dimensions brings out issues that run across the chapters, and will allow readers to catch glimpses of genuine comparative thinking. In this regard, readers are encouraged to pay additional attention to the two summarizing chapters that over and above identifying principal issues, complement and expand perspectives, raise novel questions, at times challenge premises, and frequently cast fresh light on the propositions advanced in these chapters.

We make grateful acknowledgment of a number of generous sponsors at Rice University. First and foremost, we register our gratitude to the principal sponsor of the conference, the Boniuk Institute for the Study and Advancement of Religious Tolerance. Additionally, our heartfelt thanks go to the five co-sponsors: the Ken Kennedy Institute for Information Technology, the Humanities Research Center, the Office of the Dean of Humanities, and the Departments of History and Religion. We are grateful also for the Boniuk Institute's further support in providing resources for editorial expenses associated with the current publication.

These chapters that treat the intersection of oral, scribal, and memorial aspects in the three monotheistic faiths are themselves the product of noteworthy intermedial complexities. Never fully secured as definitive properties, they underwent a series of media transformations. Initially, the papers were electronically authored and pre-circulated in advance of the conference. An important segment of the conference involved the authors' vocalization of the abstracts of their works and thereby initiating a discussion with colleagues who were already familiar with all written versions. In the aftermath of the conference the authors revised their products and submitted them to the editor of *Oral Tradition*. Subsequently, the editorial staff of the online, open-access journal reformatted the articles in compliance with electronic requirements. In their present version, the articles have once again undergone a media mutation as they were transposed from their electronic potentiality back into the print medium. In their entirety, therefore, the chapters represent an intricate communications and receptionist history which addresses auditors and readers in the intersecting worlds of oral mediation, electronic media, and printed pages.

1

Ancient and Modern Democracies

Orality, Texts, and Electronic Media

John Miles Foley

This lecture is dedicated to Werner and to my son Isaac.

INTRODUCTION

I should like to begin by expressing my gratitude to Rice University for creating this opportunity, and this moment in time, for all of us to come together in order to discuss issues I believe are both crucial and critical for a broad consortium of academic disciplines—especially during this new chapter in intellectual history in which we find ourselves struggling to correlate old and new paradigms, to make sense of the intersecting worlds of oral tradition, texts, and electronic media. For it is not merely languages, literatures, and the study of world religions that are heavily implicated by orality-literacy interactions, but also anthropology, history, philosophy, psychology, music, and many other areas of learning and inquiry.

Hearty thanks are due in particular the Boniuk Center for the Study and Advancement of Religious Tolerance, the Humanities Research Center, the Office of the Dean of Humanities, the Department of History, the Kennedy Institute for Information Technology, and the Department of Religious Studies. Let me also mention, as prominently as possible, our trusted guides for this shared enterprise: Werner Kelber and Paula Sanders; as well as each of those members of the conference *comitatus* from whom we will be hearing over the next few days, including our respondents Ruth Finnegan, and William Graham. Many thanks to one and all for your commitments and contributions.

CAVEAT AND OUTLINE

In view of the unprecedented nature of what awaits us during this seventh incarnation of the Orality–Literacy conference series, and in line with a policy of full disclosure that may appear unique during this political season, I feel it is only proper to provide a caveat and an outline before setting out on this evening's expedition.

First, the caveat. In much of what I have to say, I will be asking you to weigh some counterintuitive proposals—ideas that will at first blush seem quite unlikely and perhaps even heretical. But I emphasize that they will seem counterintuitive only because our intuition is based fundamentally on what I call *textual ideology*, the opposite to what Talya Fishman terms the "essentialist preference for the oral over the written," a phemomenon which she challenges. These ideas will appear unlikely only because we are in the hard-to-break habit of studying, analyzing, and representing oral traditions (and now the Internet) through our default medium of texts.

Without fully realizing the consequences, we have insisted on thinking about radically different, non-textual media not on their own terms, that is, but on textual terms. It is as if we were to adamantly cling to representing the history of the French language only in terms of supposedly analogical developments in Apache, Estonian, or Urdu. In such a scenario French itself becomes a secondhand subject, excused from primary examination. As part of my revisionist agenda, I will suggest nothing more outlandish than studying, analyzing, and representing media on their own terms—that is, directly, instead of through mandatory semiotic translation. Or at least as close as we can get. And we can get a lot closer than we customarily have.

Now for the outline. Since the principal theme of my remarks is democracy in media, our first step will be to examine the use and abuse of that word, especially with regard to some disabling cultural presumptions that prosper by remaining "under the radar," hidden from conscious scrutiny. From that juncture we will proceed to some large-scale, coarse-grained discriminations among three kinds of word-marketplaces or verbal "agoras": oral, textual, and electronic—or, for short, the oAgora, tAgora, and eAgora.

We will conclude with a short discussion of the *Pathways Project* and, perhaps not unexpectedly, a story.

I hasten to add a footnote here, and what would a textually driven scholar do without his footnotes? Namely, please understand that these three arenas for communication—again, the oAgora, tAgora, and eAgora—are most certainly not meant as absolute, mutually exclusive, or (perish the thought!) evolutionary. Like any imposed concept, they are *heuristics*, models to think with rather than divinely conceived, pre-existing categories. Human nature is of course more complex and interesting than any model, and I offer the three agoras merely as a pathway into our deliberations on democracy in media.

Exiting my footnote and returning to our outline, then, we will move on to thinking through—as promised—a counterintuitive thesis and a couple of taken-for-granted concepts.

Here is the superficially unlikely thesis: Oral Tradition (OT) and Internet Technology (IT) resemble one another more than either medium resembles Textual Communication. And why? Because OT and IT—unlike texts—mime the very way we think, namely, by navigating through networks of potentials. This homology, hopefully intriguing in itself, also offers us new ways to construe and represent OT realities via IT vehicles. But more of that later on.

The two concepts, which many right-thinking, well-trained scholars would consider matters settled long ago, are authorship and referentiality. But there is more to both of them than "meets the eye," to resort to an inexcusable pun. Oral traditions, like so many phenomena in the burgeoning Internet and digital world, are not singly but rather multiply authored. To use a term developed for wikis, group blogs, open data-bases, and other collective projects in the eAgora, the authorship of oral traditions is *distributed*. Performances are most immediately the product of a single person or group, of course, but even the most "original" of them (and the word "original" is itself problematic) have deep roots in how others have performed and re-performed beforehand. Assigning an oral traditional performance—or even an oral-derived text—exclusively to a single individual borders on a vicarious act of plagiarism.

And then there is the riddle of *referentiality*. To what do oral traditions refer? What is "contained" in the given performance and what is implied? If not contained, how necessarily is it implied? Is the distinction between any expectable feature being "there" and "not there" more phenomenological than discursive? How does the entextualization of oral traditions affect their ability to mean, or even their intelligibility? Toward the end of my reflections on referentiality (Part III) I will offer an example or two of how both

OT and IT depend on what is, from a textual perspective, not physically present at all. Of course, that putative absence is a false and misleading diagnosis, fostered by an endemically oblique and therefore faulty perspective. Truth within the medium is more to the point.

PART I: DEMOCRACY

Let's start with a recalibration. "Democracy" in today's popular speech is a Humpty-Dumpty word. It means whatever the speaker wants it to mean, for whatever purpose he or she wishes to use it, and it is often deployed more as word-magic to gain political or corporate advantage than as the fixed and certain concept we romantically imagine it to be.

It was not always so. The ancient Greeks, perhaps initially the historian Herodotus, coined the word δημοκρατεία from two roots as old as Homer—δημος, community; and κράτος strength, might, or power. Most fundamentally, then, "democracy" carries with it the noble, pluralistic sense of power residing in the hands of the entire community, the people at large. Its core meaning is thus not merely anti-monarchic but also anti-exclusive, anti-xenophobic, and anti-privileged—or, more to the point, inclusive, inter-ethnic, and *pro bono publico*: for the sake of the public good.

The page, in contrast, is oligarchic; it is now and always has been the domain of the oligarchy, etymologically those "few first ones" who control communication and invisibly censor the expressive channels we use to exchange knowledge, ideas, and art. The question is who those chosen few are in any given time and place.

In ancient and medieval times, with literacy not only highly restricted but also highly specialized, what was consigned to texts was available to and usable by very, very few. Homer's stories—and I take the name *Homêros* as a code-term for the oral epic tradition as a whole, an anthropomorphization of that tradition as a legend—were performed for centuries before the invention of alphabetic writing about 775 BCE. (There was, as Angelika Neuwirth might put it, a long *pre-canonical* tradition.) During that time, and arguably for centuries afterward, these stories' exclusive or principal medium was in fact oral tradition. The new technology of writing and reading did not, as we have too often presumed, conquer archaic Greece overnight, anymore than Internet and digital media have entirely dispensed with the book and page in our time. What was written down was in many cases taken out of the loop for the people at large. Just the opposite of our situation—or rather our ideological view of our situation.

Indeed, as moderns who have trouble thinking outside the default medium of the page, we have grossly overestimated the text-making and text-consuming technology of pre-Gutenberg, not to mention pre-paperback societies—the same syndrome that Richard Horsley has in mind when he points out that the "concept of Scripture assumed in standard Jewish and Christian biblical studies is . . . deeply embedded in the assumptions of modern print culture." To imagine, as so many scholars implicitly have, an Amazon.com-like literacy consisting of easily reproducible copies and a mass readership in ancient and medieval times is to subscribe to an anachronism of major proportions. A single book of Homeric epic—take any one of the 48 in the *Iliad* and *Odyssey*—required 20–24 feet of papyrus to inscribe its several hundred hexameters. Not exactly the sort of thing one could stuff into a satchel, or manipulate with acceptable ease on a well-lit library table. So it was not just a question of who possessed the literacy skills needed to use a text (again, very, very few), but even more basically how these 48 books (at minimum 960 feet of papyrus) might possibly be "read."

In the medieval period we have more (but hardly enough) information about the establishment, copying, and transmission of the works we cherish. But in some ways that only complicates matters. Brian Stock has explained the dynamics of what he calls "textual communities,"[1] which were formed around texts but were at the same time dependent for their function not on the virtually universal literacy we take for granted but on the literacy skills of a single person, who then interpreted and communicated the wisdom out of the text to the broader community. How? By shifting into oral mode, of course. We might want to compare this with what Gregor Schoeler has explained about the continuing oral mediation of Islamic texts. Whatever the case, it is hard to imagine a more determinative oligarchy than the medieval textual community. The privileged few become the privileged one, in effect.

Early medieval England also presents us with other unexpected complications. There are no literate English kings until the twelfth century, for example; and why should there be? That craft, like other crafts that supported the society and its administration, was the province of specialists whose trade it was to build, amass, and manage documents. And then there is the (for us) counterintuitive phenomenon of scribes who read formulaically and thus re-made or re-composed Old English poetry rather than copied it verbatim. This mixed mode of "singing on the page" has been confirmed in modern scenarios as well, in Finland and the Former Yugoslavia to name just two prominent sites.

1. Stock, *Implications of Literacy*.

These few examples bespeak a simple truth. Our naïve assumptions notwithstanding, texts are the furthest thing from a genuinely democratic medium in the ancient and medieval worlds. Their making and their use are controlled by oligarchies—variously constituted, to be sure, and dependent on the particular society or intra-societal group, but oligarchies nonetheless.

And what about today's world? Who constitutes the contemporary oligarchy? We can make a few observations. University presses act as ready gatekeepers for the academic community, but the levels of privilege and determinism hardly end there. Commercial presses have their own non-democratic agenda, as do learned journals and popular magazines—all of them with their own designs on how the marketplace of ideas must function. Anyone who sets pen to paper, or fingers to keyboard, works within an idiosyncratic textual scenario that foreshortens reality by predetermining the outer limits of creativity and communication. Once the precious artifact is created, it is made available only to a select few—those who can afford the price of the book, the subscription to the journal, the annual fee for the learned organization. Nor does the disenfranchising end there. Publishers and their consortiums limit circulation by limiting distribution networks (something Werner Kelber has been very helpful in reminding us about). Even within the snug confines of the Western world, it is a lot more difficult for North American scholars to gain access to French and German books and journals than it should be.

I might add an anecdote that puts another sort of disparity into relief. As our journal *Oral Tradition* has migrated online as a gratis, open-access resource, we have had firsthand experience of some powerful truths that oligarchic text-communication had hidden. Enormous numbers of new readers have come on board—at last check, more than 40,000 downloads to 108 countries have taken place; but that was not the most instructive development. Along with new readers have come new potential contributors with new agendas, people from far outside the Western sphere, from areas where, quite ironically, oral traditions are most prevalent. Their submissions to *eOT*, as we call it, are only very seldom the highly theorized, critically *au courant* essays that our academic journals conventionally demand, but rather case studies and descriptions of live performances interwoven with social context. The graduate students who serve as editorial assistants for the journal at first argued that we could not in good conscience consider publishing such "unacademic" contributions, and a lively debate ensued over what was right and proper according to professional standards. In the end, however, it proved fundamentally a question of recognizing that we had long been functioning narcissistically as an unindicted oligarchy, with an indefensibly limited agenda and what amounted to heavy censorship.

And having recognized our inadvertent act of disenfranchising, we had to take measures to move beyond it. As I put it to them that morning, "Do we really want to talk to the world about oral tradition or don't we?"

No matter the particulars, then, makers and users of texts cannot help but participate in an undemocratic, even counter-democratic enterprise. To write and to read and to publish and to consume textually is to predispose, to hold at arm's length, to confront knowledge, ideas, and art vicariously and non-immediately, to forestall emergence and right-now involvement. No medium or environment exists for very long without rules that support its activities by eliminating the clutter of innumerable alternate possibilities, and the page is no exception. In fact, the page flourishes brilliantly by severely constricting the arena for exchange. Its uniquely functional deformation of reality operates by remaining a well-kept secret.

PART II: THE THREE AGORAS

To delve further into democracy in media, let me summon a term and institution from ancient Greece, the acknowledged cradle of democratic thinking. That institution is the *agora*, or marketplace that served the population as a brick-and-mortar site for religious, commercial, and political exchange. For present purposes we will be applying it to three media: the oral (oAgora), textual (tAgora), and electronic (eAgora). I hasten to add that each of these agoras is a complex arena in itself, that each supports a variety of activities, and that, like Holly Hearon, I have no wish to commit the archetypal sin of studies in oral tradition by oversimplifying matters that deserve more nuanced modeling and explanation. Thus I stipulate from the start that just as the oAgora encompasses four flexible and expansive categories I have described elsewhere (oral performance, voiced texts, voices from the past, and written oral traditions), so tAgora transactions involve everything from manuscripts to printed pages and on to static (electronic) text files. The eAgora can of course play host to many fixed items, but in discussing its characteristic dynamics I will be primarily concerned with interactive, option-driven experiences rather than pre-set, invariable objects. The kind of eAgora commerce in which we are interested here consists of ever-evolving navigation and ongoing co-creation, not simply the paperless exchange of fixed texts.

The historical sequence of media-events sets up certain expectations about the relationships among the three agoras. The oAgora, to which David Rhoads seeks to return New Testament texts, stretches back beyond documentable history and is of indeterminate age. Writing, meanwhile, is a relatively recent invention of our species. If we plot our entire existence as *homo sapiens* on a single calendar year to simplify dating, we will see, perhaps to our surprise, that writing appears only during the second week of December, more than 90% of the way through our history. Print in the West emerges with Gutenberg's press as late as December 27th (though in the East a few species-days earlier), and Internet communication a mere 16 minutes before midnight on New Year's Eve. This media-calendar puts the more modern technologies into stark historical relief, of course, but it can also obscure the continuing importance of OT, which is per capita still the most widely employed communications technology in the world. It can also obscure the observed reality that the various technologies mix and influence one another in myriad ways, and indeed that the three agoras, or verbal marketplaces, that we have identified will each support a broad spectrum of activities. Witness David Carr's differentiation between "memory variants," "graphic variants," and "aural variants," for example. That said, and speaking in broad generalities, two of the three marketplaces—the oAgora and the eAgora—share striking resemblances. Notwithstanding the chronology of their invention, OT and IT act in several ways as matched bookends to the waning age of print. How does this homology between the oAgora and eAgora present itself? We can identify several points of comparison between the two media, which also amount to points of contrast with the tAgora.

Most fundamentally, both OT and IT consist of webs for users to navigate. Consider first the one-way tAgora trek through a predetermined sequence of words, lines, pages, chapters, and so forth.

Now consider the oAgora and eAgora, which offer us the opportunity to choose among various viable routes through a system, alternative pathways through a network. (Notice that Catherine Hezser has already developed a 'network theory,' applicable to the first two centuries of rabbinic transmission, and characterized by decentralization and oral exchange.) Oral poets don't speak text-items; they know how to manage an itinerary through the living poetic tradition, which finally consists not of a warehouse of things but of a series of choices. What story shall I tell, and how shall I tell it this time? Which genealogy shall I recount for this particular group? Which healing charm shall I use for this patient, and what shall I emphasize during this administration of the verbal treatment? How shall I mourn the passing of my sister or uncle or daughter, feeling the pain of that loss somewhat differently each time I go to the village cemetery to lament? Reacting to the idiosyncrasies of the individual occasion and audience, the performer has the freedom to shape the story or genealogy or charm or funeral lament within limits, to speak both traditionally and to the immediate moment. If we expand this working dynamic of "variation within limits" to an entire community, over time, with many performers sharing access to the expressive system, we can begin to glimpse the pathway-driven power of OT.

Nor is the concept of pathways an extraneous imposition on the reality of how oral traditions work. Homer (and his tradition) identify just such a web of resources as the core of what it means to be an [aoidos] ἀοιδός, an oral epic poet in ancient Greece. Here is the Phaeacian bard Demodokos, at lines 479–81 of Book 8 of the *Odyssey*:

> For among all mortal men the singers have a share
> in honor and reverence, since to them the Muse
> has taught the **pathways**, for she loves the singers' tribe.

His Ithakan counterpart, Phemios, makes a similar comment as he begs Odysseus for his life at lines 347–48 of Book 22:

> The god implanted all sorts of **pathways** in my mind.

The Greek word for "pathway" is οιμη, not a technical term or abstraction but a rather homely term to describe a tangible route-connection from one geographical spot to another. In this instance it is pressed into service to name the links between nodes in a story-map, the connections that constitute the network of Homeric tale-telling. The poet and his tradition are explaining the oral bard's craft not by celebrating the performer's memory or vocal abilities, but by highlighting his ability to navigate that shared network. This "inside look" into ancient Greek oral poetics bears importantly on such crucial issues as the nature of performance, the harmony of tradition and individual, the patterned language and narrative structure of Homeric epic, and so forth.

On the IT side, it is once again the network that matters. Web surfers, even those who fully intend to follow earlier itineraries precisely, are characteristically drawn to new and unanticipated experiences and opportunities for learning, simply by virtue of the connectedness and built-in options that constitute the Internet. We can read fixed texts online, to be sure, and that activity is in many ways not so different from thumbing through the pages of a brick-and-mortar book or turning the leaves of a vellum manuscript. But the web also offers the opportunity to take responsibility for charting our own course, for interacting as we go, for determining the direction if not the precise outcome(s) of our journey. And that IT navigation, like its OT counterpart, is an emergent process that happens as we proceed, and that we participate in controlling. For that reason, every iteration—though the sense of "identical repetition" embedded in that term is not quite apposite—will be cognate with earlier journeys but not identical to any of them.

In both the oAgora and the eAgora, how we manage the available, built-in options—how we co-create—will prove just as important as what those options are.

Surfing the OT and IT webs thus involves experiences that are surprisingly homologous. All explorations in both media are rule-governed; they consist of using what amounts to a special, highly coded case of language—not a textual libretto but language itself. The rules that guide the OT and IT processes are not exhaustively prescriptive; they aim at supporting creativity, not foreclosing on it. Innovation is not only possible but uniquely enabled by flexible systems of multiply connected pathways (themselves always under construction) that make up each medium.

Our everyday encounter with the Internet makes this simple point every time we click from one multi-dimensional site to another, of course. We cannot avoid following certain rules, nor can we avoid creating our own itineraries. We begin a web session by opening the browser with a start-up page (which can itself change, and is in fact likely to morph over time). From that point we may select a bookmark or type a URL into the browser in order to visit a particular site, but from that point onward the pseudo-textuality of the session begins to vanish. We can interact with the designated site, follow links to many other possible sites of interest, discover web pages that didn't exist a few weeks ago or that have been modified since our last visit, search the web by keywords for interests that develop as we explore, and in short create for ourselves an emergent experience cognate to, but in some ways also different from, prior surfing experiences.

The oAgora presents a similar set of opportunities and conditions that jointly shape in-process activities. Oral performers speak within an idiomatic framework but seldom if ever repeat themselves exactly: instead, they surf their traditions, with the recurrent, rule-governed activity generating many related but different products. What's more, audiences join in this democratic process as well. It is important to stipulate that some oral performers will limit participation according to cultural variables such as age, gender, time of performance, and other factors, just as IT participation can be limited by password protection, dedicated intranets, and the like. But generally and relatively speaking, we can characterize the oAgora as a site for democracy in verbal art, a place where the community holds sway over the exchange of knowledge, ideas, and art.

For example, consider the Basque art of oral improvisation known as *bertsolaritza*, a contest poetry practiced in a wide range of formal and informal venues in northern Spain and southern France. This fascinating tradition requires the performer to navigate through a vast and complex network consisting of many hundreds of possible melodies as well as many dozens of possible verse forms and meters—with performance commencing mere seconds after the initial, heretofore unknown, topic or prompt is announced, or in immediate response to a competitor's verse-poem. Finding a pathway through this maze of requirements is a remarkable accomplishment, and puts the lie to the longstanding and commonly held hypothesis that complex verbal expression can occur only in a textual environment. Indeed, I witnessed contest poetry that was both improvisational and traditional—as well as even more forbiddingly complicated—last summer in Sardinia as well. And if the mere fact of those Sardinian oral performances were not enough, I was confronted with an astonishing ethnographic fact—namely, that the leading oral poet from the southern part of the island, Paolo Zedda, is also a dentist who teaches folk arts at the University of Cagliari! So much for our preconceptions about oral tradition and its performers!

Back to the Basque tradition, which presents yet another instructive dimension. Although each improvisatory act of *bertsolaritza* is by definition unique and unprecedented, toward the end of the poem the audience regularly joins the *bertsolari* in singing the last few lines in unison. Performers thus respond lyrically, expertly, and spontaneously, while audiences take their part in something that doesn't exist until it is performed. Our default experience of textual communication, dependent as it is on creation and interpretation of fixed items, does not prepare us for this kind of shared improvisational phenomenon. How is it accomplished?

What makes this synchronized individual performance and group participation possible is the shared "Internet" of Basque *bertsolaritza*. Singers have learned to navigate the commonly shared pathways of the oral expressive tradition by internalizing the poetics of this improvised genre. They have learned to surf the compositional web, in other words, making decisions based on a fluent grasp of applicable patterns in music, syntax, verse-form, and rhyme. Rules govern their surfing, but those same rules are flexible and generative enough to foster the making of poetry that has never existed before the moment of its speaking. Likewise, the audience, steeped in the experience of many prior performances, has to a lesser but still substantial degree achieved a parallel fluency, a corresponding ability to surf the *bertsolaritza* tradition themselves. By following the topic development, musical pattern, rhyming scheme, and other aspects—and by applying their own experience and linguistic competence to the emerging performance—they arrive along with the poet at the structural and semantic inevitability of the last few lines. Poet and audience conclude the never-before-uttered improvisation together. Basque oral poetry is a case study in the radical democracy of the oAgora.

PART III: AUTHORSHIP AND REFERENTIALITY

How does the agora model help us understand the nature of authorship in human communication? Who fits the job description of author in each agora, and how does verbal commerce actually work in each environment?

We have known for a long time that the conventional fiction of an individual author is a limited approximation, even for a *magnum opus* confidently ascribable to a single celebrated writer. Whether we invoke "anxiety of influence" or some other critical paradigm that measures interaction between and among works of verbal art, we realize deep down that our identification of authors as original geniuses working effectively *ex nihilo* is a convenient falsehood, a lie we tell to ourselves in order to protect and maintain the twin illusions of object and stasis.

And if the myth of individual authorship amounts to an imposition on written, published, and eventually copyrighted texts, then it must apply even less successfully to works from the oAgora and eAgora. Clearly, oral performances—embedded as they are in an ongoing tradition of communications that can never produce an epitome—cannot be said to be "authored" in the sense we implicitly mean. (And here I am mindful of Werner Kelber's comments on the trajectory from multiformity and polyvalency toward chirographic control.) Nor can oral-derived texts, at any point along the spectrum from simple transcriptions of oral events to written texts that employ (and assume) an OT code, be understood as "authored" without severely misrepresenting their ontology. Corresponding sorts of observations can be made about web-based and digital communication, so much of which actually depends on the lack of a single, determinative author. The very a-textuality of oAgora and eAgora commerce is what supports their activities and makes them function as they do.

So how do we conceive of the agents for communication within these media-technologies? Who is responsible? If there is no single person in charge, how do we fit OT and IT composition and reception into our usual thinking?

The quick answer is that we can't. Although we have tried over and over again to reduce oral traditions to textual form, all that ever results is a cenotaph. Utilizing our default model and methods, which appear to have served philology, textual criticism, and the history of ideas so well, just doesn't work. Indeed, if the past twenty-five to thirty years have shown anything, it must be that we pay an enormous price for colonizing oral traditions in the name of the textual empire. But what else can we do—given that OT apparently has no real authors?

Here the eAgora comes to the rescue, with a solution based not on the twin myths of object and stasis but on the radically democratic nature of thinking and exchange within the virtual community. That solution is *distributed authorship*.

Consider two examples, one probably familiar and the other perhaps not as much so. Almost everyone here has consulted *Wikipedia*, the collective eEncyclopedia assembled by many hands and subject to continuous revision. Any given article may have been initiated by a single person, but it will also always be "under construction," as the language of web-speak puts it. Final form—no matter how polished and, to use a transparently inappropriate word, "authoritative"—is not a category in Wikipedia. It is precisely the forestalling of finality that constitutes its core dynamic, that makes it work. And, by the way, it is that same forestalling that frees such eResources from the built-in obsolescence of textuality.

The other example is *open-source software*, the unbranded species of application that is notproprietary or (dare we say it?) textually conceived. Unlike Microsoft Word, for instance, open-source instruments are freely available for sharing, rewriting, and ever-evolving use, often without financial implications. There even exists a "ten commandments" sort of doctrine that stipulates how creators and re-creators should share applications and source code, and how transmission should occur unencumbered by the customary regulations that proceed from imposed ideas of ownership (itself a curious concept) and monetized transactions. Once again, we have not one author but many, not a final product but an invitation to a process. Once again, we have democracy in the form of distributed authorship.

How does this concept play out in oral tradition? As before, let's consider some examples, one from either end of the spectrum described above.

For more than three decades I have been working on the oral epic songs collected by Milman Parry, Albert Lord, and Nikola Vujnović in the region of Stolac, in what is today called Bosnia, as well as on South Slavic materials recorded by my fieldwork team. I have focused mainly on four Parry-Lord-Vujnović individual singers (or *guslari*) and their repertoires: Halil Bajgorić, Ibro Bašić, Mujo Kukuruzović, and Salko Morić, who among them performed more than fifty epics that were either encoded on aluminum records or written down from dictation in small notebooks.

When Albert Lord assigned me the Stolac *guslari* for edition and translation, my initial impulse was conventional enough: I created a grid into which I planned to fit the performances, to be matched against their elicited repertoires and correlated with their own accounts of how and from whom they learned each item. Imagine my only-too-textual frustration when I began to realize that these individuals provided no titles (the investigators imposed the labels), no stable repertoire (they gave different lists each time they were interviewed), no unshared song or song-type (both stories and subgenres were communal), and no concept of a best or final form of any epic performance. Oh, they tried heroically to provide answers to remarkably impertinent questions such as "From whom did you learn that song?" or "How many songs do you know?" or "What makes an epic excellent?" But their responses were more efforts to please their interlocutors than anything else. Cognitively, the original fieldworkers' concerns—and also my own as I started to come to grips with this rich treasury of oral tradition—were entirely foreign to these denizens of the oAgora. They were tAgora concerns, and they simply did not make any sense.

What makes better sense is to conceive of each performance by these four individuals as a series of nodes in a network. Each *guslar* effectively surfed through a shared internet of epic, moving along familiar pathways but keeping options open as he responded to the audience, the situation, even his own frame of mind. Potential for variation is everywhere because alternatives (large and small) are everywhere; nothing is writ in stone, nor ever can be for that matter. Authorship is distributed because each singer surfs somewhat idiosyncratically, and differently each time he opens his performance-browser.

The model of an oral performance as a shared Internet that offers potentials rather than predisposed certainties helps explain my initial frustrations mentioned above. Instead of titles the *guslari* offered such kinetic descriptions as "When Alagić Alija was imprisoned in Zadar and met Velagić Alija and they escaped and returned to their homeland in the Lika..."—clearly a pathway rather than an object-label. Repertoires and sources were similarly inapposite concepts because they assumed a warehouse model, with each item labeled as a separate object made by a single individual and transmitted as a commodity. Songs and song-types were shared because the network was open to multiple individuals as a resource for creativity, but emphatically not for finality or epitomization, which would have to wait until the operative fiction of the tAgora was in place. Power to compose and to receive oral epic songs lay in the hands of the democratic community of singers and audiences, as the common prologue to these performances explicitly reveals:

Sad po tome, moje braćo draga,	Now in turn, my dear brothers,
Pa velimo da pesmu brojimo.	So we wish to count out a song.
Ej! Davno nekad u zemanu bilo,	Eh! Once it was, long ago in time,
Davno bilo, sada pominjemo	Long ago it was, now we are remembering
Pa ovome mestu i svakome.	In this place and in every other.

Everything about the compositional code, which also serves as the code for reception, is mutual, shared, democratic.

And this quality extends to the oral epic language even as it is deployed in texts, as the case of Petar Petrović Njegoš illustrates. Njegoš was in adult life the archbishop of Montenegro, a highly learned and literate man. But he grew up in a Montengrin village, where as a boy he listened to *guslari* and learned the phraseological and narrative code for oral epic-making. He learned the OT pathways, in other words. When later in his career as a religious administrator he undertook to write his own poetry—and please notice that he wrote for publication rather than performed orally—he had two basic choices. He could compose in one or more of the elite verse-forms then all the rage among European *literati*, or he could opt to use the verse-vehicle he had internalized during his youth. Well, he chose the latter, thus turning the *epski deseterac* (epic decasyllable) to purposes both traditional and new-wave, penning some poems that recounted mythic-historical events from oral tradition and others that responded to contemporary political concerns. By selecting the OT vehicle, he framed his ideas within a shared, idiomatic, democratic mode. In effect, he communicated in a code that fostered creativity via navigation within a network of potentials. And he expected his audience to be fluent in that specialized code as well. Although he wrote for publication and consumption by silent readers, Njegoš was for all intents and purposes "singing on the page." And we read him best when we read him within that context.

All this has implications for *referentiality* as well. Of course, language isn't language without referential content, without a malleable set of signifiers to conjure with and signifieds to partner with. But OT, as I have shown elsewhere, typically depends more intensively on special codes than garden-variety, everyday language. That's why the single verb *Pocmilije* ("He cried out") as the opening word in a South Slavic oral epic (after the prologue) reflexively indicates an *Odyssey*-type story to follow, whoever the *dramatis personae* turn out to be. That's why, in that same tradition, the phrase "black cuckoo" idiomatically identifies a woman either already or about to be widowed. (Perhaps this isn't so different a dynamic from what Suzanne Pinckney Stetkevych calls "rhetoric as ritual.") Within the special language or register of this kind of communication, units and patterns take on "extra" meanings that we will not find glossed in any dictionary or lexicon, tAgora instruments that they are. Referentiality in oral tradition is more than textual and more than lexical: it is metonymic, traditional, and democratic.

What is true in the oAgora is, perhaps not unexpectedly by now, true in the eAgora as well. Web addresses, or URLs, for example, also employ special codes to generate meaning. Internet addresses, such as http://www.oraltradition.org, for instance, signify little or nothing outside the specialized language of the web. But combine the "protocol" (http), the WorldWideWeb indicator (www), the domain name (oraltradition), and the domain suffix (org) and you have a unique, dedicated pathway to a much larger, multidimensional reality. At every level of performative Internet code (html, RSS feeds, Java script, and so forth), it is precisely the uniqueness, combinatory character, and generativity of dedicated codes that enable surfing.

As I suggested with a homemade proverb in *How to Read an Oral Poem*, "Oral tradition works like language, only more so." The same sort of super-idiom can be identified as the root algorithm of web expression as well. Likewise, and again adverting to a proverb from that same book, "Performance is the enabling event, tradition is the context for that event." In other words, doing and experiencing are part of the meaning; and implied, idiomatic referents are a crucial part of the communication. Again, we find the web-surfer and the OT surfer engaged in cognate pursuits: they are clicking through networks of potentials. And even those pathways that they choose not to follow on a given excursion remain a present, immanent resource that contribute to the process. Most fundamentally, then, even idiomatic referral is open, shared, and democratic.

IV: READING DEMOCRATICALLY

In the few minutes that remain I would like to introduce you to an initiative that has taken shape as I have worried over how to most effectively study and represent the analogy between oral tradition (OT) and Internet technology (IT). Only too clearly, a conventional book, although it has many advantages, runs the risk of obscuring more than it explains about this counterintuitive thesis, and so I have looked elsewhere—to something called the *Pathways Project*.

Briefly stated, the *Pathways Project* offers a network of interconnected nodes that can be read in different sequences, via different strategies, and with different emphases. It consists of two parts: a brick-and-mortar (though quite unconventional) book that will be published by the University of Illinois Press and an online, open-access facility at http://pathwaysproject.org .

First, the book. Entitled *Pathways of the Mind: Oral Tradition and the Internet*, this is a *morphing book* that can be read in not one but a number of ways. You can choose to march straight through, from page one to the end, and the presentation is configured to make sense if construed in that order. Alternatively, it is possible to consult topics attached to one of the three agoras, and to parse the book's contents from that perspective. Or the reader can opt to follow any of the several "maps" included in the introduction. These maps describe non-linear ways to construe the book's contents—by consulting a group of sections that bear on a topic or issue of importance—for example, on democracy in media. Still other readers may decide to follow pathways suggested within the short units or thought-bytes that make up the book (mostly 1000–2000 words in length), thus charting itineraries that are even more idiosyncratic. How you proceed is entirely up to you, and you can return for as many different experiences as you like. The morphing book will support multiple visits and multiple construals.

Of course, it is also at heart a book, and cannot be entirely forced out of the linear dynamic that has served book technology so well for so long. In that way, and even though the morphing book opens up options for the co-creation of emergent meaning, it also reminds us of the categorical difference between transactions in the oAgora on the one hand, and in the tAgora on the other. Books are, to our great advantage, still and always books.

The second part of the *Pathways Project, the online facility*, is not a book, and therein lies a fundamental difference. Options for "reading" the electronic network (strictly speaking, a wiki) are unencumbered by physical limitations such as spatialization, page-turning, lemmatization, and so forth. To emphasize the opportunities inherent in the network, we have built the digital architecture to foster four kinds of reading processes, the latter three of which produce practically infinite variation.

Method one: *Table of Contents*. You can, as with the morphing book, march straight through, although this strategy is much more transparently non-canonical when it is deployed electronically; it is more clearly just one of hundreds or thousands of possible sequences supported by the facility. You can glimpse this reality by looking at the righthand menu-bar, where other nodes, including a full table of contents, are always available. Or you can navigate on the fly. I should add that it takes a great deal of restraint to maintain any fixed agenda in the face of options that are just a click away at every turn, but, with a stiff upper lip, it can be done.

Method two: *The Three Agoras*. In lieu of "straight through," you can proceed according to one of the three agoras, as in the brick-and-mortar book associated with the *Pathways Project*. If you select this option, click on the chosen agora in the top menu-bar and you will be taken to a longer-than-usual background section (or node) on the nature of transactions in that arena, combined with numerous internal links to other nodes of interest. You make an initial choice of agora, and then follow the possibilities as they emerge.

Method three: *The eWorld Link-map*. Or you can decide to pursue one of the *link-maps* available in the righthand menu-bar. A *link-map* is a pre-planned routing or sequence of pathways suggested because its nodes all treat a topic that may prove useful to people wishing to explore various aspects of the OT-IT homology. *The eWorld link-map*, for instance, consists of several nodes that look at what it means to live and work and think about oral tradition in an increasingly virtual environment.

Method four: *Internal Branches*. It is not so much an algorithm for construal as a continuing option for readers plotting their own expeditions through the web of the *Pathways Project*. Branches, as I call them, are simply links within nodes that offer a detour from that particular node to pursue a related topic—always with the option of returning merely by clicking the return button in your browser. You may decide to forgo all such detours (and even the root sense of the word "detour" doesn't really work in this context), or you may choose to follow one or many of them; the itinerary of your reading experience is in your hands.

As the *Pathways Project* develops, I hope that it helps us better understand the cognitive advantages and disadvantages of various media-technologies in general, and the nature and implications of the OT-IT homology in particular.

EPILOGUE: ODEMOCRACY & EDEMOCRACY

Perhaps appropriately for a conference on orality and literacy, I will close with a story or parable. It's an oral story, to be sure, and it really did happen, though it's not terribly traditional. Like many Native American tales from oral tradition, it ponders abstract concepts by portraying them as a concrete human drama. And like folktales the world over, it teaches. Or at least it taught me a lesson that I won't forget.

One day, quite out of the ether, I received an e-mail from a certain Ćamil Bajgorić, who pronounced himself interested in reading *The Wedding of Mustajbey's Son Bećirbey*, a South Slavic oral epic I had published in two forms—as a brick-and-mortar book and as a gratis online contribution. I should point out that the online edition features a complete audio of the 1935 performance together with hyperlinked glossary and commentary, all attached to a transcription and English translation—in other words, a multimedia experience available free of charge. It seems Ćamil had discovered the online reference to my eEdition while surfing through various South Slavic sites, and was contacting me because our link wasn't working. (The problem was straightforward enough, as I quickly wrote back; he had simply caught us at a point of transition between servers.)

Now as a rule, broken web links are a dependable source of embarrassment, but in this instance the reported malfunction turned out to be a great stroke of good luck. Think about it: if the URL had functioned smoothly and invisibly, as it should have, Mr. Bajgorić could have silently accessed the eEdition without my knowledge, used it in whatever way and for whatever purpose he had in mind, and exited without a discernible trace. I would never have become aware of his interest, and I would have no story to tell. And that, as I will explain in a moment, would have been a shame.

Why? Because Ćamil Bajgorić went on to mention that the *guslar* (or epic singer) Halil Bajgorić, the performer of the epic he wished to read, was none other than his own grandfather! The grandson wanted to read the story, of course, but part of his motivation was also, shall we say, genealogical. With that kin-connection to spur us on, we quickly finished migrating the eEdition to the new server and restored the link so that the *guslar*'s grandson (and you too, if you so choose) could experience his grandfather's performance not as a text but in multimedia. Thanks to www.oraltradition.org/zbm, OT remains virtually available via IT.

Thinking back over this extraordinary sequence of events in the weeks that followed, I was struck by the fact that Halil's epic and Ćamil's request mimed the fundamental connection in the *Pathways Project*, our online facility devoted to analysis and representation of OT and IT. The real-life episode synched OT and IT in a memorable way because it bridged oral tradition and the Internet, and did so booklessly. Halil, himself preliterate, composed his epic without the cognitive prosthesis of the page, and Ćamil attended that performance via the virtual reality of the Internet. The composite paper edition—the culturally sanctioned vehicle—never figured in the interface between grandfather and grandson (at least until I sent Ćamil a copy of the book). Moreover, by reintegrating various dimensions of the song-performance—voice, music, context, commentary, etc.—into a single composite form reflective of the original composite event, the eEdition allowed the grandson a far more genuine experience of his grandfather's performance than a conventional paper edition could ever manage. Even if in facsimile, Ćamil became part of the audience for that performance.

Halil and Ćamil Bajgorić lived in vastly different worlds. One was a preliterate farm laborer from Dabrica, a tiny village in Bosnia, whose sole technology of communication was oral tradition. The other is a book-savvy and computer-literate resident of the state of Michigan devoted to learning more about his familial and ethnic identity. Although their life experiences were starkly disparate (and although they apparently never met face-to-face), each in his own way became a navigator of pathways. And in the final analysis it was precisely their parallel, homologous modes of navigation that brought them together, long after discontinuities in space and time seemed to preclude any sort of meeting.

OT and IT (or, better, OT as IT) made that connection—and made it democratically.

BIBLIOGRAPHY

Foley, John Miles. *How to Read an Oral Poem*. Urbana: University of Illinois Press, 2002.

———. *Oral Tradition and the Internet. Pathways of the Mind*. Urbana: University of Illinois Press, 2012.

———. *The Wedding of Mustajbey's Son Becirbey as Performed by Halil Bajgoric*. FF Communications 283. Helsinki: Suomalainen Tiedeakatemia, 2004.

Stock, Brian. *The Implications of Literacy: Written Language and Models of Interpretation in the Eleventh and Twelfth Centuries*. Princeton: Princeton University Press, 1983.

2

Torah on the Heart

Literary Jewish Textuality within Its Ancient Near Eastern Context

David Carr

This essay examines evidence for the interplay of memory recall and written technology in ancient Israel and surrounding cultures.[1] The focus is on recovering the processes by which ancient Israelite authors wrote and revised long-duration texts of the sort found in the Hebrew Bible. Thus, this essay does not address the process by which display, administrative, or other types of texts were written, however important those genres were. Instead, the primary emphasis is on what we can learn from other cultures, epigraphy, manuscripts, and references within the Hebrew Bible itself about the context in which such texts transmitted over long periods of time were composed and revised, texts that might be broadly described as literary-theological in

1. This essay combines review of past work and a report on work in progress. Portions of this research were presented in English at the California Biblical Colloquium on February 15, 2008, and at the Rice Conference on Orality and Literacy on April 14, 2008. My thanks go to participants in each forum for responses that helped me improve upon the work that they heard. Portions of the first part of this essay on general dynamics of orality and written textuality were presented in much earlier form at several lectures in Germany in the spring of 2005 (now published as Carr, "Mündlich-Schriftliche Bildung"). Unless otherwise indicated, the translations included in this essay are my own.

emphasis (such as the Epic of Gilgamesh, Ptah-Hotep, Homer, the Bible—with "theology" used in its very broadest sense).

Remarkably little has been written on this topic in the several centuries of biblical scholarship, especially given how much scholars have wanted to say about the stages through which the Hebrew Bible reached its present form. On the one hand, since the 1700s, scholars have developed many theories, some quite compelling, about sources and layers of redactional revision in the texts of the Pentateuch/Torah (Genesis–Deuteronomy) and other parts of the Hebrew Bible. On the other hand, very few have explored concretely how such sources were created or revised, other than to posit some general sort of transition from oral traditions/cycles to written compositions/sources/redactions. Moreover, the few studies that have addressed the specific processes of writing, however worthwhile they are have focused almost exclusively on what might be termed the "material technology" of writing: the creation and preparation of different sorts of scrolls, pens, and ink, and various sorts of scribal markings.[2] Even now, with a resurgence of focus on the "scribal" context of the Hebrew Bible in some recent and important publications,[3] much more emphasis has been put on the historical contexts of writing on the one hand and on exigencies of scroll technology on the other—for example, how long a scroll lasts.

However important those dimensions of composition are, this essay focuses on another issue that might be termed the "cognitive technology" of textual composition and revision. As will be evident in the first part of the essay, this focus comes from some parallel themes that have emerged in studies of textuality in Mesopotamia, Egypt, and Greece. Together, these themes—emerging largely independently in these different disciplines—point to education and socialization of leading elites as a primary context, if not *the* primary context, for the transmission of the kind of long-duration literature seen in the Bible, as well as literature such as Gilgamesh, the Enuma Elish, or Homer. By "long-duration literature" is meant texts—usually viewed in some way as particularly archaic/ancient, inspired/holy, and obscure/inaccessible—that are passed from generation to generation, transcending whatever their original time-bound contexts might be and being consumed by generation after generation. "Education/enculturation" is not necessarily training in a "school" that we might recognize today with a professional teacher and separate building, but more a familial or

2. See Blau, *Heilige Schrift*, and Blau, *Studien*; Breasted, *Edwin Smith Surgical Papyrus*; Eissfeldt, "Mesopotamische Elemente"; Martin, *Scribal Character*; Wilson and Wills, "Literary Sources"; Tov, *Scribal Practices*, and others.

3. See Schniedewind, *How the Bible Became a Book*; and van der Toorn, *Scribal Culture*.

pseudo-familial arrangement where a "father" taught his sons (or students seen as "sons") the ancient tradition in a part-time or apprentice-like setting alongside other activities. As will be discussed shortly, the "elites" thus educated are not just textual professionals, for example "scribes" as most conceive that word, but priestly, governmental, high-level military, bureaucratic, and other elites as part of larger-scale city-states, empires, and similar formations.

The comparative argument for these assertions is presented in much more detail in my book *Writing on the Tablet of the Heart: Origins of Scripture and Literature*. In it I argue that the main point of the textual production and reception process in the educational/ enculturational context was not to incise and revise texts on parchment, papyrus, or tablet. Rather, the aim was to "incise" such texts word for word on the minds of the next generation. A form of ancient literacy was learned, but the whole process was much more than mere learning of letters and words. It was the appropriation of an entire vocabulary of episodes, poetic lines, narrative themes, and implicit values. Written copies of texts served a subsidiary purpose in this system—as numinous symbols of the hallowed ancient tradition, as learning aids, and as reference points to insure accurate performance.

One particular emphasis of the book was on the importance of overcoming typical dichotomies between "orality" and "literacy" that continue to dominate many studies of ancient literature. Though scholars decades ago deconstructed the idea that there was a "great divide" between orality and literacy, a remarkable number of high quality publications still work with a strong distinction between the two, or at least a "continuum" with orality at one end and literacy at the other. Certainly, there are meaningful distinctions to be made between different modes of textual transmission, and for certain genres of texts—such as receipts (written) or exclusively oral legends (oral)—the distinction is still important. Nevertheless, I maintain that such distinctions obscure more than they help in the study of literature like the Bible, for the Bible was formed and used in an oral-written context. On the one hand, biblical texts and similar texts in other cultures were "oral" in the sense that they were memorized, and—in certain cases—publicly performed. On the other hand, written copies of these texts were used in this process to help students accurately internalize the textual tradition, check their accuracy and correct it, and/ or as an aid in the oral presentation of the text.

We can better imagine this process through looking at how written musical scores function in the training and performance of music. Most musicians never progress to the point where they can read a complex musical score "by sight." Instead, as a student of music one learns to read musical scores, and then gradually learns and performs progressively more difficult pieces of music. Sometimes, of course, a student practices such written music to the point where she or he can perform it by heart. Nevertheless, even if a musician has learned a piece well, he or she will often find it helpful to have a copy of the music in view to remind him or her of sections they would otherwise forget. In addition, especially in the time before electronic recording was possible, the written score was a primary way by which musical works were handed down from one generation to another accurately. In all times the written musical score functions as a learning, performance, and transmission aid in a primarily aural endeavor: making music.[4]

In *Tablet of the Heart*, I argue that the primary focus of both orality and literacy in the use of texts like the Bible was cognitive and social. Though there are reported performances of texts in select contexts for broader audiences—such as the reading of the Torah by Ezra or pan-Hellenic performances of epic poetry—the main context for their transmission and revision over time was the process of internalizing texts, word for word, within the context of ancient education. The following four quotes illustrate the cross-cultural importance of this process, each coming from a different one of the above-mentioned contexts:

> [T]he whole vocabulary of the scribal art, I will recite for you, I know it much better than you.[5]

> You are, of course, a skilled scribe at the head of his fellows, and the teaching of every book is incised on your heart.[6]

> [M]ay you engrave it on the tablets of your mind.[7]

> Write [my commandments/teachings] on the tablets of your heart.[8]

The examples could be multiplied, but this is a sampling of four quotes from four oral–written cultures where people used writing to memorize and perform predominantly oral works. The four quotes come from, respectively, Mesopotamia, Egypt, Greece, and ancient Israel.

4. For a nuanced discussion of the different sorts of roles that written music and practice play in different kinds of music, see Finnegan, *Literacy and Orality*; Finnegan, *Hidden Musicians*.

5. Edubba dialogue 1, 59, as translated by Sjöberg 1975:164.

6. Satiric Letter II, 2–3, following the rendering of Fischer-Elfert 1986:94.

7. Aeschylus, *Prometheus Bound*, 788.

8. Prov 3:3; 7:3.

Using those quotes as an entry point, let us turn now for a brief review of literary-educational systems in Mesopotamia, Egypt, and Greece. This will serve as a prelude to a preliminary report on work that I have done over the last few years on text-critical evidence for oral–written preservation and revision of ancient literature, particularly in ancient Israel.

THE COMPARATIVE ARGUMENT

Mesopotamia

I start with Mesopotamian education in a bilingual corpus of Sumerian and Akkadian works. Put briefly, there are multiple pointers in Mesopotamian literature to a writing-supported process of memorization. For example, there are some parodic pictures of ancient education, one of which includes the quote given above about "reciting the whole scribal art" or another where a fictive student in a dialogue claims that his teacher only had to show him one sign, and he could recite several others in the list from memory.[9] One tablet has 639 lines from five compositions preserved in minute script. Even with the minuscule writing on the tablet, there was not enough space on the postcard-sized tablet for all five compositions, so just the first line of various stanzas was given, with the reader expected to provide the rest from memory.[10]

That said, there are certainly ways in which Mesopotamian education and literature diverge from counterparts elsewhere. In particular, Mesopotamian education is distinguished from other forms of education by its predominant use of clay tablet technology, unusually intensive use of educational lists, and the fairly wide variety of genres of texts used later in education. Though Egypt, Israel, and Greece each used lists to a limited extent, especially in early stages of education, Mesopotamian education—as documented in particular through "type 2" tablets that combined successive educational exercises on the same artifact—featured a massive series of lists of cuneiform signs and words at the outset of the educational process, before students progressed to what we might call "wisdom works" and then on to love songs, myths, and so on.[11] Notably, these lists were among the most prominent parts of Mesopotamian education as it was practiced outside Mesopotamia in the second millennium. During that period we

9. Vanstiphout, "Dialogue," 92, lines 19–20 and 34–35.

10. Waetzoldt, "Der Schreiber als Lehrer in Mesopotamien," 36.

11. The preeminent study taking advantage of this data is Veldhuis, "Mesopotamian Canons."

find remnants of such lists in Egypt, Syro-Canaan, Hatti, Elam, and various other loci across the Near East.[12] In addition, such examples of "peripheral" cuneiform education appear to have focused on a limited group of more advanced literary texts, the Epic of Gilgamesh being among the most prominent. A variety of archaeological finds show that such cuneiform education occurred in city-states of ancient Canaan just before the emergence of ancient Israel, a training that insured the internalization of Mesopotamian lists and portions of works such as Gilgamesh by officials in towns such as Jerusalem.[13]

Egypt

The Egyptian system, of course, also lies close to Israel, and likewise played some role in the emergence of early Israelite textuality, as is evident in the Israelite appropriation of Egyptian terms for writing implements, Egyptian numerals, and the Egyptian mode of writing right to left. It is the Egyptian system that was the source of the quote, "You are, of course, a skilled scribe at the head of his fellows, and the teaching of every book is incised on your heart."[14] Many other witnesses to oral–written education could be added, such as the oft-quoted comment in the Instruction of Merikare, "Do not kill one whose excellences you know, with whom you once chanted the writings," or the conclusion to the Instruction of Ptah-Hotep, which talks of how "Memory of [the teaching's maxims] will not depart from the mouths of humankind, because of the perfection of their verses."[15]

There are a number of indications that Egypt, like Mesopotamia, had an oral–written process of education that focused on internalization and socialization of youths for elite roles. Egyptian educational literature includes frequent calls to memorize the teachings of the written texts.[16] Practice copies of Egyptian instructional texts often include red markings to aid in recitation and internalization of memorizable blocks. Even the Egyptian word for "read," *šdy*, means "read aloud," pointing to the interrelationship of both writing and orality in the educational internalization process.[17]

12. For a survey, see Carr, *Tablet of the Heart*, 47–61.

13. Horowitz et al., "Bibliographical List."

14. Fischer-Elfert, *Papyrus Anastasi I*, 94.

15. Parkinson, *Tale of Sinuhe*, 51.

16. Posener, "Manuscrits égyptiens"; Brunner, *Altägyptische Erziehung*, 74–76; Schlott, *Schrift und Schreiber*, 69; McDowell, "Student Exercises," 607; Parkinson, *Poetry and Culture*, 116–17.

17. Morenz, *Beiträge*, 43–52.

Overall, the textual-educational system in Egypt is distinguished from that in Mesopotamia by several features. As suggested before, there was far less focus on educational use of lists, with lists used only to a limited extent beginning in the New Kingdom period. Moreover, Egyptian education featured a far greater focus on use of wisdom instructions in education. Though there is some use of texts from other genres, such as the *Hymn to the Inundation* or the *Prophecy of Neferti*, the dominant texts in each period of Egyptian education were instructions attributed to great sages from ancient periods.[18]

One important way that the textual cultures of Egypt and Mesopotamia was similar is the following: they both used words for "scribe" to label people who had completed education. This similarity, however, has misled many scholars to isolate these cultures as "scribal" as opposed to supposedly more egalitarian cultures such as Greece. What is often overlooked in such comparisons is the fact that the term "scribe" in Egypt and Mesopotamia functioned similarly to that of "college graduate" in our context. It did not mean that the person was a textual professional, though that was often the case. In many if not more other instances, "scribes" in Egypt and Mesopotamia worked as priests, bureaucrats, military officials, courtiers, advisers, and so on. "Scribe" was a badge of graduation that allowed you to perform such elite roles in both Mesopotamia and Egypt. It didn't necessarily mean you spent most of your time writing and reading.[19] In this sense the focus in some recent literature on the "scribal" context of the formation of biblical literature is potentially misleading, at least insofar as it might lead some to think that all biblical texts were produced by full-time writing professionals.

Greek Textuality (Ancient and Hellenistic)

Greece, in contrast to the other cultures discussed so far, does not call its elites "scribes," and Greece uses an alphabetic writing system. On this basis many have drawn sharp distinctions between education and literacy in Greece as compared with so-called "scribal" systems in Egypt and Mesopotamia. But in fact the picture is not so clear. Early estimates of high literacy in the Greco-Roman world have been cast in doubt by William Harris's work (especially 1989). And recent studies have likewise questioned the

18. For more survey and literature, see Carr, *Tablet of the Heart*, 63–83.

19. For Mesopotamia, see Michalowski, "Ebla," 62; Vanstiphout, "Old Edubba Education," 5, 7–8; Veldhuis, *Elementary Education*, 143–44, and Gesche, *Schulunterricht*, 14–16. For Egypt, see Janssen and Janssen, *Growing up in Ancient Egypt*, 67–68; and Baines and Eyre, "Four Notes," 66–71.

supposed ease of alphabetic reading systems.[20] At least as it was learned in the ancient world, you were taught alphabets through "word images" no less numerous or counterintuitive than Egyptian hieroglyphs. Moreover, Greek students were to memorize—at least in theory—a vast bulk of Homeric and other verse.

We see reflections of this idea in the quote given above, "may you engrave it on the tablets of your mind" and other similar quotes in Greek literature.[21] For example, we see multiple references—often satirical—to the memorization of Greek literature in Aristophanes and Euripides, and Plato refers to memorization in multiple contexts as well. For example, in his *Laws* dialogue, he has a character, the "Athenian stranger," describe how students are given reading lessons in a "great number of poets" and required to "learn them by heart."[22]

Generally, the perishability of Greek writing materials means that we have few student exercises, aside from a handful of abecedaries—alphabet practice—found on broken pottery. Otherwise, we are dependent on whole works that were transmitted over time as part of classical education. Nevertheless, as if to compensate, we have a new type of data largely missing from above-discussed cultures: artistic representations of teaching and reading on sixth to fifth-century vases, including the famous Douris cup 2285 in Berlin. That image has been persuasively interpreted as a youth standing before his teacher, reciting a text of which the teacher held a copy on his lap. The text has been internalized by the student, while the written copy is used as a control to insure accurate learning.

In addition, this image and other vase representations of school scenes often have lyres on the walls, supplementing other indicators that Greece—like Mesopotamia and possibly Egypt—used the medium of music to write texts on the hearts of students (some Mesopotamian texts have musical notations, and the red marks in Egyptian seem to have been, in part, semi-musical). Music functions like the indelible marker of ancient education—a tool used to help students memorize vast quantities of material. If one is in doubt about the feasibility of a student memorizing such huge quantities of material, one need only consider the ability of a teenager to memorize thousands of lines of popular music through listening to such music on a digital player.

Greek literature also includes another pointer to the process of memorization: explicit discussion of the training of memory and means toward

20. See Davies, "Forms of Writing."

21. Aeschylus, *Prometheus Bound*, 788.

22. *Laws* 810e–11a.

that end. This includes reference to certain compositional devices used by both authors and students to compose/remember an easily memorizable text. One of these devices is the acrostic, which—among other things—helps a student in the difficult task of keeping the lines of a poem in proper order. Another such compositional/memory device is the chiastic pattern, which likewise aids in ordering. Both devices are seen not just in Greece, but also in other cultures that similarly focus on cognitive internalization of literary texts.

Once we move to Greek education in the Hellenistic period, we have a new range of data, particularly from Greek education in Egypt. The dry conditions of that country allowed the preservation of many Greek school exercises, used in the education of those who studied Greek literature in order to qualify to be a part of the Hellenistic administration. Furthermore, we have a few Greek school books from Hellenistic Egypt. Like the above-mentioned "type 2" exercises from Mesopotamia, they provide clues to the sequence of education in Hellenistic Egypt. Interestingly, as in Mesopotamia, a student in Hellenistic Egypt would start by reading, writing, and memorizing lists—this time of the alphabet and alphabetized lists of names and words. Next came gnomic "wisdom"-like material, and the students spent the rest of their education on more advanced exercises with such wisdom material along with memorization of portions of Homer (above all) and other core parts of Greek literature.

Pre-Hellenistic Israel and the Hebrew Bible

These data from other cultures, much better documented than that of ancient Israel because of a combination of larger-scale and more widespread preservation of remains (such as tablets or manuscripts preserved in the Egyptian desert), provide a far better starting point for study of textuality in ancient Israel than present-day or recent analogies. Where much biblical scholarship has been dominated by unconscious models drawn from print culture, these ancient cultures—however diverse—show the absolutely central role of the mind—especially the learning/ memorizing/composing mind—in the formation and revision of ancient literary-theological texts transmitted over generations. The more clarity we have that long-duration, literary-theological texts in other cultures were transmitted as part of an oral–written process of education and memorization, the more the burden of proof lies on someone who wants to argue that ancient Israel is the great exception.

Nevertheless, there is no need to argue that Israel is the great exception, however much biblical scholarship (with its orientation to the holy canon) often has wanted to maintain just that. Instead, it turns out that this model of textuality amidst oral–written enculturation/education correlates well with data both inside and outside the Hebrew Bible for the existence and importance of similar processes of socialization of elites through a process of oral–written internalization of ancient texts.

To be sure, any such textual-educational system in Israel was on a smaller scale than some of those systems discussed above. Moreover, like those systems, Israel probably had few if any recognizable "schools." Instead, education happened in the family or in a pseudo-familial context, probably largely on an apprentice-like model. Both epigraphic and biblical evidence show that some people—virtually all of them officer-class or above—did learn writing and used it extensively. Archaeology, for example, provides a useful supplement to biblical evidence, since digs have turned up an increasing number of abecedaries and other early school exercises from the period of ancient Israel. Indeed, we actually have more such evidence for the case of ancient Israel than we do for the case of ancient Greece. We should remember that ancient Israelite education/formation, like other such systems, was almost certainly oral as well as written, perhaps even oral primarily in many instances. As a result, the focus was not on learning to read and write. Those were only tools.

With those qualifications, the above-discussed model of oral–written education in a familial setting proves unusually illuminating in looking at the peculiar mix of data in the Hebrew Bible regarding the production and reception of texts. Examples of such data include texts from Proverbs, quoted before, about writing on the tablet of the student's heart (Prov 3:3; 7:3), or counterparts to these texts in Deuteronomy 6 and 11 now focused on the Mosaic Torah (Deut 6:6–9; 11:18–21), or oft-cited texts from Isaiah that speak of sealing Isaiah's alternative "Torah" on the hearts of his son/students (Isa 8:16–18; 30:9–11), various references to the memorization of written "songs" in ancient Israel (see the Song of Moses; Deut 31:19, 22; 32:44–46), the promise in Jeremiah that God will write the new covenant on the heart of Israel (Jer 31:33–34), Ezekiel's "eating the scroll" as an image of internalization of a written message (Ezek 2:9–3:3), mention of God's Torah being written on the inmost parts of the Psalmist in Psalm 40:9, and many, many other reflections of oral–written education in the writings of the Hebrew Bible.[23] And this does not begin to encompass the evidence for

23. Much of the most important evidence is surveyed in Carr, *Tablet of the Heart*, 122–61.

such oral–written education in Ben Sira, Qumran materials, Pseudepigrapha, Josephus, Philo, and other Second Temple sources.[24]

To be sure, there is more emphasis in the biblical tradition on "hearing" than on the "writing" and "reading" of biblical texts, let alone the education of students in such texts. Nevertheless, this biblical emphasis on "hearing" and "speaking" must be put in context. The point was not writing and reading texts written on parchment or papyrus, the point was writing the texts of the ancient tradition "on the hearts" of the student, having them "hear" and internalize them. Therefore, we should not be surprised at the elusive way in which written texts feature in many ancient Israelite discussions of learning. This is a contrast to today's writing- and print-focused educational culture. When we look for educational enterprises in the ancient world, most scholars are predominantly focused on written texts. For ancient cultures such as Israel such copies of texts were aids to memorization and numinous symbolic tokens of tradition. Within this oral-primary culture, even the texts themselves primarily thematized hearing and remembering.

MANUSCRIPT EVIDENCE FOR THE ROLE OF MEMORY IN TRANSMISSION OF TEXTS

That said, there is another way in which ancient Israelite writing can be used as a way of uncovering the memorization and internalization process by which biblical texts were formed: analysis of text-critical and other variants in the transmission of biblical literature. In a seminal article penned in 1930, Milman Parry noted that past studies of classics had been hampered by a model that presupposed that Homeric epics had been created and transmitted through a purely literary process of writing and copying texts. Such scholars aimed to reconstruct the earliest written text of Homer through eliminating various errors that occurred through careless copying by ancient scribes. In response, Parry objected:

> How have they explained the unique number of *good* variant readings in our text of Homer, and the need for laborious editions of Aristarchus and of the other grammarians, and the extra lines, which grow in number as new papyri are found?[25]

24. Again, see Carr, *Tablet of the Heart*, 201–85, for more detail.

25. Parry, "Oral Verse-Making I," 75–76, reprinted in Parry, *Homeric Verse*, 268. See also his discussion of some such variants, Parry, "Oral Verse-Making I," 112–14, reprinted in Parry, *Homeric Verse*, 297–98, and his further comments in Parry, Oral Verse-Making I," 46–47, reprinted in Parry, *Homeric Verse*, 361.

Parry went on to elaborate on the idea that memorized and performed texts exhibit a different sort of variation from written traditions that are transmitted purely through graphic copying. The latter sort of traditions will show variations that are often the result of visual errors of copyists—graphic variants: a skipped line, misinterpreted letters, and so on. The lists of such errors are prominent in almost any text-critical handbook. Typically the result of such a copying error is a text that is garbled, where at least one or the other variant does not make sense. But Parry noticed that the earliest manuscripts of Homer are characterized by another sort of variation, one where both variants make sense: *good* variants (emphasis in Parry's original). Moreover, he noted how dynamic the tradition was, again pointing to a process of free updating and adaptation rather than copying. These indicators—preserved in the written records of Homeric verse—pointed to an earlier or concomitant process of memorization and recitation.

Parry's comments were preliminary. He was working from hunches about what might constitute markers of orally transmitted texts. Yet his suggestions coincide in a remarkable way with an equally seminal study in another discipline published just two years after his article (based on studies done years prior): Frederic Bartlett's experimental psychological study *Remembering*. In the process of observing his subjects' results in reproducing texts, Bartlett observed some of the sorts of variation that Parry intuitively saw as characteristic of orally transmitted traditions. One set of Bartlett's experiments focused on changes introduced by a single individual as he or she attempted repeated recall of a text over ever greater periods of time. Though the variation was greater than in the Homeric manuscripts, one thing was common: Bartlett's students produced variant versions of the tradition that made sense, indeed they often transformed the tradition so that it made more sense to them. Bartlett termed this processing of the tradition in memorization the "effort after meaning."[26] In another series of experiments, Bartlett studied "serial reproduction," that is, reproduction of a variety of sorts of texts down a chain of different persons. In some ways the changes were similar to those seen in repeated reproduction of a text by the same individual: abbreviation, loss of specific names and numbers, rationalization. Nevertheless, depending on their genre, many such texts underwent massive transformations, at least initially in the process. They were radically abbreviated and sometimes completely reversed. Certain kinds of texts or parts of texts often survived. For example, students radically revised virtually all

26. Bartlett, *Remembering*, 84.

parts of one story given to them, but often remembered one striking line in it: "Lawn tennis has often been described as a mutual cocktail."[27]

Building on these experiments, Bartlett argued for the essentially reconstructive character of memory. The recall seen in Bartlett's subjects was not a sort of blurry reflection of an exact image of a text. It was not as if each person remembered 10–100 percent of the exact words of a given text. Rather, the sort of variation seen in both repeated and serial reproduction reflected how each person built his or her recalled version of a text out of what they understood of a text. The result of this "effort after meaning," especially when multiple people engaged in this sense-making process, was radical transformation. Yet Bartlett also found that this transformation process had limits, limits often reached within three or four reproductions of a given story by different subjects. Once a story had reached a certain form among the tradents, it often did not change much. For example, a fifteen-line paragraph presenting an argument about the modification of the species is abbreviated by the third stage to nine successive versions quite close to the following two-line summary: "Mr. Garlick says isolation is the cause of modification. This is the reason that snakes and reptiles are not found in Ireland."[28] It was as if the readers had adapted this and other texts to their expectations and memory structures so that they reached a relatively fixed form.

Though Bartlett's experiments produced higher variation than that seen in the early Homeric manuscripts mentioned by Parry, subsequent memory research has discovered a number of real-life strategies that social groups use to preserve oral tradition with less variation. For example, using poetic form to compose a text aids in the recall of that text. Someone reciting a poem knows that the correct text must follow a certain rhyme, meter, and/or other poetic device. Therefore, the poetic form of Homer and many other traditions aids in the recall of those traditions. In addition, many societies undergird the memorization of texts through linking them to music, so that a performer can match the correct text with the given music. Oral tradents in many cultures transmit texts of highly familiar genres, made up of familiar formulae and/or other literary elements. Whereas Bartlett had his students memorize a Native American story completely outside their tradition and frame of reference, a Homeric rhapsode or his contemporary equivalent could guide his reproduction of a given tradition by following

27. Ibid., 150–54.

28. Bartlett, *Remembering*, 121–35.

the generic and other constraints that he knew through acquaintance with the tradition.[29]

Indeed, Parry was one of the earliest and most influential scholars to identify the importance of such elements in oral transmission. His study of both Homeric and Yugoslavian epic argued that oral tradents reconstructed such traditions by building on their extensive repertoire of rhythmic formulae and other poetic structures. Furthermore, Parry, Lord, and others argued that "accuracy" of such recall was redefined in such situations. Such reciters do not have electronic means to verify whether or not a given performance matches another one word-for-word. Most performers do not aim for such reproduction in any case. Their virtuosity was measured by their mastery of formulae, tropes, and outlines of the epics, along with an ability to produce a masterful whole out of them.

Thus, even though Homeric rhapsodes, Yugoslav bards, and other native performers can produce texts with less variation than Bartlett's students, such real-life textual virtuosos cannot and do not aim for absolute verbatim accuracy. Rather, both they and their audiences know when a given performance varies excessively from what they consider the key formulaic, generic, and other constraints of the tradition. In this way Bartlett's experiments in serial reproduction failed to reflect the communal dimension of real-life situations of serial transmission of oral tradition. In Bartlett's single-line series of student reproductions, there was no way for multiple knowers/ hearers of a tradition to correct mistakes made at a given stage. Once a crucial part of a given story was lost by one student, that part could not be reconstructed by others later in the chain. But in actual oral transmission, a given performance is heard by others who share knowledge of the tradition. Performers can correct each other, and an audience can respond negatively if a part deemed essential is left out. This network of reinforcing processes is not and cannot be focused on verbatim accuracy. Nevertheless, it can prevent some of the more radical shifts seen in Bartlett's experiments with students who were trying to memorize texts in artificial situations.

Even so, the early manuscript tradition of Homer shows a level of agreement that surpasses anything that would be achievable through purely oral transmission—even a process reinforced by poetry, music, and other oral tactics. Empirical studies of recall—both of supposed examples of "photographic"/eidectic memory and of societies claiming total recall of their oral traditions—have not been able to document human ability to recall extensive tracts of text without the reference aid of written texts. In a

29. For an excellent summary of a range of psychological and anthropological studies bearing on textual recall, see Rubin, *Memory*.

series of studies done in the 1980s, Ian Hunter argued that the human brain does not retain the capacity to memorize more than fifty words without the aid of written or other memory aids.[30] And though anthropologists have discovered some cases of virtual verbatim recall of ritual and/or musically accompanied texts, these cases are isolated and feature the memorization of relatively brief texts. The main example of possible verbatim recall of more extensive tradition is the Hindu Vedic tradition, but unfortunately its early, exclusively oral transmission is not documented.

This has implications in interpreting the data seen in early Homeric manuscripts. Though Parry and others documented numerous examples of variation in lines or words of the Homeric corpus, the bulk of the lines parallel each other closely in a way that resembles transmission that must be undergirded in some way by writing. Thus the variants reflect a possible ongoing process of reproducing the tradition in memorized (or partially memorized) form, but the process of memorization is undergirded by writing-supported training and/or correction. This supposition is strengthened by the fact that the corpus is far larger than can be transmitted verbatim in exclusively oral form. The few documented examples of verbatim transmission in exclusively oral contexts focus on short texts. But the Homeric corpus comprises thousands of lines. Huge swaths of text in that corpus are verbally parallel, while the areas of variation are limited.

Thus, in the case of ancient textual materials such as Homeric epic or the Bible, we must contend with a mix of oral and written dynamics. To the extent that they were copied, they will manifest the sorts of verbal agreement and graphic variation seen in literary transmission. Yet to the extent that exemplars of the tradition or parts of the tradition were reproduced from memory, we will also see the kinds of variation typical of recall of textual material in human memory: substitution of synonymous terms, radical adaptation of the tradition, and so on. In what follows, these phenomena will be referred to as "memory variants," thus distinguishing them from the sorts of variants created through copying, "graphic variants," as well as from variants more typical of dictation, "aural variants."

STUDY OF MEMORY VARIANTS IN THE HUMANITIES (ESPECIALLY THE ANCIENT NEAR EAST)

In the years since Parry and Bartlett's seminal work, scholars in a number of branches of humanities have found such "memory variants" in manuscript

30. Hunter, "Lengthy Verbatim Recall (LVR) and Tape-Recorder Memory"; Hunter, "Lengthy Verbatim Recall."

traditions, even if they did not use that term. West's and Apthorp's work found many similar "good variants" in early Homeric manuscripts, along with other larger-scale variations, such as harmonization, typical of manuscripts transmitted through memory.[31] Sisam, Baugh, Duggan, Olsen, Allen, Doane, Zumthor,[32] and others have found similar phenomena in medieval and early modern European manuscripts. Such manuscripts paralleled each other over extended sections, yet they included or omitted minor words, varied in use of prepositions, substituted synonyms of words for each other, inflected words differently, varied in spelling of words in common, and occasionally featured minor and more significant variation in word order or larger sections. We even see similar evidence arising in musicology, such as work by Hendrik van der Werf,[33] who found that the manuscript tradition for medieval *chansons* features the sorts of variation characteristic of transmission in memory: substitution of equivalent wording, omission of words, lines, and stanzas, variation in spelling, word order, and even stanza order.

These are not the types of errors produced by a scribe who visually copies the original manuscript, producing a graphic parallel to the earlier exemplar. Instead, they are the kinds of variation typical of a scribe reproducing a text, at least in part, through memory. The qualification "in part" is important, because it is easily possible that a scribe might both consult a manuscript visually and reproduce other parts of it from memory, even when copying it virtually from beginning to end. We will see a probable example of this phenomenon from the Dead Sea Scrolls later in this essay. Moreover, different contexts are important for the appearance of memory variants. Within later Jewish tradition, for example, reference manuscripts were produced through a careful process of graphic copying (accompanied by singing!), but Jewish scholars still internalized biblical tradition and often would cite it from memory—rather than copying it—in producing other works, thus producing memory variants.

Before moving further into evidence from Judaism and older Israel-Judah, a brief survey of work on memory variants in ancient cultures is in order, with a focus on the cultures of the Mediterranean and Ancient Near East discussed previously. One thing that emerges in such a survey is how isolated the different studies are. Very few studies build on earlier ones, and discussion is usually confined to a given sub-discipline. For example, already in 1937, Axel Volten published a study of the Egyptian Instruction

31. West, *Ptolemaic Papyri of Homer*; Apthorp, *Manuscript Evidence*.

32. Sisam, "Notes"; Sisam, *Studies*; Baugh, "Improvisation"; Baugh, "Middle English Romance"; Duggan, "Role of Formulas"; Olsen, *Poetic Craft*; Allen, *King Horn*; Doane, "Ethnography"; Zumthor, *Essai*.

33. Van der Werf, *Chansons*.

of Anii that surveyed a series of errors typical of oral transmission, such as synonyms, unexplained loss of suffixes, and substitution of similar sentences. Though he does not appear aware of Parry's early article on oral-cognitive transmission of Homeric epic, Volten argued that a process of memorization would explain both these errors and some rearrangements of sections that happens in the textual tradition. Forty years later Günter Burkard published a book that was, in some ways, a response to Volten's work but no more conscious of the broader range of research on forms of transmission over previous decades in classics and literary studies. Burkard argued that memory errors were more characteristic of the earliest stage of tradition, such as in the early Instruction of Ptah-Hotep, rather than being predominant in later instructions, such as Anii.[34] Still, he found many short-term memory errors in the transmission of Old and Middle Kingdom instructions, many of which revealed New Kingdom students attempting the sort of "seeking after meaning" in older texts that was seen in Bartlett's experiments. Most significantly, Burkard was not arguing against the role of memory in transmission of traditions, but against an exclusively oral model. According to his theories, students used written exemplars to memorize the texts, but sometimes produced copies or portions of copies from memory. This oral-written model would explain the mix of graphic and memory errors in the manuscripts he studied.

Assyriology does not have, as far as I know, extensive studies of oral-written variants. Nevertheless, the transmission history of many Mesopotamian texts, including memory variation from edition to edition of those texts, is unusually well documented because the clay tablets on which they were written survived well. Many scholars of those texts have commented in passing on manuscript variants that probably result from memory or oral transmission. For example, in dialogue with Scandinavian-school scholars who posited an exclusively oral transmission history of biblical texts up to the post-exilic period, Geo Widengren noted how Mesopotamian *šu-ila* prayers preserved some variants that indicated interaction between orality and textuality.[35] Louis Levine notes in passing some synonymous and other variants that show Assyrian scribes treating inscriptions with striking freedom, and Bendt Alster briefly comments on how variants of the Lugalbanda tradition reflect an oral background.[36] Finally, Niek Veldhuis drew directly on Rubin's and other work on memory to theorize about memory dynamics surrounding the early transmission of early Mesopotamian lexical lists,

34. Burkard, *Textkritische Untersuchungen.*

35. Widengren, "Oral Tradition and Written Literature," 219.

36. Levine, "Inscriptions of Sennacherib," 72; Alster, "Lugalbanda," 63–64.

while also noting the diminishment of such memory dynamics in the later transmission of Mesopotamian literature.[37]

The above is just a sampling of observations of a much broader phenomenon. The Mesopotamian tradition contains a number of examples of multiply transmitted traditions. Virtually any time one compares parallel versions of cuneiform texts, as in—for example—Jeffrey Tigay's parallel comparisons of verbally parallel portions of the Gilgamesh epic, one finds plentiful examples of the sorts of memory variants discussed above: word order shifts, substitutions of lexical equivalents, minor shifts in grammar or prepositions, rearrangement of lines, and so on.[38] In addition, I surveyed and discussed a set of such variants in the Descent of Ishtar tradition in my *Writing on the Tablet of the Heart*.[39]

Ancient Israel did not have as extensive a scribal apparatus as either Egypt or the Mesopotamian kingdoms, and aside from the Bible, little literature from Israel or surrounding areas has survived. Israelite scribes wrote on more perishable materials than their Mesopotamian counterparts, and the climate of Israel meant that virtually no papyri from the ancient Israelite period survived (in contrast to Egypt where more papyri did survive). Nevertheless, as we will see, there are some data with which one can work, and this has been explored by a few scholars. A key early example is Helmer Ringgren's classic 1949 study of parallel versions of biblical poems. In this study he compared the parallel versions of several psalms and prophetic poems, classifying the variants by whether they were likely graphic errors, conscious alterations or updating, dictation, or other errors. Another, more recent example would be Raymond Person's article, "The Ancient Israelite Scribe as Performer," where he examines several examples of synonymous variants in the various versions of the Isaiah-Hezekiah narrative and builds on Doane's work on the "scribe as performer" (see above) to argue that such variants show the "oral mindset" of ancient Israelite scribes.[40] He also suggests that the sort of variation seen in the Qumran 1QIsa[a] scroll may reflect the same sort of oral mindset.

37. Veldhuis, *Elementary Education*, 131–41 and Veldhuis, "Mesopotamian Canons."

38. Tigay, *Evolution*, 58–68, 218–22.

39. Carr, *Tablet of the Heart*, 42–45.

40. Person, "Scribe as Performer"; rpt. in rev. form in Person, *Deuteronomic School*, 83–97.

MANUSCRIPT EVIDENCE FOR THE ORAL-WRITTEN TRANSMISSION AND REVISION OF ANCIENT SEMITIC TRADITIONS

Building on these studies, I have undertaken a comprehensive study of written traditions transmitted in parallel in the ancient Near East, with a particular focus on literary-theological traditions from Mesopotamia and ancient Israel. Building on work by Jerrold Cooper, Jeffrey Tigay, and others,[41] I have compiled parallel versions of the major Mesopotamian epics and inscriptions for which we have multiple editions, analyzed Abba Bendavid's biblical parallels and some of Primo Vannutelli's parallel version of the biblical histories,[42] and produced parallel versions of the major Qumran documents, such as the community rule, 4QRP, the Temple Scroll, and divergent early editions of biblical books, such as that found in 4QSam[a]. The following is a report on this work in process. Three preliminary findings are worth mention.

First, the phenomenon of memory variation is prevalent throughout these traditions. Though I am not myself an Assyriologist and thus am not equipped to evaluate such variants in Mesopotamian traditions, I can say that Tigay's lists of memory variants, along with numerous shifts in the order of lines in Mesopotamian texts, suggest that Mesopotamian texts were transmitted, at least in part, through a writing-supported process of internalization. On the biblical side, the Israeli linguist Tamar Zewi found numerous instances where Samuel-Kings and Chronicles vary in both directions in whether active or passive verbs are used to express similar content.[43] This and several similar cases involve syntactic variation that does not appear to be linked to diachronic shifts in the Hebrew language or differences in the semantic content. Moreover, they are not the kinds of shifts that typically occur in an environment focused exclusively on graphic copying of texts. Rather, they are examples—surveyed by a linguist without apparent investment in any model for the creation of this literature—of cognitive transformations that occur in texts transmitted, at least in part, through memory.[44]

41. Especially Cooper, "Gilgamesh Dreams of Enkidu"; Tigay, *Evolution*; George, *Babylonian Gilgamesh Epic.*

42. Bendavid, *Parallels*; Vannutelli, *Libri.*

43. Zewi, "Biblical Parallels," 240–41.

44. These examples could be multiplied through survey of work by biblical scholars, including scholars building cases for specific models of the relationship of the traditions of Chronicles and Samuel-Kings. For example, though Steven McKenzie, *Deuteronomic History*, repeatedly posits all kinds of graphic and ideological reasons for variation between Chronicles and Samuel-Kings in his detailed study of the relationship between the traditions, he also acknowledges a number of cases where the alternatives are so

Many more examples of such transformations have been uncovered by my survey of parallel editions of biblical correspondences and parallel editions at Qumran. Indeed, on the basis of this survey, it appears that the number of probable memory variants is far greater than that of probable graphic or aural variants.

The second major phenomenon that I have observed in this survey of documented revision of ancient texts is an overall "tendency toward expansion." In Mesopotamia, we see evidence of this expansion in the Sumerian king list, Hammurapi decree, and the Anzu, Atrahasis, and Gilgamesh epics. In ancient Israelite literature the relative dating of documented cases is more debated, but some of the clearer cases of documented expansion of otherwise verbatim parallels can be found in the proto-Samaritan Pentateuchal manuscripts, 4QRP, longer versions of Esther and Daniel, and probably the Jeremiah tradition. In some cases, such as the elimination of the barmaid's speech in the Gilgamesh tradition or the omission of large swaths of the Samuel-Kings tradition in Chronicles, later tradents do seem to have abbreviated, rather than expanded, their precursor tradition in some respects. Moreover, as many have observed, the royal inscription tradition in Mesopotamia often abbreviated narrations of earlier regnal years in favor of a consistent focus on the most recent one. Nevertheless, each such case has specific circumstances that explain the exception. The overall trend toward preservation and expansion of reproduced ancient traditions is clear.[45]

---

semantically similar that the originality of either reading is difficult to determine. One of several instances occurs in the versions of Solomon's prayer, where McKenzie, *Deuteronomic History*, 150, says that it is impossible to determine whether the reading of the Masoretic Text of 1 Kgs 8:29 (יומם after לילה) is original, or the reading of 2 Chr 6:20 and the Old Greek of 1 Kgs 8:29 (יומם occurs before לילה). Similarly, McKenzie, *Deuteronomic History*, 139, notes that either למלך (the Masoretic Text of 2 Kgs 10:10 and 2 Chr 9:9) or לשלמה (the OG of 2 Kgs 10:10) could be original.

45. It should also be noted that psychologists such as Bartlett, *Remembering*, and anthropologists have documented an opposing tendency toward abbreviation of traditions known/learned in exclusively *oral* form, a tendency leading toward focalization of central and unusual elements and elimination of elements deemed irrelevant. Furthermore, there are numerous examples of later authors drawing in a highly selective way on earlier traditions in the process of producing entirely new texts. Such appropriation of content is particularly characteristic of appropriation of material across a language barrier, as in the appropriation of narrative elements from earlier Sumerian Gilgamesh traditions in the Old Babylonian Gilgamesh epic. In all these cases the later tradition draws on the contents of the earlier tradition and often fragments of wording from such traditions, but the tradent does not reproduce long stretches of the precursor tradition and the resulting text lacks verbal agreement across long stretches. The later tradition may be longer at some points or shorter in others, but it does not come under the heading of this "trend toward expansion." It is not a reproduction of a written tradition known/learned in written form.

The third overall trend, again noted by some previous scholars, is that of harmonization, usually harmonization of one part of a given text to another section of what is understood to be the same text. Years ago, Cooper wrote an article on harmonization of Gilgamesh's two dreams about Enkidu in the Standard Babylonian version of the Gilgamesh epic,[46] and Tigay and Hans Jürgen Tertel have added a number of other examples of harmonization in the Gilgamesh and other major Mesopotamian epics.[47] Similarly, the proto-Samaritan and Temple scroll traditions feature other examples of harmonization of biblical laws.[48] Sometimes memory variants in these harmonizations can help us almost see into the scribe's workroom as he compiles the scroll. For example, starting in line 11 of the fifty-first column, the Temple Scroll reproduces large swaths of the Deuteronomic law in sequence, starting with the law of the courts in Deut 16:18–20. Aside from the law of the king, these later columns of the temple scroll have laws from Deuteronomy as the base text, which are then supplemented by fragments from Leviticus, Numbers, and other parts of Deuteronomy. One pattern that starts to emerge in these laws is the presence of relatively more memory variants in the portions of Scripture added from other loci in Deuteronomy and Leviticus.

For example, when Deut 22:6 is part of the base text reproduced in the Qumran Temple Scroll[49] (65:4), it is virtually identical with the Masoretic Text (with the exception of an added את), but in 52:6, where Deut 22:6 is drawn on selectively to enrich another passage in Deuteronomy, the wording varies more.[50] Similarly, in 11QT 2:1–15 (conflating Deut 7:25 in 2:7–11); 52:7–21 (conflating Deut 17:5 in 55:21), and 11QT 66:8–16 (adding material from Lev 20:21, 17; 18:12–13), the Temple scroll follows the base text much more closely than the biblical material that is being used to enrich or expand that base text. This may indicate that the author(s) of these portions of the Temple Scroll often graphically consulted a copy of Deuteronomy in producing the main text, but depended more on memory to enrich that main text with biblical passages distant from the pericope being reproduced. This matches what we know about the technology of scroll reading. Scrolls are unwieldy, and it is much easier to consult a scroll

46. Cooper, "Gilgamesh Dreams of Enkidu."

47. Tigay, *Evolution*, 93–100, 224–29; Tertel, *Text and Transmission*, 33–36, 43–54.

48. Tigay, "Conflation."

49. Hereafter Qumran Temple Scroll will be abbreviated as 11QT.

50. The different level of preservation of 22:6b was pointed out in Yadin, *Temple Scroll*, 233 (Hebrew orig. 1977).

graphically when reading or copying it from beginning to end, than to skip around, looking for isolated citations.

Overall, these documented cases of transmission of tradition provide invaluable glimpses into the minds of the tradents, showing how they regarded and processed the texts passed down to them from others. The massive verbatim agreement between these examples testifies to the probable use of writing to support the transmission of these traditions, since exclusively oral-cognitive tradition produces wider forms of variety than most examples mentioned here. Yet the presence of memory variants testifies to the occasional use of memory to transmit the traditions as well. In some cases such memory variants may have been produced when scribes reproduced an entire text from memory, having mastered it as students. Yet other dynamics may have been involved as well. In the case of the temple scroll and other texts as well we see a particular density of memory variants in places where a scribe inserts elements of another text—possibly from memory—into a broader context, such as elements of laws from Leviticus into a context in Deuteronomy. In other cases a scribe may draw on memory of another text to clarify the one being reproduced, replacing an archaic or otherwise odd term in the given text with a more contemporary or understandable term from its parallel. And then there may just be cases where memory variants in a section of text, such as the Ten Commandments, may betray a scribe's use of memory to reproduce that portion of text, while using graphic modes to reproduce others.

CONCLUDING REFLECTIONS ON BROADER PRINCIPLES AND METHODOLOGICAL IMPLICATIONS

One feature these three phenomena of oral–written transmission have in common is the overall focus of ancient tradents on preservation of written words from the past. Usually, this meant that they reproduced traditions with virtually no change. To be sure, as we have seen, such reproduction without change could include a variety of memory variants: changes of wording, order, or non-significant shifts in grammar or syntax. And graphically copied traditions could include various copyists' errors. Nevertheless, if we are to look empirically at the documented transmission of ancient texts, the first and most important thing to emphasize is the following: the vast majority of cases involve reproduction of earlier traditions with no shifts beyond the memory or graphic shifts surveyed so far. At the least, tradents aimed for preservation of the semantic content of traditions. Often, with time, traditions such as the later Mesopotamian and Jewish traditions developed various techniques for insuring more precise preservation of the tradition, often through processes of graphic copying and various techniques of proofing copies.

Amidst this overall trend toward preservation of ancient written tradition, two main trends of revision have emerged. Both are consistent in some way with the push toward preservation. First, we have seen how, as a general rule, ancient scholars who were producing a new version of an ancient tradition either preserved it unchanged (aside from memory or graphic variants) or expanded it. The other major sort of preservation amidst revision is the tendency of many ancient scholars to harmonize ancient traditions. Scholars reproducing ancient traditions had learned them well enough to recognize inconsistencies and divergences between different parts of them. Commands given early in the epic might not be executed precisely later in the story, or the execution might not be reported at all. Speeches might be partially, but not completely, parallel to one another. Laws on a given topic might be scattered broadly across a given work and/or be inconsistent. As we have seen, some scholars reproducing these traditions dealt with these phenomena by combining and/or harmonizing the divergent traditions. Commands and their executions would be made to match; speeches made parallel; laws joined and conformed to each other, and so on. Sometimes this process may have led to contraction of traditions, thus contradicting the above-described tendency of scholars to preserve and expand traditions. Yet this tendency can be seen nevertheless as another sort of preservation of traditions. I suggest that such harmonization involved what might be understood as a "hyper-memorization" of tradition where different parts of a textual tradition (or broader corpus) were understood to be so sacrosanct that they were not allowed to contradict each other.

Thus the push toward preservation of tradition combines in different ways with the "striving after meaning" (so Bartlett) that tradents do when reproducing traditions they cherish. At some stages, tradents may understand themselves to be producing "the same" tradition, when the product actually might appear quite different to an outsider. A narrative is expanded, a law is harmonized, a word in a proverb is exchanged for another; maybe divine designations, Yahweh and Elohim, are exchanged.

The fluidity that could occur amidst the push toward preservation of ancient texts has significant implications for multiple disciplines, certainly, and especially for biblical studies. For example, "textual criticism" in biblical studies and other parts of the humanities often has meant the attempt to establish the earliest "text" of a given composition. Yet, how much can we seek an earlier fixed text, if such good variants were in play over against each other at the earliest stages? Similarly, biblical scholars often have identified possible earlier sources of biblical books on the basis of divergent designations for God. Yet, if such divine terms (such as "Elohim" and "Yahweh") were taken to be equivalent designations of one and the same deity, they may well have been exchanged with one another by scribes. Thus variation between them in Hebrew texts often may reflect cognitive variation, not variation between an "Elohim" and "Yahweh" source. Finally, some biblical scholars have argued for dating biblical texts on the basis of linguistic features found in them. Yet, might linguistic marks often taken as clues to the datings of biblical books actually be signs that some less authoritative manuscript traditions were allowed to float and be linguistically updated in a way that other, more authoritative manuscript traditions, say for the Torah, were not?

It is not as if everything is chaotic. Clearly meaningful distinctions can be made between stages of textual transmission, with an overall tendency seen in Mesopotamia, Egypt, and Israel from more transmission of texts via memory earlier on to ever-increasing focus on exact, graphic copying of texts later on, as they achieve more authority. That said, even at late stages of transmission, scholars seem to have internalized the written texts that they carefully copied, and often depended on memory to reproduce those texts in a variety of contexts—whether citing them, inserting them into a parallel law, or even reproducing them as part of a new literary whole. Moreover, the widespread presence of memory variants in the early transmission of biblical literature up into the late Second Temple period should lead us to re-envision the process of composition, revision, and early reception of biblical literature and reevaluate some more graphic, exclusively text-based models that undergird contemporary exegetical methods.

BIBLIOGRAPHY

Allen, Rosamund S., ed. *King Horn: An Edition Based on Cambridge University Library Ms. Gg. 4.27(2)*. Garland Medieval Texts 7. New York: Garland, 1984.

Alster, Bendt. "Lugalbanda and the Early Epic Tradition in Mesopotamia." In *Lingering Over Words: Studies in Ancient Near Eastern Literature in Honor of William L. Moran*, edited by Tzvi Abusch et al., 59–72. Harvard Semitic Studies 37. Atlanta: Scholars, 1990.

Apthorp, Michael J. *The Manuscript Evidence for Interpolation in Homer*. Heidelberg: Winter, 1980.

Baines, John, and Christopher J. Eyre. "Four Notes on Literacy." *Göttinger Miszellen* 61 (1983) 65–96.

Bartlett, Frederick C. *Remembering: A Study in Experimental and Social Psychology.* Cambridge Psychological Library, 1932. Reprinted, Cambridge: Cambridge University Press, 1995.

Baugh, Albert C. "Improvisation in the Middle English Romance." *Proceedings of the American Philosophical Society* 103 (1959) 418–54.

———. "The Middle English Romance: Some Questions of Creation, Presentation, and Preservation." *Speculum* 42 (1967) 1–31.

Bendavid, Abba. *Parallels in the Bible.* Jerusalem: Carta, 1972. [Heb.]

Blau, Ludwig. *Studien zum althebräischen Buchwesen und zur Biblischen Literatur- und Textgeschichte.* Strasbourg: Trübner, 1902.

———. *Zur Einleitung in die Heilige Schrift.* Tübingen: Trübner, 1894.

Breasted, James H. *The Edwin Smith Surgical Papyrus.* Oriental Institute Publications. Chicago: University of Chicago Press, 1930.

Brunner, Helmut. *Altägyptische Erziehung.* Wiesbaden: Harrassowitz, 1957.

Burkard, Günter. *Textkritische Untersuchungen zu Ägyptischen Weisheitslehren des Alten und Mittleren Reiches.* Ägyptologische Abhandlungen. Wiesbaden: Harrassowitz, 1977.

———. "Mündlich-Schriftliche Bildung und die Ursprünge Antiker Literaturen." In *Lesearten der Bibel: Untersuchungen zu einer Theorie der Exegeses des Alten Testaments,* edited by Helmut Utzschneider and Erhard Blum, 183–98. Stuttgart: Kohlhammer, 2006.

Carr, David M. *Writing on the Tablet of the Heart: Origins of Scripture and Literature.* New York: Oxford University Press, 2005.

Cooper, Jerrold S. "Gilgamesh Dreams of Enkidu: The Evolution and Dilution of Narrative." In *Essays on the Ancient Near East in Memory of Jacob Joel Finkelstein,* edited by Maria de Jong Ellis, 39–44. Hamden, CT: Archon, 1977.

Davies, Anna Murpurgo. "Forms of Writing in the Ancient Mediterranean World." In *The Written Word: Literacy in Transition,* edited by Gerd Baumann, 23–50. Oxford: Clarendon, 1986.

Doane, Alger N. "The Ethnography of Scribal Writing and Anglo-Saxon Poetry: Scribe as Performer." *Oral Tradition* 9 (1994) 420–39.

Duggan, Hoyt N. "The Role of Formulas in the Dissemination of a Middle English Alliterative Romance." *Studies in Bibliography* 29 (1976) 265–88.

Eissfeldt, Otto. "Mesopotamische Elemente in den Alphabetischen Texten aus Ugarit." *Syria* 39 (1962) 36–41.

Finnegan, Ruth. *The Hidden Musicians: Music-Making in an English Town.* Cambridge: Cambridge University Press, 1989.

———. *Literacy and Orality: Studies in the Technology of Communication.* Oxford: Blackwell, 1988.

Fischer-Elfert, Hans-Werner. *Die Satirische Streitschrift des Papyrus Anastasi I.* Vol. 1, *Übersetzung und Kommentar.* Ägyptische Abhandlungen. Wiesbaden: Harrassowitz, 1986.

George, Andrew R. *The Babylonian Gilgamesh Epic: Introduction, Critical Edition, and Cuneiform Texts.* Oxford: Oxford University Press, 2003.

Gesche, Petra D. *Schulunterricht in Babylonien im Ersten Jahrtausend v. Chr.* Alter Orient und Altes Testament 275. Münster: Ugarit, 2001.

Harris, William V. *Ancient Literacy.* Cambridge: Harvard University Press, 1989.

Horowitz, Wayne, et al. "A Bibliographical List of Cuneiform Inscriptions from Canaan, Palestine/Philistia, and the Land of Israel." *Journal of the American Oriental Society* 122 (2002) 753–66.

Hunter, Ian M. L. "Lengthy Verbatim Recall (LVR) and the Myth and Gift of Tape-Recorder Memory." In *Psychology in the 1990's: In Honour of Professor Johan von Wright on His 60th Birthday, March 31, 1984*, edited by K. M. J. Lagerspetz and P. Niemi, 425–40. Amsterdam: North Holland, 1984.

———. "Lengthy Verbatim Recall: The Role of Text." In *Progress in the Psychology of Language*, vol. 1, edited by Andrew W. Ellis, 207–35. Hillsdale, NJ: Erlbaum, 1985.

Janssen, Jac J., and Rosalind M. Janssen. *Growing up in Ancient Egypt*. London: Rubicon, 1990.

Levine, Louis D. "Inscriptions of Sennacherib." In *History, Historiography, and Interpretation: Studies in Biblical and Cuneiform Languages*, edited by Hayim Tadmor and Moshe Weinfeld, 58–75. Jerusalem: Magnes, 1983.

Martin, Malachi. *The Scribal Character of the Dead Sea Scrolls*. 2 vols. Bibliothèque du Muséon 44–45. Louvain: Louvain University Press, 1958.

McDowell, Andrea G. "Student Exercises from Deir el-Medina: The Dates." In *Studies in Honor of William Kelly Simpson*, edited by Peter Der Manuelian, 601–8. 2 vols. Boston: Museum of Fine Arts, 1996.

McKenzie, Steven L. *The Chronicler's Use of the Deuteronomistic History*. Harvard Semitic Monographs 33. Atlanta: Scholars, 1984.

Michalowski, Piotr. "Language, Literature, and Writing at Ebla." In *Ebla 1975–1985: Dieci anni di studi linguistici e filologici. Atti del Convegno Internazionale (Napoli, 9–11 ottobre 1985)*, edited by Luigi Cagni, 165–75. Naples: Istituto Universitario Orientale, 1987.

Morenz, Ludwig D. *Beiträge zur Schriftlichkeitskultur im Mittleren Reich und in der 2. Zwischenzeit*. Ägypten und Altes Testament. Wiesbaden: Harrassowitz, 1996.

Olsen, Alexandra Hennessy. *Speech, Song, and Poetic Craft: The Artistry of the Cynewulf Canon*. New York: Lang, 1984.

Parkinson, Richard B. *Poetry and Culture in Middle Kingdom Egypt: A Dark Side to Perfection*. Athlone Publications in Egyptology and Ancient Near Eastern Studies. New York: Continuum, 2002.

———. *The Tale of Sinuhe and Other Ancient Egyptian Poems, 1940–1640 BC*. Oxford: Clarendon, 1997.

Parry, Milman. *The Making of Homeric Verse: The Collected Papers of Milman* Parry. Edited by Adam Parry. Oxford: Clarendon, 1971.

———. "Studies in the Epic Technique of Oral Verse-Making: I. Homer and Homeric Style." *Harvard Studies in Classical Philology* 41 (1930) 73–147.

———. "Studies in the Epic Technique of Oral Verse-Making: II. The Homeric Language as the Language of an Oral Poetry." *Harvard Studies in Classical Philology* 43 (1932) 1–50.

Person, Raymond F., Jr. "The Ancient Israelite Scribe as Performer." *Journal of Biblical Literature* 117 (1998) 601–9.

———. *The Deuteronomic School: History, Social Setting, and Literature*. Studies in Biblical Literature 2. Atlanta: Society of Biblical Literature, 2002.

Posener, Georges. "Sur l'emploi de l'encre rouge dans les manuscrits égyptiens." *Journal of Egyptian Archaeology* 37 (1951) 75–80.

Ringgren, Helmer. "Oral and Written Transmission in the Old Testament: Some Observations." *Studia Theologica* 3 (1949) 34–59.

Rubin, David C. *Memory in Oral Traditions: The Cognitive Psychology of Epic, Ballads, and Counting-Out Rhymes*. New York: Oxford University Press, 1995.

Schlott, Adelheid. *Schrift und Schreiber im Alten Ägypten*. Munich: Beck, 1989.

Schniedewind, William M. *How the Bible Became a Book*. Cambridge: Cambridge University Press, 2004.

Sisam, Kenneth. "Notes on Old English Poetry: The Authority of Old English Poetical Manuscripts." *Review of English Studies* 22 (1946) 257–68.

———. *Studies in the History of Old English Literature*. Oxford: Clarendon, 1953.

Sjöberg, Åke W. "The Old Babylonian Edubba." In *Sumerological Studies in Honor of Thorkild Jacobsen*, edited by Stephen J. Lieberman, 159–79. Assyriological Studies 20. Chicago: University of Chicago Press, 1975.

Tertel, Hans Jürgen. *Text and Transmission: An Empirical Model for the Literary Development of Old Testament Narratives*. Beihefte zur Zeitschrift für die alttestamentliche Wissenschaft 221. Berlin: de Gruyter, 1994.

Tigay, Jeffrey H. "Conflation as a Redactional Technique." In *Empirical Models for Biblical Criticism*, edited by Jeffrey H. Tigay, 61–83. Philadelphia: University of Pennsylvania Press, 1985.

———. *The Evolution of the Gilgamesh Epic*. Philadelphia: University of Pennsylvania Press, 1982.

Toorn, Karel van der. *Scribal Culture and the Making of the Hebrew Bible*. Cambridge: Harvard University Press, 2007.

Tov, Emanuel. *Scribal Practices and Approaches Reflected in the Texts Found in the Judean Desert*. Studies on the Texts of the Desert of Judah 5. Leiden: Brill, 2004.

van der Werf, Hendrik. *The Chansons of the Troubadours and Trouvères: A Study of the Melodies and Their Relation to the Poems*. Utrecht: A. Oosthoek's Uitgeversmaatschappij, 1972.

Vannutelli, Primo. *Libri Synoptici Veteris Testamenti*. Rome: Pontifical, 1931.

Vanstiphout, Herman L. J. "The Dialogue Between an Examiner and a Student." In *The Context of Scripture*, vol. 1, *Canonical Compositions from the Biblical World*, edited by William W. Hallo and K. Lawson Younger, 592–93. Leiden: Brill, 1997.

———. "On the Old Edubba Education." In *Centres of Learning: Learning and Location in Pre-Modern Europe and the Near East*, edited by Jan Willem Drijvers and Alasdair A. MacDonald, 3–16. Brill's Studies in Intellectual History 61. Leiden: Brill, 1995.

Veldhuis, Niek. *Elementary Education at Nippur: The Lists of Trees and Wooden Objects*. Groningen: Styx, 1997.

———. "Mesopotamian Canons." In *Homer, the Bible and Beyond: Literary and Religious Canons in the Ancient World*, edited by Margalit Finkelberg and Guy G. Stroumsa, 9–28. Jerusalem Studies in Religion and Culture 2 . Leiden: Brill, 2003.

Volten, Aksel. *Studien zum Weisheitsbuch des Anii*. Det Kongelige Danske Videnskabernes Selskab, Historisk-filologiske Meddelelser. Copenhagen: Levin & Munksgaard, 1937.

Waetzoldt, Hartmut. "Der Schreiber als Lehrer in Mesopotamien." In *Schreiber, Magister, Lehrer: Zur Geschichte und Funktion eines Berufsstandes*, edited by Johann G. von Hohenzollern and Max Liedtke, 25–50. Bad Heilbrunn: Julius Klinkhardt, 1989.

West, Stephanie. *The Ptolemaic Papyri of Homer*. Cologne: Westdeutscher, 1967.

Widengren, Geo. "Oral Tradition and Written Literature among the Hebrews in the Light of Arabic Evidence, with Special Regard to Prose Narratives." *Acta Orientalia* 23 (1959) 201–62.

Wilson, Andrew M., and Lawrence Wills. "Literary Sources of the Temple Scroll." *Harvard Theological Review* 75 (1982) 275–88.

Yadin, Yigael. *The Temple Scroll: Text and Commentary*. Jerusalem: Israel Exploration Society, 1983 [Heb. orig., 1977].

Zewi, Tamar. "Biblical Parallels and Biblical Hebrew Syntax." *Zeitschrift für Althebraistik* 17 (2006) 230–46.

Zumthor, Paul. *Essai de poétique médiévale*. Collection Poétique. Paris: Seuil, 1972.

3

Guarding Oral Transmission

Within and Between Cultures

Talya Fishman

Like their rabbinic Jewish predecessors and contemporaries, early Muslims distinguished between teachings made known through revelation and those articulated by human tradents. Efforts were made throughout the seventh century—and, in some locations, well into the ninth—to insure that the epistemological distinctness of these two culturally authoritative corpora would be reflected and affirmed in discrete modes of transmission. Thus, while the revealed Qur'an was transmitted in written compilations from the time of Uthman, the third caliph (d. 656), the inscription of hadith, reports of the sayings and activities of the Prophet Muhammad and his companions, was vehemently opposed—even after writing had become commonplace. The zeal with which Muslim scholars guarded oral transmission, and the ingenious strategies they deployed in order to preserve this practice, attracted the attention of several contemporary researchers, and prompted one of them, Michael Cook, to search for the origins of this cultural impulse.

After reviewing an array of possible causes that might explain early Muslim zeal to insure that hadiths were relayed solely through oral transmission,[1] Cook argued for "the Jewish origin of the Muslim hostility to

1. See Cook, "Opponents," 491–512.

the writing of tradition."[2] The Arabic evidence he cites consists of warnings to Muslims that hadith inscription would lead them to commit the theological error of which contemporaneous Jews were guilty: once they inscribed their *Mathnā*, that is, Mishna, Jews came to regard this repository of human teachings as a source of authority equal to that of revealed Scripture.[3] As Jewish evidence for his claim, Cook cites sayings by Palestinian rabbis of late antiquity and by writers of the geonic era, which asserted that extra-revelationary teachings are only to be relayed through oral transmission.[4]

Occasioned by Cook's remarks, this paper argues that exhortations to guard oral transmission, whether articulated by Jews or by Muslims, were not expressions of any essentialist preference for the oral over the written, but, rather, historically contingent utterances that addressed the particular political, theological, or social needs of their proponents. When the nascent communities of rabbinic Jews and Muslims distinguished between the authoritative corpora of knowledge that each possessed, they did so in response to specific challenges. The technological and behavioral strategies they adopted in order to maintain these distinctions were ones they had inherited from Hellenistic culture. And when pockets of Jews and Muslims exhorted preservation of oral transmission well after the formative periods of their respective cultures, they were not echoing innate cultural predispositions to "oralism" in the "hollow" manner of "revivalists," but were responding to specific stimuli.[5]

In order to put to rest the claim of Jewish culture's putative preference for oral over written transmission, the first part of this study will reconstruct the historical contexts within which Jewish endorsements of oral transmission were formulated, both in antiquity and in the period of the Geonim, that is, the "Eminences" who presided over post-talmudic rabbinical academies in the area of Baghdad between the seventh and eleventh centuries. The second part will discuss performative strategies that rabbinic Jews used in order to tag certain corpora as "oral," even when the latter clearly existed as written texts. Widespread use of inscribed texts of *oral matters* did not alter rabbinic society's need to preserve a classification that distinguished

2. Ibid., 442, 501–3; 498 n. 560; 509.

3. Ibid., 501–3; and Ibn Saʿd, *Ṭabaqāt*, v, 140; iii, 1. Ibn Saʿd relates two relevant accounts: one is related by Ṣufyān al-Thawrī (d. 778) on the authority of Ibn Shihāb al-Zuhrī (d. 742), and the other was reported by ʿAbd Allāh ibn al-ʿAlāʾ of Damascus (d. 786), a student of al-Qāsim ibn Muḥammad (d. 728), who was a grandson of the first caliph. The passages are discussed in Goldziher, "Disputes," 59–60; Wegner, "Islamic and Talmudic Jurisprudence," 34; Cook, "Opponents," 502; Musa, *Hadith as Scripture*, 23–24; Fishman, "Claims," 71–73.

4. Cook, "Opponents," 498–518.

5. Ibid., 439.

sharply between two types of transmission, and it did not diminish the cultural meaning of this taxonomy. Finally, stimulated by studies on early Muslim resistance to hadith inscription undertaken by Cook, Menahem Kister, and Gregor Schoeler,[6] the third part will ruminate on the timing and regional specificity of admonitions to guard the oral transmission of tradition that were articulated in eighth- and ninth-century Iraq by Muslims and Jews alike.

DISPARATE JEWISH MOTIVES FOR CHAMPIONING ORAL TRANSMISSION

Third-century rabbis claimed that "Oral Torah," extra-scriptural tradition, had been revealed at Sinai along with Scripture itself,[7] and they promulgated rules to regulate the production, handling, transmission, and use of such *oral matters* on the one hand, and of *written matters*, or Scripture, on the other. The regulations they formulated are mirror images of one another; practices prescribed for one type of knowledge are proscribed for the other (*b. Tem.* 14b; *b. Git.* 60b):

> R. Judah ben Nahmani, the interpreter of Resh Lakish, discoursed as follows: It is written: [Exod 24:27], "*Write you these words/matters*," and it is written [*ibid.*], "*for according to the mouth of these words/matters*." What are we to make of this? It means: The matters [*devarim*] that are written you are not at liberty to say by heart, and the matters [*devarim*] that are oral you are not at liberty to say/recite in writing.[8]

The articulation of these strictures should be viewed within the context of the intense factionalism that characterized Jewish society after the Second Temple's destruction in 70 CE. At a time when the very definition of the biblical canon was a subject of ferocious debate, the rabbinic regulations established boundaries that could be experienced in the public arena. The first ruling, stipulating that a particular corpus of tradition could only be transmitted by a lector chanting from the written text, offered public display

6. Ibid.; Kister, "La taqra'u l-qur'ana"; Schoeler, "Schriftlichen oder mündlichen Überlieferung"; Schoeler, "Oral Torah and Hadit."

7. Jaffee, "Oral-Cultural Matrix," 54; Jaffee, *Torah in the Mouth*, 140–67.

8. Translation mine. The earliest source for this tradition, a *beraita*, appears in *Tanna devei Rabi Yishma'el*. See Lieberman, *Yevanit ve-Yavnut*, 213–24; Epstein, *Mavo le-Nusah ha-Mishna*, i, 692–706; Elon, *Mishpat 'Ivri*, i, 208–10; Baumgarten, "Unwritten Law"; Gerhardssohn, *Memory and Manuscript*, 122; Gandz, "Dawn of Literature"; Zlotnick, "Memory and the Integrity."

to the scope—and the limits—of the "approved" scriptural corpus. Writings that other Jews of the time revered as inspired texts, but that rabbis pointedly excluded from the biblical canon, could not be liturgically performed. Indeed, the second-century Palestinian sage R. Akiba warned that anyone reading liturgically from *sefarim hitzoniyyim*, that is, writings deemed external to the rabbinic canon (for example, from the Aprocrypha), would lose his share in the World-to-Come (*y. Sanh.* 10:1).[9] By insuring that only texts to be venerated as Scripture would be performed aloud, the first regulation served to publicly mark the boundaries of the rabbinically defined canon. It was, in this sense, a marker of communal and theological identity.

Beyond this, however, the rabbis' requirement that the Bible be transmitted only through the declaimed reading of an open text served to mechanically arrest certain tendencies that occur naturally in the course of a tradition's transmission. Where propagation of tradition's content is the goal of instruction, linguistic formulations are fluid, even labile. Under such circumstances, clarificatory or interpretive perspectives tend to be incorporated into the body of the tradition itself, since the purpose of transmission is to relay meaning.[10] The insistence that certain traditions be transmitted only through direct reading (and not through oral paraphrase) served to curb natural tendencies toward linguistic slippage and the accretion of explanatory comments. Moreover, at a time when non-rabbinic Jews were producing works of so-called "re-written Bible" (such as the *Book of Jubilees*), this dictum prevented the "seepage" of extra-biblical interpretations or insights into the corpus of written Torah, shoring up the boundary between them and preventing later teachings from being mistaken for Scripture itself.

When viewed in tandem with the first regulation, the second regulation, which stipulates the mode of transmission appropriate for *oral matters*, promoted the agenda of rabbinic Jews in several ways. It insured that the teachings of the rabbis, unlike those of their Jewish contemporaries who claimed revelation, would be positioned as insights external to the revealed word of God. The distinctness of rabbinic *midrash* from the corpus of *written matters* was predicated on the assumption that Scripture's precise formulation was already fixed and immutable; in this sense, *midrash* authorized the Scriptural text it engaged. Finally, by giving their own extra-biblical

9. Menahem Haran, "Mi-ba'ayot ha-qanonizatzya shel haMiqra," 247, adds in a footnote that this observation had been made previously by Yehezkel Kaufman and Nahman Krochmal.

10. This phenomenon is boldly illustrated, for example, in Fishbane, *Biblical Interpretation*.

traditions equal billing with Scripture, the dicta's parallel formulation bestowed authority upon the rabbis, the tradents, and teachers of *oral matters*.[11]

The ascription of these paired rabbinic dicta to the time of Resh Laqish (c. 200–c. 275) complements Martin Jaffee's determination that the concept of "Oral Torah" emerged in the third century,[12] and should assist in parrying the hypothesis that the rabbis promoted this construct only in reaction to what they perceived as Christianity's co-optation of Scripture.[13] The rabbinic ascription of greater value to Oral Torah than to Written Torah, prominent in the midrashic narratives equating *Oral Torah* with pedigree (*y. Pe'ah* 2:16 (17a); *y. Meg.* 4:1 (74d); *y. Ḥag.* 1:8 (76d)), undoubtedly was a response to the Christian claim to being *verus Israel*,[14] but there is no reason to construe the actual rabbinic distinction between *written matters* and *oral matters* as one that was born of an interfaith polemical encounter.

Assertions that orally transmitted rabbinic teachings were superior to those learned from written texts were also made, with vehemence, by Jews in the circle of the Babylonian Geonim between the eighth and eleventh centuries. From a doctrinal standpoint, these remarks merely reinforce the second of the paired ancient dicta, but as historical records they indicate that rabbinic Jews felt some anxiety about the locus of rabbinic authority at a time when inscribed rabbinic texts had become more widely accessible.

Although the Baghdadi *yeshivot* headed by the Geonim were the acknowledged headquarters of rabbinic Judaism during this period (a status reaffirmed twice a year at month-long academic convocations that brought Jewish students from all over the world to the geonic academies), rabbinic communities far from Baghdad (including those of Al-Andalus, Sicily, Kairouan, and Palestine) appear to have been largely self-sufficient, not only administratively, but juridically as well.[15] As the inscribed Babylonian Talmud became more widely available, Jews in several communities came to regard it as a reference work for adjudication. The composition of Maghribi talmudic commentaries in the eleventh century that focused on the clarification of

11. Hezser, *Jewish Literacy*, 201, notes that "while the *concept* of the 'Oral Torah' was specifically rabbinic, its *function* seems to have been similar to the Pharisees' presentation of their own views as 'ancestral traditions' and the Essenes' lack of distinction between their own legal and exegetical extrapolations and the biblical text itself: namely, to demonstrate that they are 'the legitimate and only legitimate heir to biblical Israel.'"

12. Jaffee, *Torah in the Mouth*, 67.

13. Yisrael Yuval has made this argument in oral conversation.

14. Indeed, one midrashic iteration of this motif contrasts the writings of Jews not with those of Christians (or Muslims), but with the archives of pagan Hellenists.

15. Ben Sasson, *Qayravan*.

applied law greatly abetted this process,[16] but Jews remote from the geonic academies appear to have made legal decisions on the basis of inscribed texts of *oral matters* even before these works were created.

Adjudication from such inscriptions elicited harsh criticism. If we are to believe a claim made in the early ninth century by the Babylonian Jew Pirkoi ben Baboi,[17] Yehudai Gaon had sought, in the 760s, to impress upon Palestinian Jews that legal teachings encountered in Talmud could not be construed on their own as actual prescriptions for practice. The only talmudic legal teachings that possessed such authority were those vetted by living masters, who were the links in the chain of tradition. Reporting on Yehudai Gaon's message, Pirkoi wrote:

> And Yehudai, of blessed memory, also said that, never, when you asked me something, did I ever tell you anything other than that which has a proof from the Talmud and that I learned as a *halakha le-maʿaseh* [i.e., as actually implemented legislation] from my teacher, and my teacher from his teacher. But any matter for which there is proof in the Talmud, but for which I did *not* have [testimony] from my teacher or from his teacher, as a *halakha le-maʿaseh*, I did *not* say to you. [I have] only [said] that which has a *halakha* [legal tradition] in the Talmud, and that I had received as a *halakha le-maʿaseh* from my teacher—in order to uphold the tannaitic teaching [cf. *b. B. Bat.* 130b], "one does not derive applied *halakha* from Scripture, nor *halakha* from Mishna, nor *halakha* from Talmud, until they [i.e., the teachers] instruct him that it is a *halakha le-maʿaseh*—and *then* he should go and perform the deed."[18]

Taking up Yehudai's mantle, Pirkoi begged the Jews of ninth-century Kairouan to recognize that applied Jewish law could not simply be derived from the consultation of written texts. In keeping with the Talmud's own instruction, he wrote, a legal teaching was prescriptively authoritative only if a living master asserted that it was one to be implemented in practice. Babylonian Jews, who were instructed by the Geonim, used this method of vetting, claimed Pirkoi, but the Jews of Kairouan did not. The latter, he lamented, had been influenced by the practice of Palestinian Jews, a population that wrongly derived applied law from nothing but inscribed rabbinic

16. Ta Shma, *Ha-Sifrut ha-Parshanit.*

17. See Ginzberg, "Pirqoi ben Baboi"; Spiegel, "Le-farashat ha-polmos shel Pirqoi ben Baboi." Reservations about Pirkoi's credibility are discussed in Ben Sasson, *Qayravan*, 171 and 241, n. 287.

18. My translation differs somewhat from that offered in Brody, *Geonim of Babylonia*, 179.

texts. According to Pirkoi, the Jews of Palestine had succumbed to this faulty practice because repressive Byzantine rule had made it difficult for them to perpetuate oral transmission. Once there were no longer masters who were living links in the chain of tradition, he wrote, the Jews of Palestine had come to rely on written inscriptions of *oral matters*, notwithstanding the fact that these had been intentionally sequestered:[19]

> Some of them found texts of Mishna and parts of Talmud that were hidden [*genuzin*], and each one engages with it [i.e., the text] and interprets it in accord with his own ideas [and with] whatever arises in his heart. For they did not apprehend it from earlier sages who would teach them *halakha le-maʿaseh*.[20]

In short, Palestinian Jewry's reliance on inscriptions of *oral matters* that were uncorroborated by living testimony was an unfortunate by-product of its beleaguered circumstances. It was, in Pirkoi's words, a "custom of oppression."[21]

Echoes of the battle waged by Yehudai Gaon and Pirkoi ben Baboi—their denigration of reliance on inscribed rabbinic teachings and championing of teachings that were orally transmitted—may be discerned in later writings of the geonic period. When, around 998, Jewish immigrants from Italy arrived in Kairouan and raised questions about the local Kairouanese practice of blowing shofar on Rosh HaShana, R. Yaakov ben Nissim of Kairouan turned to R. Hai Gaon in the Babylonian academy of Pumbeditha for clarification.[22] When the students in Kairouan had read the relevant talmudic passage and found corroboration for the challenge of the newcomers, wrote R. Yaakov, they came to realize that the pattern of shofar-blasts that prevailed in their community differed from that described in the text.[23] This discovery had shaken Kairouanese confidence in their own local traditions. How could they know which practice was truly correct—that which they

19. See Ginzberg, *Geonica*, ii, 53, 559; Levin, "Mi-sridei ha-Geniza B," 403; Danzig, *Sefer Halakhot Pesuqot*, 19–22.

20. Cited in Spiegel, "Le-farashat ha-polmos shel Pirqoi ben Baboi," 245. For a different interpretation of this passage, see Friedman, "Pirqoi ben Baboi," 250–51. Muslim passages with possibly related *topoi* are cited in Cook, "Opponents," 472 and 505.

21. Ginzberg, "Pirqoi ben Baboi," ii, 559–60.

22. Levin, *Otsar Ha-Geonim*, 43 (RH Responsa 117, 61–62); Ben Sasson, *Qayravan*, 173.

23. They discovered that their own practice reflected compliance with an ordinance that had been implemented by the amora, R. Abbahu *b. Roš Haš.* 33b.

had been told by their ancestors, or that which was inscribed in the Talmud? The answer, wrote Hai Gaon, was obvious:[24]

> That practice by which we fulfill our obligation and the will of our Creator is established and certain in our hands. That which we do is a legacy which has been deposited, transmitted, and received in tradition from fathers to sons, for continuous generations in Israel from the days of the prophets unto the present time.[25]

After affirming the local practice handed down by ancestors through mimesis and oral transmission, Hai Gaon proceeded to address the larger epistemological issue by illuminating what was really at stake:[26]

> How do we know *at all* that we are commanded to blow [the shofar] on this day? [Moreover,] regarding the essence of the *Written* Torah, how are we to know that it is indeed the Torah of Moses, that which he wrote from the mouth of the Almighty, if [we do] not [know this] through the mouth [i.e., attestation] of the Community of Israel? After all, those who testify to it are the same ones who testify that, through [performance of] this deed, we have fulfilled our obligation, and [who testify that] they received this by means of tradition, from the mouths of the prophets, as Torah transmitted to Moses at Sinai. It is the words of the multitudes that testify to [the authority] of each *mishna* and every *gemara*.

As Hai pointed out in his impassioned responsum, the authoritativeness of any tradition is not guaranteed by the text in which it is inscribed, but only by catholic Israel's acceptance of that tradition. Universal social endorsement, that is, consensus, bears witness to a tradition's authenticity and is the source of its authority:[27]

> Greater than any other proof is: [*b. Ber.* 45a] "*go out and see what the people do.*" *This* is the principle and the basis of authority! [Only] *afterwards* do we examine everything said about this issue in the Mishna or Gemara. Anything that arises from them and that can help to explain what we want is fine, but if there is nothing in it [Mishna or Gemara] which aligns with our wishes,

24. Levin, *Otsar Ha-Geonim*, 43 (RH Responsa 117, 61–62).

25. My translation of this passage differs from the overlapping sections translated in Groner, *Legal Methodology*, 16–17.

26. Levin, *Otsar Ha-Geonim*, 43 (RH Responsa 117, 62).

27. Ibid.

> and if it is not clarified through proof, this [i.e., the teaching of Mishna and Gemara] does nothing to uproot the principle [of following universal practice].

Hai's rule asserts that legal teachings in the talmudic text are to be taken into account only when they corroborate tradition as practiced. Custom and consensus, both non-textual criteria, determine the legal applicability of a talmudic opinion.

Impressing this epistemological hierarchy on his readers, Hai urged them to reflect on it in a more philosophical vein, quite apart from issues of applied law:[28]

> We must acknowledge this principle even when we are not compelled by need on the occasion of performing a commandment. After all, it is in this [principle] that we find the great proof that it [i.e., the practice in question] was fulfilled in keeping with the law transmitted to Moses at Sinai.

Hai's claim that consensus is a source of law (as, indeed, *ijmāʿ* is in Islamic legal theory)[29] seems to describe a *modus operandi* that had been in effect for generations, for even early geonic responsa conclude with the formulaic affirmation, "this is the *halakha* and this is the custom," indicating that the decision just rendered was informed by both of the necessary legal conditions.[30]

To sum up, each of the endorsements of oral transmission examined above must be understood as a response to a discrete set of social or political provocations. While it is true that Jews touted the mere existence of an oral tradition as a sign of theological preeminence when they were assessing their status in the context of interfaith polemics, the rabbis' initial decision to distinguish Oral Torah from Written Torah by enforcing disparate modes of transmission did not portray oral transmission as superior to writing. It was, instead, a strategic move designed to consolidate rabbinic identity and authority in the wake of the Temple's destruction, at a time when disparate groups of Jews jockeying for power were defining their relationships to the past. By the same token, rabbinic endorsements of oral transmission were formulated in the geonic period—a time that witnessed the rise of Islam

28. Levin, *Otsar Ha-Geonim*, 43 (RH Responsa 117, 62).

29. However, consensus does not seem to have had the status of a formal source of law in the Talmud. See Ben Sasson, "Jewish Community in Medieval North Africa," ii, 20, n. 18. On the geonic conjoining of "consensus" with "tradition," see Libson, "Observations," 95; Sklare, *Samuel ben Hofni Gaon*, 162–64. Sklare notes (164) that Rabbanites took the position of the majority as indicative of consensus, whereas Karaites did not.

30. Libson, "Observations," 91.

and the emerging scrutiny of hadith—as Jews attempted to work out the relative degrees of authority wielded by living tradents on the one hand, and by the inscribed Talmud on the other. Each of the above-mentioned utterances was a response to specific challenges; none points to any essential Jewish "preference" for oral transmission or to an innate cultural "hostility to writing."

THE CULTURAL TECHNOLOGY OF "PHANTOM TEXTS"

As is obvious from the preceding remarks, inscriptions of *oral matters* did circulate in rabbinic circles in antiquity and in the geonic period. Indeed, the Talmud itself makes references to inscriptions of extra-biblical traditions in the realm of both *halakha* (legal matters)[31] and *aggada* (non-legal teachings).[32] How could these practices have existed so openly, in the face of the third-century dictum? There are, in effect, several answers.

Certain rabbinic passages portray such inscriptions as lamentable but necessary evils, concessions to human frailty and to the corrosive force of forgetfulness. Though suboptimal, the consultation of the written texts of *oral matters* was excused as something necessary for the greater good—a situation anticipated and legitimated in the Psalmist's teaching, "It is time to act for the Lord, for they have regarded Your law as void" (Ps 119:26).[33]

A non-apologetic explanation may be reconstructed from a combination of philological and historical evidence. The awkwardly formulated prohibitive dictum intentionally links together seemingly incompatible verbs: "Matters that are oral you may not *say* in *writing*" ("Devarim she-bi'al peh i attah rashai *li-omran bikhtav*"). The key to this strange locution was provided by Saul Lieberman one half-century ago: he noted that Palestinian rabbis availed themselves of a distinction that was made by others in Hellenistic societies between a *syngramma*, an authorized edition of a book, on the one hand, and a *hypomnêma*, on the other, that is, the notes which an individual inscribed for his private use. Lieberman pointed out that the paired rabbinic dicta of the third century identified Scripture as the lone corpus occupying the category of *syngrammata*, or *written matters*, and designated extra-biblical teachings as *hypomnêmata* or *oral matters*.[34] When

31. For example, *b. Hor.* 14a re: *pashat, garas viteretz.*

32. For example, *b. Pesaḥ* 62b; *b. Tem.* 14b.

33. See, for example, *b. Tem.* 14b.

34. Lieberman, *Hellenism in Jewish Palestine*, 87ff., 204ff.; Gerhardssohn, *Memory and Manuscript*, 159.

oral matters are understood as teachings that can exist in writing, but are merely an individual's private notes—and not as official data intended for public knowledge—the awkward formulation of the second rabbinic dictum comes to assume a precise meaning: "Matters that are oral you may not *say* in *writing*."[35] When closely scrutinized, it is clear that this ruling does not prohibit the writing of *oral matters*, but rather the recitation of *oral matters* from their inscriptions.

But if both *oral matters* and *written matters* existed in inscribed form, how was one to distinguish between one type of text and the other? The difference in taxonomic status was partly reflected in their respective sites of preservation: inscriptions of *oral matters* were not to be exhibited in public places, but were instead to be sequestered. The Babylonian Talmud refers several times to a *megilat setarim*, literally "a scroll-to-be-sequestered," a type of inscription that may be thought of as a phantom text; while none denied its existence, it was ascribed no social, political, or cultural authority. Lieberman's understanding of the *hypomnêma* as a feature of Hellenistic culture has found corroboration in Yaakov Elman's observation that all talmudic references to a *megilat setarim* were made by Palestinian sages, and in Cook's claim that the "oralist" passages in ancient rabbinic writings are all ascribed to Palestinian rabbis.[36]

The use of the *megilat setarim* and the cultural understanding of the function of such phantom texts persisted well beyond the third century. This would stand to reason, given recent research by Yaakov Zussman showing that *oral matters* really were transmitted orally through the end of the amoraic period (around the year 500, in Babylonia), and given Nahman Danzig's claim that Talmud continued to be transmitted orally even later, in the geonic *yeshivot*.[37] Such written inscriptions, called *nushaot*, were used as *aides-mémoires* in the academies, but they possessed nothing of the cultural authority of *girsaot*, that is, of oral formulations learned from a master.[38] Indeed, through the eleventh century, pedagogic emphasis in these post-talmudic academies was on "putting [the traditions] in their mouths," that

35. Cf. Ibn Ḥazm's claim that prophetic reports are a form of divine revelation that is not "recited," although it is "read," Musa, *Hadith as Scripture*, 78 .

36. It also supports the hypothesis that rabbinic culture's insistence on the transmission of Scripture only from the reading of written texts was intended to fix (cf. the Muslim use of "shackle") the still-labile language of Scripture in the culturally contentious environment of post-70 Palestine. See Elman, "Orality," 54, n. 5; and Cook, "Opponents," 498–500.

37. Zussman, "Torah she-be-'al pe"; and Danzig's claim, "MiU-Talmud 'al Peh le-Talmud Bi-khtav."

38. Y. Brody, "Sifrut ha-geonim," 290–91; and R. Brody, *Geonim of Babylonia*, 156–57.

is, of enabling the students to recite them.[39] Along these lines, it may be possible to read Pirkoi's attack on Palestinian Jews for ascribing excessive authority to buried inscriptions of Mishna and Talmud, as a critique of this community's use of *megilot setarim* ("scrolls-that-are-to-be-sequestered") for purposes that went beyond mnemonic consultation.[40]

The persistence of a specific etiquette for handling *megilot setarim* (that is, *hypomnêmata*), behaviors that marked the inscriptions in question as mere "jottings" that fell below the radar screen of official writing,[41] helps to explain how the concept of *oral matters* could continue to remain culturally meaningful over the course of centuries, notwithstanding the fact that corpora bearing this designation were routinely encountered in textual form.

A particularly cogent illustration of this arrangement may be gleaned from Sherira Gaon's late tenth-century *Epistle*, the earliest Jewish work to describe the formation of the ancient rabbinic corpora of Mishna, Midrash, Tosefta, and Talmud. One recension of this seminal document (labeled "Spanish" because of the provenance of its manuscripts) portrays the Mishna as having been inscribed by Rabbi Judah the Patriarch around the year 200. The other recension (labeled "French"), thought by contemporary scholars to be the version that more closely reflects geonic attitudes,[42] insists that Rabbi Judah only arranged the Mishna, giving the corpus a fixed oral formulation. Yet a careful reading of even the "Spanish" recension reveals that the Mishna's status as a corpus of *oral matters* remained uncompromised even after its inscription. While readers of this version[43] learned that Rabbi Judah the Patriarch had actually written the Mishna, they also learned that (a) this sage continued, throughout his life, to amplify the Mishna's teachings in unscripted, oral exposition, and that (b) the written Mishna continued to be learned by heart and transmitted from memory, even after it was written.[44]

The practice of memorizing inscriptions of rabbinic law and of transmitting them by heart—along with oral elaboration and explanation—persisted

39. From Sherira Gaon's description of his son Hai's method of instruction, in Brody, *Geonim of Babylonia*, 55.

40. *Pace* Mordecai Akiva Friedman. The Talmud recounts, for example, that when a Targum on Job, an inscribed text of oral matters, was found, he disapproved and caused it to be hidden away. *b.* Šabb. 115a; *y.* Šabb. 16a; *t.* Šabb. 14; BT Soferim 5, 15.

41. Drory, *Reshit ha-Haga'im*.

42. See Beer, "Sherira Gaon"; Friedman, "Terumat ha-geniza"; Zussman, "'Torah she-be-ʿal pe,'" 214, n. 18 and 234, n. 26.

43. Including, for example, Maimonides, as is evident in Blau, *Teshuvot ha-Rambam* (Responsum 442: "What is the source of our knowledge of how our Saintly Master wrote the Mishna?").

44. Sherira Gaon, *Iggeret*, 59.

among Sephardi jurists through the sixteenth century, if not later. In this manner, Sephardi Jews continued to affirm the taxonomic status of *oral matters*, even though they encountered these as written texts.[45]

In short, the classificatory distinction between *written matters* and *oral matters* continued to be culturally meaningful to Jews long after it proved unfeasible to transmit the latter solely through oral transmission. Written texts of rabbinic teachings were hardly shunned; their assignment to the role of "cueing devices" insured on the one hand that *oral matters* would not be forgotten, and on the other that they would never be mistaken for Scripture itself.

RESISTANCE TO HADITH INSCRIPTION: ABBASID-UMAYYAD RIVALRY

Early Muslims sought to reinforce the distinction between the revealed teachings of the Qur'an and hadith, human records of what the prophet Muhammad had said and done. Muslims initially proclaimed that such extra-revelationary teachings were not be committed to writing,[46] and like rabbinic Jews—though not because of them—they undertook many strategies to preserve the oral status of hadith when such teachings were privately inscribed.[47] Arabic acknowledgments that inscription was an unfortunate but necessary concession to the inadequacy of human memory go hand in hand with dismissals of the resultant jottings as mere "notes" (*ʾaṭrāf*).[48] Those who produced such notes were enjoined to erase them or, at the very least, to keep them hidden with one's personal possessions.[49]

45. On the use of this practice by Maimonides in the twelfth century and by R. Joseph Caro in the sixteenth century, see Fishman, *Becoming the People of the Talmud*.

46. See Schoeler, "Oral Torah and Hadit," 117–18; Cook, "Opponents"; Musa, *Hadith as Scripture*.

47. See Schoeler, "Oral Torah and Hadit," 113; Cook, "Opponents," 476–81; 504–7. Though Cook, 504, seems to assume that Muslims engaged in such practices because Jews did, the treatment of *hypomnêmata* in manners that emphasized their unofficial status was a legacy of the Hellenistic culture to which both Jews and Muslims were heirs.

48. See Schoeler, "Oral Torah and Hadit," 113 and Cook, "Opponents," 488. Such *ʾaṭrāf* (literally, "extremities" or "tips") were abbreviated written notes in which only the beginning and the end of a hadith were recorded.

49. Even the standard Prophetic tradition against the writing of hadith points to the safety nets that might be employed. On erasure, "notes," and the sequestration of jottings in the house, see Schoeler, "Oral Torah and Hadit," 116; and Cook, "Opponents," 488.

Nonetheless, in the second decade of the eighth century, by which time few of the Prophet Muhammad's companions were alive, Umayyad caliph ʿUmar II (717–20), commissioned the production of an official collection (*tadwīn*) of hadith; he portrayed this project as a stop-gap measure that was designed to stave off the loss of tradition.[50] According to certain Islamic narratives, the scholars who were recruited for this project balked at participating in the inscription of hadith, but were compelled to do so by the Umayyad rulers.[51] Nonetheless, even after its "shackling," that is, inscription,[52] the transmission of hadith under optimal circumstances continued to take place by means of the process of *samʿa*, or auditing.[53]

Researchers have noted with perplexity that, even after the hadith collections of Muslim and Bukhari had entered circulation, opposition to the writing of hadith persisted in the Iraqi garrison towns of Basra and Kufa well into the ninth century.[54] Anti-inscriptionist arguments articulated in the 720s[55] undoubtedly nourished this strangely perduring phenomenon, but it seems historically appropriate to presume that these regionally limited protests of the ninth century were responses to some geographically specific stimulus.[56] A compelling hypothesis set forth in 1989 by Schoeler addresses this historical problem. Noting that the scholars of Basra and Kufa were renowned as the best keepers of tradition, either because or in spite of the fact that they had no books, Schoeler posited that their ninth-century fulminations against the inscription of hadith served to impugn the juridical legitimacy of the recently overthrown Umayyad dynasty of Syria.[57]

50. Written hadith compilations had been created on an occasional basis for the private use of Umayyad rulers of Damascus from the death of the second caliph Umar I; Schoeler, "Oral Torah and Hadit," 121; and Cook, "Opponents," 489. Schoeler, "Oral Torah and Hadit," 122, describes Umar II as having played the role for hadith that the third caliph, Uthman, played for Qur'an itself. Interestingly, this caliph was also the protagonist of several anti-inscriptionist tales.

51. Schoeler, "Oral Torah and Hadit," 122, 125–26; Cook, "Opponents," 460.

52. The major shift occurred during the time of al-Zuhrī (d. 757). See Abbott, *Studies*, ii, 53, 80, 184, 196; Schoeler, "Oral Torah and Hadit," 129; Cook, "Opponents," 439.

53. Schoeler, "Oral Torah and Hadit," 129.

54. Musa, *Hadith as Scripture*, 12, n. 40; Cook, "Opponents," 482–90; Schoeler, "Oral Torah and Hadit," 114–15.

55. The debate emerged upon Umar II's death in 720. Schoeler, "Oral Torah and Hadit," 125.

56. However, Cook prefers to see the regional opposition of this late period as having been motivated by the same "oralist" attitudes that had prevailed earlier in all centers of Islam Cook, "Opponents," 441–90. Yet he also seems to link the late resistance to hadith inscription to conservatism that had prevailed in Basra in earlier times, ibid., 450–58.

57. Schoeler, "Oral Torah and Hadit," 126.

With the emergence of their own caliphate in 750, Abbasid scholars of Iraq condemned the Umayyads as power-hungry rulers who had permitted political aims to take precedence over religious goals. According to this Abbasid narrative, the Umayyads' quest to dominate had led them to cavalierly abandon a taboo that had done so much to preserve the distinction between the human records of hadith and the revealed Qur'an. Not surprisingly, the Abbasids deliberately refashioned the social and political hierarchy when they came to power, and pointedly installed scholar-jurists as the leaders of Islamic society.[58]

Schoeler's hypothesis[59] may shed light on a poorly understood development within contemporaneous Jewish culture. What specific historical circumstances triggered the critiques of the Jews of Palestine leveled by Yehudai Gaon in the eighth century and by Pirkoi ben Baboi in the ninth? The framing of Pirkoi's *Epistle* as but another instance of a longstanding rivalry between Babylonian and Palestinian Jews that harks back to talmudic times fails to address this question.[60] In thinking about the flare-up in rivalry between Babylonian and Palestinian Jews in the second half of the eighth and early ninth centuries, it may be worth noting that Jews from elsewhere referred to Palestinian Jews by the metonymic label of *Shami*, or "Damascenes."[61] Might it be that Jews connected with the Babylonian gaonate in the half-century after the rise of the Abbasid caliphate were swept up in a broader cultural struggle that pitted Muslims of their region against Syro-Palestinian rivals? Iraqi jurists first discredited compilations of hadith commissioned by the Umayyads in the decades following the Abbasid rise to power,[62] when Yehudai Gaon is reported to have made his appeal to the Jews of Palestine.

Like Abbasid jurists, rabbinic leaders of this time and place vehemently criticized co-religionists on the Mediterranean's eastern shore for relying on written inscriptions of oral traditions, rather than on living embodiments of

58. Coulson, *History of Islamic Law*, 36–52.

59. Cook, "Opponents," 474–93, disputes his argument, rejecting this possibility on doubts of the historicity of the accounts in question and finding no indication of hostility in the traditions cited.

60. Gafni, *Land, Center and Diaspora*, 97, 41–57; and Gafni, "Expressions." Indeed, by the time that Pirkoi excoriated the Jews of Palestine for perpetuating the "habits of persecution" they had developed under the restrictive conditions of Byzantine Christian rule, the community in question had been living under Muslim rule for more than a century and a half!

61. In the years following the Abbasid revolution, Jews of Palestine featured prominently alongside of Umayyads in uprisings staged against the Abbasids. See Gil, *History of Palestine*, 280–83.

62. Schoeler, "Oral Torah and Hadit," 114.

tradition. Indeed, Pirkoi's proud claim that geonic Jews of Babylonia learn only from living authorities dovetails with a well-identified, if elusive, cultural phenomenon: at the precise historical moment when other Baghdadi intellectuals were deeply immersed in book culture and its propagation,[63] Babylonian geonim doggedly avoided the dominant trend and continued to transmit Talmud through oral instruction. None of the explanations proffered for this phenomenon—neither the geonic impulse to control legal information,[64] nor their desire to uphold third-century tannaitic dicta—[65]exclude, detract from, or pre-empt the possibility that the rise of the Abbasid dynasty emboldened Iraqi Jews and Muslims to discredit the juridical status of their erstwhile challengers in Umayyad territory.

BIBLIOGRAPHY

Abbott, Nabia. *Studies in Arabic Literary Papyri.* 3 vols. Oriental Institute Publications 75–77. Chicago: University of Chicago Press, 1957–72.

Baumgarten, J. M. "The Unwritten Law in the Pre-Rabbinic Period." *Journal for the Study of Judaism* 3 (1972) 7–29.

Beer, Moshe. "Iyyunim le-Iggeret Sherira Gaon." *Shenaton Bar Ilan* 4–5 (1967) 181–95.

Ben Sasson, Menahem. "Jewish Community in Medieval North Africa." 2 vols. PhD diss., Hebrew University, 1983.

——. *Tsemih at ha-Qehilah ha-Yehudit be-Artsot ha-Islam: Qayravan, 800–1057.* Jerusalem: Magnes, 1996.

Blau, Yehoshua, ed. *Teshuvot ha-Rambam.* 3 vols. Jerusalem: Meqitse Nirdamim, 1957.

Brody, Yerahmiel. "Sifrut ha-geonim ve-ha-teqst Ha-talmudi." *Mehqere Talmud* 1 (1990) 237–303.

Brody, Robert. *The Geonim of Babylonia and the Shaping of Medieval Jewish Culture.* New Haven: Yale University Press, 1998.

Cook, Michael. "The Opponents of the Writing of Tradition in Early Islam." *Arabica* 44 (1997) 437–530.

Coulson, Noel James. *A History of Islamic Law.* Edinburgh: University of Edinburgh Press, 1964.

Danzig, Nahman. *Mavo le-Sefer Halakhot Pesuqot.* New York: Bet Midrash la-Rabbanim be-America, 1993.

——. "MiU-Talmud ʿal Peh le-Talmud Bi-khtav." *Sefer Ha-Shana Bar Ilan* 30–31 (2006) 49–112.

Drory, Rina. *Reshit ha-Haga'im shel ha-Sifrut ha-Yehudit ʿim ha-Sifrut ha-ʾArvit ba-Meʾah ha-ʾAśirit.* Tel Aviv: HaQibbuts haMeuhad, 1988.

Elman, Yaakov. "Orality and the Redaction of the Babylonian Talmud." *Oral Tradition* 14 (1999) 52–99.

63. Toorawa, *Ibn Abī Ṭāhir Ṭayfūr.*

64. Elman and Ephrat, "Yeshiva and Madrasa."

65. Fishman, *Becoming the People of the Talmud.*

Elman, Yaakov, and Dafna Ephrat. "The Growth of the Geonic Yeshiva and the Islamic Madrasa." In *Transmitting Jewish Traditions: Orality, Textuality, and Cultural Diffusion*, edited by Yaakov Elman and Israel Gershuni, 107–38. New Haven: Yale University Press, 2000.

Elon, Menachem. *Mishpat 'Ivri: Toldotav, Meqorotav ve-'Eqronotav*. 3 vols. Jerusalem: Magnes, 1978.

Epstein, Jacob Nahum. *Mavo le-Nusah ha-Mishna*. 2 vols. Jerusalem: Magnes, 1948.

Fishbane, Michael. *Biblical Interpretation in Ancient Israel*. Oxford: Oxford University Press, 1988.

Fishman, Talya. *Becoming the People of the Talmud: Oral Torah as Written Tradition in Medieval Jewish Cultures*. Philadelphia: University of Pennsylvania Press, 2011.

———. "Claims about the Mishna in the *Epistle* of Sherira Gaon: Islamic Theology and Jewish History." In *Beyond Religious Borders: Interaction and Intellectual Exchange in the Medieval Islamic World*, edited by David M. Freidenreich and Miriam Goldstein, 65–77. Philadelphia: University of Pennsylvania Press, 2012.

Friedman, Mordecai Akiya. "'Al ta'anat Pirqoi ben Baboi be-devar metziat sefarim genuzim shel ha-Yerushalmi." *Sinai* 83 (1978) 250–51.

———. "'Al terumat ha-geniza le-heqer ha-halakha." *Madda'ei ha-Hayahadut* 38 (1998) 277–94.

Gafni, Isaiah. "Expressions and Types of 'Local-Patriotism' Among the Jews of Sasanian Babylonia." In *Irano-Judaica II*, edited by Shaul Shaked and Amnon Netzer. Jerusalem: Ben Zvi Institute, 1990.

———. *Land, Center and Diaspora: Jewish Constructs in Late Antiquity*. Sheffield: Sheffield Academic, 1997.

Gandz, Solomon. "The Dawn of Literature." *Osiris* 7 (1939) 261–522.

Gerhardssohn, Birger. *Memory and Manuscript: Oral Tradition and Written Transmission in Rabbinic Judaism and Early Christianity*. Translated by Eric J. Sharpe. Uppsala: Gleerup, 1961.

Gil, Moshe. *A History of Palestine, 634–1099*. Translated by Ethel Broida. Cambridge: Cambridge University Press, 1992.

Ginzberg, Louis. *Geonica*. 2 vols. New York: Jewish Theological Seminary, 1909.

———. "Pirqoi ben Baboi." In *Ginzei Shekhter*, vol. 2, *Geonic and Early Karaitic Halakah*, 139–47, 504–72. New York: Jewish Theological Seminary, 1928.

Goldziher, Ignaz. "Disputes Over the Status of *Ḥadīth* in Islam." Translated by Gwendolyn Goldbloom. In *Ḥadīth: Origins and Developments*, edited by Harald Motzki, 55–66. Aldershot, UK: Ashgate, 2004.

Groner, Tsyi. *The Legal Methodology of Hai Gaon*. Chico, CA: Scholars, 1985.Haran, Menahem. "Mi-ba'ayot ha-qanonizatzya shel haMiqra." *Tarbiz* 25 (1955–56) 245–71.

Hezser, Catherine. *Jewish Literacy in Roman Palestine*. Texts and Studies in Ancient Judaism 81. Tübingen: Mohr/Siebeck, 2001.

Ibn Saʿd, Muhammad. *Kitāb al-Ṭabaqāt al-Kubrā*. Translated by Eduard Sachau. 9 vols in 15 parts. Leiden: Brill, 1904–40.

Jaffee, Martin S. "The Oral-Cultural Matrix of the Talmud Yerushalmi: Comparative Perspectives on Rhetorical Paideia, Discipleship, and the Concept of Oral Torah." In *The Talmud Yerushalmi and Graeco-Roman Culture*, vol. 3, edited by Peter Schäfer, 7–61. Tübingen: Mohr/Siebeck, 1998.

——. *Torah in the Mouth: Writing and Oral Tradition in Palestinian Judaism, 200 BCE–400 CE*. Oxford: Oxford University Press, 2001.

Kister, Menahem J. "Lā taqra'ū l-qur'āna 'alā l-muṣḥafiyyīn wa-lā taḥmilū l-'ilma 'ani l-ṣaḥafiyyīn: Some Notes on the Transmission of *Ḥadīth*." *Jerusalem Studies in Arabic and Islam* 22 (1998) 127–62.

Levin, Binyamin Menasseh. *Otsar Ha-Geonim: Teshuvot Geonei Bavel u-Ferushehem 'al pi Seder ha-Talmud*. 13 vols. Jerusalem: Hebrew University, 1928–43.

Levin, Binyamin Menasseh. "Mi-sridei ha-Geniza B: Ma'asim Le-Vnei Yisrael." *Tarbiz* 2 (1931) 383–410.

Libson, Gideon. "Observations on Halakha and Reality in the Gaonic Period: *Taqanah*, *Minhag*, Tradition, and Consensus." In *The Jews of Medieval Islam: Community, Society, and Identity*, edited by Daniel Frank, 67–99. Leiden: Brill, 1995.

Lieberman, Saul. *Hellenism in Jewish Palestine: Studies in the Literary Transmission, Beliefs, and Manners of Palestine in I Century B.C.E.–IV Century C.E.* New York: Jewish Theological Seminary, 1950.

——. *Yevanit ve-Yavnut be-Erets-Yisrael: Mehqarim be-Orhot Ḥayim be-Erets Yisrael be-tequfat ha-Mishnah ve-ha-Talmud*. Jerusalem: Mosad Bialik, 1962.

Musa, Aisha. *Ḥadith as Scripture: Discussions on the Authority of Prophetic Traditions in Islam*. London: Palgrave/Macmillan, 2008.

Schoeler, Gregor. "Oral Torah and Hadit: Transmission, Prohibition of Writing, Redaction." In *The Oral and the Written in Early Islam*, edited by James E. Montgomery and translated by Uwe Vagelphol, 111–41. London: Routledge, 2006.

——. "Weiteres zur Frage der schriftlichen oder mündlichen Überlieferung der Wissenschaften im Islam." *Der Islam* 66 (1989) 38–67.

Sherira Gaon. *Iggeret Sherira Gaon*. Edited by Binyamin Menasseh Levin. Haifa: Godla-Ittskovski, 1921.

Sklare, David. *Samuel ben Hofni Gaon and His Cultural World: Texts and Studies*. Leiden: Brill, 1996.

Spiegel, Shalom. "Le-farashat ha-polmos shel Pirqoi ben Baboi." In *Harry Austryn Wolfson Jubilee Volume on the Occasion of His Seventy-fifth Birthday*, vol. 1, edited by Shalom Spiegel, 243–74. Jerusalem: American Academy for Jewish Research, 1965.

Ta Shma, Yisrael. *Ha-Sifrut ha-Parshanit la-Talmud be-Eropah uvi-Tsefon Afrikah: Korot, Ishim Ve-Shit ot*. Jerusalem: Magnes, 1999.

Toorawa, Shawkat M. *Ibn Abı Tāhir Tayfūr and Arabic Writerly Culture: A Ninth-Century Bookman in Baghdad*. London: Routledge Curzon, 2005.

Wegner, Judith Romney. "Islamic and Talmudic Jurisprudence: The Four Roots of Islamic Law and Their Talmudic Counterparts." *American Journal of Legal History* 26 (1982) 25–71.

Zlotnick, Dov. "Memory and the Integrity of the Oral Tradition." *Journal of Ancient Near Eastern Studies* 16–17 (1984–85) 229–41.

Zussman, Yaakov. "'Torah she-be-'al pe'—peshuta ke-mashma'a." In *Mehqere Talmud*, vol. 3, *Muqdash li-Zikhro shel Profesor Ephraim Elimelech Urbach*, edited by Yaakov Zussman and David Rosenthal, 289–385. Jerusalem: Magnes, 2005.

4

The Interplay between Written and Spoken Word in the Second Testament as Background to the Emergence of Written Gospels

Holly E. Hearon

Christianity is a faith rooted in the written and the spoken word. However, the precise relationship between the written and the spoken word in the period of Christian origins has been a matter of much debate. Past studies have viewed the written and the spoken word as belonging to differentiated social worlds and modes of thought.[1] In recent years a more nuanced understanding of the interplay between written and spoken words and worlds has begun to emerge.[2] Following this trend, I attempt, in this essay, to draw a kind of "contour map" of the textual world of the Second Testament with respect to written and spoken words, tracing where and how references to written and spoken words occur and the interplay between them. To assist in charting this territory, I employ as a compass references to the uses of written and spoken word found in Greek and Roman sources. My focus, then, is on primary sources rather than studies of these sources in secondary literature. While I include the broad range of texts in the Second Testament, the cornerstone of my study is Luke-Acts. The goal of this exercise is to gain insight into the different ways written and spoken words were per-

1. For example, Ong, *Orality and Literacy*; Kelber, *Oral and Written Gospel*.

2. For example, Byrskog, *Story as History*; Jaffee, *Torah in the Mouth*; Kirk, "Manuscript Tradition."

ceived, encountered, and experienced in early Christian communities, and to explore what insight this may offer into the emergence of written gospels. This is self-consciously only an initial exploration of the territory, intended to lay the groundwork for a larger and more comprehensive project.

WORDS SPOKEN AND WRITTEN

The complex relationship between spoken word and written word was recognized and commented on in the first-century CE Mediterranean world. Quintilian observed that writing, reading, and speaking "are so intimately and inseparably connected that if one of them be neglected, we shall waste the labor which we have devoted to the others."[3] Theon similarly encouraged the young *rhetor* both to listen to written words read well and develop skill at crafting spoken words through the practice of writing words.[4] These comments, of course, are addressed to orators, members of the social and literary elite, whose goal is to attain eloquence in speaking. Nonetheless, they suggest that when we encounter a written text, such as the Second Testament, it is important to consider how these written words stand in relation to spoken words, and what this relationship may tell us about how both written and spoken words are perceived, encountered, and employed.

Illustrations of the close relationship between written and spoken words are found within the Second Testament itself. Written texts "speak": "Now we know that whatever the law says [λέγω] . . . it speaks [λαλέω] so that every mouth might be silenced" (Rom 3:19).[5] Reading is not a silent activity, but a re-oralization of written words: "Philip, running up [to the chariot] heard him reading . . ." (Acts 8:30; see also Rev 1:3). Spoken word is employed to corroborate written word: "Therefore we have sent Judas and Silas who themselves by word of mouth will announce the same things [written in this letter]" (Acts 8:17). In these examples, the boundary between written and spoken words is porous. The written word is perceived as having voice, a voice that is vocalized in the act of reading. Yet it is a voice that is dependent on living voices in order to assume agency, which is demonstrated by the third example.[6] This suggests that written word is perceived as being, more or less, an extension of spoken word. Additional examples

3. Quintilian, *Institutio Oratoria* 10.1.2 (Butler, LCL).

4. "Exercises of Aelius Theon," in Kennedy, *Progymnasmata*, 5–6.

5. All translations of the Greek New Testament are by the author.

6. The written text expresses agency to the degree that it demonstrates a point of view; however, this agency is limited unless the point of view is taken up by living voices.

of this complex relationship between written and spoken word are found in Luke-Acts: for example, writing on a tablet (πινακίδιον) is substituted for the voice (Luke 1:63) while letters are written in the absence of physical presence (ἐπιστέλλω . . . ἐπιστολή [Acts 15:20, 30; 21:25; 23:25, 33]).

If written word is encountered as an extension of spoken word, the question then arises whether the reverse is also true: that is, is spoken word perceived as being, more or less, an extension of the written word? There are notably few examples to suggest that this is the case. One is found in Acts 12:21 where Herod Agrippa delivers a public address (δημηγορέω). The instructions of Theon and Quintilian to orators suggest that such an address may have its source in the careful practice of writing. Thus this particular spoken word may be perceived and encountered as an extension of written word. Elsewhere, in Luke 24:27, Jesus interprets (διερμηνεύω) the events of his passion in relation to scripture. The correlation between Jesus' life and the scriptures is intended to demonstrate continuity. It could be argued, then, that here also spoken word is both perceived and encountered as an extension of written word. It is less clear that this same claim could be made when, for example, Paul engages in debate on the basis of the scriptures (διαλέγομαι [Acts 17:2; 18:4, 19; 19: 8, 9]). In the latter instance, there are competing claims over the interpretation of the written text, thus emphasizing the distance between written word and spoken word.

In contrast to the few examples cited above, the prominent and distinctive place of spoken word (independent of written word) is revealed in the rich and varied vocabulary dedicated to speech acts. While the speech delivered by Herod in Acts 12:21 may well be an extension of written word, other speeches are marked by their distinctly oral aspect: e.g., προσφωνέω "to call out" (Luke 23:20; Acts 21:40; 22:2) and ἀποφθέγγομαι "to express oneself orally with focus on sound rather than content" (Acts 2:4, 14; 26:25).[7] This oral aspect is emphasized also in teaching (διδάσκω [e.g., Luke 4:15; 5:3; 13:32; Acts 5:42; 11:26]), proclamation (κηρύσσω [e.g., Luke 4:44; 8:39; Acts 8:5; 15:21]), debate (διαλέγομαι [e.g., Acts 17:2; 18:4, 19; 19:8, 9]), discussion (διαλαλέω [Luke 1:65; 6:11]), storytelling (Luke 16:1–9; 11:1–7), and the circulation of rumors (e.g., Luke 7:17; Acts 9:42). Acts 17:21 offers a particularly vivid description of this oral/aural environment from the view on the street: "Now all the Athenians and the foreign visitors took pleasure in nothing more than telling or hearing something new." Collectively, these references draw attention not only to the dominant role of spoken word within the narrative world of Luke-Acts, but also the range of functions

7. Danker, *Greek–English Lexicon*, 887, 125.

associated with spoken word. It constitutes the primary way in which words are both encountered and employed.

While spoken word sometimes finds expression through written word, there are instances where written word appears to be encountered as just that—written word. In these instances, emphasis is placed on written word as a witness or record: scrolls (βίβλια) preserve words so that the same words can be read in different contexts (Luke 4:16–20), magic spells are recorded for consultation in books (βίβλος [Acts 19:19]), debts are recorded in promissory notes (γράματτα [Luke 16:6, 7]), censuses are compiled for the purposes of taxation (ἀπογραφή [Luke 2:2; Acts 5:37]), inscriptions identify the status of objects such as coins (Luke 20:24), an edifice (ἐπιγραφή [Acts 17:23; cf. Rev 21:12]), and a cross (ἐπιγραφή [Luke 23:38]). It could be argued, in these examples, a reversal of roles between written and spoken word is found from that described earlier: where Judas and Silas corroborated written word (Acts 15:26), in the examples cited here, the stable witness of written word functions to corroborate spoken word. This suggests a stability to written word that may be perceived as absent in spoken word.[8]

These introductory comments highlight the complex relationship between written and spoken word. At times this relationship is porous, the one mode of verbalization being perceived and encountered as an extension of the other. At other times, the two words function independently of one another. The dominant role, however, resides with spoken word; it is as spoken word that most words are encountered and employed. While spoken word may find expression as written word, it is, more often than not, written word that is perceived, encountered, or employed as an extension of spoken word.

SOCIAL DIMENSIONS OF SPOKEN AND WRITTEN WORD

As the description in the preceding section suggests, references to written and spoken word are not merely descriptive of media worlds and their functions; they also point to social divisions that are attendant in expressions of spoken and written word. The range of activity undertaken as spoken word in Luke-Acts, for example, reveals a hierarchy of speech determined by a convergence of power, status, and access within specific social contexts. Herod, for example, is depicted addressing a public forum (Acts 12:21), while Pilate uses public speech to exercise crowd control (Luke 23:20). These speech acts demonstrate that these two figures not only hold positions of status that grant them access to the crowds, but also power

8. Stability is not to be confused with reliability. Stability refers to a fixed text.

associated with that status to command the attention of the crowds. So, too, does Paul within the context of the synagogue, where he is said to speak out boldly (παρρησιάζομαι [Acts 14:3; 18:26; 19:8]). In Athens, however, he speaks [φημί] with little persuasive effect, while in Ephesus the town scribe (γραμματεύς) must intervene in order for Paul to address a crowd in the context of a public forum. In these social contexts, Paul has access, but little status and even less power.

Teaching takes place largely within specific communities (e.g., synagogues [Luke 4:31; 6:6], the Temple in Jerusalem [Acts 4:2; 5:21, 25, 42], the ἐκκλησία [Acts 11:26; 15:35; 18:11]), by individuals who have acquired status within those communities (e.g., Jesus, Stephen, Peter, Paul). Here the example of Apollos is interesting (Acts 18:24–28). He is described as "eloquent," "well versed in the scriptures," and an effective debater; yet Priscilla and Aquila find his initial proclamation to be not wholly accurate and offer correction. Thus, Apollos has power (as a speaker and debater) and access, but his status is limited because of the faulty content of his speech. Proclamation, in contrast to teaching, is represented as a more public activity, broadcast for those "with ears to hear" (Luke 3:3; 8:1; 9:2; 12:3; 24:47; Acts 8:5; 28:31). Although proclamation, too, tends to be associated with persons who have acquired status within the community, converts also may bear witness to their experience through proclamation; so, for example, the leper whom Jesus heals (Luke 8:39 par. Mark 1:45; cf. Mark 5:20; 7:36). Here power resides not so much in the person as in his or her testimony, which may, ultimately, accrue power to the person as he or she gains status on the basis of said testimony.

Spoken word is not limited to individuals. Questioning, discussions, and debates occur within groups, small and large, and point to the collective nature of spoken discourse. These activities are sometimes employed within narratives to give special prominence to individual voices by calling attention to them; that is, those voices that raise questions, spark controversy, or prompt discussion invite our attention as well. Within groups, spoken word also finds expression through storytelling. This activity is often only alluded to: for example, someone comes to Jesus for healing, presumably because he or she has heard stories of other healings, or word spreads through the countryside, perhaps as rumor, but told as story. As in Athens, people are eager to be the first with new words to speak to one another, particularly when there is something exciting or controversial to capture their attention. This can, for a few brief minutes, accord an otherwise anonymous individual status, by virtue of access to an audience and power, if their story or testimony is accepted as credible. Nonetheless, such informal storytelling was not limited to the illiterate masses; it was a prominent and popular form of spoken word that crossed class boundaries.[9]

Although spoken word as a medium is universally accessible to those who are able to speak, it is nonetheless circumscribed by a convergence of social context, power, status, and access. Not everyone has the power, status, or access to speak in every context. Certain speech acts are restricted: a leper may proclaim, for example, but not deliver a public address (δημηγορέω). Paul may teach within a community of believers (διδάσκω [Acts 18:11]), but facing a crowd in the Areopagus he proclaims (κηρύσσω [Acts 17:23]), not as one who has status but, like the leper, as one whose status will be based on the perceived credibility of his testimony.

Written word, like spoken word, reflects social divisions. Among the *different kinds* of written texts named, the greatest number consists of legal documents of the sort necessary for the administration of government and social relations. Some references, such as the promissory note cited above (γράμματα [Luke 16:6, 7; cf. Matt 25:19]), reflect exchanges that would have been engaged in on a day-to-day basis by those in trade or small business owners. Others include the census identified above in Luke-Acts; elsewhere in the Second Testament are references to a bond of indebtedness (χειρόγραφον [Col 2:14]) and a certificate of divorce (βιβλίον ἀποστασίου) [Mark 10:4 par. Matt 19:7; cf. 5:31]).[10] Letters could also serve administrative functions, providing introductions, or offering commendation (e.g., Acts 9:2; 15:30; 23:25, 33; cf. Rom 16:1–3; Phil 2:19–24). These various written texts represent public records of one kind or another that define social relationships, marking out the boundaries between them. This is true whether or not those bound by the documents can read them. In this respect, the documents are perceived and encountered as something more than words written; like inscribed coins and edifices, they function like a seal and imbue the written word with the power and authority of the person who issues or authorizes the document.[11]

This is reflected in the way in which the words used to identify these documents are taken over and employed to describe religious images and ideas. For example, the writer of Colossians says that Christ has erased the "record" (NRSV) that stood against them, using a technical term for a bond of indebtedness (χειρόγραφον [Col 2:14]). The word ἀπογράφω, used for taking a census in Luke 2:1–5, describes in Hebrews 12:23 the list of the

9. Hearon, "Storytelling"; Hearon, *Mary Magdalene Tradition*, 43–100.

10. For the purposes of this paper I am engaging in only a cursory way the genre represented by the texts of the Second Testament.

11. So also Jaffee, *Torah in the Mouth*, 16.

firstborn who are enrolled in the heavenly Jerusalem. Similarly, names of the saints are said to be recorded in the "book of life" (βίβλος ζωῆς [Phil 4:3; Rev 3:5; 20:12, 15]).[12] Employing the image of a letter of commendation, Paul writes: "You reveal that you are a letter of Christ, prepared by us, written not with ink, but with the spirit of the living God, not on tablets of stone, but on tablets of human hearts" (2 Cor 3:2; cf. 2 Cor 3:7). In the same way, the language used of inscriptions on coins, signs, and edifices, ἐπιγραφφή / ἐπιγράφω, describes how the law is inscribed on human hearts (Heb 8:10 and 10:16, quoting Jer 31:33 LXX; cf. Rom 2:15). In these instances, written word represents something more than words written; rather the words represent the power to effect what is written. It is not the words, however, that have this power; rather the power resides with the one who cancels the bond of indebtedness and writes the names in the book of life.[13] It is worth noting that when these written words are taken over as religious images, they are translated into positive images, perhaps because they represent a challenge to imperial power.

Not all written word assumes the iconic status represented by these examples. The letters of Paul, it may be argued, more nearly resemble day-to-day exchanges than administrative directives, despite Paul's status as an apostle.[14] Nonetheless, it is striking that, in terms of the *kind of written words that are named* in the Second Testament, it is these administrative documents that dominate: written words that in one way or another give order to life and underscore the patterns of authority that are embedded in the social structure. That the references to these administrative documents are few in number is a reminder that the authority to order social life also was embedded in a very few persons. Therefore, and in contrast to spoken word, the *kinds of written word* named in the Second Testament are not universally accessible, but are even more narrowly circumscribed by power and status.

Nonetheless, it is important to bear in mind that not all written texts are viewed the same way. The mere fact that something is written says little. It is important to understand how the particular written word is perceived,

12. Note that the book cited in Acts is a "book of magic," that is, a text that contains words of power.

13. Revelation is a quintessential example of this phenomenon. John is instructed by Jesus to write what he sees in a book, the words of which are described as a prophecy (1:7); if anyone takes anything away from the prophecy, they forfeit their share in the tree of life (22:18–19). Within the prophecy a scroll is opened that unleashes judgment upon the earth (5:1–2).

14. Only 2 Peter 3:16, a late text, begins to ascribe to the letters of Paul an iconic status as scripture.

encountered, and employed. Within the texts of the Second Testament, the majority of the kinds of written word that are named are perceived and encountered less as written word than as a symbol that is closely tied to the power and status of the person who "speaks" the word written.

THE HEBREW SCRIPTURES AS WRITTEN AND SPOKEN WORD

Without doubt the greatest number of references to written word occur in relation to the texts that constitute the Hebrew Bible.[15] The variety of expressions employed to identify these texts points to the different ways in which they were perceived and encountered. Notably, in only two instances is reference made to the physical or material nature of the Hebrew scriptures as written word. In Luke (4:17–20), Jesus is handed the scroll (βιβλίον) of the prophet Isaiah. He unrolls the scroll, finds "the place where it was written" (εὗρεν τὸν τόπον οὗ ἦν γεγραμμένον), rolls up the scroll, and returns it to the attendant. A similar passage in Acts (8:26–35) offers a study in contrast. Here the emphasis is placed on reading, yet no reference to the physical nature of the written word is made. The eunuch is described, instead, reading a "passage of the scripture" (ἡ περιοχὴ τῆς γραφῆς). The eunuch asks Philip about whom the prophet speaks (λέγω), Philip "opens his mouth" (ἀνοίξας . . . τὸ στόμα αὐτοῦ) and goes on to proclaim the good news (εὐαγγελίζομαι), beginning with the scripture (ἡ γραφή). Although reading occurs in both passages, only in Luke is this act linked to a tactile experience of the scroll.

Hebrews 9:19 also contains a reference to a scroll (βιβλίον) (of the law). Here, however, it is not the contents of the scroll to which attention is drawn, but what the scroll represents. The writer states that Moses sprinkled both the scroll and the people with blood to seal the (old) covenant between God and the people; in the same way, Christ, through his own blood, seals the (new) covenant. The scroll, in this passage, serves an iconic function, an image of the old that is replaced by the new (Christ). The Lukan passage, in contrast, brings Jesus and the scroll together in order to underline that the one is the fulfillment of the other (so Luke 24:44). The physical presence of the scroll provides a "body" for the "voice" of the written text.[16]

15. Of the remaining references to written word, the majority are found in the letters of Paul (e.g., "I wrote to you.")

16. Hebrews 10:7 refers to a scroll (ἐν κεφαλίδι βιβλίου) in a quote from the Psalms (41:7–8 LXX). The sole reference to the "book of the law" (βιβλίον τοῦ νόμου) is found in a quote from Deuteronomy 26:27 in Galatians 3:10. It is unclear whether

In relatively few places the written word is referred to as a book (βίβλος): of Moses (Mark 12:26), of the prophet(s) (Luke 3:4; Acts 7:42), of the psalms (Luke 20:42; Acts 1:20). In these instances the emphasis is less on the physical aspect of the written word than on the kind of composition it represents.[17] Although the references to "book" would seem to describe the text as a whole, in these examples particular verses are singled out for quotation in a verbal exchange or discourse, drawing attention to the "voice" of the text. This dimension of written text is highlighted particularly in Luke 20:42, where the writer states "as David says [λέγει, present tense] in the book of Psalms." Thus "books" may contain written words that speak as a living voice.[18]

This dimension of "voice" is picked up in references to "oracles" or "sayings." In Acts 7:38, Stephen speaks of the "living oracles" (λόγια ζῶντα) received by Moses in order that he might give them "to us," while Paul speaks of the Jews having been entrusted with the "oracles of God" (λόγια τοῦ θεοῦ [Rom 3:2; see also Heb 5:12; 1 Pet 4:11]). In each instance, the expression assumes that what is written is encountered as an active voice, speaking in and to the present. Thus the written word transcends time and space; but more than that, it is represented not so much as a written word as a "living voice." Since these examples do not single out specific passages or words as "living oracles" (in contrast to the examples in the preceding paragraph), the phrase (perhaps in contrast to βίβλος) is shown to connote the nature of the written word as a whole. In this respect, it speaks to how the written word is perceived and encountered broadly as spoken word rather than to the function of specific words.

A similar idea is expressed in the phrase "that which is spoken through the prophet," which is encountered numerous times, and most particularly in Matthew (e.g., Matt 3:3; 8:17; 12:17; 21:4; cf. Luke 1:70; Acts 2:16; 3:2; John 1:23). It may be worth noting that Matthew employs the phrase "written by the prophet" only twice. One instance is a parallel passage shared with Mark (11:10, par. Mark 1:2). The other is found only in Matthew (2:5). The latter stands out because it occurs in the midst of a series of fulfillment

---

the reference in 2 Tim 4:13 to "scrolls" (βιβλία) refers to books of the Bible. Although normally translated as "book," both John 20:30 and 21:35 employ the word (βιβλίον), elsewhere translated as scroll.

17. Danker, *Greek–English Lexicon*, 176. This is brought out by comparison with Acts 19:19, which employs βίβλος in reference to books of magic. The nature of the book is defined by "magic" rather than "book."

18. Fitzmyer, "Old Testament Quotations," 10–12, notes that the language of "speaking" functions as an introductory formula for Old Testament quotations in both the Qumran texts and New Testament.

quotes surrounding the birth Jesus, all of which are "spoken through the prophet(s)" (Matt 1:22; 2:15, 17, 23) and given (written) voice in the context of the narrative by the narrator. In 2:5, however, the chief priests and scribes report to Herod what has been "written by the prophet" concerning the birth of the Messiah. This suggests that spoken word and written word are being played off one another. Since all of these words are considered true from the perspective of the narrator, the distinction is to be found in the speaker and audience: that is, those who believe that Jesus is the Messiah versus those who do not. In this instance (2:5) Herod does not believe that Jesus is the Messiah; thus the scriptures remain a written word, bearing no living voice that speaks to the present.[19] This same idea may be signaled by the phrase "the one who has ears, let him hear" (e.g., Matt 11:15; 13:9 par. Mark 4:9 and Luke 8:8; 13:16 par. Luke 10:24; 13:43). Luke (9:4) offers a more emphatic rendition: "you! put these words in your ears."[20]

One of the most frequent designations of the Hebrew Scriptures is as writing. Here a cluster of expressions is found: e.g., the writing (ἡ γραφή); the writings (αἱ γραφαί); the written code (τὸ γράμμα);[21] Moses wrote (Μωϋσῆς ἔγραψεν); it is written (in the law; in the prophets) (γέγραπται; ἐστίν γεγραμμένον); the things written (τὰ γεγραμμένα).[22] Alongside these expressions is a large number of references to the reading of scripture. Together, these expressions and references seem to describe a context in which scripture is encountered and engaged specifically as written word. Yet a closer examination of these references reveals a more complex picture.

The majority of references to reading in the Second Testament involve the reading of scripture;[23] of these nearly half describe scripture being read aloud on the Sabbath (Luke 4:16–17; Acts 13:15, 27; 15:21; cf. 2 Cor 3:14, 15) or in public (1 Tim 4:13). With the exception of Luke 4:16–17, the reader is not identified. Rather, the emphasis is placed on the text that is being heard. In one instance the reading of scripture occurs as an act of private

19. Elsewhere, Matthew will use the phrase "that which is written" (e.g., 11:10; 21:13; 26:24, 31).

20. Werner Kelber, in his analysis of orality and textuality in Paul, sees a similar dynamic at work (*Oral and Written Gospel*, 140–83).

21. In Paul, γράμμα always has a negative connotation (Rom 2:27; 7:6; 2 Cor 3:6–7). 2 Timothy (3:15), in contrast, speaks of the "holy writings" (ἱερὰ γράμματα) (cf. Rom 1:2), an expression that comes to the fore following the first century CE (Schrenk, *TDNT* 1:763–64).

22. This language functions formulaically, as evidenced by the presence of parallel language in the Qumran texts (Fitzmyer, "Old Testament Quotations," 7–10).

23. Other references are to reading letters (e.g., Acts 23:34; 2 Cor 1:13; Eph 3:4). In three instances, context indicates that the letters are to be read aloud (Acts 15:31; Col 4:16; 1 Thess 5:27); so too the final reference to reading: Rev 1:3.

devotion (Acts 8:28, 30, 32) by a high-status retainer; nonetheless, it is read aloud and becomes an opportunity for interpretation by another. The other references to reading occur in oral contexts where Jesus, engaging others in debate, asks "have you not read?" (Mark 2:25 [par. Matt 12:3, 5, Luke 6:3]; Mark 12:10 [par. Matt 21:42]; Mark 12:26 [par. Matt 22:31]; Matt 19:4; Luke 10:26). In each instance, those engaged are religious leaders: Pharisees, chief priests, scribes, elders, Sadducees. In other words, those who are identified as readers belong to the retainer class. Thus those who encounter "that which is written" as a written word on a scroll are a small and well-defined group. Further, it is not clear that the phrase "have you not read" means "have you not (literally) picked up the scroll and run your eyes over the words?" It could mean "have you not heard read," since the scriptures are consistently described as being encountered as written word read aloud. A different but perhaps not dissimilar situation is represented by the letters of Paul. Here "that which is written" is reinscribed as written word within the letter. Yet the letter will be read aloud (1 Thess 5:27; Col 5:16). Thus the written word appears to be experienced most often as spoken word.

This picture is underscored when other references to the Scriptures as written word are brought into consideration. The passages cited above where the phrase "have you not read?" occurs identify the scriptures as written word, but give them voice as spoken word in the context of oral debate (see also Luke 20:17). Similarly, Paul is described arguing over the scriptures in a synagogue (διαλέγομαι [Acts 17:2]), while Apollos confutes the Jews, demonstrating from scripture that Jesus is the messiah (ἐπιδείκνυμι; διακατελέγχομαι [Acts 8:28]). Apollos is described as "competent" in the scriptures (δυνατός [Acts 18:24–25]), a term more nearly associated with exhortation than education.[24] Elsewhere the Jews "search" (ἐραυνάω [John 5:39 (cf. 7:52)]) or "examine" (ἀνακρίνω [Acts 17:11]) the scriptures. This does not necessarily assume access to or reading of a written text. Quintilian describes how memorization of a text can occur through hearing as well as reading.[25] Elsewhere, he identifies one of the purposes of memorization as ongoing reflection on the text, so that what is memorized is "softened and . . . reduced to pulp."[26] Thus, oral engagement of words "written" on the memory may well be what is described here. This appears to be what is taking place in John, when the crowds engage in discussion over what the scriptures say (7:40–42), and in Luke, when Jesus opens the disciples' minds

24. Danker, *Greek–English Lexicon*, 264.

25. Quintilian, 11.2.33–34 (Butler, LCL).

26. Quintilian, 10.1.9 (Butler, LCL).

to the scriptures (διανοίγω [Luke 24:45]), interpreting the things about himself written there (διερμηνεύω [Luke 24:47; see also Acts 8:35]).

Thus, although the scriptures are described as written texts, this designation has less to do with how they are encountered or employed than how they are perceived: that is, as a stable text (in the sense of permanent rather than fixed) that can be appealed to as a common basis of identity. As written word, the Hebrew Scriptures may share the iconic status identified above that appears to be distinctive to some kinds of written word. Alongside this perception of the text as "written," however, is the experience of the written text as, principally, a spoken word that is read aloud, heard, and remembered. This is also how the text is most often employed: it is quoted in discourse and appealed to in debate. Equally strong is both the perception and encounter of the text as a living voice that continues to speak to the present (so Luke 20:27: "Moses wrote for us . . ."; Rom 15:4: "For whatever was written in former days was written for our instruction . . ."). The Hebrew Scriptures, therefore, are representative of the complex relationship between written and spoken word. They are perceived of as both written word and spoken word (as having "voice"), yet they are most often encountered and employed as spoken word. This is an important insight to hold onto.

THE WRITTEN AND SPOKEN WORD IN PROCLAMATION AND TEACHING

An understanding of how the Hebrew Scriptures are perceived, encountered, and employed is important for assessing the relationship between written and spoken word in proclamation and teaching. It was asserted earlier that these activities are lodged firmly in the sphere of spoken word. This is because proclamation and teaching are, themselves, encountered and employed as spoken word. However, proclamation and teaching, in some instances, also engage the Hebrew Scriptures. The question arises, then, of how the relationship between written and spoken word is understood in these contexts.

The language of proclamation refers principally to the activity (as opposed to content) by which "good news" is proclaimed broadly (e.g., Mark 13:10; 14:9; Matt 10:27 par. Luke 12:3; Rom 10:14–15).[27] Although it is intended to invite a response, within the world of the narratives proclamation is presented as an open-ended invitation, with no explicit response

27. The content of proclamation is variously described as "good news" (e.g., Matt 4:17; 10:7; Luke 8:1; 9:2), forgiveness of sins (Luke 24:47), the Messiah (Acts 8:5; 10:36), Christ crucified (1 Cor 1:23).

recorded (but see Heb 4:6). While most often it is those in designated positions of leadership (e.g., Jesus, disciples) who are depicted proclaiming the word, those who have received God's beneficence may themselves become proclaimers of the good news (Mark 1:45; 5:20; Luke 8:39).

In Acts 8:35 Philip proclaims the good news about Jesus "beginning with the scriptures." Here, the written word becomes the basis for the spoken word or proclamation. Similar examples are found in Luke 4:18, where scripture becomes the basis of Jesus' proclamation concerning himself (cf. Luke 24:44–45), and Matthew 3:1, where John grounds his proclamation in a quote from Isaiah (cf. Rom 10:8, 15). In the examples from Luke 4:18 and Acts 8:35 the scriptures are read aloud, while in Matthew 3:1 they are quoted from memory. Thus in all three instances both the scriptures and the proclamation are encountered as spoken word. Yet the scriptures represent a stable word, which the proclamation (as a spoken word that exists only in the moment) does not. However, by rooting the proclamation in a written word, the word proclaimed is linked to the voice generating the written word, that is, the one who has the power to effect the words written (see the earlier discussion).

A different kind of example is found in Acts 15:21. Here it is said, "For Moses from generations of old in every city has had those who proclaim him in the synagogues on every sabbath *because* [emphasis added] he is read aloud" (ἀναγινωσκόμενος, read as a causal participle). In this instance the reading of the written word is itself viewed as a form of proclamation. This stands in contrast to the examples in the previous paragraph where the written word forms the *basis* for the proclamation. A similar relationship between written and spoken word may be evidenced in the Gospel of Mark. The opening verse of that Gospel identifies what follows as "good news" (εὐαγγέλιον); that is, an announcement or proclamation. Using Acts 15:21 as an analogy, it is the speaking of the word that transforms the written word into proclamation, a spoken word ("because he is read aloud" [Acts 15:21]). The Gospel of Mark, then, when read aloud, would itself be viewed as a form of proclamation. That the written text itself would be perceived as proclamation is less clear. The example from Acts suggests that proclamation requires the agency of a living voice.

Proclamation may be linked directly to teaching (see esp. Matt 4:17, 23; 9:35; 11:1), which is often explicitly associated with the Hebrew Scriptures. Scripture is described as useful for teaching (2 Tim 3:16); Jesus admonishes the crowds to both teach (διδάσκω) and do the commandments (ἐντολαί [Matt 5:19; cf. 19:16 par. Mark 18:19 and Luke 18:18]); Paul asserts that "those things written" in the law (νόμος) were written for our instruction (νουθετέω [1 Cor 10:11; see also Rom 15:4: διδασκάλιον]); Paul debates (διαλέγομαι) those in the synagogue "from the scriptures" (Acts 17:2, 17; 18:4, 19; 19:8, 9; 20:7,9; 24:12, 25; cf. 18:28), while the Jews "examine" (ἀνακρίνω) the scriptures to see whether what Paul says is true (Acts 17:11). In addition, people identified as "teachers of the law" are among those present when Jesus is teaching (νομοδιδάσκαλος [Luke 5:17; cf. Acts 5:34; 1 Tim 1:7: "those who desire to be teachers of the law"]), Paul is described as one instructed (παιδεύω) in the law (Acts 22:3), while in Romans 2:18 Paul identifies his imaginary interlocutor as one who is instructed in the law (κατηχέω [cf. Rom 2:21; Luke 1:4]), and Hebrews 5:12 admonishes the readers, saying that although they ought to be teachers (διδάσκαλοι), they need instead someone to instruct them (χρείαν ἔχετε τοῦ διδάσκειν ὑμᾶς) in the oracles of God.

Among these references to teaching, few explicitly demonstrate how the scriptures are engaged in teaching. This picture must be gleaned by inference. Apart from the Ethiopian eunuch (Acts 8:27–28), the reading of scripture is always described as an oral event in a public setting (e.g., Luke 4:16–17; Acts 13:27; 15:21; 1 Tim 4:13). Similarly, although Luke depicts Jesus reading from the scroll in the synagogue (4:16–17), elsewhere Jesus is universally described as quoting from scripture, making scriptural allusions, or directing people to consider what they have "read" in the law in exclusively oral contexts. There is nothing to point to the consultation of the physical text. Thus it appears that the scriptures are encountered through words read aloud, remembered, spoken, debated, refuted, and exchanged.

In writing about education Quintilian observes: "For however many models for imitation he may give them from the authors they are reading, it will still be found that fuller nourishment is provided by the living voice, as we call it, more especially when it proceeds from the teacher himself who . . . should be the object of their affection and respect."[28] Loveday Alexander also concludes from her studies of scientific manuals that the "oral teaching tradition is more important than written sources."[29] This would appear to be supported by the examples cited above. Thus, although there is a clear relationship between written and spoken word within the broader context of teaching, in the case of teaching the scriptures it could be ventured that spoken word translates the written word into a living voice.[30] That is to say, the written word is encountered and experienced as, literally, a living voice that cannot be separated from the authority of the person who gives the written word "voice." Further, the discussion and debate that surrounds this

28. Quintilian, 2.2.8 (Butler, LCL).

29. Alexander, *Preface to Luke's Gospel*, 205, cf. 82–85.

30. Jaffee, *Torah in the Mouth*, 8, 25.

written word now spoken suggests that although the written word (scripture) represents a stable word, it is the interpretive dimension that is worked out as spoken word that is of primary concern.

An interesting example of the complex relationship between written and spoken word in teaching and proclamation is found in connection with the phrase "word of God" (λόγος τοῦ θεοῦ). In a few texts, the phrase unambiguously refers to Torah: Mark 7:13 par. Matt 15:3; John 10:35; Rom 9:6. In each of these texts, emphasis is placed on the "word" as that which cannot be set aside (that is, it is a stable word). The book of Revelation appears to distinguish between written and spoken word by making a clear distinction between "the word of God and the *testimony* [emphasis added] of Jesus" (1:2, 9; 6:9; 20:4).[31] Elsewhere, the phrase "word of God" refers to the gospel/good news—that which is proclaimed—(e.g., John 1:14; Acts 6:7; 17:13; 1 Cor 14:36), and it is as "the good news" that the word of God is taught (but only in Acts 15:36; 6:32; 17:13; 18:5; 18:11). This dual function of the phrase "the word of God" likely arises from scrutiny of the scriptures in order to interpret the death and resurrection of Jesus (e.g., Luke 24:45; 1 Cor 15:3–4). The result, however, is oral teaching and proclamation. The active force of the phrase is brought out in two additional texts: Hebrews 4:12, where the "word of God" is described as "living," and 2 Peter 3:5 and 7, where it is described as the generative power that gave birth to creation.

An examination of the language of tradition (παράδοσις; παραδίδωμι) gives additional support to the contention that this teaching of the gospel as "word of God" is a primarily oral enterprise.[32] This language occurs rarely and almost exclusively in polemical contexts (e.g., Mark 7:13 par. Matt 11:27; 1 Cor 11:17–26; 15:1–8; 2 Thess 3:6). Writers employ the language of tradition when they are defending themselves against the teachings of others, attempting to establish group identity, make a claim for continuity, or reinforce community boundaries. In nearly all of these instances, reference to specific traditions is notably absent. It is not the content of the tradition that is persuasive, then, but the appeal to tradition as something held in common and, by extension, the interpersonal relationships it references. Thus the language of tradition serves its own distinct rhetorical function. This function is further signaled by the association of tradition or traditions with individuals. Here it becomes evident that it is not simply traditions or teachings that are in competition with one another; the honor and authority of individuals are at stake as well. The polemics in which the language

31. I say "appears" because the distinction may in fact be between a stable or fixed word on the one hand and a proclaimed word on the other.

32. Hearon, "Traditions and the Traditioning Process."

of tradition is employed, therefore, are polemics that are not "primarily concerned with content, but with interpersonal relationship."[33]

This emphasis on persons is reflected in the references to conflicts that arise over teaching within the narrative world of the Second Testament. In many instances the conflict occurs between Jesus and religious leaders, variously identified as the chief priests, scribes, and Pharisees (e.g., Mark 12:13–14; Matt 16:12; Luke 23:4; John 7:35). However, there are also numerous examples of conflicts that arise between competing groups within the Jesus movement. For example, Paul warns the Romans to "keep an eye on those who cause offenses and dissensions contrary to the teaching that you learned" (16:7); the writer of Titus complains of those who are "upsetting households by teaching that which is not fitting" (1:11); and John of Patmos brings charges against those "who hold to the teaching of Balaam" (2:14) and of the Nicolaitans (Rev 2:15).[34] Among those about whom concerns are raised are women. The author of 1 Timothy writes, "I permit no woman to teach or to have authority over a man; she is to keep silent" (2:12), while the author of Titus issues a positive command, counseling older women to be "teachers of what is good," teaching young women to "love their husbands, love their children, to be temperate, pure, good household managers, and obedient to their husbands" (2:3–5). The prohibition against women teaching indicates, almost certainly, that women are in fact teaching men as well as women (see the earlier example of Prisca). In contrast, the instructions concerning what older women should teach younger women suggest an attempt to regulate both what women teach and whom they teach. This, in turn, suggests that women are transmitting traditions that are accepted by some as authoritative and viewed as generative of sound faith and practice.[35]

This competitive environment, in which teachers and their teachings are pitted against one another, perhaps offers a context for the movement from spoken to written word. In the opening verses of the Gospel of Luke, the author says that what is written represents those things in which "Theophilus" has already received instruction (κατηχήθης). According to Alexander, the written word was often "regarded simply as a more permanent form of the teaching already given orally" and was to be distributed among those who had already received this teaching.[36] From this perspective, the Gospel of Luke is not an end in itself, but a written word that is intended to sup-

33. Tannen, "Oral/Literate Continuum," 2–3.

34. Other examples are found in Eph 4:14; Col 2:22; 1 Tim 1:3; 4:1, 11; 6:2, 3; 2 Tim 4:3; Heb 13:9; 2 Pet 2:1; 1 John 9, 10.

35. Hearon and Maloney, "Voices of the Women."

36. Alexander, "Living Voice," 234.

port and be engaged in tandem with spoken word. Something like this may be suggested in Mark 13:14, where the narrator addresses the reader with the words "let the reader understand" (par. Matt 24:15). It is possible that here the reader is also being engaged as interpreter or teacher in a context where the written word is read aloud to a group. The writer of Luke states that he has employed both written (ἐπεχείρησαν ἀνατάξασθαι διήγησιν) and oral sources (αὐτόπται) in composing the Gospel. What the written sources are remains a mystery—possibly "Q," but perhaps also scripture.[37] The oral sources are described as "eyewitnesses and servants of the word." Alexander proposes that αὐτόπται is best understood as a reference to "those who know the facts at first hand" rather than to forensic witnesses.[38] This would support the idea that the Gospel represents not a transcript of the teachings of Jesus, but a memory-log of the teachings as represented by those reputed to know these teachings at first hand.[39] Imbedded in this passage may be an attempt to correct those who, like Apollos, know "the Way," but not quite accurately.

While caution should be exercised in lumping together the four Gospels under a single heading, it is worth noting that all four do show some signs of functioning within this teaching model. As in the Gospel of Luke, the writer of John's Gospel draws attention to the written nature of the text (John 20:30–31; 21:24–25). However, it is striking that, with one exception (19:20 [reading the sign on the cross]), there are no references to reading anywhere in John's Gospel. Rather, the writer speaks of the disciples remembering the scriptures and the words that Jesus has spoken (2:17, 22; 12:15; 15:20; cf. Acts 11:16; 20:35; Jude 1:17; Rev. 3:3). In contrast to Luke and John, Matthew and Mark draw no attention to their texts as written word.[40] However, in each of these Gospels emphasis is placed on Jesus' role as teacher (e.g., Mark 2:13; 4:2; 6:1–6 par. Matt 13:53–58; Matt 4:23; 23:10). It is the language of teaching, for example, that is used in the stories that inaugurate Jesus' ministry in each Gospel: "and they were astonished at his teaching, for he was teaching them as one having authority" (Mark 1:22); "and opening his mouth he began teaching them and said" (Matt 5:2).

37. This may be suggested by the repetition of the word ὑπηρέτης in Luke 4:20—its only other occurrence in the Gospel—where it is used to describe the one who attends the scroll.

38. Alexander, *Preface to Luke's Gospel*, 120–22.

39. Quintilian writes in this regard: "For our whole education depends upon memory, and we shall receive instruction all in vain if all we hear slips from us," 1.1.i (Butler, LCL).

40. I take the language in Matthew's opening verse as an echo of Genesis 5:1 (βίβλος γενέσεως) referring to a list, or account, of the genealogy of Jesus.

Quintilian may offer here an interesting possibility for viewing the relationship among the Gospels. Commenting on the importance of learning to paraphrase, he writes: "But I would not have paraphrase restrict itself to the bare interpretation of the original: its duty is to rival and vie with the original in the expression of the same thoughts."[41] This remark invites consideration of the possibility that Matthew and Luke, and perhaps even John, should be viewed as paraphrases that "rival and vie" with the Gospel of Mark. Regardless of whether or not this is the case, the context of teaching offers one possible impetus for the movement within early Christian communities from spoken to written word. It is a context that is, at the least, consistent with the interaction between written and spoken word as evidenced within the texts of the Second Testament.

CONCLUSIONS

To return to the image of a "contour map" with which I began this article, what might such a map of spoken and written word in the texts of the Second Testament look like? Recognizing that any construct of this sort is imperfect at best, I would propose that such a map could be constructed by representing spoken word as water and written word as dry land. On this map one would find a world with very little dry land and a great deal of water. There would be a few mountains representing written texts whose function is primarily iconic. There would also be some marshland where spoken word engages or becomes an extension of written word. At some points this land might be fairly extensive; at other points, quite sparse. However, the prevailing impression made by the map would be of a vast expanse of lakes and waterways, edged around by marshland giving way to a very few islands of dry land, punctuated only occasionally by a mountain.

It is the marshland that has been the primary focus of this paper. In order to gain insight into the relationship between written and spoken word as described in the texts of the Second Testament, I have examined closely how written and spoken are perceived, encountered, and employed. What this examination has revealed is that written word overlaps spoken word in significant ways: it is perceived as having "voice," yet it is a voice that is ultimately dependent on living voices (spoken word) for vocalization, agency, and corroboration. "Agency" and "corroboration" may extend from confirmation, to explanation, to (in the case of the Hebrew Scriptures) proclamation and teaching. At what point, however, does the "voice" of the text

41. Quintilian, 10.5.v (Butler, LCL); "Exercises of Aelius Theon" in Kennedy, *Progymnasmata*, 62–64.

become the "voice" of the speaker? Here the perceived relationship between written and spoken word becomes very porous. The written word may represent no more than a template, a reference point, or a starting point for the agent of the spoken word. Further, for many people the written word would not be a part of experience or consciousness. To the degree that written word is in view, its perceived stability may project authority onto the word spoken and proclaimed, assigning, by extension, a status to the speaker greater than s/he might otherwise experience.

In terms of encounter, written word, as described in the texts of the Second Testament, is encountered almost exclusively as a spoken word that is read aloud or recited from memory. Very little attention is given to the physical or visual dimension of written word. Rather, words that might be seen as describing physical dimensions of the written word reference other aspects of the text. For example, the word "book" (βίβλος) is always modified (e.g., "of Moses"), so that emphasis is placed on the kind of composition rather than the physical aspect of the composition. The Hebrew Scriptures as "the writings" are often read, but they are read aloud, "read" from memory, interpreted, and debated. Thus, although they are described as written word, they are encountered and employed as spoken word. I propose, therefore, that their designation as written word or "writings" has less to do with how they are encountered or employed than with how they are perceived: as a word that is stable. In the few instances where a written word is not described in relation to voice or vocalization, it seems to assume an iconic function. In these examples the written word serves administrative functions (e.g., a bill of divorce, a record of debt) or as an identity marker (e.g., on a coin). In these instances emphasis is placed on written word as a permanent record. It is possible that the Hebrew Scriptures serve in this way as well; yet the degree to which the Scriptures are debated, interpreted, and reinterpreted underscores the "living" dimension of the voice that is ascribed to the text.

In terms of how written word is employed, we again find overlap with spoken word. There are some instances where the emphasis appears to be on writing as inscription to the extent that the "written word" is employed as a permanent record or stable word. However, in the contexts described in the texts of the Second Testament, that which is written is most often employed as a point of engagement for spoken word that goes beyond that which is written. This would be the case, for example, in the speech that Herod delivers (Acts 12:21) or the letter that is delivered by Judas and Silas (Acts 8:17). It is most clearly the case in proclamation and teaching. In these instances written word is employed as the basis of and in the service of spoken word. The ascription of voice to written word suggests that some written word is perceived as an extension of spoken word, pointing to the dialectic between the two. It is also the case that spoken word may be perceived as an extension of written word; yet when there are competing interpretations, teachings, or proclamations, it is possible that the spoken word may be perceived as at some distance from the written word. In these instances, the stable nature of written word comes to the fore. The authority given to the spoken word in relation to written word may, in these cases, be dependent upon the convergence of power, status, and access enjoyed by any one individual (or written text) within a specific social context.

What can these insights into the complex relationship between written and spoken word offer in terms of our understanding of the emergence of written gospels within early Christian communities? First, they suggest that we need to view these written texts as being closely intertwined with spoken word. They reflect, on the one hand, the engagement of the Hebrew Scriptures (written word) as words read aloud and remembered, and as spoken word that is taught, proclaimed, and debated. They also reflect spoken word (proclamation and teaching) that finds its basis in experience recounted as spoken word; that is, spoken word that is independent of written word. Nonetheless, it is possible that this spoken word engages themes or images recorded in written word (the Hebrew Scriptures) that are encountered and employed primarily, if not exclusively, as spoken word, depending on the social context. Second, they suggest that these written texts would have been perceived as in some way an extension of spoken word. I propose that at one point the Gospel of Mark may have been perceived as a form of proclamation *when it was read aloud*. The work of Alexander, echoing Quintilian, argues that the written Gospels also may have served as an extension of spoken word by supplementing the living voice of the teacher. In this respect, the different gospels may reflect the divergent voices of teachers within early Christian communities. This view is consistent with the context of teaching described within the texts of the Second Testament. Third, and finally, our findings suggest that we should exercise caution in ascribing iconic or canonical status to the written gospels prior to fourth- and fifth-century debates. Rather, we should assume that these written texts continued to be employed in a complex, dialogical relationship with spoken word in a variety of social contexts that would have brought to the fore competing voices seeking to understand how the voice of the written text might engage and be engaged by the living voices of the day.

BIBLIOGRAPHY

Alexander, Loveday. "The Living Voice: Skepticism towards the Written Word in Early Christian and in Graeco-Roman Texts." In *The Bible in Three Dimensions: Essays in Celebration of Forty Years of Biblical Studies in the University of Sheffield*, edited by David J. A. Clines et al., 221–47. Journal for the Study of the Old Testament Supplements 87. Sheffield: Sheffield Academic, 1990.

———. *The Preface to Luke's Gospel: Literary Convention and Social Context in Luke 1.1–4 and Acts 1.1*. Society for New Testament Studies Monograph Series 78. Cambridge: Cambridge University Press, 1993.

Byrskog, Samuel. *Story as History, History as Story: The Gospel Tradition in the Context of Ancient Oral History*. Wissenschaftliche Untersuchungen zum Neuen Testament 123. Tübingen: Mohr/Siebeck, 2002.

Danker, Frederick William, ed. *A Greek-English Lexicon of the New Testament and Other Early Christian Literature*. Chicago: University of Chicago Press, 2000.

Fitzmyer, Joseph A. "The Use of Explicit Old Testament Quotations in Qumran Literature and in the New Testament." In *Essays on the Semitic Background of the New Testament*, 3–58. London: Chapman, 1971.

Hearon, Holly E. *The Mary Magdalene Tradition: Witness and Counter-Witness in Early Christian Communities*. Collegeville, MN: Liturgical, 2004.

———. "Storytelling in Oral and Written Media Contexts of the Ancient Mediterranean World." In *Jesus, the Voice, and the Text: Beyond the Oral and the Written Gospel*, edited by Tom Thatcher, 89–110. Waco, TX: Baylor University Press, 2008.

———. "Traditions and the Traditioning Process: A Re-assessment of Second Testament Written Remains." Paper presented at the Orality and Literacy Conference, Regis University, Denver, October 21, 2006.

Hearon, Holly E., and Linda M. Maloney. In *Distant Voices Drawing Near: Essays in Honor of Antoinette Clark Wire*, edited by Holly E. Hearon, 33–52. Collegeville, MN: Liturgical, 2004.

Jaffee, Martin S. *Torah in the Mouth: Writing and Oral Tradition in Palestinian Judaism 200 BCE–400 CE*. New York: Oxford University Press, 2001.

Kelber, Werner H. *The Oral and the Written Gospel: The Hermeneutics of Speaking and Writing in the Synoptic Tradition, Mark, Paul, and Q*. 1983. Reprinted, Bloomington: Indiana University Press, 1997.

Kennedy, George A., trans. "The Exercises of *Aelius Theon*." In *Proygymnasmata: Greek Textbooks of Prose Composition and Rhetoric*, edited and translated by George A. Kennedy, 1–72. Atlanta: Society of Biblical Literature, 2003.

Kirk, Alan. "Manuscript Tradition as a *Tertium Quid*: Orality and Memory in Scribal Practices." In *Jesus, the Voice, and the Text: Beyond the Oral and the Written Gospel*, edited by Tom Thatcher, 215–34. Waco, TX: Baylor University Press, 2008.

Ong, Walter J. *Orality and Literacy: The Technologizing of the Word*. London: Routledge, 1982.

Pliny. *Letters and Panegyricus*. 2 vols. Loeb Classical Library. Translated by Betty Radice. Cambridge: Harvard University Press, 1972.

Quintilian. *The Institutio Oratoria of Quintilian*. Translated by H. E. Butler. Loeb Classical Library. Cambridge: Harvard University Press, 1980.

Schrenk, Gottlob. "γράφω, γραφή, γφάμμα, ἐπι-, προφράφω, ὑπόγραμμος." In *Theological Dictionary of the New Testament*, edited by Gerhard Kittel, 1:742–73. Translated by Geoffrey W. Bromiley. Grand Rapids: Eerdmans, 1964.

Tannen, Deborah. "The Oral/Literate Continuum in Discourse." In *Spoken and Written Language: Exploring Orality and Literacy*, edited by Deborah Tannen, 1–16. Norwood, NJ: Ablex, 1982.

5

Oral and Written Communication and Transmission of Knowledge in Ancient Judaism and Christianity

Catherine Hezser

In antiquity, when no telephones, postal services, and internet connections existed, the transfer of information and knowledge depended on direct or indirect contacts and personal mediation.[1] If one wanted to ask someone's advice or tell him or her something, one would either have to go and visit that person oneself or send an oral or written message through an intermediary.[2] Only face-to-face communications would guarantee the reliable transmission of the words and opinions of one person to another, whereas mediated messages would always be suspected of misrepresentation or even forgery. Face-to-face communication could easily be conducted with one's immediate neighbors and fellow villagers or townspeople. In the case of more distant communication partners, a larger effort would have to be made to reach them. In such cases, communication would be intrinsically linked to mobility, either one's own or that of one's messengers.[3] Only the

1. See also Menache, "Introduction," 5.

2. For the biblical period see Zwickel, "Kommunikation und Kommunikationsmöglichkeiten"; Meier, *Messenger*.

3. Claudia Moatti, "Translation, Migration, and Communication," 109, has pointed out that Moses Finley's view of ancient societies as face-to-face societies has sometimes obscured the aspect of movement and mobility. But these two aspects of ancient societies are not incompatible; on the contrary, the necessity of face-to-face contacts to communicate messages would involve and even increase mobility among

most mobile members of a particular social group, and those who had the greatest access to mobile intermediaries, would be able to establish and maintain contacts over longer distances. One may assume that those who sat at the nodal points of the local, country-wide, or international communication system would be the most powerful members of their respective social circles.

In the following we shall investigate the forms and modes of communication reflected in Jewish and early Christian literary sources from the Roman period. We shall focus on Josephus, the New Testament, and rabbinic sources here. The various forms of communication and transmission of knowledge were always context-specific, serving the respective individuals and groups to reach their particular goals. Communication among early Christians was closely linked to the empire-wide expansion of Christianity. In the case of rabbis, communication with distant colleagues helped to establish a province-wide decentralized rabbinic network, which would eventually be able to collect and transmit traditions to later generations of scholars in both the Land of Israel and the Diaspora.

COMMUNICATION AMONG REBEL LEADERS IN JOSEPHUS' *VITA*

In his autobiographical *Vita*, Josephus is quite explicit about the exchange of information among his fellow rebel leaders. This information can either be correct and beneficial or false, misleading, and potentially dangerous to the extent of threatening the recipient's life. Most often, such military information is said to have been transmitted by messengers.

The messenger himself is sometimes not mentioned directly at all: Jesus "sent and requested" (*Vita* 106), or "the news was reported to me in writing" (319), a "messenger" or "courier" is called (89, 90, 301) or identified as a relative, a freedman or household slave, a soldier, or elder and community leader as part of an embassy, sometimes accompanied by an armed cohort. This means that the potentially most reliable and trustworthy person would have been chosen as an intermediary.[4] Sometimes the trust in messengers would be disappointed, though. They could leak the message or information to one's enemies or they could be caught on the road and prevented from reaching the recipient. In the case of oral messages, the information could be forgotten, changed, or falsified. Thus, using an intermediary never guaranteed the safe and correct transmission of a message,

some segments of society.

4. Hezser, *Jewish Literacy*, 265–66.

but there was often no alternative if the sender could not travel himself and meet the recipient face to face.

The purposes for which messages were transmitted ranged from the pragmatic and trivial to issues of public concern. We have to assume that the form of the message, that is, its oral or written format, varied in accordance with the purposes for which it was sent and the respective circumstances. For example, the approach of enemies or supporters would be announced by a messenger orally: "A messenger arrived and whispered to Jesus that John was approaching with his troops" (301; see also 90). Or Josephus sent a courier to Tiberias to let people know that he was approaching (90). On another occasion a deserter of Jesus is said to have come to Josephus to tell him of Jesus' impending attack (107). These were messages of immediate military significance that had to be kept confidential and were meant for one particular recipient only, in contrast to rumors, which are usually presented as false and fictitious oral messages (different from rumors in the Gospels; see below) whose very purpose was to reach a larger audience. For example, "A rumor had now spread throughout Galilee that I [Josephus] was intending to betray the country to the Romans" (132).

In contrast to incidental oral messages, letters were deemed necessary to confirm Josephus in his leadership role. After having received letters from the Jerusalem authorities confirming him in his position, Josephus allegedly sent delegates to Jonathan and his supporters to inform them of the "written orders" that they should quit "giving orders to the bearer to take pains to discover how they intended to proceed" (312). The written correspondence between Josephus and the Jerusalem leaders is also reported elsewhere (62), where Josephus allegedly asked the Jerusalem leaders how to proceed in Galilee. Whether these reports are historically reliable and such correspondence actually took place is another question, but the texts suggest that information of an official nature would be transmitted in writing.

Sometimes Josephus may have claimed that written communication took place in order to present himself as superior to other rebel leaders. For example, John is said to have written to Josephus to ask him for permission to go to the hot baths in Tiberias "for the good of his health." Josephus, who was at the Galilean village of Cana at that time, "went so far as to write separate letters to those whom I had entrusted with the administration of Tiberias, to prepare a lodging for him and any who might accompany him, and to make every provision for them" (85–86). Letters of recommendation and support are commonly written by patrons for their subordinates. On another occasion, John is said to have written Josephus a letter defending himself and his actions (101), thereby expressing allegiance to him. Similarly, Jesus is said to have "sent and requested my [Josephus'] permission to come and pay me his respects" (106). References to letters of request, support, and recommendation are used to enforce the notion that others were dependent on Josephus here.

While oral messages could also be false and misleading, letters are often associated with plots in Josephus' writing. In contrast to oral messages, letters could be shown to others and used as evidence against someone. For example, Josephus repeatedly refers to forged letters asking townspeople for military support but actually leading them into a trap (284–85). He admits to have used such means himself to mislead competing rebel leaders (324). Jonathan is said to have "laid a plot to entrap me, writing me the following letter," asking him [Josephus] to meet him with few attendants in the village where he stayed (216–18). The message carrier allegedly arrived in the middle of the night and asked for an immediate reply. Josephus made him drunk instead, so that he would reveal the plot against him. In such cases only oral comments extracted from someone who is no longer able to keep face and hide the sender's true intentions can reveal the true meaning and purpose of the written message.

Altogether then, Josephus purports to have exchanged a large amount of oral and written communication with fellow and competing rebel leaders, townspeople, and the Jerusalem authorities. We do not know to what extent his allegations are historically reliable. He may have used such references partly to present himself as superior to his colleagues and to claim the Jerusalem leaders' support for his actions. Nevertheless, it becomes clear that written communication was considered more official and forceful than oral messages but at the same time prone to falsification and misuse. Oral messages, on the other hand, were used in more urgent and confidential circumstances. They may also have been considered more honest and reliable, if one could trust the bearer or force him to reveal the sender's true intentions.

COMMUNICATION IN EARLY CHRISTIANITY

Interestingly, written communication through letters is mentioned neither in the three synoptic Gospels nor in the Gospel of John, very much in contrast to Acts and the Pauline letters, where we find a number of such references. While Mark mentions on a number of occasions (Mark 1:21, 39; 6:2) that Jesus *taught* in the synagogues in Galilee (see also Matt 4:23, 9:35, 13:54; Luke 4:15–17, 4:44), only Luke lets him read from a written scroll of Isaiah in the synagogue at Nazareth (Luke 4:17). Luke is also the only Gospel that mentions the postpartum inscription of the baby's name by his father (Luke 1:63). It therefore seems that only Luke, who lived and wrote in a Hellenistic (and probably upper-class) context, would automatically assume that Jesus and other important early Christian figures could read and that he was literate. In Mark and Matthew, on the other hand, the emphasis is very much on Jesus' oral teaching, whereas reading and writing are never mentioned.[5]

According to John 7:15, when Jesus taught in the Jerusalem Temple, his fellow Jews were amazed and said: "How does this man know letters, having never learned?" John thereby stresses the higher, spiritual authority of Jesus' teaching (v. 16), which is not based on the written word of the Hebrew Bible. The assumption is that a Jewish scholar's learning would be based on the knowledge he gained from his reading of the scriptural text, whereas a Christian teacher's power goes back to the source of Scripture itself and is therefore independent of letters and writing. A similar distinction between letter and spirit also underlies Paul's writing.

In the three synoptic Gospels all communication between Jesus and his disciples, sympathizers, and local Jewish communities is conducted orally. In order to spread his message and reach a larger number of people, Jesus and his disciples are therefore said to have constantly traveled, especially within Galilee, but also between Galilee and Judaea, at least at the beginning and end of his career. The emphasis on direct contacts between Jesus and his interlocutors made his frequent change of place necessary. As Gerd Theissen and others have stressed, this practice of traveling and teaching may be a reflection of the work of early Christian wandering charismatics who tried to imitate Jesus' restless activity.[6]

The references to Jesus' (and his disciples') travels are so numerous in the Gospels that they cannot be listed here. The reasons for the constant departures and arrivals are usually not specified, unless Jesus tries to escape the Jerusalem authorities or the masses who allegedly pursued him. The private hospitality that he and his travel companions received in the various villages and towns they entered is frequently mentioned. Wherever they arrive, Jesus is said to have addressed the masses and/or talked to his disciples. Rumors are said to have played an important role in spreading knowledge about him and his healing faculties. For example, Mark 1:28 reports that the rumor about Jesus' ability to drive out evil spirits spread everywhere throughout Galilee, and, according to Luke 4:14, when Jesus returned to Galilee "a report about him spread through all the surrounding country."

5. Fox, "Literacy and Power," 127, assumes that Jesus' teachings were first transmitted orally, probably until the 60s CE. See also Kelber, *Oral and Written Gospel*, 65; Ong, "Text as Interpretation," 12–18.

6. Theissen, *Studien zur Soziologie des Urchristentums*, 79–105.

The rumors prepare the stage for Jesus' more specific teaching and healing activity.[7] References to such rumors spreading to areas outside the Jewishly defined Land of Israel, for example to Syria (Matt 4:24), may anticipate later Christian teachers' missionary activities among gentiles.

Although most of the contacts between Jesus and his interlocutors consist of face-to-face communication, occasionally intermediaries and messengers are mentioned whom others sent to Jesus. For example, when a Roman centurion wanted Jesus to heal his sick slave, "he sent some Jewish elders to him, asking him to come and heal his slave" (Luke 7:3). Later, when they reach the centurion's house, he "sent friends" outside to deliver a message (v. 6). According to Matt 22:16, the Pharisees "sent their disciples to him" to ask whether one should pay tax to the emperor. The Gospel writers were probably familiar with the practices of upper-class Romans (Luke) and rabbis (Matt) using friends or disciples as messengers to gain information. One may perhaps understand the traditions about Jesus' sending out his disciples (Matt 10:5ff; Luke 9:1–2) in a similar vein. The difference is that, according to the Gospels, Jesus was represented by his followers after his death only, whereas rabbis already had their views spread through traveling disciples during their lifetime. In both cases the oral teaching of the master is deemed superior to that of the transmitting student.

The practice of letter-writing seems to have been adopted once early Christianity entered the Hellenistic milieu. In Acts, letters are mentioned several times. The first reference relates to the time shortly before Saul's conversion, when he allegedly asked the Jerusalem high priest to send letters to synagogues in Damascus to act against Jewish Christians (Acts 9:2; cf. 22:5). This letter-writing can be understood within the context of relationships between the high priest and Jewish Diaspora communities. Before 70 CE letters were probably sent from the Jerusalem center to the periphery and vice versa, with a clear notion of the center's superior authority.

Interestingly, Acts attributes a similar practice to Paul and other leaders of the early Jewish-Christian community in Jerusalem. Acts 15:23–29 transmits a letter that apostles and elders are said to have sent to Antioch through Paul, Barnabas, Silas, and Judas as its representatives and intermediaries. The letter is addressed to gentile Christian "brothers" in Antioch, Syria, and Cilicia. It serves as a letter of recommendation for Judas and Silas, a warning against "false" apostles who were not sent by the Jerusalem authorities, and a prescription to observe the Noahide Laws. Judas and Silas

7. On a number of occasions Jesus is said to have tried to prevent such rumors from spreading, see for example, Mark 1:44, 5:43. Reports about rumors may have been meant to enhance Jesus' significance: his divine powers developed a force on their own that he did not initiate himself.

were supposed to add their oral commentary to the information contained in the letter (v. 27). They allegedly stayed in Antioch for some time before returning to Jerusalem (v. 33). Paul and Barnabas, on the other hand, are said to have started major missionary journeys from Antioch then (v. 36ff). Differences between Acts and the Pauline letters concerning the itineraries of the journeys are much discussed among scholars but cannot be dealt with in this context. What needs to be stressed here is the Jerusalem center's alleged use of an "official" letter to claim authority over the practices and beliefs of the Diaspora communities before 70 CE.

From an early stage onward, Paul's missionary activity in the Diaspora seems to have involved both intensive traveling and personal visits, delivering his teaching and instruction orally, as well as communication by means of letters in his absence as a supplement to his presence at certain places. Although they sometimes give the impression of stylized theological tractates, the Pauline letters themselves are the main testimony of Paul's attempts to maintain contact with Christian communities[8] over more or less large distances by means of written communication. The exchange of letters between Paul and Diaspora communities also meant that the Jerusalem center's claim to superior authority had been broken. Paul created a network of Diaspora communities that became independent of Jerusalem and maintained connections among each other instead (cf. the greetings and recommendations at the end of Pauline letters). Such a decentralized network would especially have developed after 70 CE.

Obviously not every member of the gentile Christian Diaspora communities would have been able to read the Pauline letters him- or herself. These letters were intended to be read out loud to the assembled (house) communities by their literate sub-elite leaders or by specially appointed readers.[9] Direct connections through letters would be established among community leaders on behalf of and as representatives of their local Christian co-religionists. These leaders, and especially Paul, would at least try to maintain control over lay Christians' beliefs and practices and divert attention from competitors ("false" apostles) who orally proclaimed alternative

8. The term "community" is used here to refer to groups or gatherings of Christians at various places; it does not imply organization and institutionalization. For reservations about the usage of the term for early Christians, see Hopkins, "Christian Number," 198–99.

9. On (Christian) sub-elites and their literacy levels, see Ibid., 209–10. On his missionary journeys Paul repeatedly stayed in the houses of fellow Christians, and so-called "house"-churches or local gatherings of Christians took place in the houses of sufficiently well-off community members. Those who opened their houses to gatherings and served as the main local contacts for "international" authorities such as Paul are likely to have been seen as local leaders by their fellow Christians.

teachings.[10] In this way, letters would still function as a means of executing authority and control, although the center had shifted from a particular locale (Jerusalem) to a Christian "holy man" (Paul). The fact that Pauline Christianity eventually became dominant will have been partly due to the publication and publicity, that is, the repeated copying, circulation, and oral reading, of his particular theological message.[11]

Later bishops and church leaders maintained extensive correspondences among themselves and with Christian communities.[12] Stanley K. Stowers even calls early Christianity "a movement of letter writers,"[13] a phenomenon that will have contributed greatly to the gradual expansion and dispersion of Christianity in the first four or five centuries CE (44). Letters among Christian religious leaders also seem to have served another function: "Through letters, the bishops, elders, deacons, and teachers sought consensus through dialogue and conflict. They drew boundaries of developing self-definition; they gave praise and blame to one another; they developed an articulate religious philosophy for the church" (44–45). That is, the exchange of letters helped develop Christian theological ideas and ethical recommendations. Despite the entirely oral beginnings of Christianity in the early Jesus movement, the very character and identity of Christianity would develop only later on the basis of stenographed sermons,[14] written communication, and the transmission of such written records to later generations of Christians. The oral teachings were not recoverable in their "original" form. What survived was their written reformulation and transformation.

COMMUNICATION AMONG RABBIS

A development that is similar in some regards and different in others can be observed for rabbinic Judaism. After 70 CE a Temple- and Jerusalem-centered Judaism turned into a decentralized, countrywide movement of

10. See also Botha, "Greco-Roman Literacy," 211, who notes that this "'political' side of Paul's letters has received little attention, how he uses writing to control and influence others and to promote a (probably) minoritarian viewpoint."

11. McGuire, "Letters and Letter Carriers," 150.

12. In the second and third centuries this seems to have especially been the case for city bishops such as Origen and Cyprian, who had secretaries at their disposal to write the letters for them (Fox, "Literacy and Power," 135 and 141). McGuire, "Letters and Letter Carriers," 150, calls the mid-fourth to the mid-fifth century "the golden age of patristic epistolography," and he stresses that "many more letters would have been written than those that survived" (151).

13. Stowers, *Letter Writing*, 15.

14. Maxwell, *Christianization and Communication*.

like-minded Torah scholars and teachers who supported one another but also competed with each other.[15] Holiness was no longer found in a particular institution or place, but was represented by each individual rabbi himself. By establishing relationships with other rabbis at more or less distant places and by attracting students and sympathizers among the populace, rabbis created a broad network of exchange and communication that covered the Galilee as well as the coastal region and even Babylonia from the third century CE onwards. Such a network between rabbis who resided at different locations could be created and maintained in only two ways: on the one hand through travel, mutual visits, and direct contacts, and on the other through the exchange of written messages in the form of letters. Rabbinic literature provides ample evidence of rabbinic communication over distances and the exchange of halakhic knowledge among rabbis. The very fact that rabbis established such a mobile and lively communication network must be considered the basis of the eventual transmission and collection of traditions and the creation of rabbinic documents.

In both tannaitic and amoraic documents at least some rabbis are presented as very mobile.[16] Far from being sedentary teachers or established leaders of local communities, these rabbis seem to have traveled for many different purposes, which were probably partly linked to their worldly professions. In contrast to early Christian missionaries, rabbis did not travel for missionary reasons, nor did they value travel as a means towards achieving a higher level of spirituality as did the later itinerant monks. Their mobility gave them an opportunity to visit colleagues and to discuss halakhic matters with them. For rabbis who lived in many different locales and did not have immediate access to their colleagues, such travels provided the best opportunity to engage in halakhic discussions with other scholars and to thereby develop *halakhah* (rabbinic rules and regulations) itself. The development of the Roman road system in the province of Syria-Palestine would have made their travels easier.[17] Colleagues and friends provided hospitality in addition to the inns available to travelers.[18]

Already in the Mishnah and Tosefta rabbis are frequently said to have visited each other. Usually the reason for the visit is not further specified,

15. Hezser, *Social Structure*, 171–80.

16. Tannaitic documents, such as the Mishnah and the Tosefta, contain traditions attributed to rabbis from the time between 70 and approximately 200 CE; amoraic documents, such as the Talmud Yerushalmi and aggadic midrashim, contain traditions as well as amoraic traditions associated with rabbis assumed to have lived from the third to the first half of the fifth century.

17. Roll, "Roads and Transportation," 1166–70.

18. Rosenfeld, "Innkeeping."

since the later transmitters and editors would consider it irrelevant. They were interested in the halakhic discussions and opinions of the respective rabbis only. Therefore the narratives that report such visits have very brief introductions and focus on the oral discussions and debates among rabbinic colleagues. The impression is that the topics discussed came up incidentally rather than having been planned from the outset. Yet such incidental discussions on visits that may have been undertaken for entirely different, profane reasons were obviously transmitted orally to later generations of scholars and became part of written collections of traditions. The following story can serve as an example (*m. Kil.* 6:4):

> It happened that R. Yehoshua went to R. Yishmael to Kefar Aziz, and he showed him a vine that was trained over part of a fig tree. He said to him: May I put seed under the remainder [of the tree]? He said to him: It is permitted. And he brought him up from there to Bet Hameganiah and showed him a vine that was trained over part of a branch and a trunk of a sycamore tree in which there were many branches. He said to him: Under this branch it is prohibited [to put seed], but [under] the rest it is permitted.[19]

The reference to R. Yehoshua's visit to his younger colleague R. Yishmael in Kefar Aziz is mentioned only briefly at the beginning of the story to set the scene. We do not know the purpose of R. Yehoshua's visit, whether he went to Kefar Aziz to meet his colleague or merely passed by this village on his journey to another destination. The halakhic discussion allegedly developed incidentally, when the rabbis walked in R. Yishmael's garden or vineyard and looked at some of his plantings. The younger R. Yishmael asks his older and more experienced colleague whether a certain practice would violate the rules concerning mixed seeds. Their walk and R. Yehoshua's halakhic instructions continue. Only the orally exchanged and transmitted halakhic views were relevant to later generations of scholars.

Such stories are more numerous in the Tosefta.[20] For example, R. Yehoshua allegedly "went to R. Yochanan b. Zakkai in Beror Hayil and townspeople would bring them figs" (*t. Maʿaś.* 2:1). R. Yehoshua's ass drivers approach R. Yehoshua to ask him whether they have to tithe their produce and he pronounces his halakhic opinion on the matter (*idem*). In another story R. Halafta is said to have gone to R. Gamliel II in Tiberias and "found him sitting at the table of Yochanan b. Nazif. And in his hand was the scroll of Job in translation and he was reading in it" (*t. Šabb.* 13:2). R. Halafta

19. All translations of rabbinic texts are my own.

20. The Tosefta is a collection of tannaitic traditions in addition to the Mishnah.

reminds R. Gamaliel II of his grandfather R. Gamliel the Elder, who refused to even touch a translated biblical scroll when sitting on the stairs of the Temple Mount (*t. Šabb.* 13:2). Again, certain practices with which a rabbi is confronted on his journey give rise to the formulation of halakhic opinions on a variety of issues. The practice of a colleague at another location is corrected and/or criticized. Only direct contacts between distant rabbis would enable such confrontations between variant opinions and practices. Such contacts would also allow rabbis to learn about other rabbis' views and exegeses. According to *t. Soṭah* 7:9, R. Yochanan bBeroqah and R. Eleazar Hisma were on their way from Yavneh to Lydda and visited R. Yehoshua in Peqi'in. R. Yehoshua allegedly took this opportunity to ask them about what was taught in the study house in Yavneh and they tell him about R. Eleazar bAzariah's teaching. In this case, R. Yehoshua would only know of R. Eleazar bAzariah's exegesis through the mediation of his visiting colleagues from another location.

Such references to the exchange of halakhic and exegetical knowledge through direct contacts between rabbis from different locations are especially numerous in the later Talmud Yerushalmi and amoraic midrashim. This may partly be due to the literary style of these documents, which incorporated more narrative traditions. It may also be a reflection of the expansion of the rabbinic movement and the increase of rabbis' mobility and mutual visits. Rabbis are said to have visited each other to help prepare or attend family events (for example, *y. Ber.* 2:4, 5a: "R. Chiyya, R. Issa, [and] R. Ammi went to make a marriage canope for R. Eleazar. They heard the voice of R. Yochanan [teaching]"; *y. Ber.* 2:8, 5c: "When R. Bun b. R. Chiyya died, R. Zeira went up and gave a condolence speech on his behalf"; *y. Ber.* 6:5, 10c: "R. Yona and R. Yose went to the banquet of R. Hanina of Anat"), to pay sick calls (e.g., *y. Pe'ah* 3:9, 17d; *y. ʿAbod. Zar.* 2:3, 41a), or to work with their colleagues (e.g., *y. Šabb.* 2:1, 4d).

Rabbis are also often said to have "walked on the road" together or to have gone to visit bathhouses. Most often, the reasons for rabbis' mutual visits are not stated explicitly, but such direct contacts almost always led to the discussion of *halakhah*, the observance of certain practices, or the transmission of exegetical insights. Although we cannot take such stories literally as historical evidence of particular rabbis' actual meetings with particular colleagues, the frequency of such traditions in different forms, addressing different subjects, makes it quite likely that travel and mutual visits were the social contexts in which the oral exchange of halakhic and exegetical knowledge between spatially separated rabbis took place.

In addition to direct contacts through visits of rabbinic colleagues, indirect contacts were established through messengers and intermediaries.

Students, colleagues, friends, and relatives could function as messengers. The literary sources do not always specify whether oral or written messages were delivered. Occasionally, however, letters are directly mentioned. As in the case of rabbinic travel and mutual visits, references to messengers and (written) notes are much more common in amoraic than in tannaitic documents.

Already in the Mishnah there are references to students citing traditions in the name of their teachers (for example, *m. ʿErub.* 1:2: "In the name of R. Yishmael a student said before R. Aqiba") and the notion that two or more students' memory of the same tradition makes it more trustworthy (cf. *m. ʿErub.* 2:6: "R. Ilai said: I heard from R. Eliezer: . . . And I went around among his disciples and looked for a partner for myself [in having heard and memorized these teachings] but did not find [any]"). Especially interesting is the following tradition concerning communication between Palestine and Babylonia in the tannaitic period (*m. Yebam.* 16:7):

> R. Aqiba said: When I went down to Nehardea to intercalate the year I found Nechemiah of Bet Deli. He said to me: I have heard that in the Land of Israel they do not allow a woman to [re] marry on the basis of [the testimony of] one witness, except for R. Yehudah b. Baba. And I answered him: That's right. He said to me: Tell them in my name: . . . . I have received [a tradition] from R. Gamliel the Elder, that they permit a woman to [re]marry on account of one witness. And when I came and recounted the words before R. Gamliel he rejoiced over my words and said: We have found a fellow for R. Yehudah b. Baba [i.e., someone who transmits the same teaching heard from R. Gamliel the Elder] .

The story relates that when R. Aqiba came to Babylonia, he met a fellow Palestinian, Nechemiah of Bet Deli, who claims to know Palestinian rabbinic views on the remarriage of widows, with which R. Aqiba is also familiar. Interestingly, this person also claims to have knowledge of a teaching of R. Gamliel the Elder that only one Palestinian sage (R. Yehudah b. Baba) is said to have remembered. The tradition seems to have been new to R. Aqiba himself, who nevertheless carried it back to Palestine and confronted R. Gamliel the Elder's grandson with it. The latter is glad to have found confirmation of a tradition that until then had rested on the memory of only one Palestinian sage.

Although the story cannot be taken literally as a historical record of encounters between the mentioned individuals, it nevertheless reveals rabbinic notions about oral memory and the oral transmission of traditions across borders. It also shows how precarious such transmission was:

deceased sages' views could easily be forgotten or remembered by one student only. If there was only one witness to a view, there was no certainty that he had remembered it correctly. Therefore, a second independent testimony would be all the more valuable. The Mishnah does not tell us how Nechemiah of Bet Deli would have gained knowledge of the mentioned Palestinian rabbinic views. The reference to the Galilean village of Bet Deli indicates his Palestinian origin, so he must be a Palestinian who emigrated to Babylonia at some stage in his life. Neusner's suggestion that he studied with R. Gamliel in Jerusalem before 50 CE seems to overstate the matter,[21] but contacts between a Palestinian immigrant to Babylonia and Palestinian rabbis are certainly assumed here. Such immigrants would have been able to spread Palestinian views in Babylonia and to tell their Palestinian contacts about Babylonian views, a practice that was still exceptional in the tannaitic period but became commonplace from the third century CE onward.

There is no reference to the transmission of written messages or letters among rabbis in the Mishnah, neither within the Land of Israel itself nor between Israel and the Diaspora. This contrasts with the famous story in *t. Sanh.* 2:6, according to which R. Gamliel I and elders were sitting on the steps of the Temple Mount with Yochanan the scribe, dictating letters to Diaspora communities concerning the intercalation of the year, an issue relevant for the festival calendar. This is the only letter directly mentioned in the Tosefta, however, and it is presented as an official letter, sent by Jerusalem rabbinic authorities to Diaspora communities, much like the letters sent to Diaspora Christian communities by the Jewish-Christian Jerusalem authorities mentioned in Acts. Within rabbinic circles, there are several references to oral testimonies instead (for example, *t. Demai* 3:1: "R. Yose bHameshullam testified in the name of R. Nathan, his brother, who said in the name of R. Eleazar Hisma"; *t. Šeb.* 5:12: "R. Yehudah bIsaiah the perfumer testified before R. Aqiba in the name of R. Tarfon that balsam is subject to the [laws of the] Seventh Year"). The tannaitic evidence suggests, then, that orality rather than writing played a dominant role in the transmission of rabbinic traditions throughout the first two centuries CE.[22]

Although oral communication continues to be important in amoraic times, and while rabbinic travels and visits to distant colleagues even increased at that time, as pointed out above, there are many more references to letters and written messages in amoraic than in tannaitic sources, and the use of written communication seems to have increased both within the Land of Israel and especially between Israel and the Diaspora in late

21. Neusner, *Jews in Babylonia*, 52.

22. Hezser, *Jewish Literacy*, 267–75.

antiquity. For the first time we encounter a situation similar to that of Josephus, who claims to have exchanged written notes with other rebel leaders on various occasions. First, there are direct references to letters in amoraic documents. Second, rabbis are now frequently said to have "sent to" colleagues through intermediaries, a formulation that is sometimes followed by the verb "he wrote."

Only a few examples for the exchange of letters can be provided here. In connection with the intercalation of the year, "Rabbi sent him [Hananiah, who had moved to Babylonia] three letters through R. Yitzhaq and R. Natan" (*y. Sanh.* 1:2, 19a), criticizing his practice. After receiving the first two letters, he is said to have honored the letter-bearers; when he received the third, "he wanted to treat them with contempt" (*idem*). This behavior seems to have been quite typical for recipients who received bad messages. Elsewhere R. Hiyya bBa is said to have asked R. Eleazar to intervene with R. Yudan the patriarch to ask him to write a letter of recommendation for him, since he wanted to move abroad (probably to Babylonia) to make a living (*y. Ḥag.* 1:8, 76d; for a variant version see, *y. Moʿed Qaṭ.* 3:1, 81c). When Yehudah bTavai had fled to Alexandria, Jerusalemites allegedly wrote a letter to Alexandria concerning him (*y. Sanh.* 6:8, 23c). The Babylonian Rab is said to have written a letter to the Palestinian patriarch Rabbi concerning the case of the daughter of Absalom's support after her divorce (*y. Giṭ.* 46d).

In many of these cases, letters are imagined to have been employed in communication between greater distances in quasi-official contexts: intercalation of the calendar, court appeals, recommendations, threats of excommunication, exchanges between the patriarch and exilarch, or community issues. But elsewhere in the Yerushalmi, written messages are also said to have been employed sometimes among rabbis for the "minor" purpose of discussing halakhic issues or asking colleagues halakhic questions. The formulation "sent and asked" is commonly used in the Yerushalmi and may refer to both oral and written messages. Sometimes the written nature of the message is directly mentioned, as in the following case (*y. Qidd.* 3:14, 64d):

> R. Tanhum b. Papa sent [and] asked R. Yose [concerning] two cases from Alexandria, one about an unmarried woman and one about a married woman [who had sexual relationships with an improper man]. Concerning the married woman he sent [and] wrote to him: "A *mamzer* shall not enter the congregation of the Lord" [Deut 23:2]; concerning the unmarried woman he sent [and] wrote to him: "It seems that you are not careful about holy Israelite girls." He said to R. Mana: Take and sign [the letters], and he signed. He said to R. Berekhiah: Take [and] sign, but he did not accept.

Wilhelm Bacher and Jacob Lauterbach considered the letter mentioned in this tradition a forerunner of the later *responsa* of the Gaonic period.[23] Interestingly, the correspondence concerns cases from Alexandria in Egypt that were allegedly brought before the Palestinian R. Yose for decision. It is not explicitly said whether R. Tanhum bPapa sent a written or oral message to R. Yose to request his help in the mentioned cases. R. Yose's answer (negative in the first and positive in the second case) is said to have been submitted in writing. In order to make his views more authoritative, he is said to have asked two other rabbis, among them his former student R. Mana, to sign the letter with him. The tradition does not cite the letter in full but merely mentions phrases most relevant to the decision. In the Talmud the discussion continues: R. Berekhiah is said to have eventually changed his mind, at a time when it was too late, since the letter had already been sent off.

According to Bacher and Lauterbach, "This story shows that often questions were settled by a single letter, as was later the case with the Geonim, who exchanged a series of responsa" (*ibid.*). Unfortunately, we do not know how common this practice was in the amoraic period, despite the Babylonian Talmud's (infrequent) use of the formula "they sent from there," that is, halakhic messages or decisions from Palestine to Babylonia (*b. Giṭ.* 66a, 73a; *b. Zebaḥ.* 87a; *b. ʿArak.* 22a), without specifying the written or oral nature of such messages. That written requests for halakhic information were occasionally sent from Babylonia (and also other Diaspora locations?) to the Land of Israel is certainly imaginable, but how frequent and legally authoritative such messages actually were remains uncertain.[24]

In the Yerushalmi the formula "sent and asked" usually appears without reference to the oral or written nature of the message. Sometimes the transmitters and editors of these traditions may have imagined the message to have been transmitted in written form, but in (most?) other cases an oral message may have been envisioned, especially if communication within the Land of Israel (rather than between Israel and the Diaspora) was involved. When a rabbi is said to have "sent to" a Palestinian colleague to request an answer to a halakhic question, such a question and answer could have been exchanged in writing or orally. In either case an intermediary would have been necessary to transmit the message. Such messengers are usually not mentioned, however. The later tradents may have considered a reference to students' transmission of their teacher's messages too insignificant

23. See www.JewishEncyclopedia.com.

24. From the Palestinian rabbinic side there would obviously have been an interest in transmitting such traditions and claiming such authority.

or self-evident to mention explicitly. Yet occasionally the identity of the intermediary is specified, though: for example, R. Gamliel sent to R. Yehoshua through R. Aqiba (*y. Roš. Haš.* 2:8, 58b); R. Zeira sent to R. Nahum though R. Yannai bR. Yishmael (*y. Taʿan.* 2:2, 65c); R. Shmuel bYitzhaq sent R. Yaqob bAha to ask before R. Hiyya bBa (*y. Yebam.* 12:2, 12d). Such references are rare in comparison with the many traditions not specifying the messenger, however.

Altogether, then, both mobility and visits among rabbis, as well as direct and indirect oral and written communication among them, seem to have increased in the amoraic period, from the third to early fifth century CE. The increase in literary references to these phenomena may partly be due to the sheer volume of amoraic in comparison to tannaitic literature and the larger corpus of narrative traditions in the Talmud Yerushalmi as compared to the Mishnah and Tosefta. On the other hand, we know that the rabbinic movement expanded and diversified in the amoraic period and that rabbis were increasingly present in the cities of Roman Palestine, in addition to their presence in villages.[25] If there were more rabbis at more places, there would have been more reasons and opportunities to contact those colleagues who lived outside of one's hometown.

Another reason for the many reported visits may have been rabbis' increased participation in the late Roman "culture of mobility." A number of ancient historians have already stressed that late antiquity was characterized by the greater mobility of a larger segment of the population: not only soldiers and Roman officials but also merchants, monks, bishops, philosophers, teachers, students, tourists, pilgrims, and health-seekers traveled on the roads.[26] Rabbis seem to have increasingly been affected by the "travel bug" and recognized its advantages: travel allowed them to establish and maintain direct contacts with distant colleagues and thereby create a network of communication throughout the province as well as with rabbis in neighboring regions.[27]

Especially from the third century onwards, direct contacts between rabbis were supplemented by indirect communications through oral and written messages. Together, these contacts allowed rabbis to receive answers

25. On the expansion and diversification of the rabbinic movement, see Cohen, "Rabbi"; on the gradual urbanization and the continued importance of villages, see Hezser, *Social Structure*, 157–65; on Galilean villages' participation in cultural and economic developments, see Edwards, "Identity and Social Location."

26. See Casson, *Travel*, 122; McCormick, "Byzantium on the Move"; André and Baslez, *Voyager*, 7, speak of "une culture voyageuse."

27. For a book-length study on the relationship between mobility and communication in ancient Judaism, see Hezser, *Jewish Travel*.

to halakhic questions and cases, identify similar or divergent opinions, and transmit their views to more or less distant colleagues and through students to later generations. A rabbinic dispute could emerge only once different opinions were identified. Discussions of *halakhah* depended on direct or indirect contacts among rabbis. Since the rabbinic movement was decentralized and no regular meetings between rabbis (like the Christian synods) took place, such informal visits and meetings and individual contacts were the only way in which halakhic opinions could be exchanged. The establishment of such a travel and communication network can be considered the social basis of the eventual collection, fixation, and editing of rabbinic traditions that eventually developed into written documents.

It should be noted at the end of this discussion that not all rabbis would have participated in the communication network in a similar way. Not all rabbis would have been able to engage in (extensive) travel or had traveling students who could function as intermediaries. Rabbis whose mundane profession involved travel could visit rabbinic colleagues most easily and even sojourn with them on their way. Those rabbis who had the most significant contacts, who sat at the nodal points of the communication network, were probably most powerful within the movement. They would have been able to gather the largest inventory of halakhic knowledge and determine which views to pass on to others and which to delete from memory.[28] For the Middle Ages, Sophia Menache points to a model "in which the amount of information assimilated by the different social strata correlated with their social status and the political functions they fulfilled."[29] The existence of communication channels as such constituted only the basis; whether and to what extent actual communication took place depended on the individual rabbi's initiative. Those who were most powerful within the rabbinic network, such as the patriarch R. Yehudah ha-Nasi, will have tried to monopolize the communication, a phenomenon that may be reflected in later rabbinic traditions' identification of him as the editor of the Mishnah.

CONCLUSION

Both the early Jesus movement and the rabbis of the first few centuries CE seem to have relied on face-to-face contacts and direct oral communication

28. For an application of network theory to late antique pagan intellectuals, see Ruffini, "Late Antique Pagan Networks." He points out that "the chief characters" all had extensive networking connections over provincial distances, especially connecting Egypt and Greece. Connections were maintained directly but also through fourth- and fifth-degree contacts.

29. Menache, "Introduction," 7.

to establish contacts with colleagues, students, sympathizers, and others. In order to establish such contacts with people at more distant places—colleagues willing to discuss halakhic issues in the case of rabbis; people to whom they could spread their message in the case of the early Jesus movement—mobility and travel were often necessary. Only those early Christian missionaries who were ready to leave their hometowns would be successful in their missionary activity, a phenomenon realized by the "wandering charismatics" and especially Paul. Similarly, only those rabbis who established and maintained contacts with their colleagues at different locations would be able to discuss and develop their halakhic knowledge and gain support for their opinions. They would be able to spread their own views and amalgamate knowledge collected through such contacts. Accordingly, the most mobile and communicative rabbis would be the ones whose traditions would survive and who would actively participate in the transmission and eventual collection of their colleague-friends' views.

When Christianity entered the Greco-Roman realm, letters seem to have been increasingly employed, a process that started with Paul and reached its summit with the extensive correspondences of the church fathers and bishops of the fourth and fifth centuries, which were eventually published. In Palestinian Judaism it seems to have taken longer until the advantages of written correspondence were recognized, and this practice seems never to have caught on as much as in late antique Christianity and the Greco-Roman world. We noticed a dramatic increase in references to letters in amoraic in comparison with tannaitic literature. Yet even in amoraic times letters seem to have been mainly employed for semi- or quasi-official purposes and in order to transfer information over long distances, between Palestine, Babylonia, Syria, and Egypt. Nevertheless, the rabbinic movement seems to have expanded in late antiquity and with it the rabbinic communication network. Both oral and written messages were increasingly sent through intermediaries to supplement face-to-face contacts. Both direct and indirect contacts helped to develop, preserve, and transmit rabbinic *halakhah*, while early Christian communication helped develop Christian theology. In both cases those religious leaders who sat at the nodal points of the communication network would have had most control over this development.

The most likely Greco-Roman analogy would be communication networks among philosophers. Like rabbis, philosophers put a great emphasis on oral instruction and on oral discussion and disputes.[30] They established schools at various places throughout the Roman Empire. Whereas the cit-

30. Alexander, "Living Voice."

ies of Sepphoris, Tiberias, and Caesarea in Palestine and Sura, Pumbedita, and Nisibis in Babylonia seem to have developed as the most significant locations of rabbinic activity in late antiquity,[31] Athens and Alexandria were the focal points of pagan philosophical life. According to Ruffini, all major philosophical figures of the fifth and sixth century CE (the period of his investigation) "had extensive connections to both Alexandria and Athens, and provided links between the pagan intellectual communities in Egypt and Greece."[32] Such connections would be established primarily through visits and direct oral communication and secondarily through written communication by means of letters. They would have had a major impact on the development of views and would eventually determine whose views were considered worthy of being transmitted to other locations and to later generations of readers.

BIBLIOGRAPHY

Alexander, Loveday. "The Living Voice: Scepticism Towards the Written Word in Early Christian and in Graeco-Roman Texts." *Journal for the Study of the Old Testament* 87 (1990) 221–47.

André, Jean-Marie, and Marie-Françoise Baslez. *Voyager dans l'Antiquité.* 2nd ed. Paris: Fayard, 1993.

Botha, Pieter J. J. "Greco-Roman Literacy as Setting for New Testament Writings." *Neotestamentica* 26 (1992) 195–215. Reprinted in *Orality and Literacy in Early Christianity*, 39–61. Biblical Performance Criticism Series 5. Eugene, OR: Cascade Books, 2012.

Casson, Lionel. *Travel in the Ancient World.* 2nd ed. Baltimore: Johns Hopkins University Press, 1994.

Cohen, Shaye J. D. "The Rabbi in Second Century Jewish Society." In *The Cambridge History of Judaism*, vol. 3, *The Early Roman Period*, edited by William Horbury et al., 922–77. Cambridge: Cambridge University Press, 1999.

Edwards, Douglas R. "Identity and Social Location in Roman Galilean Villages." In *Religion, Ethnicity, and Identity in Ancient Galilee: A Region in Transition*, edited by Jürgen Zangenberg et al, 357–74. Wissenschaftliche Untersuchungen zum Neuen Testament 210. Tübingen: Mohr/Siebeck, 2007.

Fox, Robin Lane. "Literacy and Power in Early Christianity." In *Literacy and Power in the Ancient World*, edited by Alan K. Bowman and Greg Woolf, 126–48. Cambridge: Cambridge University Press, 1994.

Hezser, Catherine. *Jewish Literacy in Roman Palestine.* Texts and Studies in Ancient Judaism 81. Tübingen: Mohr/Siebeck, 2001.

———. *Jewish Travel in Antiquity.* Texts and Studies in Ancient Judaism 144. Tübingen: Mohr/Siebeck, 2011.

31. There is a large amount of literature on contacts between Palestinian and Babylonian sages in late antiquity. See, for example, Oppenheimer, "Contacts."

32. Ruffini, "Late Antique Pagan Networks," 241.

———. *The Social Structure of the Rabbinic Movement in Roman Palestine*. Texts and Studies in Ancient Judaism 66. Tübingen: Mohr/Siebeck, 1997.

Hopkins, Keith. "Christian Number and Its Implications." *Journal of Early Christian Studies* 6 (1998) 185–226.

Josephus. *Life*. Vol. 1. Translated by H. St. J. Thackeray. Loeb Classical Library 186. Cambridge: Harvard University Press, 1926.

Kelber, Werner H. *The Oral and the Written Gospel: The Hermeneutics of Speaking and Writing in the Synoptic Tradition, Mark, Paul, and Q*. Reprinted, Bloomington: Indiana University Press, 1997.

Lauterbach, Jacob Zallel. "She'elot u-Teshubot." In *The Jewish Encyclopedia: A Descriptive Record of the History, Religion, Literature, and Customs of the Jewish People from the Earliest Times*, edited by Isidore Singer, 11:240–50. New York: Ktav, 1907.

Maxwell, Jaclyn L. *Christianization and Communication in Late Antiquity: John Chrysostom and His Congregation in Antioch*. Cambridge: Cambridge University Press, 2006.

McCormick, Michael. "Byzantium on the Move: Imagining a Communications History." In *Travel in the Byzantine World*, edited by Ruth Macrides, 3–29. Aldershot, UK: Ashgate, 2002.

McGuire, Martin R. P. "Letters and Letter Carriers in Christian Antiquity." *Classical World* 53 (1960) 148–200.

Meier, Samuel A. *The Messenger in the Ancient Semitic World*. Harvard Semitic Monographs 45. Atlanta: Scholars, 1988.

Menache, Sophia. "Introduction: The Pre-History of Communication." In *Communication in the Jewish Diaspora: The Pre-Modern World*, edited by Sophie Menache, 1–14. Brill's Series in Jewish Studies 16. Leiden: Brill, 1996.

Moatti, Claudia. "Translation, Migration, and Communication in the Roman Empire: Three Aspects of Movement in History." *Classical Antiquity* 25 (2006) 109–40.

Neusner, Jacob. *A History of the Jews in Babylonia*, vol. 1, *The Parthian Period*. South Florida Studies in the History of Judaism 217. Atlanta: Scholars, 1999.

Ong, Walter J. "Text as Interpretation: Mark and After." In *Orality, Aurality, and Biblical Narrative*, edited by L. H. Silverman, *Semeia* 39 (1987) 7–26.

Oppenheimer, Aharon. "Contacts between Eretz Israel and Babylonia at the Turn of the Period of the *Tannaim* and the *Amoraim*." In *Between Rome and Babylon: Studies in Jewish Leadership and Society*, edited by Nili Oppenheimer, 417–32. Texts and Studies in Ancient Judaism 108. Tübingen: Mohr/Siebeck, 2005.

Roll, Israel. "Roads and Transportation in the Holy Land in the Early Christian and Byzantine Times." *Jahrbuch für Antike und Christentum: Ergänzungsband* 20/2 (1995) 1166–70.

Rosenfeld, Ben-Zion. "Innkeeping in Jewish Society in Roman Palestine." *Journal of the Economic and Social History of the Orient* 41 (1998) 133–58.

Ruffini, Giovanni. ""Late Antique Pagan Networks from Athens to the Thebaid." In *Ancient Alexandria between Egypt and Greece*, edited by William V. Harris and Giovanni Ruffini, 241–57. Columbia Studies in the Classical Tradition 26. Leiden: Brill, 2004.

Stowers, Stanley K. *Letter Writing in Graeco-Roman Antiquity*. Library of Early Christianity 5. Philadelphia: Westminster John Knox, 1986.

Theissen, Gerd. *Social Reality and the Early Christians: Theology, Ethics, and the World of the New Testament*. Translated by Margaret Kohl. Minneapolis: Fortress, 1992.

———. *Studien zur Soziologie des Urchristentums.* Wissenschaftliche Untersuchungen zum Neuen Testament 19. Tübingen: Mohr/Siebeck, 1983.

Zwickel, Wolfgang. "Kommunikation und Kommunikationsmöglichkeiten im Alten Israel aufgrund biblischer und ausserbiblischer Texte." In *Bote und Brief: Sprachliche Systeme der Informationsübermittlung im Spannungsfeld von Mündlichkeit und Schriftlichkeit*, edited by A. Wagner, 113–23. Nordostafrikanisch/westasiatische Studien 4. Frankfurt: Lang, 2003.

6

Oral and Written Aspects of the Emergence of the Gospel of Mark as Scripture

Richard A. Horsley

Jewish and Christian, and especially Protestant Christian, emphasis upon the sacred book and its authority have combined with scholarly interests and techniques, as well as the broader developments in the modern West . . . to fix in our minds today a rather narrow concept of scripture, a concept even more sharply culture-bound than that of "book" itself.

—William A. Graham (1987)

Mark's Gospel . . . was composed at a desk in a scholar's study lined with texts . . . In Mark's study were chains of miracle stories, collections of pronouncement stories in various states of elaboration, some form of Q, memos on parables and proof texts, the scriptures, including the prophets, written materials from the Christ cult, and other literature representative of Hellenistic Judaism.

—Burton Mack (1988)

It was not necessary that the Gospel performer know how to read. The performer could learn the Gospel from hearing oral performance . . . It is quite possible, and indeed even likely, that many Gospel performers were themselves illiterate . . . It was certainly possible for an oral performer to develop a narrative with this level of structural complexity . . . In Mark the number of interconnections between parts of the narrative are quite extraordinary.

—Whitney Shiner (2003)

The procedures and concepts of Christian biblical studies are often teleological. The results of the historical process are assumed in study of its early stages. Until recently critical study of the books of the New Testament focused on establishing the scriptural text and its meaning in the context of historical origins. Ironically that was before the texts became distinctively authoritative for communities that used them and were recognized as Scripture by established ecclesial authorities. Such teleological concepts and procedures obscure what turn out to be genuine historical problems once we take a closer look.

How the Gospels, particularly the Gospel of Mark, came to be included in the Scriptures of established Christianity offers a striking example. On the earlier Christian theological assumption that Christianity as the religion of the Gospel made a dramatic break with Judaism as the religion of the Law, one of the principal questions was how the Christian church came to include the Jewish Scriptures in its Bible. We now see much more clearly the continuity of what became Christianity with Israel. The Gospels, especially Matthew and Mark, portray Jesus as engaged in a renewal of Israel. The Gospel of Matthew is now generally seen as addressed to communities of Israel, not "Gentiles."[1] And while Mark was formerly taken as addressed to a "Gentile" community in Rome, it is increasingly taken as addressed to communities in Syria that understand themselves as the renewal of Israel.[2]

Far more problematic than the inclusion of the Jewish Scripture (in Greek) is inclusion of the Gospels in the Christian Bible. The ecclesial authorities who defined the New Testament canon in the fourth and fifth centuries were men of high culture. The Gospels, however, especially the Gospel of Mark, did not meet the standards of high culture in the Hellenistic and Roman cultural world. Once the Gospels became known to the cultural elite, opponents of the Christians such as Celsus, in the late second century, mocked them for their lack of literary distinction and their composers as ignorant people who lacked "even a primary education."[3] Fifty years later, the "church father" Origen proudly admitted that the apostles possessed

1. Saldarini, *Matthew's Christian Jewish Community*, 1994.

2. Horsley, *Hearing the Whole Story*, 2001.

3. *Contra Celsum* 1.62

"no power of speaking or of giving an ordered narrative by the standards of Greek dialectical or rhetorical arts."[4] Luke had asserted, somewhat presumptuously perhaps, that he and his predecessors as "evangelists" had, in the standard Hellenistic-Roman ideology of historiography, set down an "orderly account" of events in the Gospels. Origen, who knew better, had to agree with Celsus that the evangelists were, as the Jerusalem "rulers, elders, and scribes" in the second volume of Luke's "orderly account" said about Peter and John, "illiterate and ignorant" (ἀγράμματοί εἰσιν καὶ ἰδιῶται, Acts 4:13).

Nor would the Gospels, again especially Mark, have measured up as Scripture on the model of previous Jewish scriptural texts. The Gospels stand in strong continuity with Israelite-Jewish cultural tradition; indeed they portray Jesus and his followers as its fulfillment. Yet they do not resemble any of the kinds of texts included in the Jewish Scriptures or other Jewish scribal compositions, whether books of Torah (Deuteronomy), books of history (Judges; 1–2 Kings), collections of prophecies (Isaiah, Amos), collections of instructional wisdom (Proverbs 1–9; Sirach), or apocalypses (Daniel). Rather the Gospels tell the story of a popular leader they compare to Moses and Elijah who focused on the concerns of villagers in opposition to the political and cultural elite and who was gruesomely executed by the Roman governor.

Consideration of the *oral and written* aspects of scripture may be one of the keys to addressing the question of how the Gospels, particularly the Gospel of Mark, became included in the Bible by the ecclesial authorities of established Christianity in the fourth and fifth centuries. Only contemporary with or after the Gospel's official recognition as part of Scripture do we find Christian intellectuals producing commentaries that are more than spiritualizing allegories or moralistic homilies on Gospel passages. Research in a number of interrelated (but often separate) areas is coalescing to suggest that the Gospel of Mark developed in a largely oral communication environment and was performed orally in communities of ordinary people in ever-widening areas of the Roman empire, such that it became *de facto* authoritative and revered among Christian communities. In both the situation of the Gospel's origins and the circumstances of its regular recitation, written texts were known and respected as authoritative. Recent research suggests that it was through repeated oral performance that it gained wide authority among the people as the basis on which it was included in the Bible.

4. *Contra Celsum* 1.62

Evidence for both the written and oral functioning of the Gospel of Mark is fragmentary and often indirect. Yet there may be sufficient evidence to consider the following oral and written aspects of the emergence of the Gospel of Mark as scriptural:

- the Gospel's relation to Scripture in comparison with scribal cultivation of Scripture
- the predominantly oral communication environment (and oral-memorial cultivation of Israelite cultural tradition) in the Gospel's origin among ordinary people
- the oral (in relation to the written) cultivation of the Gospel in the second and third centuries prior to its official inclusion in the Christian Bible
- the features of the Gospel that made it memorable and performable
- the Gospel's resonance with hearers in historical context

An appropriate preface to these steps is to note the loosening grip of print culture on scriptural studies.

LOOSENING THE HOLD OF PRINT CULTURE ON THE CONCEPT OF SCRIPTURE

The concept of Scripture assumed in standard Jewish and Christian biblical studies is problematic as well as narrow because it is so deeply embedded in the assumptions of modern print culture. Only recently have a small number of biblical scholars begun to "catch on" to the ground-breaking research and analysis of colleagues such as William Graham, on the oral as well as written functioning of the Qur'an and the Bible, and Werner Kelber, on oral and written aspects of New Testament texts. Such work as theirs has now set some of the key terms of the discussion. If, with Graham and Kelber, we move behind the print culture on which our eyes are usually fixed, what is meant by scripture becomes wider and more diverse. In the Middle Ages, Christian Scripture cannot be confined to what was inscribed on codices or scrolls in Hebrew, Greek, and/or Latin translation. The latter, broken into more easily memorable sections, was commonly learned and recited orally by priests and monks. If we are to deal with such oral aspects of scripture, then our concept must obviously include texts in oral performance. And we must take into account different forms of written scripture (a necessary redundancy) and different forms of oral appropriation. Perhaps the "most common denominator" will be the contents of the text, whether in oral-memorial or written (or visual) form. Moreover, there has often been a close relationship between the oral and the written cultivation of scriptural texts. Recent work in related fields has revealed the remarkable interrelation between orality and scribal practice with regard to other authoritative (although perhaps not scriptural) texts in medieval Europe.[5] Oral cultivation has often affected the continuing development of written texts as scribes with memorial knowledge of the text made new written copies.

Conceptually, once we back away from the modern print-cultural definition of scripture, it is more satisfactory and more historically accurate to say that the text of scripture functioned as much (or more) in scribal memory and oral recitation as in (but not independent of) writing on scrolls. Correspondingly the term "text" then would refer to the contents that are learned and recited as well as written on scrolls (as in older usage; see OED; and compare the Latin *textus*, that which has been woven, texture, and even context; also the Greek verb ῥάπτω, "to stitch," behind the compound ῥαψῳδέω, "to recite"). When we want to use "text" to refer more specifically to either a text in memory and recitation or a written text, we could "mark" it as "written text" or "oral text" for clarity. Graham called for this move in the use of the term "text" twenty years ago in reference to Walter Ong's observation regarding the relentless domination of textuality understood according to print-culture in the scholarly mind.

At least the contents of Christian scripture, particularly the Gospels, far from being limited to the literate elite, have functioned in significant ways among ordinary people. The functioning of scripture among ordinary people is difficult to get a handle on. What would scripture have meant for medieval peasants who could not read Latin and perhaps rarely heard texts read or recited, even in Latin? Scripture as written on codices was something very holy and mysterious possessed by the Church hierarchy in cathedrals and monasteries. At least some medieval peasants, however, were not ignorant of the contents of scripture as stories, symbols, and significant figures. They heard about these in homilies, perhaps on particular saints' days, and saw them in murals and statues that decorated even tiny rural chapels. Early print editions of the Biblia *pauperum* contain replicas of murals on chapel walls that display scenes from the Gospels flanked by the analogous scenes from the "Old Testament"—a popular version of what Auerbach wrote about in his essay on *Figura*.[6] When the contents of the Gospels in particular were suddenly made accessible in oral performance to

5. Carruthers, *Memory*; Clanchy, *Memory to Written Record*; Doane, "Ethnography," and others.

6. Auerbach, *Scenes*.

non-literate peasants in the late Middle Ages they "came alive," for example among the Lollards in England, the followers of Jan Hus in Bohemia, and the peasants in southwest Germany in 1524–25.[7] For non-literate people it may be difficult to distinguish between scripture and cultural memory. What we are after is relationships of people and scripture, looking at the different functions of scripture in various circumstances.

MARK'S RELATION TO JUDEAN SCRIPTURES IN COMPARISON WITH SCRIBAL CULTIVATION

The standard view of the Gospel of Mark in New Testament studies rooted in the assumptions of print culture is that it was "written" by an "author" on the basis of written sources. On the standard assumption of general literacy, particularly in Jewish society, and the availability of books of the Hebrew Bible ("the Law and the Prophets," "Old Testament"), Mark was supposed to have "quoted" from books such as Isaiah, Jeremiah, and the Psalms. Recent research in a number of areas can now be brought together to construct quite a different picture that takes the relationship of oral communication and written texts more fully into account. In that different picture, moreover, the Gospel of Mark seems to stand at some distance from the scribal culture in which written Judean texts were cultivated.

First, studies have now documented extensively that literacy in Roman Judea was perhaps even more limited than in the Roman empire generally.[8] Beyond scribal circles, communication was almost completely oral, ordinary people having little use for writing. Insofar as writing was limited to the cultural elite in second-temple Judea,[9] the cultivation of written texts was concentrated in circles of scribes who had taken on this role and responsibility in the service of the Jerusalem temple-state.[10]

Second, recent analysis of different "kinds" of writing in Judea, the ancient Near East, and in Greece and Rome have made us sensitive to how particular written texts may have functioned.[11] We cannot assume that texts were written to be "studied" and "interpreted," as in scholarly print-culture.

7. Aston, *Lollards and Reformers*; Deanesly, *Lollard Bible*; Blickle, *Reformation to Revoltion*; Scribner, *Simple Folk*.

8. Achtemeier, "*Omne verbum sonat*"; Botha, "Greco-Roman Literacy"; Harris, *Ancient Literacy*; Hezser, *Jewish Literacy*.

9. Hezser, *Jewish Literacy*.

10. Carr, *Tablet of the Heart*; Horsley, *Galilee*; and Horsley, *Scribes, Visionaries, and Politics*.

11. Niditch, *Oral World and Written Word*.

Scrolls were expensive, cumbersome, and difficult to read, unless one was already familiar with the text. Besides being relatively inaccessible, however, some ancient writings were not intended for regular consultation. They had other statuses and functions.[12] Some were laid up in temples or palace storerooms as specially inscribed texts. Some of those were also "constitutional" in function. Books of Mosaic torah, for example, were "found," recited publicly in Jerusalem, and then presumably redeposited in the Temple (2 Kings 22:3—23:24; Nehemiah 8) to legitimate great reforms in the Judean temple-state.

Third, as a result of the discovery of the Dead Sea Scrolls, it is now evident that the authority of the books that were later included in the Hebrew Bible held what might be called relative authority in Judean society. Close study of the scrolls of the books of the Pentateuch and the Prophets that were later included in the Hebrew Bible has shown that in late second-temple times they existed in multiple textual traditions and that each of those textual traditions was still developing.[13] Judging from the relative number of copies of those books found in the caves at Qumran, compared with the number of copies of other books, such as Jubilees and alternative books of Torah found there, the books later defined as biblical shared scriptural status with a wide range of texts.[14] Their authority, as well as their texts, was still developing. The written "books of Moses," moreover, also shared authority with the ordinances promulgated by the Pharisees that were included as part of official state law under some high priests.[15]

Most important for consideration of the oral as well as written aspects of the Judean scriptures may be the recent recognition that scribes themselves were engaged in oral cultivation of texts. Just as in the ancient Near East and under the monarchy of Judah, in later second-temple times scribes not only learned writing and made written copies of texts, but also learned texts mainly by recitation.[16] Texts were thus "written on the tablet of their heart," with their character as obedient servants of the temple and palace shaped accordingly. Martin Jaffee explained that cultivation of texts by the Pharisees, the scribal-priestly community at Qumran, and later the rabbis was as much oral as written (or oral–written). Following Jaffee's analysis of a key passage in the Community Rule from Qumran (1QS 6:6–8), it is clear

12. Horsley, *Scribes, Visionaries, and Politics.*

13. Ulrich, *Dead Sea Scrolls and Origins.*

14. Horsley, *Scribes, Visionaries, and Politics.*

15. Josephus, *Antiquities* 13:296–98, 408–9.

16. Jaffee, *Torah in the Mouth*; Carr, *Tablet of the Heart*; Horsley, *Scribes, Visionaries, and Politics.*

that in their nightly meetings the scribes and priests at Qumran were not "studying" a book of Torah by poring over a scroll as much as reciting a book of Torah that was also inscribed on their memory. Such scribal communities appropriated scripture by ritual recitation.[17] As Graham pointed out, "the 'internalizing' of important texts through memorization and recitation can serve as an effective educational or indoctrinational discipline."[18]

All of these results of recent research conspire to undermine the previously standard construction of the late second-temple Judean scriptures as readily accessible and widely known to a largely literate society by reading. Instead, the books later recognized as biblical, along with other authoritative written texts, were known mainly in circles of scribes who both learned them by recitation and copied them on scrolls.

The Gospel of Mark, however, does not fit this emerging picture of oral–written scribal knowledge and cultivation of Judean scriptures. The feature of the Gospel that offers the obvious "test case" is provided by Mark's references to what are presented as passages of scripture. In the previously standard construction of biblical studies, it has been assumed that Mark and the other "evangelists" were "quoting" from written texts of scripture. When we reexamine these references in the Gospel apart from the assumptions of print culture, however, it is difficult to find clear indications that written texts were involved. Indeed it is not clear that Mark's knowledge of the content of scripture is derived from scribal or scribal-like cultivation of scripture that involved written texts in close relation to oral recitation.

The Gospel of Mark introduced "quotes" and some of its other references with the formula "(as) it is written" (γέγραπται; 1:2; 7:6; etc.). We can presumably conclude from this formula at least that the Gospel derives from a society in which the existence of authoritative written texts was widely known, even that their existence in writing gave them a special authority. A study of the frequent use of the formula in the *Didachê* ("The Teaching of the Twelve Apostles," discovered in the nineteenth century) concluded that it is an appeal to the scripture as authority, while the "quotation" may be from memory.[19] That a prophecy or a law was "written" on a scroll, especially if it was in a revered text (ostensibly) of great antiquity, gave it an added aura of authority, for ordinary people as much as for the literate elite. Virtually all of the instances where the Gospel of Mark uses the formula are references to a prophecy now being fulfilled. That it stands "written" lends authority to the prophecy and its fulfillment in John or Jesus (Mark 1:2–3;

17. Horsley, *Scribes, Visionaries, and Politics*, 115–17.

18. Graham, *Beyond the Written Word*, 161.

19. Henderson, "Didache and Orality."

9:12–13; 14:21, 27) or to Jesus's application of the prophecy to the Pharisees or the high priests (7:6–7; 11:17). In several cases "it is written" is simply a general appeal to authority, with no particular "quotation" given (9:12–13; 14:21).

In the few cases in Mark where particular words or phrases are quoted, they do not appear to have involved consultation of a written text. In two cases the "quotes" are composites from two different prophets. Mark 1:2–3, ostensibly quoting "the prophet Isaiah," begins with lines from Malachi (words similar to what we know in our written texts of Malachi 3:1 and Isaiah 40:3), and the anonymous "quotation" in Mark 11:17 includes lines from both Isaiah and Jeremiah (similar to what we know in Isaiah 56:7 and Jeremiah 7:11). We recognize that the anonymous "quotation" in Mark 7:6–7 derives from Isaiah (although the citation is not very close to written texts of Isaiah 29:13; similarly Isaiah 6:9–10 in Mark 4:12). And in Mark 14:27 the short line supposedly quoted from Zechariah 13:7 looks like proverb that may have been well-known, even before Zechariah. The best explanation for all of these cases, particularly the ones of composite "quotations" and the proverb, would seem to be that Mark's knowledge of this material is oral-memorial and not from examination of written texts. But it is oral-memorial knowledge that does not appear close to what we would expect of scribes whose knowledge would presumably have been closer to one or another of the written textual traditions.

The other supposed quotations of scripture in Mark are a mixed bag of recitations of oral traditions (with no indication that they also stand in scripture) and/or polemical references in which Jesus states that the authority of what the literate scribes should know very well actually supports his position, or references to scripture as addressed to the (literate) elite but not to the ordinary people for whom Jesus is speaking. In two episodes of the Gospel, Jesus recites "the commandments (of God)" as commonly known oral tradition, against the scribes and Pharisees from Jerusalem who have voided God's word and the man who has by implication violated the commandments by accruing great wealth (7:9–13; 10:17–22). Jesus's followers' spontaneous singing of a well-known psalm and his reference to the ecstatic David's declaration in the words of another well-known psalm are similarly derived from oral tradition. At three different points Mark's Jesus challenges the Pharisees, high priests and scribes, and Sadducees, respectively, with the phrase "have you never/not read," claiming that their written text supports his action or position against theirs (Mark 2:25; 12:10; 12:26). In all cases the historical incident or statement by God or psalm would almost certainly have been common knowledge in oral tradition, and especially in the incident about David and the bread from the altar, "Jesus's" version is strikingly different from what the Pharisees would have "read" in any of the variant written versions. In the only places where Mark refers to Moses as having "written," it was for the Pharisees or the Sadducees (10:3–5; 12:19), and by implication not for ordinary people.

This analysis of the "quotations of scripture" in Mark suggests that the Gospel had a complex relation to Judean scripture that was part of a wider cultural tradition. The Gospel and its audience knew of the existence of authoritative written texts. The Gospel not only viewed the written texts as authoritative, finding their fulfillment in Jesus's mission, but appealed to them as supporting its (Jesus's) position against that of the scribes who should have known them well because they could read. The Gospel's citations of lines ostensibly "written" in scripture, however, show significant differences from what we could expect in scribal (oral–written) cultivation of the texts, judging from the varying versions found in the ancient MSS.

Some of the Markan references previously classified as "quotations of scripture," however, can now be understood as derived from commonly known oral tradition. The overall picture that can be derived from examination of Mark's references is of a very broad knowledge of Judean/Israelite cultural tradition that includes knowledge of the existence of authoritative written texts, limited and sometimes rough knowledge of the contents of those texts, and the assumption that some commonly known historical incidents and teachings of Moses are included in those written texts.

THE IMPORTANCE OF ORAL COMMUNICATION IN THE ORIGIN OF THE GOSPEL

This comparison of references to Israelite tradition in Mark's Gospel with Judean scribal oral–written cultivation of scriptures points to two further and related features of the Gospel: its origins in and orientation toward ordinary people and the corollary, the origins and development of the Gospel in an oral communication environment.

As suggested by its references to tradition, Mark is not a scribal text, but focused on a popular prophet leading a movement of ordinary people. The people involved in the story, and evidently its audience as well, are located in the villages of Galilee and surrounding territories in Syria (villages of Tyre, Caesarea Philippi, and the Decapolis), not Jerusalem, from which scribes and Pharisees "come down" to oppose Jesus. There is even a notable language difference, since Peter is recognized apparently by his "up-country" dialect (presumably of Aramaic; Mark 14:70). After Jesus's confrontation with the high priests and scribes and his Roman execution in

Jerusalem, the audience is directed back to rural Galilee (Mark 14:28; 16:7). This open ending signals where the story continues among its audience.

This story of a leader-and-movement that emerged among villagers and expanded in ever-widening circles among other ordinary people was thus heavily dependent on oral communication, as indicated by ever more extensive research that finds literacy limited mainly to scribal and administrative circles. Under the standard view rooted in assumptions of widespread literacy, it was not possible to explain the development of a Gospel story of Jesus engaged in a renewal of Israel in the absence of knowledge of the Hebrew Bible/Judean scripture, presumed to be *the* medium through which Israelite tradition was known. It now appears that written copies of scriptural books (in Hebrew) were not generally available and that ordinary people (who spoke Aramaic) could not have read them anyhow. Yet ordinary people were by no means ignorant of Israelite tradition or dependent on the scribes and Pharisees to mediate it.

The historian Josephus recounts several incidents in Galilee during the great revolt against Roman rule in 66–67 CE that have been claimed as evidence that Galilean villagers knew and observed "the Torah" (note the vague term). Closer examination of his accounts, however, indicates that the Galileans' actions were rooted in the basic principles of the Mosaic Covenant, which would presumably have been well-known and observed among Israelite peoples, and not in more specific ordinances or regulations of teachings in one or another books of the Pentateuch.[20] The popular movements in 4 BCE and in the great revolt of 66–70 CE, whose participants acclaimed their respective leaders as "kings,"[21] were evidently following the same cultural pattern carried in the cultural memory of the popular acclamation of the young David as messiah.[22] Similarly, the popular movements led by "prophets" in mid-first century (*Antiquities* 18:85–87; 20:97–98 and 19–71; *War* 2.259–63) were evidently informed by another common cultural pattern carried in the popular memory of Moses and Joshua.[23]

These movements were drawing on what anthropologists have termed the "little tradition" cultivated orally in Galilean and Judean village communities, in contrast to the "great tradition" cultivated (orally and in writing) in Jerusalem.[24] . Parallel to the official cultivation of a cultural repertoire by literate experts serving the Jerusalem temple-state was a popular tradition

20. Horsley, *Galilee*, 128–57.

21. According to Josephus' accounts in *Antiquities* 17:271–85 and *War* 2:55–65.

22. See 2 Samuel 2:1–5; 5:1–5; Horsley, "Messianic Movements."

23. Horsley, "Prophets of Old."

24. Scott, *Domination and the Arts of Resistance.*

cultivated orally among the people. Although difficult to document, there was surely interaction among the two, which shared many stories, historical legends, covenantal laws (for example, the decalogue), prophecies, and prophetic heroes (for example, Elijah). But we should not imagine that the Judean and Galilean peasants who formed those popular movements, including the movements in response to the prophetic teachings and practices of Jesus of Nazareth, were directly familiar with the contents of "the Law and the Prophets," nor were they in possession of and regularly reading from scrolls inscribed in Hebrew. Instead, they had for generations cultivated their own often localized popular Israelite tradition that articulated and grounded their own interests and concerns.

As story about and derived from (and addressed to) a popular movement, the Gospel of Mark emerged from and belonged to the "little tradition."[25] And as the developing Gospel was performed in communities of the expanding movement, it resonated with the hearers by referencing the popular tradition.[26] The Gospel thus portrays Jesus as a new Moses and Elijah in multiple sea crossings, feedings in the wilderness, healings, appointing twelve disciples who carry on his mission, and addressing people in new (Mosaic) covenantal teaching. None of these episodes need to refer to scripture since they are rooted in and resonate with a popular tradition long cultivated orally among the people.

ORAL COMMUNICATION, ORAL PERFORMANCE, AND ORAL-WRITTEN TEXTS IN THE CONTEXT IN WHICH MARK WAS CULTIVATED

Contrary to the standard operating assumption of New Testament studies rooted in print culture, oral communication and oral recitation of texts, not the reading and writing of texts, prevailed in the early centuries during which the Gospel of Mark gained authority among communities of Christians. This can be seen in communications in the Hellenistic-Roman world in general, in the communities of Christ in particular, and in the evidence for the oral recitation of texts such as Mark that were eventually included in the New Testament. The Gospel of Mark thus continued to be performed orally in communities of ordinary people even after written copies existed and became fairly widely distributed through repeated recitation and repeated copying.

25. Horsley, *Hearing the Whole Story*, 118 and 157–76.

26. Here I am indebted to the theory of performance developed in Foley, *Immanent Art*; Foley, *Singer of Tales in Performance*; and Foley, *How to Read an Oral Poem*.

Below the level of the literate elite, the vast majority of people had little or no need for writing, as noted above for Galilee and Judea. Communication generally was oral and cultivation of cultural traditions was oral. To appreciate that cultivation of texts was oral among ordinary people it may help to recognize that the cultivation of texts was also oral among the literate elite. Just as texts were learned and cultivated by oral recitation by scribes in Judea, so in Hellenistic and Roman literate circles texts that were written were processed orally, with written texts playing ancillary, monumental, and authorizing roles. Public recitation was the principal means of "publishing" a composition. "Reading" a cumbersome chirograph required prior knowledge of the text inscribed on it. Students of virtually any subject learned by recitation and memorization. Those who composed texts did not "write" them as "authors" do in print culture, but dictated them to a secretary or scribe.[27]

One of the foundational assumptions of modern New Testament studies is that "early Christianity" was a literate culture. It is indeed impressive that Christian communities possessed written copies of some of their revered texts already in the second century. Yet the few early Christian references to oral and/or written communication indicate that the communities of Christ and their nascent intellectual leadership did not just prefer orality, but were even reticent about or suspicious of writing.[28] In the early second century Papias, bishop of Hierapolis, declared,

> I inquired about *the words* of the ancients, what Andrew or Peter or Philip or Thomas or James or John or Matthew or any other of the Lord's disciples *said*, and what Ariston and the elder John, the Lord's disciples, were *saying*. For I did not suppose that things from books (ἐκ τῶν βιβλίων) would benefit me so much as things *from a living and abiding voice* (ζώσης φωνῆς καὶ μενούσης).[29]

Papias' statement indicates both the oral mode of communication and the high valuation placed on the direct oral continuity of communication from the Lord through the previous two generations of disciples. The erudite early theologian Clement of Alexandria apologized for committing the teaching of the church to writing. He was clear that written notes are weak and lifeless compared with oral discourses. The former served only

27. Graham, *Beyond the Written Word*, 30–44; Small, *Wax Tablets of the Mind*; Hezser, *Jewish Literacy*.

28. Achtemeier, "*Omne verbum sonat*"; Alexander, "Living Voice"; Botha, "Greco-Roman Literacy"; Shiner, *Proclaiming the Gospel*.

29. Eusebius, *Historia Ecclesiastica*, 3.39.3–4.

instrumental purposes such as aiding the memory or preventing the loss of important teaching. And some teachings could be communicated only orally. It was dangerous to write them down, for they might fall into the hands of those who would misunderstand what he was trying to communicate.[30]

The Shepherd of Hermas presents a fascinating illustration of the function of "books" among the Christ-believers who were non-literate or semi-literate. In the "visions" section of this second-century text produced by a prophet in Rome, Hermas receives a visit from a heavenly revealer:

> She said to me, "Can you take this message to God's elect ones?" I said to her, "Lady, I cannot remember so much; but give me the little book to copy." "Take it," she said, "and give it back to me." I took it and went away to a certain place in the country, and *copied everything, letter by letter, for I could not distinguish the syllables* [μετεγράψαμεν πάντα πρὸς γράμμα οὐχ γὰρ τὰς σύλλαβας] So when I had finished the letters of the little book, it was suddenly taken out of my hand; but I did not see by whom.[31]

This scene stands in the revelatory tradition known from earlier Enoch texts, the book of Daniel, and the book of Revelation, a tradition that includes heavenly books shown to visionaries, thus lending their visions the highest authority of divine writing.[32] Hermas' vision reflects knowledge of how new copies of written copies of texts were made, and then returned to the one from whom they were borrowed.[33] Later the "ancient lady" had "additional words" for Hermas to "make known to all the elect." Hermas is to send two books, respectively, to Clement and Grapte, who would exhort the widows and orphans. Meanwhile Hermas was to "read it [the book] with the elders in charge of the assembly" (Vis. 2.4.2–3). But Hermas does not know how to read the book, as he has already indicated in the way he describes his copying ("letter by letter, since I could not distinguish the syllables"). He cannot make out the syllables so that he knows how the text sounds, that is, he cannot reoralize the written text in a recitation, he cannot read. In immediate "literary" context as well as in the general cultural context, it seems clear that Hermas' "reading," like Grapte's exhortation, was an oral performance of a text known in memory. At least some of the "authors" of the revered "writings" of the apostolic and sub-apostolic "fathers" were not

30. Shiner, *Proclaiming the Gospel*, 18; Haines-Eitzen, *Guardians of Letters*, 105.

31. "Shepherd of Hermas," Vis. 2.1.3–4.

32. Niditch, *Oral World and Written Word*; Horsley, *Scribes, Visionaries, and Politics*, 89–130.

33. Haines-Eitzen, *Guardians of Letters*, 21–40.

literate. The point is that cultivation (learning and appropriation) of texts was by oral recitation or performance.

This further communication of his revelation by the non- or semi-literate Hermas and Papias's highest valuation of "the living voice" also illustrates the third point about how oral communication predominated in the context in which Mark would have been performed. Most valuable to the subsequent generations of Christ-believers was the direct chain of oral recitation of the "words of the Lord." Written books were of secondary, ancillary value. From his close investigation of the performance of texts in the Hellenistic-Roman world, Whitney Shiner concluded that a "reader" of the Gospels did not need to know how to read from a codex: "The performer could learn the Gospel from hearing oral performances or by hearing others recite it."[34] Justin Martyr reports that at Sunday assemblies "the memoirs of the apostles or the writings of the prophets are read for as long as time permits."[35] Hippolytus says that "Scripture was read at the beginning of services by a succession of readers until all had gathered . . . This practice lasted at least to the time of Augustine." He comments that many people had learned to recite (large portions of) the Gospels themselves from hearing them recited in services.[36]

As in both Judean culture and Hellenistic-Roman culture generally, early Christians committed texts to memory in order then to recite or perform them orally. Such performers probably included some who were semi-literate. Already in the second century, and certainly in the third and fourth centuries, at least some Christians possessed craft literacy, and were copyists, secretaries, "calligraphers." Origen's wealthy patron provided him with copyists and (women) calligraphers. That example, of course, also indicates that even craft literacy was not especially common. As we know from the fourth-century report by Epiphanius (67.1.1–4 and 67.7.9), even the professional copyist, Hieracas, in Leontopolis in Egypt, memorized the Old and New Testaments in order to recite and comment on the texts. Or, to come at this from another angle, the striking lack of evidence "regarding copyists involved in reproducing [written] Christian texts prior to the fourth century is itself instructive."[37] Copies of books were not readily available. Whoever wanted a written copy of a text had to ask someone who possessed it to have a copy made and send it along. Written copies of texts were revered, hence in demand. But texts were usually cultivated orally.

34. Shiner, *Proclaiming the Gospel*, 26.

35. Ibid., 45.

36. Ibid., 45 and 107.

37. Haines-Eitzen, *Guardians of Letters*, 38–39.

Detailed recent investigations by text critics are now confirming that oral recitation was probably the predominant form of appropriation and further cultivation of revered authoritative texts such as the Gospels in Christian communities. David Parker and others are recognizing that manuscripts from the second and third centuries are extremely varied: "The further back we go, the greater seems to be the degree of variation."[38] The majority of so-called "textual variants" of Christian books originated in the first two centuries, in the relatively free transmission process: ". . . while readers of the Gospels have got used to the idea that there are differences between [the gospel texts], they have largely overlooked the fact that there are often as great, if not greater, variations between the manuscript copies of each Gospel."[39] There is a growing awareness that manuscripts cannot be neatly grouped into distinctive traditions or versions. The evidence is too varied, even chaotic. Text critics have characterized the fluid state of the texts as "uncontrolled," "unstable," "wild," "free," suggesting unlimited flexibility and even randomness.[40] Parker and Haines-Eitzen suggest this evidence may indicate that oral cultivation of the texts influenced and was reflected in the copying of the texts, a suggestion that invites further exploration. It appears that through the second and third centuries Mark, like the other Gospels, continued to be performed orally from memory. Not until the Church suddenly became eagerly responsive to the imperial state, with the initiative coming from Constantine himself, did bishops such as Eusebius order "fifty copies of the divine scriptures . . . for the instruction of the church, to be written on well-prepared parchment by copyists most skillful in the art of accurate and beautiful writing."[41]

THE GOSPEL OF MARK AS MEMORABLE AND PERFORMABLE

To have been continuously performed, and to have resonated with the people, such that it became widely used, the Gospel of Mark must have been memorable and performable in significant ways. Exploration of Mark as oral performance has barely begun among Gospel scholars. Yet there have been some suggestive probes, and the results and implications of these can be summarized here.

38. Parker, *Living Text*, 188.
39. Ibid., 197; Haines-Eitzen, *Guardians of Letters*, 76.
40. Haines-Eitzen, *Guardians of Letters*, 106–7.
41. Cited in Gamble, *Books and Readers*, 79 n.132.

Drawing on and Adapting Israelite Tradition and Larger Cultural Patterns

Much of the literary analysis that was borrowed by Gospel interpreters in the 1970s and 1980s was developed to deal with modern prose fiction. The assumption was that students were reading novels (or a Gospel) for the first time and not familiar with the story. In the assemblies of Christ where Gospels were performed in the late first and second-third centuries, however, both the performer and the community of listeners were already familiar with the story and/or the Jesus-speeches. I want to focus briefly on two key implications of the already familiar story, partly to counter the persistence in New Testament studies of the belief that the Gospels made a decisive break with "Judaism," and the residual habit of focusing mainly on text-fragments such as individual sayings or episodes.

Precisely because the Gospel was an oft-told story, both the performers and the audiences were familiar not only with the Gospel story, but also with the Israelite tradition(s) in reference to which it resonated. Israelite cultural tradition traveled in and with the Gospel story. Hearers were thus on familiar cultural ground, since Mark's story, for example, began with Jesus receiving a call and undergoing a test in the wilderness, as had Moses and Elijah, the founding prophet of Israel and the prophet of renewal, respectively. They would almost have expected Jesus then to call protégés, as Elijah had called Elisha to help expand his renewal of Israel, and of course there should be twelve disciples in a program of renewal of Israel (Mark 1:16–20, 3:13–19, and 6:7–13). Like Moses, Jesus led sea-crossings and presided over feedings in the wilderness for a people without sufficient food, and like Elijah he performed healings (Mark 5–8). Again in the recapitulation of Moses, he not only knew and recited the covenant commandments, but he also gave renewed covenantal teaching for revitalized community life (Mark 10:2–45).

Israelite tradition also offered roles other than that of the prophet like Moses or Elijah that Jesus could have been adapting, such as that of the young David who, acclaimed "messiah" by his followers, led them against foreign conquerors, an issue with which several episodes in Mark's Gospel struggle. Israelite prophets such as Elijah and Jeremiah, moreover, had boldly opposed the oppressive rulers of the people and had been persecuted and hunted down. In more recent Judean tradition, those who had been martyred in resisting the foreign emperor's attempt to control or interfere with the traditional Mosaic covenantal way of life had been vindicated by God. In any number of ways that we who are not as familiar with Israelite tradition do not even "get," the episodes of the Gospel story and even the sequence of the episodes of the Gospel story were already familiar in the cultural memory of Jesus's followers, at the center of which was Israelite tradition. Those who performed and heard the Gospel in Greek-speaking villages a few generations later and who were now using those same Scriptures as their own would been aware of how the story of Jesus resonated with stories and prophecies that had become part of their cultural memory.[42]

The other key implication is implicit in the first. While biblical scholars have standardly focused on tiny text-fragments (isolated sayings or verses) and drawn connections between one verse and another, both narratives and prophetic oracles in the scriptures are rooted in, express, and adapt larger cultural patterns. As noted above, the popular prophetic and messianic movements in Judea and Galilee at the time of Jesus were informed by the cultural patterns carried in Israelite traditions of Moses-Joshua and the young David.[43] Both of those same broader cultural patterns can be discerned to be operative in Mark's story, which portrays Jesus as a new Moses and struggles with whether and how Jesus was a messiah like David. To take the other most evident example, the broad pattern of Mosaic covenant that was clearly operative in the texts produced by the Qumran community (the Community Rule and the Damascus Rule) can be discerned in and behind the series of dialogues in Mark 10:2–45 as well as in Matthew's "sermon on the mount."[44] The point here is that the Israelite cultural memory out of which the Gospel of Mark developed included such broad cultural patterns, and their adaptation in Mark's Gospel make it memorable and performable, thus contributing to its taking root in communities of early Christians.

Oral Narrative Features and Devices

In his ground-breaking *Oral and Written Gospel*, Werner Kelber enabled us to appreciate most of the Jesus-stories that were the components of the Gospel of Mark as oral performances. Many of his observations about those oral components of Mark also apply to the Gospel as a whole. Since Kelber's study, others such as Pieter Botha and Joanna Dewey have furthered the discussion of the oral features of the Markan narrative.[45]

42. On cultural/social memory, see Kelber, "Case of the Gospels," and Kirk and Thatcher, *Memory, Tradition, and Text*.

43. Horsley, "Popular Messianic Movements" and Horsley, "Prophets of Old."

44. Horsley, *Hearing the Whole Story*, 177–202.

45. Kelber, *Oral and Written Gospel*; Botha, "Mark's Story"; Dewey, "Gospel of Mark." The following paragraphs draw upon Horsley, *Hearing the Whole Story*, and Horsley, "Oral Performance and Mark."

In a discussion of "Mark's Oral Legacy," Kelber identifies several key features of oral style in the narrative of Mark's Gospel.[46] These same features, such as formulaic connective devices (like "and," "immediately," "and again," which are usually omitted in English translations) also link together the many episodes of the Gospel. While some of these connectives may have been present already in oral stories that became incorporated into the overall narrative, the latter may have stimulated some of them as well. The effect is an action-packed narrative of "one thing after another."

Another feature that contributes to the oral performative character of Mark's Gospel is the plethora of folkloristic triads in the narrative.[47] The healing stories unfold in three steps. Parables often have three steps. That Peter denies Jesus three times and even that Jesus asks the disciples to watch with him three times might be explained as derived from stories that Mark incorporated. Yet, as Kelber pointed out, there are recurrent appearances of threes that cannot be accounted for in this way. Jesus predicts his arrest, execution, and rising three times, clearly a structuring element in the middle step of the narrative focusing on Jesus and the disciples. The narrative distinguishes three disciples for special focus, and Jesus enters Jerusalem three times. Both are structural features in the overall story.

In addition to the formulaic connectives and various triads, the Gospel includes various devices of "narrative maneuvering," such as the well-known Markan "sandwich" technique of juxtaposing two stories, one framing the other. The scribes' charge that Jesus works in the power of Beelzebul is framed by Jesus's family's concern that he is possessed (3:20–35); the healing of the woman who had been hemorrhaging for twelve years is framed by the healing of the twelve-year-old dead young woman (5:21–43); Jesus's prophetic demonstration against the Temple is framed by the cursing of the fig tree (11:12–25); and Jesus's trial before the high priesthood is framed by Peter's denial (15:52–72). In this device of oral storytelling the core episode and the framing episode reinforce and interpret each other.

A similar but somewhat more complex oral narrative device is the concentric or chiastic structuring of several stories. Most striking, and most carefully studied, is the arrangement of the five episodes (of healing—eating—celebrating—eating—healing) in 2:1—3:6.[48] Without elaborating on the remarkable patterning in these five episodes, let me point out that they display many connections with the contents and themes of the Gospel as a whole. Healing (including exorcism) and eating (including the wilderness

46. Kelber, *Oral and Written Gospel*, 64–70.

47. Ibid., 66.

48. Dewey, *Markan Public Debate.*

feedings and covenantal meal at passover) are two of Jesus's principal activities throughout Mark's narrative. Both actions anticipate but also manifest the coming of the kingdom of God (that is, the renewal of Israel), the overall theme of the Gospel. This sequence of five episodes also exemplifies how Jesus's actions challenge the dominant order centered in Jerusalem as represented by the scribes and Pharisees. This is also central to the dominant plot of the Gospel as a whole. Again, it is typical of oral narrative that particular sequences of episodes or stanzas exemplify, in microcosm, the overall theme or plot of the narrative.

Another example of the oral "narrative maneuvering" may be the reiteration of a pattern already current in the pre-Markan oral tradition in the second major narrative step of the story. Close readers of Mark discerned behind the sequence of episodes in Mark 4:35–8:26 two "chains" of stories that have the same order.[49] The first consists of a sea-crossing, an exorcism, two healings (arranged in one of Mark's "sandwich" formations), and a wilderness feeding (4:35–41; 5:1–20; 5:21–24 and 35–43; 5:24–34; 6:30–44). The second (6:45–52; 7:24–30; 7:31–37; 8:1–10; 8:22–26) has the same sequence, except that it inverts the last two stories in order to frame the next major narrative step (8:22—10:52) with healing of blind figures at the beginning and end. This is yet another feature that would aid in oral performance and hearing.

By themselves, without insertion of other episodes, those sets of stories clearly represent Jesus as enacting the renewal of Israel as a prophet like Moses and Elijah, the great founder (sea-crossing and wilderness feeding) and renewer (healings) of Israel, respectively, in the popular Israelite cultural memory. By inserting additional episodes into these chains, the Markan narrative expands their message of the renewal of Israel. For example, in the mission of the twelve (representative of the twelve tribes), Mark's Jesus further confirms that his program of the kingdom of God is a renewal of Israel. And the story of Herod Antipas's arrest and execution of the Baptist illustrates what happens to prophets engaged in a renewal of Israel and, more specifically, prefigures what is about the happen to Jesus. Thus the materials inserted into the "chains" enable the listeners to hear that the message of the chain and that of the whole story are the same, that is, the renewal of Israel over against the rulers of Israel.

49. Achtemeier, "*Omne verbum sonat.*"

The Overall Narrative Structure of the Gospel of Mark

On the basis of these implications of Kelber's earlier work and others' insights, we can discern the narrative structure and structuring elements that must have made the Gospel of Mark a most memorable and performable text in the first several generations of its use. I will delineate the overall structure and then comment on how the "infrastructure" would help make the Gospel easily memorable. (I am aware of the irony of continuing to use visual-spatial metaphors such as "structure" and chapter-and-verse numbers to "locate" sections of a text.)

The Narrative Steps in the Gospel of Mark

OPENING: John's announcement, Jesus's baptism and testing in wilderness (1:1–13)

THEME: Jesus (as prophet) proclaims that the Kingdom of God is at hand (1:14–15)

FIRST STEP: Jesus launches renewal of Israel in Galilee (1:16—3:35)

SPEECH: Jesus teaches the mystery of the kingdom in parables (4:1–34)

SECOND STEP: Jesus like Moses/Elijah continues renewal of Israel (4:35—8:21/26)

THIRD STEP: Jesus debates his role and renews covenant (8:22/27—10:52)

FOURTH STEP: Jesus proclaims divine judgment of Temple, high priests (11:1—13:1–2)

SPEECH: Jesus speaks about future, exhorting solidarity, and not being misled (13:3–37)

FIFTH STEP: Jesus's last supper, arrested, trial; crucifixion by the Romans (14–15)

OPEN ENDING: direction back to "Galilee" for continuation of movement (16:1–8)

Except for the two pauses for the speeches, the overall narrative consists of one episode after another linked with "ands" and frequent references to "immediately." As noted above, all of the narrative steps included devices that provided some intermediate patterning. In the first step (after the obligatory first move, for a prophet like Elijah, of calling protégés to assist him), Jesus enters the assembly (συναγωγή) in the village of Capernaum (1:21) and then returns "home" to Capernaum (2:1), again enters the assembly (3:1), and again goes "home" (3:19), at fairly evenly timed intervals in the narrative. As noted just above, the next narrative step (4:35—8:21/26) is organized around two series of five episodes in the same sequence that recapitulate the prophetic acts of Moses and Elijah (sea-crossing, exorcism, two healings, and a wilderness feeding), except that the last two in the second series are reversed to provide an episode of healing a blind person as an opening to frame the next narrative step. The third step in the narrative is structured by the three announcements of Jesus's arrest, crucifixion, and rising that serve as foils to the dialogue episodes in this section. This step closes with another healing of a blind man that corresponds to the transitional episode from the previous narrative step, a framing that sets off the increasing blindness of the disciples to what Jesus is doing and its implication. In the fourth narrative step Jesus enters Jerusalem three times, first in a seemingly "messianic" demonstration, then in a demonstration that announces God's condemnation of the Temple, and then for a sustained confrontation with the ruling high priests and their representatives. The climactic narrative step features two "sandwich" or framing devices: first, the high priests' resolve to arrest and kill Jesus and Judas's betrayal frame the last supper; and second, Jesus's prayer in Gethsemane followed by Peter's denial frames Jesus's trial.

In addition to the "infrastructure" of the narrative steps, there are numerous links between and across the narrative steps, including repetitions of themes that drive home the message. Between the second and third, and the third and fourth narrative steps, and between the fourth narrative step and the second speech, are episodes that make them overlap. These episodes belong to the previous step, but also begin the next step or speech (the healing of the first blind person, the healing of the second blind person, and the prophecy of the destruction of the Temple). In the first narrative step, after an exorcism and several healings and disputes with the scribes or Pharisees, the latter conspire with the Herodians against Jesus, announcing clearly what is coming in the climax of the story. In the second narrative step, introduced by Herod Antipas's question about Jesus's identity, comes the episode in which Herod beheads John, again prefiguring the climax of the story with the arrest and execution of Jesus. In the third narrative step, the same question about Jesus's identity and Peter's adamant answer that he is "the messiah" introduces Jesus's first announcement that he will be executed, prompting Peter's protest and Jesus's sharp rebuke "get behind me, Satan."

Additional links are evident between the first and second narrative steps and the second and third steps. After calling the first four disciples and then naming the full twelve, suggesting a renewal of Israel, in the first step, Jesus then heals two women, one hemorrhaging for twelve years and the other twelve years old, suggesting a renewal of Israel, and then commissions the twelve to expand his program of preaching and healing among the villages of Israel, in the second step. After Jesus does Moses-like and Elijah-like actions in the second narrative step, he then appears on the mountain with Moses and Elijah in the third narrative step. In links and repetitions such as these, the overall narrative is tied together and the performer (and audience) has cues and other devices that make the sequence of "one thing after another" come up in memory and flow out in plotted sequence.

In its various narrative devices of connectives and maneuvering, its adaptation of familiar cultural patterns, and the many connectives of its narrative structure, the Gospel of Mark was memorable and performable in the oral communication context of early Christian communities. Further exploration of Mark's narrative in oral performance should open up additional memorable and performable aspects of the Gospel.

MARK'S RESONANCE WITH HEARERS IN CONTEXT

As a performed text, the Gospel of Mark would have resonated with its hearers in particular historical (performance) contexts. In his discussion of "Mark's Oral Legacy," Kelber also reminds us that oral communication is embedded in its context, which has not only cultural and aesthetic aspects but political and economic ones as well. In fact, "nonlinguistic features have priority over linguistic ones."[50] Oral communication receives powerful ideological and situational support from its context as it resonates with the hearers. For Mark's Gospel we are attempting to understand not only its origins but also its continuing performance in early Christian communities in Syria, Egypt, Asia Minor, and so on. Whitney Shiner makes the important observation that in oral performance the narrative happens simultaneously in two worlds, the imagined world of the narrative and the concrete social world of the performance context. In contrast with a silent modern reader who perceives dialogue as taking place within the story world of a text, the ancient hearers of Mark would have heard dialogue within their own situation as well. There was thus "a partial collapse between the narrative dialogue and the audience."[51]

To appreciate the performance context of communities of Christ among peoples subject to the Roman empire and how the narrative may have resonated with them, modern Western scholars need to cut through at least two layers of blockage. One is the heavy layer of Christian supersessionism and anti-Judaism according to which Mark and Matthew have been read. As noted above, in these texts no split has yet taken place between "Christianity" and "Judaism." Both are stories of the fulfillment of Israel that has now expanded to include other, non-Israelite peoples (and there, indeed, are the seeds of subsequent supersessionism). The division evident in the texts is between the rulers and the ruled, not between "Jews" and

50. Kelber, *Oral and Written Gospel*, 75.

51. Shiner, *Proclaiming the Gospel*, 171.

"Christians." There is no question that some "Christian" texts (Luke-Acts) were playing up the Roman destruction of Jerusalem as God's punishment for the Judean rulers' collaboration in the killing of Jesus. But that is not true of all texts.

The other obstruction to our understanding is our own different social location and historical situation. If we listen with the ears of ancient people who were poor and under heavy obligation for rents or taxes to the wealthy and powerful local magnates, perhaps we can sense how both particular episodes and the whole Gospel story would have resonated with them. Mark repeatedly represents Jesus criticizing the powerful and their representatives for their demands on and exploitation of the poor. He accuses them of "devouring" widows' houses and of urging villagers to "dedicate" to the Temple the economic resources they need locally to "honor their father and mother" (Mark 12:38–40 and 7:9–13). Mark has Jesus insisting on cooperative non-exploitative economic life in their communities, in keeping with the covenantal commandments (versus the negative example of wealthy fellow seeking "eternal life"). "It is easier for a camel to go through the eye of a needle than for someone who is rich to enter the kingdom of God" (Mark 10:25).

The parable of the tenants in Mark's Gospel (Mark 12:1–9) offers an illustrative episode that, working creatively from Israelite cultural tradition, would have resonated with virtually any community in antiquity. Many of the rural hearers may have become tenants of their creditors as a result of spiraling debts; and many of the urban hearers or their parents may well have migrated into the city because they or their ancestors had lost their land to absentee landlords. The parable builds on the "song of the vineyard" that Isaiah had used to indict the wealthy for their exploitation of the peasants and seizure of their land. Jesus's parable dramatizes the sharp conflict between the wealthy absentee landlords, often also the rulers, and their tenants, who had been forced off their land that the landlords now controlled. Poor listeners would have been sympathetic with the tenants. But "Jesus" turns the parable against the wealthy rulers, with the implication that the vineyard/land will be given to others, that is, to those whom the wealthy landlord has exploited.[52] The parable of the tenants as applied is a virtual microcosm of the whole Gospel story, which portrays Jesus carrying out a renewal of the people over against the rulers of the people. Mark's narrative that focuses on the renewal of the people of Israel was recognizably

52. There is no indication in Mark that the "others" are "Christians" who are replacing "the Jews." It is clear that they are the ordinary people addressed throughout the story.

representative of the similar conflict in other areas of the Roman empire where it was performed.

In sum, the Gospel of Mark was not a good candidate to become scripture according to the prevailing models and standards either of Judean scribal circles or of Greco-Roman intellectual circles. As a story about a popular prophetic leader of a renewal movement among ordinary people in Galilee, it was evidently regularly performed orally among other communities of ordinary people in an ever-widening radius. Having become revered and authoritative for the broad base of the Christian movement during the second and third centuries, Mark was among the popular texts defended by the nascent Christian literate intellectuals against their cultural detractors. With strong resonance among the populace, these ordinary people's stories were also eventually acknowledged by the emergent hierarchy of the established Church as integral to the canon of the New Testament that was added to the Jewish scriptures in Greek as Christian Scripture. But what led to their inclusion in the canon was their repeated oral performance as increasingly authoritative, scriptural texts in the second and third centuries before standardized written copies were widely available.

BIBLIOGRAPHY

Achtemeier, Paul J. "*Omne verbum sonat*: The New Testament and the Oral Environment of Late Western Antiquity." *Journal of Biblical Literature* 109 (1990) 3–27.

Alexander, Loveday. "The Living Voice: Scepticism Towards the Written Word in Early Christianity and in Graeco-Roman Texts." In *The Bible in Three Dimensions: Essays in Celebration of Forty Years of Biblical Studies in the University of Sheffield*, edited by David J. A. Clines, 221–47. Journal for the Study of the Old Testament Supplements 87. Sheffield: JSOT Press, 1990.

Aston, Margaret. *Lollards and Reformers: Images and Literacy in Late Medieval Religion*. London: Continuum, 1984.

Auerbach, Erich. *Scenes from the Drama of European Literature: Six Essays*. New York: Meridian, 1959.

Blickle, Peter. *From the Communal Reformation to the Revolution of the Common Man*. Studies in Medieval and Reformation Thought 65. Leiden: Brill, 1998.

Botha, Pieter J. J. "Greco-Roman Literacy as Setting for New Testament Writings." *Neotestamentica* 26 (1992) 206–27. Reprinted in *Orality and Literacy in Early Christianity*, 39–61. Biblical Performance Criticism Series 5. Eugene, OR: Cascade Books, 2012.

———. "Mark's Story as Oral Traditional Literature: Rethinking the Transmission of Some Traditions about Jesus." *Hervormde Teologiese Studies* 47 (1992) 304–31. Reprinted in *Orality and Literacy in Early Christianity*, 163–90. Biblical Performance Criticism Series 5. Eugene, OR: Cascade Books, 2012.

Carr, David M. *Writing on the Tablet of the Heart: Origins of Scripture and Literature*. Oxford: Oxford University Press, 2005.

Carruthers, Mary J. *The Book of Memory: A Study of Memory in Medieval Culture.* Cambridge Studies in Medieval Literature 10. Cambridge: Cambridge University Press, 1990.

Clanchy, M. T. *From Memory to Written Record: England 1066–1307.* 2nd ed. Oxford: Basil Blackwell, 1993.

Deanesly, Margaret. *The Lollard Bible and Other Medieval English Versions.* Cambridge: Cambridge University Press, 1966.

Dewey, Joanna. "The Gospel of Mark as an Oral–Aural Event: Implications for Interpretation." In *The New Literary Criticism and the New Testament*, edited by Elizabeth Struthers Malbon and Edgar V. McKnight, 248–57. Sheffield: Sheffield Academic, 1994.

———. *Markan Public Debate: Literary Technique, Concentric Structure, and Theology in Mark 2:1–3:6.* Chico, CA: Scholars, 1980.

Doane, Alger N. "The Ethnography of Scribal Writing and Anglo-Saxon Poetry: Scribe as Performer." *Oral Tradition* 9 (1994) 420–39.

Epiphanius. *The Panarion of St. Epiphanius, Bishop of Salamis (Selected Passages).* Translated by Philip Amidon. New York: Oxford University Press, 1990.

Epp, Eldon Jay. "The Multivalence of the Term 'Original Text' in New Testament Textual Criticism." *Harvard Theological Review* 92 (1999) 245–81.

Eusebius. *Historia Ecclesiastica.* Loeb Classical Library. 2 vols. Translated by Kirsopp Lake. Cambridge: Harvard University Press, 1926–32.

Foley, John Miles. *How to Read an Oral Poem.* Urbana: University of Illinois Press, 2002.

———. *Immanent Art: From Structure to Meaning in Traditional Oral Epic.* Bloomington: Indiana University Press, 1991.

———. *The Singer of Tales in Performance.* Voices and Performance in Text. Bloomington: Indiana University Press, 1995.

Gamble, Harry Y. *Books and Readers in the Early Church: A History of Early Christian Texts.* New Haven: Yale University Press, 1995.

Graham, William A. *Beyond the Written Word: Oral Aspects of Scripture in the History of Religion.* Cambridge: Cambridge University Press.

Haines-Eitzen, Kim. *Guardians of Letters: Literacy, Power, and the Transmitters of Early Christian Literature.* Oxford: Oxford University Press, 2000.

Harris, William V. *Ancient Literacy.* Cambridge: Harvard University Press, 1989.

Henderson, Ian H. "Didache and Orality in Synoptic Comparison." *Journal of Biblical Literature* 111 (1992) 283–306.

Hezser, Catherine. *Jewish Literacy in Roman Palestine.* Texts and Studies in Ancient Judaism 81. Tübingen: Mohr/Siebeck, 2001.

Horsley, Richard A. *Galilee: History, Politics, People.* Valley Forge, PA: Trinity, 1995.

———. *Hearing the Whole Story: The Politics of Plot in Mark's Gospel.* Louisville: Westminster John Knox, 2001.

———. "'Like One of the Prophets of Old': Two Types of Popular Prophets at the Time of Jesus." *Catholic Biblical Quarterly* 47 (1985) 435–63.

———. "Oral Performance and Mark: Some Implications of *The Oral and Written Gospel*, Twenty-Five Years Later." In *Jesus, the Voice, and the Text: Beyond the Oral and Written Gospel*, edited by Tom Thatcher, 45–70. Waco, TX: Baylor University Press, 2008.

———. "Popular Messianic Movements around the Time of Jesus." *Catholic Biblical Quarterly* 46 (1984) 471–93.

———. *Scribes, Visionaries, and the Politics of Second Temple Judea*. Louisville: Westminster John Knox, 2007.

Horsley, Richard A., with Johnathan A. Draper. *Whoever Hears You Hears Me: Prophets, Performance, and Tradition in Q*. Harrisburg, PA: Trinity, 1999.

Jaffee, Martin S. *Torah in the Mouth: Writing and Oral Tradition in Palestinian Judaism, 200 BCE—400 CE*. New York: Oxford University Press, 2001.

Josephus. *Jewish Antiquities*. Translated by H. St. John Thackeray and Ralph Marcus. Vols. 4–9. Loeb Classical Library. London: Heinemann, 1930.

———. *The Jewish War*. Translated by H. St. John Thackeray. Vols. 2–3. Loeb Classical Library. London: Heinemann, 1927.

Kelber, Werner H. "The Case of the Gospels: Memory's Desire and the Limits of Historical Criticism." *Oral Tradition* 17 (2002) 55–86.

———. *The Oral and the Written Gospel: The Hermeneutics of Speaking and Writing in the Synoptic Tradition, Mark, Paul, and Q*. 1983. Reprinted, Bloomington: Indiana University Press, 1997.

Kirk, Alan, and Tom Thatcher, eds. *Memory, Tradition, and Text: Uses of the Past in Early Christianity*. Semeia Studies 52. Atlanta: Society of Biblical Literature, 2005.

Lake, Kirsopp, ed. and trans. "The Shepherd of Hermas." In *The Apostolic Fathers*, vol. 2, , 1–306. Loeb Classical Library. Cambridge: Harvard University Press, 1959.

Mack, Burton L. *A Myth of Innocence: Mark and Christian Origins*. Philadelphia: Fortress, 1988.

Niditch, Susan. *Oral World and Written Word: Ancient Israelite Literature*. Library of Ancient Israel. Louisville: Westminster John Knox, 1996.

Ong, Walter J. *Orality and Literacy: The Technologizing of the Word*. London: Methuen, 1982.

Parker, D. C. *The Living Text of the Gospels*. Cambridge: Cambridge University Press, 1997.

Saldarini, Anthony J. *Matthew's Christian Jewish Community*. Chicago Studies in the History of Judaism. Chicago: University of Chicago Press, 1994.

Scott, James C. *Domination and the Arts of Resistance: Hidden Transcripts*. New Haven: Yale University Press, 1990.

———. "Profanation and Protest: Agrarian Revolt and the Little Tradition." *Theory and Society* 4 (1977) 1–38, 211–46.

Scribner, Robert W. *For the Sake of Simple Folk: Popular Propaganda for the German Reformation*. Oxford: Oxford University Press, 1994.

Shiner, Whitney. *Proclaiming the Gospel: First-Century Performance of Mark*. Harrisburg, PA: Trinity, 2003.

Small, Jocelyn Penny. *Wax Tablets of the Mind: Cognitive Studies of Memory and Literacy in Classical Antiquity*. London: Routledge, 1997.

Ulrich, Eugene. *The Dead Sea Scrolls and the Origins of the Bible*. Studies in the Dead Sea Scrolls and Related Literature. Grand Rapids: Eerdmans, 1999.

7

The History of the Closure of Biblical Texts

Werner H. Kelber

PROLOGUE

In an essay entitled "Technology Outside Us and Inside Us,"[1] Walter Ong developed the basic principles of a media-sensitive hermeneutics that have informed my work over the years and that provide a theoretical underpinning for this paper. Writing and print, as well as electronic devices, according to Ong's thesis, are technologies that produce something in the sensible world outside us but also affect the way our minds work. Handwriting slowly undermined and partially replaced the predominantly oral lifeworld, print drastically altered major aspects of Western civilization, and the electronic medium is about to usher in a transformation of global dimensions. External changes have always been plainly in evidence, especially at epochal threshold events such as the alphabetic revolution in ancient Greece around 700 BCE,[2] or the fifteenth-century shift from script to print[3]—events that scarcely left a single sphere of human activities untouched. But, and this is Ong's point, we have not been sufficiently aware of the depths to which media technologies have penetrated the human psyche:

1. Ong, "Technology Outside Us and Inside Us."
2. Havelock, *Literate Revolution*.
3. Eisenstein, *Printing Press*.

> Writing, print, and electronic devices of various sorts are all devised to deal, directly or indirectly, with the word and with thought itself. Of all technologies, they affect man's interior most. Indeed, in a curious way they enter into man's interior itself, directly affecting the way in which his consciousness and unconsciousness manage knowledge, the management of his thought processes, and even his personal self awareness.[4]

For some time now my own work in biblical studies has examined ways in which our ritualized print habits of reading and writing, editing and authoring have—until recently—stylized our perceptions of ancient and medieval modes of communications. All along, a concern of mine has been to highlight the magnitude of what I have termed the typographical captivity that has shaped our methodological tools, sharpened our critical methods, and swayed our assumptions about ancient texts. In terms of media sensibilities it is no exaggeration to claim that print was the medium in which modern biblical scholarship was born and raised, and from which it has acquired its formative methodological habits, its intellectual tools, and, last not least, its historical theories. For all practical purposes, it was not handwritten manuscripts but the print Bible—the first mechanically constructed major book of print technology—that has served, and continues to serve, as the centerpiece of modern biblical scholarship.

Mindful of the power of media in the ancient and medieval past, in modernity and in current biblical scholarship, this paper attempts an overview of the history of the biblical texts from their oral and papyrological beginnings all the way to their triumphant apotheosis in print culture. In macrohistorical perspectives, a trajectory is observable that runs from scribal multiformity, verbal polyvalency, and oral, memorial sensibilities toward an increasing chirographic control over the material surface of biblical texts, culminating in the autosemantic print authority of the Bible.

THE *MOUVANCE* OF TRADITION

A few years ago David Carr published an exceedingly ambitious book that discusses ways in which people in ancient Near Eastern civilizations produced, worked, and lived with texts, or, more specifically, ways in which

4. Chirography, typography, and electronics are, for Ong, an "interiorized phenomenon, something registering inside humans," affecting cognitive faculties, patterning thought processes, altering modes of discourse and research, reinforcing, complexifying, and even deconstructing reasoning processes. Ong, "Technology Outside Us and Inside Us," 191, 194.

writing and literature functioned orally, scribally, and memorially in predominantly educational contexts. In *Writing on the Tablet of the Heart*, Carr has constructed a paradigm of the ancient verbal arts that will serve as a useful starting point for my deliberations.[5]

Writing, texts, and literacy, Carr suggested, have to be understood as core constituents of educational processes. From Mesopotamia to Egypt, and from Israel to Greece and into the Hellenistic period, literacy and education were closely interconnected phenomena. Indeed, literacy and education were virtually synonymous as long as it is understood that neither concept conveys what it has come to mean in the print culture of European and North American modernity. Concepts derived from the contemporary experience of literacy in the West are too narrowly focused on the technical ability to read and write. In the ancient Near Eastern cultures what mattered most was the kind of literacy that went beyond alphabetic competence to include training in and mastery of the tradition. A literate person was not necessarily an alphabetically skilled individual but one knowledgeable in the tradition. Education likewise entailed more, and often something other, than training in the rudiments of writing and reading. The principal aim of education was the internalization of texts in people's minds and hearts for the purpose of generating and/or reinforcing what today we might call the cultural identity of a people. Skilled scribes were expected to possess or acquire mastery of their core writings by way of memorization and recitation. Scrolls, therefore, functioned less as reference systems or text books and more as memory devices or, to use Carr's preferred term, as instruments of "enculturation."

Carr's "enculturation" model has no counterpart in today's Western world of communications and is, I should like to claim, unlike many conventional concepts of textual composition and transmission currently in use in the scholarly study of ancient Near Eastern, classical, and biblical literature. Recitation and memorization, essential features for Carr's reconstruction, are predominantly unacknowledged in the historical, critical paradigm, and the oral, performative dimension is still regularly bypassed. Biblical criticism, with rare exceptions, tends to view the tradition predominantly as a literary one, imagining a tight nexus of textual interfacing, implying that oral performance was a mere variant of writing. Disposed to put the emphasis on writing and texts, the historical paradigm tends to predicate a textual world that is both constituted and constrained by literary predecessors and datable sources.[6]

5. Carr, *Tablet of the Heart*.

6. Umberto Eco in *The Name of the Rose*, 286, has memorialized the premise of

Carr's "enculturation" paradigm seeks to capture the behavior of the ancient manuscript tradition, biblical texts included, from a new angle. A whole edifice of historical conceptual tools is at stake. Ideas formed around editing, copying, revision, and recension are all subject to rethinking and may be used only with reservation. Notions about authorship, tradition, composition, and originality or authenticity, all deeply entrenched in the historical paradigm, require reconsideration. One of the corollaries of Carr's model is that the materiality of communication as it manifests itself in the technology of writing and in the physical format and layout of writing surfaces is taken into serious account. For example, one needs to devote more critical thought to the fact that the scroll was virtually useless for strictly literary information retrieval, source critical extrapolations, reference checks, and cross-referencing. It was useful mainly to people who knew more or less what to look for, to people, in other words, who had already stored the content in their minds and hearts. In short, Carr's "enculturation" paradigm summons us to construct a new theory of the verbal arts in the ancient communications world.

There can be no question that texts were in fact subject to a high degree of literal copying; many were stored and consulted for reference purposes. And yet the notion that scribes exclusively copied extant texts in literal fashion, or juggled multiple texts that were physically present to them, is in many instances not a fitting model for the communications dynamics in the ancient world. The core traditions in particular, namely those texts that mattered most educationally, were not consistently carried forward by way of literal copying. Rather, scribes who were literate in the core curriculum carried texts as mental templates. They had ingested the tradition consisting of one or more texts and were thus able to write or rewrite the tradition without any need for a physical text. Importantly, rewriting, namely the reactivation of texts, was a hallmark of the ancient enculturation process. Thus when the historical paradigm discovers textual stratification, postulating literary sources, stages, or layers, one will in many, though not all, instances more aptly speak of compositional phases characteristic of the process of rewriting culturally significant traditions.

It is difficult to arrive at a historically valid terminology that captures the dynamics of what appears to have been a generally fluid, oral–scribal, and memorial transmission. Biblical studies in particular still lack the language to define appropriately the ancient media paradigm of the interfacing of orality and scribality with memory. I have found the designation

intertextuality: "Until then I thought each book spoke of the things, human and divine, that lie outside books. Now I realized that not infrequently books speak of books: it is as if they spoke among themselves."

of *mouvance*[7] helpful in describing the nature of the Jewish and Christian biblical traditions, especially in their respective initial stages. The term was initially coined by the medievalist Paul Zumthor,[8] who applied it to the manuscript tradition of French medieval poetry. Observing a high level of textual variation involving not only modifications of dialect and wording but also more substantial rewritings and the loss, replacement, or rearrangement of whole sections of a piece, he introduced *mouvance* to characterize this textual mobility.[9] Authorial anonymity and textual mobility were, in his view, connected features. Anonymity suggested that a text was not regarded as the intellectual property of a single, individual author but was subject to recurring rewritings. By analogy, large parts of the ancient Near Eastern and Mediterranean textual tradition, including the early manuscript traditions of both the Hebrew Bible and the New Testament, may be understood as *mouvance*, that is, as a living tradition in a process of persistent regeneration.

JEWISH AND CHRISTIAN TEXTUAL PLURIFORMITY

Rethinking the Jewish and Christian biblical tradition from the perspective of *mouvance*, I commence with a reflection on the genesis of the Masoretic *textus receptus*, the normative text of the Hebrew Bible. When we study the Hebrew Bible we are handed the Masoretic text, and when we learn elementary Hebrew we are confronted with Tiberian Hebrew, the linguistic system of the Masoretic scholars who produced the text between the seventh and tenth century CE. All biblical scholars, Jews and Christians alike, grow up on the Masoretic *textus receptus*, a text, moreover, that was reproduced numerous times in carefully handwritten copies. We are all familiar with the conventional picture, prevalent in many introductions to the Bible, of a Jewish scribe bent over his manuscript while copying the Torah in meticulous fashion. This picture of the scribal expert, reinforced by its reproduction in countless print textbooks, continues to affect the conventional understanding of Judaism as a religion of the book. Sensibility to oral–scribal dynamics is bound to modify and certainly complicate this picture.

7. To my knowledge, Alan Kirk, "Manuscript Tradition," was the first to apply the term to Second Temple Judaism, to early Christianity, and to the early rabbinic tradition.

8. Zumthor, *Oral Poetry*.

9. As Zumthor described it, the medieval poetic material spread both temporally and geographically "not merely by virtue of the text's physical movements as it circulates in manuscripts or in the mouths of reciters and is handed down to posterity, but also as a result of an essential instability in medieval texts themselves"; ibid., 45–46.

It is well known that prior to the discovery of the Dead Sea Scrolls no single manuscript of the Hebrew Bible/Old Testament existed that was older than the ninth century CE. With the availability of the Dead Sea Scrolls we have been unexpectedly projected back to an early state in the making of what came to be the Hebrew Bible. Written roughly between the first century BCE and the first century CE, these Scrolls are a millennium removed from what used to be the oldest available copy of the Masoretic text. A past hidden from us for centuries has been lifted into historical consciousness and has facilitated a new approach to the compositional history of the Masoretic text.

Scholarship has had some difficulty facing up to the new textual realities that were provided by the Scrolls. How deeply it was beholden to conventional patterns of thought may be demonstrated by the example of the famous Isaiah scroll, one of the best preserved among the Dead Sea manuscripts. Millar Burrows,[10] eminent representative of the first generation of Qumran experts, observed a remarkable agreement between the ancient Isaiah scroll and its Masoretic textual version. In some cases, where the Isaiah scroll differed from the *textus receptus* (in terms of orthography, morphology, and lexical items), he postulated copying mistakes that pointed to an inferior textual quality of the ancient scroll. In other cases, he judged variants of the ancient scroll to be superior and adopted them as a means of amending and improving the Masoretic standard. In either case, therefore, he was inclined to evaluate the ancient Isaiah scroll not as an entity in its own right, but rather from the perspective of the established norm of the *textus receptus*, eager to assert that the text of the Isaiah scroll "confirms the antiquity and authenticity of the Masoretic text."[11] In short, the centrality of the Masoretic *textus receptus* was the criterion for scholarly judgments.

Burrows' eminent textual scholarship, one recognizes in retrospect, operated under distinct text critical and theological premises. As far as text criticism was concerned, he held that its primary objective was "to detect and eliminate errors in the text as it has come down to us, and so to restore, as nearly as possible, what was originally written by the authors of the books."[12] In different words, text criticism, in his view, was designed to recover the original text. It is a premise ill-suited, we shall see, to comprehend and appreciate the copious nature of the manuscript evidence. Theologically, he insisted that in spite of the fact that the transmission of scriptural texts has "not come down to us through the centuries unchanged," the "es-

10. Burrows, *Dead Sea Scrolls.*

11. Ibid., 314.

12. Ibid., 301.

sential truth and the will of God revealed in the Bible, however, have been preserved unchanged through all the vicissitudes in the transmission of the text."[13] This, too, represents a position that is not well suited to face up to the nature of tradition as it appeared in light of the Dead Sea Scrolls. Burrows' premises generated an optical illusion that made us see the new textual evidence as something other than it really was.

> As more and more variables of biblical texts were identified at Qumran, the notion of a single, normative text existing in the period roughly of the first century BCE was increasingly called into question. A sense of *mouvance* and active transcription of tradition is ever more difficult for us to overlook. Textual pluriformity had to be accounted for as a phenomenon sui generis. Few experts have taken it more seriously than Eugene Ulrich,[14] the chief editor of the Qumran scrolls. Far from disregarding, explaining away, or rationalizing textual variability, he along with others has moved it to center stage: "The question dominating the discussion of the history of the biblical text is how to explain the pluriformity observable in the biblical manuscripts from Qumran, the M[asoretic] T, and the versions."[15] Textual pluriformity is now a dominant issue.

The scholarly assimilation of the new textual evidence is still very much in progress. As a result of some fifty years of intense academic labors, however, a number of points seem certain. One, the textual condition of the Dead Sea Scrolls is not specific to that community but appears to be typical of Judaism in general at that period in history. By and large, the fuller textual evidence with regard to scriptural texts—the Dead Sea Scrolls, the Samaritan Pentateuch, the Septuagint, the New Testament, and Josephus in his dealings with scriptural materials—"demonstrate[s] bountifully that there were variable literary editions of the books of Scripture in the Second Temple period."[16] As far as the ancient scriptural traditions are concerned, variability does not represent an exceptional behavior. Two, one needs to exercise caution in stigmatizing the variants as secondary, aberrant, deficient, wild, or non-biblical. All too often, these are judgments based on the criterion of later standards of normativity. Textual pluriformity was an acceptable way of textual life at that time. Three, the textual situation at Qumran does not reveal text critical efforts in the sense of comparing and

13. Ibid., 320.
14. Ulrich, *Dead Sea Scrolls.*
15. Ibid., 80.
16. Ibid., 9–10.

selecting variants for the purpose of arriving at a norm. The community appears to have lived in textual pluriformity. Four, there is no evidence for the Masoretic *textus receptus* having achieved the status of normativity in the Second Temple period. Textual pluriformity was a way of life at a time when both Christianity and rabbinic Judaism were in their formative stages. Five, the text critical search for "the original text" is not only fraught with technical, philological difficulties but, more importantly, contrary to the dynamics of the textual realities on the ground.[17] Six, just as many of us have come to question the notion of "normative Judaism" prior to the Second Revolt, 132–35 CE, so will we now have to be skeptical about the concept of a single "normative biblical text" in that period. Seven, the consequences of Roman imperialism were devastating: destruction of Qumran in 68 CE, destruction of the Jerusalem temple in 70 CE, destruction of Masada in 74 CE. The political realities at the time were anything but conducive to sustained scholarly labors aimed at accomplishing a standard text. Eight, scribes were not merely copyists loyal to the letter of the text, but creative traditionists as well. This is the point where the picture of scribes meticulously copying the Torah needs to be modified. Nine, clearly there is in Second Temple Judaism broad reference to the Law, and the Law and the Prophets, but we should not think of them as "biblical" authorities as if "the Bible" in its canonized sense had already been in existence. In the words of James Barr, "the time of the Bible was a time when the Bible was not yet there."[18] Not only was "the Bible" not in existence, but at Qumran, Enochic literature was no less important than Deuteronomy, and Jubilees just as vital as Isaiah. Ten, we can be certain that in the Second Temple period two or three textual editions of the Pentateuch were in circulation. But when we accord them canonical or semi-canonical status, we are probably making retrospective judgments reconfiguring history according to later developments and categories.

Perhaps the Qumran evidence may be assimilated into a new historical paradigm as far as the relations between the Masoretic norm and scriptural (rather than biblical) traditions were concerned. Instead of imagining a densely intertextual web with the Masoretic text at center stage and biblical manuscripts gravitating toward it, we might envision multiple scriptural versions, including what came to be the Masoretic norm, finding their hermeneutical rationale in recitation, oral explication, and memorization, with

17. Ulrich, *Dead Sea Scrolls*, 15, has raised a crucial question for the reconceptualization of the project of text criticism: "should not the object of the text criticism of the Hebrew Bible be, not the single (and textually arbitrary?) collection of Masoretic texts of the individual books, but the organic, developing, pluriform Hebrew text—different for each book—such as the evidence indicates?"

18. Barr, *Holy Scripture*, 1.

some textual bodies such as the Pentateuch and prophetic literature assuming authoritative significance.

It is in the context of this scribal, scriptural environment of textual *mouvance* that we will have to grasp the early Jesus tradition as an insistently pluriform phenomenon. In terms that are sensitive to media realities, one might say Jesus of Nazareth presented himself as a vocal, rhetorical authority. Viewing him as an aphoristic, parabolic teacher, historical critical scholarship has made great efforts in retrieving the *ipsissima verba*, his so-called original sayings. Let us see how the search for the original sayings looks from the perspective of genuinely oral sensibilities. When Jesus, the aphoristic, parabolic teacher, recited a story or saying at one place, and then journeyed to another place to recite, with audience adjustments, that same story or saying to a different audience, this second performance cannot be understood as a secondary version, or copy, of the original rendition. Rather, the second rendition is as much an authentic performance as the first one. This suggests that the notion of the one original word makes no sense in oral performance. Likewise, the concept of "variants" is problematic as far as oral performers in the ancient world are concerned because there is no one "original" from which variants could deviate. In the predominantly oral culture in which Jesus operated, each oral rendition of a story or saying was an original, indeed the original. While historical critics are inclined to sift through the textual tradition in search of the one original, oral culture operates with a plurality of originals. More is involved here than a mere change from singular to plural. The coexistence of multiple original renditions suggest *equiprimordiality*, a principle that reflects cultural sensibilities that are quite different from and contrary to the notion of the one, original speech. One of the first Western scholars to conceptualize the notion that in oral tradition there was no such thing as an original rendition and variants thereof was Albert Lord.[19]

The early chirographic rendition of the Jesus tradition, no less than the scribal tradition preceding the Masoretic text, is characterized by a remarkable pluriformity. In both instances, fixation on an assumed textual normativity or originality has blinded us from grasping and appreciating the existent scribal tradition in its own right and on its own terms. As far as the early papyrological evidence of Jesus sayings is concerned, it appears to be characterized by fluidity rather than by foundational stability. The text critic David Parker has stated the case provocatively: "The further back we go, the greater seems to be the degree of variation . . ." Parker adds that this situation is "not an unfortunate aberration" but rather "part of the way in

19. Lord, *Singer of Tales*, 101.

which they [the Christian scribes] copied their codices."[20] While his is not the only way to explain the phenomenon of scribal fluidity, Parker's observation nonetheless appears at variance with historical critical premises about tradition. While historical and textual criticism by and large operates on the assumption of a foundational text at the beginning, the actual scribal evidence on the ground suggests pluriformity at the outset and something akin to a foundational text at a later, secondary stage in the tradition. The analogy to the early history of the textual tradition of the Hebrew Bible is striking.

If, by way of an example cited by Parker,[21] one sifts through the papyrological evidence of Jesus's sayings on marriage and divorce, one recognizes that the problem is not simply one of explaining the differences among Mark 10, Matthew 5 and 19, and Luke 16, an issue well known to biblical scholars. Assessment of the full scribal evidence confronts us with both an amount and degree of variability that goes far beyond Markan, Matthean, and Lukan adaptations and is not readily explicable by a single textual genealogical tree that would take us back to the one root saying. The recovery of the original rendition would seem to be an unattainable goal. In Parker's words, "a single authoritative pronouncement [by Jesus on marriage and divorce] is irrecoverable."[22] Perhaps one should add that the project of retrieving the single original saying is contrary to the intentions of the early tradition. We have no excuse for reducing the tradition to simplicity where there is complexity, and for claiming single originality where there are multiple originalities.

It is worth noting that the reason for the *mouvance* of the Jesus tradition is not that these sayings were considered unimportant. To the contrary, as Parker rightly observed, the "basic reason for the complexity in the passages [on marriage and divorce] . . . and in many others of Jesus's sayings is precisely the importance accorded them."[23] Issues pertaining to marriage, divorce, and remarriage have been pressing ethical concerns in the past as much as they are urgent matters for our modern churches. But it is precisely the great importance attributed to these matters that accounts for the variability in the rendition of the sayings tradition. In Carr's terms, texts that mattered most in terms of educational knowledge and cultural identity were most likely to be subject to frequent rewritings. It was precisely because of the ever-present relevance of sayings on marriage, divorce, and remarriage

20. Parker, *Living Text*, 188.

21. Ibid., 75–94.

22. Ibid., 183.

23. Ibid., 75.

that a verbatim transmission was not the most desirable mode of securing the tradition. To transmit Jesus's word(s) faithfully meant to keep them in balance with social life, needs, and expectations. In paraphrasing a statement by Ong (in response to a student's question as to why Jesus did not resort to writing), one might say that his (Jesus's) sayings were considered far too important to be frozen into scribal still life.

It is easier to explain, Parker observed, what the early Jesus tradition is not, and "harder to find a suitable language to describe what it is."[24] If we say that this tradition eschewed stability, we have characterized it negatively from the point of view of later developments. If one describes it, with Parker, as a "free" and "living" tradition,[25] one has arrived at an appropriately positive definition but still lacks explanation for the phenomenon. In a footnote, Parker himself adduces Ong's observation that "manuscripts, with their glosses and marginal comments . . . were in dialogue with the world outside their own borders. They remained closer to the give-and-take of oral expression."[26] The validity of Ong's remark manifests itself with particular force in the case of the early scriptural traditions of both the Hebrew Bible and the Jesus tradition. When viewing the early scribal tradition of Jesus sayings from the perspective of oral–scribal dynamics, it appears to be operative at the intersection with speech, or, more precisely perhaps, it has every indication of being enmeshed with and empowered by oral dynamics. In four ways at least, this early scribal tradition functioned in keeping with the oral, performative sensibilities: first, like oral performance, the early scribal tradition was made up of variables and multiforms; second, it was constituted by plural originals rather than by singular originality; third, it sought, despite its chirographic materiality, to stay with the flux of temporality; and fourth, it enacted tradition that was not transmission per se, but composition in tradition. Both in terms of compositional intent and audience adjustment, the early scribal tradition of Jesus sayings still operated according to basically oral dynamics.

One should take note here that the model of Second Temple scribalism, insofar as it is characterized by pluriformity and oral dynamism, has been observed in the rabbinic tradition as well. Taking advantage of the developing field of orality-scribality studies, recent books by Martin Jaffee and Elizabeth Shanks Alexander have genuinely advanced our understanding of the scribal production and transmission, recitation, and reception of

24. Ibid., 200.

25. Ibid., 188.

26. Ibid., 188 n. 7; Ong, *Orality and Literacy*, 132.

the rabbinic texts.[27] At Qumran and in the post-70 CE rabbinic tradition, Jaffee explained, the scrolls functioned in an oral-traditional environment, where they were publicly recited and in a secondary discourse explicated. Rabbinic scribes and teachers drew on the oral-performative tradition for textual compositions that in turn were subject to re-oralization. In Jaffee's view, we should imagine the rabbinic tradition as "a continuous loop of manuscript and performance,"[28] which never yielded a ground zero on the basis of which the original construction of the one authentic text was recoverable. In keeping with Jaffee's approach, Alexander used the oral conceptual lens to focus not, or not exclusively, on the transmissional and interpretive processes of the Mishnah, the foundational document of rabbinic Judaism, but primarily on its "performative effect," trying "to imagine what would result from performing its materials."[29] Developing a concept of the ancient transmitters of the early rabbinic materials as active shapers rather than passive tradents of the tradition, she concluded that the pedagogical benefit of the mishnaic performances lay not merely in the transmission of content but in "imparting a method of legal analysis"[30] that trained the students to practice modes of legal analysis on their own.

When set against the background of the ancient Near Eastern and Mediterranean culture of communication, the performative-chirographic dynamics of the early scriptural materials of the Hebrew Bible, the Jesus sayings, and the rabbinic tradition make good sense: by and large they were embedded in an oral biosphere where scribal–oral–scribal interfaces were the rule. It was the operative logic of these traditions to reactivate (not repeat!) themselves rather than to reach for closure. To comprehend their operations, especially in their early stages, we should think of recurrent performativity rather than intertextuality.

CODEX AND CANON

Undoubtedly, the well-documented early use of the codex in the Christian tradition provided a technological innovation that was to be instrumental in ushering in wide-ranging cultural changes. Many of these changes were slow in coming and not immediately effective. On the macro-level the

27. Jaffee, *Torah in the Mouth*; Alexander, *Transmitting Mishnah*. An early driving force in approaching rabbinics from hermeneutical and oral–scribal perspectives was Fraade, *Tradition to Commentary*.

28. Jaffee, *Torah in the Mouth*, 124.

29. Elizabeth Shanks Alexander, *Transmitting Mishnah*, 169.

30. Ibid., 171.

codex paved the way for the media transfer from the chirographic to the typographic identity of the book, unwittingly mediating the Bible's eventual apotheosis in print culture. On the micro-level it served as a convenient storage place for depositing numerous texts in a single book, and provided more efficient access than the scroll. No doubt, insofar as the codex supplied the base for multiple and miscellaneous textual items in a single volume, it created the material condition for the biblical canon. However, the causal connection between codex and canon must not be pressed too far. Illustrious fourth-century codices such as Sinaiticus, Alexandrinus, Vaticanus, and the fifth-century Ephraemi Rescriptus, for example—frequently invoked as illustrations of unified Bibles—tend to blind us into assuming that volumes containing the whole Bible were common practice. Yet, not only were these codices "not produced as one volume in our sense of the word,"[31] but books carrying the whole Bible were the exception rather than the rule in ancient and medieval history. Even complete Greek New Testaments were relatively rare. The full canonical implications of the codex were only slowly realized and in the end it was print technology that finalized the canonical authority of the Bible.

But the format of the codex had a more subtle, less widely acknowledged impact on verbal art and on human consciousness. Compared with the scroll, it provided a more stable material surface that in turn encouraged experimentation with the newly acquired writing space. Below we shall have occasion to observe how techniques for formatting and arranging materials were developed that, combined with the convenient page-turning practice, were ideally suited to focus the mind on comparative readings and cross-referencing, and to encourage habits that in turn affected the perception of texts and textually perceived traditions. Thus, in taking advantage of the book format and exploring its writing space, the codex created opportunities for textuality to come into its own. In terms of the principles enunciated in Ong's essay on "Technology Outside Us and Inside Us,"[32] cited at the outset, one could say that the codex helped interiorize textuality in ways not previously experienced.

Canonicity is a topic that has for a long time commanded wide-ranging interests in biblical studies, the history of religion, and more recently in literary criticism.[33] It seems agreed that the canonization of both the Jewish and the Christian Bible was a process that extended over centuries.

31. Parker, *Living Text*, 195.

32. Ong, "Technology Outside Us and Inside Us."

33. Zahn, *Geschichte des Neutestamentlichen Kanons*; Leipoldt, *Geschichte des Neutestamentlichen Kanons*; Kümmel, *Introduction to the New Testament*, 334–58; Gamble, *New Testament Canon*; von Hallberg, *Canons*.

The Jewish canon came into existence roughly between 200 BCE and 200 CE, a period that is partially synchronous with Second Temple Judaism. The Christian canon reached a semblance of agreed uniformity in the fourth century, but a dogmatic articulation of canon and canonical authority did not occur until the Council of Trent (1546 CE).

In the case of the Christian canon, something of a modern scholarly consensus about the criteria and rationale for canonicity appears to have been reached. Among the criteria, apostolicity, orthodoxy, and customary usage of texts are cited by many. The reasons for canon formation are usually seen in a defense against Marcionism, gnosticism, and Montanism. One notes that the overall argument falls along the lines of orthodoxy versus heresiology, categories that are no longer quite fashionable in current historical scholarship.

From a broadly cultural perspective one might suggest that canon formation, both in Judaism and in Christianity, has to be understood against the background of the ideational and textual pluralism that was characteristic of Second Temple Judaism. Jan Assmann has seen this quite clearly.[34] The need for canonicity, he reasoned, arises out of the experience of an excessive textual pluralism and lack of ideational uniformity that undermine the raison d'être of the tradition. In that situation, the canon responds to the "need to prevent that 'anything goes,' a fear of loss of meaning through entropy" ("Bedürfnis, zu verhindern, dass 'anything goes,' eine Angst vor Sinnverlust durch Entropie").[35] The selective privileging of texts, therefore, manifests a will to curtail entropy, that tendency, lodged in the tradition, toward diffusion and exhaustion of energy. To define this particular canonical function, Assmann has coined the phrase of the "Bändigung der Varianz,"[36] a taming of the phenomenon of variance. From this perspective, one may view the canon as a means of safeguarding tradition by controlling and defining it, and thereby (re)asserting the cultural identity of a people. Canonicity thus understood signified an approach to the pluriform oral–scribal tradition via selectivity and exclusivity. It secured cultural identity, but it did so, and this is a crucial argument of this essay, at the price of closing the textual borders. Viewed against the *mouvance* of the Jewish and Christian textual tradition, the creation of the canon marks a principally authoritative and unmistakably reductive move.

In highlighting early triumphs of textual rationality, we are turning to Origen's *Hexapla* and Eusebius' *Canon Tables*. In the words of Anthony

34. Assmann, *Das kulturelle Gedächtnis*, 103–29.

35. Ibid., 123.

36. Ibid.

Grafton and Megan Williams, Origen's *Hexapla* "was one of the greatest single monuments of Roman scholarship, and the first serious product of the application to Christian culture of the tools of Greek philology and criticism."[37] In the perspectives we have been developing, the *Hexapla* is a prime example of a sophisticated utilization of the potentials of the codex by way of experimenting with format and layout and implementing new forms of textual arrangements. It is, in the words of Grafton and Williams, a "milestone in the history of the book," even though "its form, its contents, and above all its purpose remain unclear."[38]

As the titular designation implies, the *Hexapla* was a codex, or rather a series of almost forty codices, that arranged different versions of the text of the Jewish Bible in six parallel, vertical columns: the Hebrew version, the Greek transliteration of the Hebrew rendition, the Greek versions of Aquila (a proselyte to Judaism), Symmachus (an Ebionite), the Septuagint (LXX), and Theodotion (a Hellenistic Jew), in that order. There is now broad agreement that what prompted the massive project of the *Hexapla* was the conundrum of textual pluriformity that Origen encountered. "The reason for the *Hexapla*," states Ulrich, "was that the multiplicity of texts and text traditions proved problematic for one espousing the principle that, because the text was inspired, there must be a single text of the Bible."[39] Grafton and Williams express themselves more cautiously: "Only in its original context of almost unlimited textual and translational variety can we fully appreciate the nature and function of the *Hexapla*."[40]

Yet, granted textual pluriformity and variability, precisely how is one to understand and appreciate the rationale for constructing the *Hexapla*? What did Origen intend to accomplish by undertaking a textual enterprise of such colossal proportions? From our perspective, we recognize that he was himself not as well informed about the pluriformity of textual versions and traditions as we are today. He assumed, for example, that the Hebrew text type was identical with that from which the LXX had been translated, whereas current scholarship suggests that neither the LXX nor the Masoretic text are homogeneous, and that the textual character in both traditions changes from book to book. But Origen was sufficiently aware of textual pluriformity of biblical texts to embark upon the intellectually demanding, economically expensive, and physically grueling work of selecting,

37. Informed sensitivity to the media dimensions of scroll and codex places the work by Grafton and Williams, far above the conventional philological and theological approaches to patristics. See Grafton and Williams, *Transformation of the Book*, 131.

38. Ibid., 87.

39. Ulrich, *Dead Sea Scrolls*, 225.

40. Grafton and Williams, *Transformation of the Book*, 130.

reproducing, and collating six versions of the Bible. Indeed, "the complex *mise-en-page* of the Hexaplaric columns must have presented significant logistical challenges to the scribes who created and reproduced them."[41] Scholars generally share the view that Origen's principal purpose was a sound text that could serve as a reliable basis both for Christians themselves and for their disputes with the Jews. While this may well have been Origen's ultimate goal, it is not directly evident from the Hexaplaric arrangement. As a matter of fact, constructing a single text is precisely what he did not do. Rather than composing a standard text, he exposed his readers to a textual pluriformity, albeit on a drastically reduced scale. Could one perhaps interpret Origen's masterpiece the way Eusebius appears to have read it—as a concession that in fact no single authoritative text could be reconstructed,[42] or that it was up to readers to sort things out for themselves? Be that as it may, in juxtaposing texts one next to the other, and in inviting comparative reading, Origen constructed a textual universe that constituted a virtual counter-model to the *mouvance* of the performative tradition.

Origen's innovative use of parallel columns in his *Hexapla* appears to have provided Eusebius with a model for his *Canon Tables*.[43] In principle, Eusebius' tables constituted something of a numerical grid that captured all four gospels. He had divided the gospel texts into small sections and then supplied each section with a number as well as a reference to its location in the tables. The tables themselves consisted of ten columns, each carrying the section numbers marked on the margin of the gospel texts. In this way, table one numbered the sections common to all four gospels; tables two to four those sections common to three gospels, tables five to nine those common to two gospels; and table ten listed section numbers with no apparent parallels. Something else altogether was in play here than the rewriting of texts, namely the mathematization of texts. By virtue of the numerical logic, an entirely new approach to reading and understanding the four gospels was introduced. Comparative thinking across the gospel narratives was now a possibility. But it was accomplished at the price of imposing a numerical logic that enclosed the gospels into a tight system or, better perhaps, into the illusion of a closed system. What Eusebius and his staff of secretaries and notaries had constructed was a strictly documentary environment of such logical persuasion and on such perfect a scale that the mind has to remove itself from the project to discern its artificiality. The

41. Ibid., 105.

42. See Ibid., 170: "Eusebius read the *Hexapla* as Origen had meant it to be read: as a treasury of exegetical materials, some of them perplexing, rather than an effort to provide a stable, perfect text of the Bible."

43. Nordenfalk, *Die Spätantiken Kanontafeln*.

Canon Tables had no basis in the real life of the gospels nor did they leave any room for social engagement, for participation in the oral–scribal–oral loop, or for compositional involvement in memorial processes. No wonder Grafton and Williams entertained the view that Eusebius was anticipating aspects of the modern library system. His experimentation with systems of information storage, they wrote, "represented as brilliant, and as radical, a set of new methods for the organization and retrieval of information as the nineteenth-century card catalogue and filing systems would in their turn."[44]

MEMORY AND MANUSCRIPT

From later perspectives, it is evident that codex and canon, *Hexapla* and *Canon Tables*, were harbingers of things to come. At the time, however, the cultural potential of the new formatting techniques provided by the codex was far from being fully explored. It would take centuries for the scribal medium to optimize its material resources, and for human consciousness to interiorize scribal technology. The immense textual compilations accomplished by Origen and Eusebius were peak performances standing out in a culture that by and large remained heavily beholden to oral, scribal, and memorial *modi operandi*.

As suggested above, codex and canon did not immediately translate into a universally acknowledged authority of the Bible as a single, unified book. To the extent that textual uniformity was an essential ingredient of the authoritative Bible, medieval manuscript culture, even though it had advanced beyond the scribal technology of the Second Temple period, was by its very nature not qualified to produce identical copies because it was "of the essence of a manuscript culture that every copy is different, both unique and imperfect."[45]

Moreover, throughout patristic and medieval times the Bible was operational more often in plural form than as solitary authority. Collections of the Minor Prophets, for example, or a clustering of the Psalms into the Psalter, and of the gospels into gospel books enjoyed broad usage. Missals, breviaries, and lectionaries, widely used as service books in the medieval church, tended to disperse biblical texts into *lectiones*. There was a sense, therefore, in which the biblical tradition in the Middle Ages was experienced more as a collection of many books and a plurality of auditions than as a single text between two covers.

44. Grafton and Williams, *Transformation of the Book*, 230.

45. Parker, *Living Text*, 188.

One will further have to remember that for the longest part of its existence the Bible was largely present in the lives of the people as an oral authority: proclaimed, homiletically interpreted, listened to, and internalized. Nor did the oral proclamation always emanate from the Bible itself. The *Book of Hours*,[46] for example, composed of psalms and biblical quotations, was often a household's sole book, known from memory by millions and recited aloud at each of the eight traditional monastic hours of the day. Duffy's claim is thus very much to the point: "If we are to understand the point of contact between people and the written word [of the Bible] in the late Middle Ages, there is no more fundamental text than the *Book of Hours*."[47]. While the chirographic Bible was rare in the hands of lay people, much of its content flourished via the *Book of Hours* in the hearts of millions.

Last but not least, the Bible's authority coexisted on equal footing with that of the councils and the oral and written tradition. On theological grounds, the medieval church operated with a plurality of authorities. For a millennium and a half, therefore, there was no such thing as the sole authority of the Bible in Western Christendom. It was only with print technology, and accompanying theological developments, that a standardized text and duplication of that text was a feasible proposition. *Sola scriptura*, we may safely claim, was a concept technically unworkable and theologically unthinkable prior to the invention of printing.

The oral authority of the Bible brings us to the phenomenon of memory. Regarded since ancient times as the wellspring of civilized life, it was a continuing force in the Middle Ages, a period in Western history that was in fundamental ways a memorial more than a documentary culture.[48] It was by no means uncommon for people to have instant recall of biblical texts, whether they had memorized them from start to finish, or whether they were in command of a selection of passages, or merely knew a series of aphorisms and stories. Augustine stands for many theologians who were entirely comfortable in combining the rigors of the manuscript culture with the demands of memory. Peter Brown has vividly described his bookish environment: "on the shelves, in the little cupboards that were the bookcases of Late Roman men, there lay ninety-three of his own works, made up of two hundred and thirty-two little books, sheaves of his letters, and

46. Duffy, *Marking the Hours*.

47. Ibid., 42.

48. Credit for the modern rediscovery of the force of memory in Western civilization, from antiquity to the rise of the sciences, goes to Frances Yates' *The Art of Memory*. Mary J. Carruthers has almost singlehandedly reconceptualized medieval studies from the perspective of memory in her classic work *The Book of Memory*. Both books have exerted a profound influence on the humanities and to a degree on the social sciences.

perhaps covers crammed with anthologies of his sermons, taken down by the stenographers of his admirers."[49] But the man who surrounded himself with books, many of which he had composed himself, was persuaded that the quality of his intellect was intricately linked to the powers of memory. Writes Brown: "His memory, trained on classical texts, was phenomenally active. In one sermon, he could move through the whole Bible, from Paul to Genesis and back again, via the Psalms, piling half-verse on half-verse."[50] Augustine's competence in and cultivation of memory was essential not only for his retention of knowledge and mental composing, but, in the end, for the quality of his thought. Memory and manuscript interacted in ways we can hardly imagine today.

For more than a millennium, roughly from the time of the sack of Rome (410 CE) to the invention of printing (ca. 1455 CE), a general shift from oral, rhetorical sensibilities to a developing chirographic control over the organization and growth of knowledge is observable. Manuscripts increasingly became important tools of civilized life, and from the eleventh century onward an ever-growing scribal culture shaped the processes of learning. Brian Stock has meticulously documented the world of communications and cultural transformations in the high Middle Ages. It is a complex story. Oral–scribal–memorial interfacing dynamics constituted "not one but rather many models, all moving at different velocities and in different orbits."[51] There was the high culture of the papacy and monasticism, of the chanceries and diplomacy, of jurisdiction, and above all of scholasticism. Undoubtedly, those were orbits that excelled in thinking and formulating complex philosophical, theological, legal, and linguistic ideas, often with signal keenness of intellect. Theirs was a culture of written records that both benefited from and contributed to the developing chirographic communication. But one must guard against facile premises concerning links between a developing medieval documentary life and a restructuring of consciousness. The processes entailed in the interiorization of medieval scribalism are intricate, raising deep questions regarding the interfacing of the materiality of language and knowledge with mind and memory. In the most general terms, however, it seems fair to say that relentless scribal labors enhanced the textual base of knowledge; that knowledge, insofar as it was managed by a working relationship with manuscripts, was apt to become detached from the oral, traditional biosphere; that in the minds of the literate elite, "oral

49. Brown, *Augustine*, 428.

50. Ibid., 254.

51. Stock, *Implications of Literacy*, 34.

tradition became identified with illiteracy";[52] and that knowledge processed scribally would foster comparative and critical thought. But it needs to be restated that this mutual interpenetration of scribal technology and human thought is observable predominantly among the chirographic elite. Thus while professional scribality began to exercise effects on mind and consciousness, and the Bible became the most studied book in the West whose language and contents permeated medieval language, literacy still remained the privilege of few, and reading and writing did not instantaneously result in literate intellectualism. And this is the other part of the complex medieval communications world: the chirographic technology was, and continued to be, a tedious, backbreaking business.[53] By typographical standards, writing one letter after the next, and word after word, was exceedingly slow work, and the time spent on completing a manuscript of average length was inordinate. And so was the price of a manuscript. The copying of existing manuscripts aside, the manufacture of new texts was usually the result of a division of labor. There was the *dictator* or intellectual initiator of a text who was frequently unable to write himself/herself. There was secondly the *scriptor* who in taking dictation may or may not have had an intellectual grasp of what he or she was writing. Moreover, medieval Bibles for the most part did not have chapter and verse divisions. It was only around 1200 CE that the first chapter divisions were introduced into biblical manuscripts, and around 1500 CE that biblical texts began to be atomized into individually numbered sections or even verses. Neither the rabbis nor Augustine, neither Maimonides nor Thomas Aquinas ever cited "the Bible" the way typographic folks do.

Nor did medieval intellectuals read the Bible quite the way we do. Reading was still widely, although not exclusively, practiced as an oral activity. To be sure, some aids to the visual apperception of biblical texts were in usage. Punctuation symbols and the beginnings of word and chapter division, initially introduced in support of oral recitation, in fact imposed a visual code that was to facilitate silent reading habits. Still, far into the High Middle Ages reading was regarded as something of a physical activity, requiring good health and robust energy. In short, reading was associated with dictation and recitation more than with private reflection.[54]

Standing in a complex communications web of chirographic technology, memory, oral recitation, and homiletic exposition, the Bible was

52. Ibid., 12.

53. Troll, "Illiterate Mode of Written Communication."

54. Saenger, "Silent Reading"; Achtemeier, "*Omne verbum sonat*"; Gilliard, "More Silent Reading."

anything but a closed book with a single sense. Augustine's hermeneutics, for example, could strictly hold to the theory of a divinely inspired and unified book of the Bible, while at the same time keeping entirely aloof from literalism. He had no patience with those who thought the Word of God was plain and obvious for all to grasp. What a misunderstanding of the Bible that was! How could one incarcerate the immense mysteries of the Book into the prison house of the single sense? Veiled in mystery as the Bible was, it served to inspire hearers and readers to reach out for newer and deeper senses hidden beneath, between, or above the literal sense. Impressively articulated in his classic *De Doctrina Christiana*, the seven steps of hermeneutics were less a matter of exegetical discernment and more of spiritual exercises that would take hearers from the fear of God to piety, the love of God and love of neighbor, to justice, mercy, the vision of God, and all the way to a state of peace and tranquility.[55]

Augustine's conviction of the plural senses of the Bible was widely shared in the Middle Ages. The classic theory of interpretation that dominated large segments of Western Christendom espoused the fourfold sense of biblical texts: the literal or plain sense, the oblique or allegorical sense, the homiletical and often ethical sense, and the spiritual sense that gestured toward deeper or higher realities.[56] Whether one acknowledged this fourfold sense, or merely practiced a twofold sense, or inclined toward a threefold interpretation, the spiritual sense was in all instances accorded the position of priority. That the biblical text was open to plural senses was entirely taken for granted. Such was the nature of truth that it comprised multiple senses. It was as if the experience of textual pluralism had been projected onto hermeneutics. Allen Orr's conclusion that biblical literalism appeared late in the history of Christianity, and in connection with the Reformation and the so-called Counter-Reformation, has much to commend it.[57] And both the Reformation and the Counter-Reformation, we shall see, marked a period that was closely tied in with the print medium.

THE WORD MADE PRINT

There were intellectual forces at work in medieval culture that directed the focus toward texts and developed a textually grounded (theo)logic to unprecedented heights. Around the turn of the thirteenth to the fourteenth century William of Ockham (1285–1349? CE), a Franciscan monk from

55. Robertson, Augustine, *On Christian Doctrine*, 38–40.

56. Lubac, *Exégèse médiévale.*

57. Orr, Review of *Living with Darwin.*

Surrey County in England whose skepticism toward philosophical realism moved the particular, the experiential, and the contingent to the center of inquiry, explored the notion of distinctiveness, including the distinctive nature of texts.[58] Scripture, indeed all texts, he reasoned, were operating according to something akin to an intrinsic linguistic economy, and the operations of the mind—everybody's mind—were such that they could access the internal textual logic via the *cognitio intuitiva*. From the perspective of media sensibilities, we observe an intellectualism that is fully at home in the prevailing chirographic culture and thoroughly exploiting its inner resources.[59] In nominalism, of which Ockham was a prominent representative, the notion began to assert itself that the full potential of biblical texts was to be found less in their oral proclamation and auditory reception than in their very own textual economy. With Ockham, the closure of the biblical text was about to receive a hermeneutical, indeed theological justification. That premise of the closed text was soon to garner powerful technological support through the print medium.

Between 1452 and 1455 CE Johannes Gutenberg produced the first print Bible, henceforth universally known as the 42-line Bible. It is not immediately obvious why he selected a book as monumental in scope as the Bible to implement a technology that was very much in its infancy. At first glance, print's technical effects of duplication appear to point to the propagation of faith as his principal objective. But many arguments speak against it. The casting of close to 300 different characters was labor-intensive and hiked up the price of the print Bible.[60] Moreover, Latin, the language of the Vulgate, was no longer marketable; few people could actually read the Latin print Bible. Last but not least, Gutenberg's undertaking was not a commissioned project and for this reason required vast capital investments. Analogous to developments we observe at the launching of the electronic medium, the print medium effected the entrée of entrepreneurship into the communications world. Capitalism took hold of the new medium with a vengeance. A new technological and economic culture was emerging that was not infrequently predicated on substantial financial risk-taking. In Gutenberg's case, the print Bible brought its master no economic profit

58. Adams, *William of Ockham*; Leff, *William of Ockham*.

59. Carruthers, *Memory*, 158, observed that Ockham's "whole scholarly life until 1330 was spent in the greatest of European universities, his circle the most 'bookish' of the time." When, following the papal interdiction in 1330, Ockham lived isolated in Munich, he repeatedly complained that he had been deprived of access to all the books he needed to consult.

60. Ruppel, *Johannes Gutenberg*; Kapr, *Johannes Gutenberg*.

whatsoever. As is well known, he died a poor man, enmeshed in lawsuits and unable to pay his debts.

To the viewers and readers of the first major machine-made book in Western civilization, the most striking feature was sameness and proportionality. Prior to the invention of printing, sameness in this sense of complete identity had never been experienced. No one jar was like the other, and no two manuscripts were quite alike. The copies of Gutenberg's two-volume Vulgate represented models of stunning sameness, setting the highest standards of calligraphic virtuosity. By virtue of their unprecedented spatial formatting and finality of precision they expressed a sense of unearthly beauty. Michael Giesecke, who aside from Elizabeth Eisenstein has written the most comprehensive, modern work on the technology and cultural implications of print technology, has suggested that aesthetics, in particular the Renaissance ideal of beauty in the sense of complete proportionality, must have been uppermost in the mind of Gutenberg.[61]

Owing to the duplicating effects of typography, textual pluriformity was now being effectively challenged by the ideal of uniformity. Theology and biblical scholarship were increasingly operating in a media environment that was losing touch with Jewish and Christian textual pluriformity. One either viewed the *mouvance* of tradition as something that had to be remedied text critically, or one was beginning to lose sight of it altogether. In short, the notion of *mouvance* was supplanted by what was to become the icon of textual stability. Moreover, the Bible's complete standardization, combined with its breathtaking beauty, projected a never before visualized model of authority. Indeed, it was in part at least this technically facilitated uniformity that contributed to the Bible's unprecedented authority. But again, it was an authority that was accomplished at the price of isolating the Bible from its biosphere. The printed pages, in all their perfectly proportioned beauty, created the impression that sacred Scripture was closed off in a world of its own—uniformly spatialized, consummately linearized, and perfectly marginalized—a world, that is, where in the words of Leo Battista Alberti any alteration of any kind would only distort the harmony. Now, but only now, was it possible to visualize the premise of *sola scriptura*, not merely to conceptualize it theologically.

61. Giesecke, *Der Buchdruck in der frühen Neuzeit*, 141–43, cites a programmatic statement concerning the Renaissance ideal of beauty by the Italian architect and art historian Leo Battista Alberti 1404–72 in *De re edificatoris*, Florence, 1485: "Beauty is a harmony of all component parts, in whichever medium they are represented, juxtaposed with such a sense of proportionality and connectivity that nothing could be added or altered that would not distort it" Giesecke's trans. See also Eisenstein, *Printing Press*, 2 vols.

It is often pointed out that the Protestant Reformers still exhibited profoundly oral sensibilities with respect to Scripture. *Sola scriptura* notwithstanding, Scripture remained a living presence for all of them. Martin Luther, Martin Bucer, John Calvin, Thomas Cranmer, William Tyndale, and others spoke and wrote a scripturally saturated language because they were at home in Scripture and Scripture in them. Their respective theological positions remained fully cognizant of and sympathetic toward the power of oral proclamation. Luther never viewed his vernacular translation simply as a linguistic feat, but rather as a Pentecostal reenactment of the bestowal of the Spirit.[62] The presence of scriptural orality in the theology of the Reformers cannot be in doubt.

At least as significant, however, was the influence of the print medium. The typographic apotheosis of the Bible deeply affected the Reformers' theological thinking on scriptural authority, tradition, memory, interpretation, and numerous other features. Seven hermeneutical and theological developments, all of them in varying degrees bound up with the new medium, were instrumental in bringing about tension and conflict with the oral, scribal, memorial world of verbalization. One, the rejection of the fourfold sense of the Bible aided and abetted the rationale for the closure of biblical texts. Two, the increasingly high regard for the *sensus literalis* jeopardized the hermeneutical pluralism cultivated by the medieval church. Three, the repudiation of allegory—the very figure that generates worlds of correspondences—was a contributing factor toward reducing biblical interpretation to intra-textual literalism. Four, the unprecedented elevation of the Bible to *sola scriptura* conjured up the notion of the Bible as a freestanding monolithic artifact detached from tradition. Five, Luther's premise of *scriptura sui ipsius interpres* paved the way toward closing off the Bible into its own interior textual landscape. Six, the steady marginalization of memory effected a shifting of the interpretation of the Bible toward a fully textualized, documentary model. Seven, perhaps most ominously, the rejection of tradition, this larger-than-textual life of communal memory, disconnected biblical texts both from their vital sustenance and their performance arena. To be sure, some of these features had been anticipated, implicitly or explicitly, in the manuscript culture of ancient and medieval theology, and especially in nominalism's *via moderna* of the fourteenth and fifteenth centuries. One cannot make print the sole determinant of these developments. But the Word made print, namely, the inauguration of the medium that "is comfortable only with finality,"[63] heavily contributed toward view-

62. Newman, "Word Made Print," esp. 117–23.

63. Ong, *Orality and Literacy*, 132.

ing the Bible as a closed book, or, better perhaps, toward fantasizing it as a closed book. Typography was a major, although not the only, factor that effectively reified the biblical texts and generated a high degree of plausibility for thinking of the Bible as an authority that was standing on its own.

No doubt, these are extraordinary developments not only with respect to the status and interpretation of the Bible, but for Western intellectual history in general. In their aggregate, they amounted to an unprecedented elevation of scriptural authority seeking to hold Scripture firmly to its chirographic space and thereby depriving it of the oxygen of tradition. It is not entirely surprising that links between the severe reductionism instituted by the sixteenth-century Reformers and nineteenth- and twentieth-century fundamentalism have been drawn. In a recent study, James Simpson developed the thesis that the Reformers were the protagonists not (merely) of modern liberalism, but of modern fundamentalism as well.[64] He is convinced that the rise of what he calls sixteenth-century fundamentalism was intrinsically linked with the power of the high tech of the fifteenth century. Simpson is not the first one to offer observations of this kind. In the past, Eisenstein has advised us to project not merely the single trajectory of Humanism, Renaissance, and Reformation toward Enlightenment and modernity, but to acknowledge other trajectories as well.[65] Fundamentalism in the sense of literal interpretation and inerrancy of the Bible, Eisenstein observed, while strictly speaking a late nineteenth- and twentieth-century Protestant, North American phenomenon, was in the age of Erasmus "just beginning to assume its modern form."[66] Unless we recognize this development, she stated, "the appearance of fundamentalism in the age of Darwin or the holding of the Scopes trial in the age of Ford become almost completely inexplicable."[67] Needless to say, for Eisenstein the genesis of sixteenth-century fundamentalism is closely allied with the printing press and its impact on the formatting, reading, and interpreting of the Bible. On the whole, however, Eisenstein exercised a careful balance in recognizing print's consequences for better and for worse: "The impact of printing on the Western scriptural faith thus pointed in two quite opposite directions—toward 'Erasmian' trends and ultimately higher criticism and modernism, and toward more rigid orthodoxy culminating in literal fundamentalism and Bible Belts."[68]

64. Simpson, *Burning to Read.*

65. Eisenstein, *Printing Press.*

66. Ibid., I, 366.

67. Ibid., 440.

68. Ibid., 366–67.

Luther, it is well known, was fully conscious of the unprecedented potential of the print medium: "Typography is the final and at the same time the greatest gift, for through it God wanted to make known to the whole earth the mandate of the true religion at the end of the world and to pour it out in all languages. It surely is the last, inextinguishable flame of the world."[69] We know that he was in possession of print copies of Johann Reuchlin's *De Rudimentis Hebraicis,* of a Hebrew Bible (first published by the North Italian Jewish Soncino press in 1488) and of Erasmus' Greek New Testament. To a large extent, therefore, his work of Bible translation was carried out with the assistance and on the basis of print materials. About Luther's translation of the New Testament while sequestered at the Wartburg Castle (1521–22 CE), Eisenstein writes: "Clearly he was better equipped by printers than he would have been by scribes during his interval of enforced isolation."[70] Additionally, he utilized printed copies of the Bible and the New Testament as tools for proclamation, propaganda, and polemic. But he could not have anticipated the full impact the print Bible would have on the religious, social, and political landscape of Europe. No medium escapes the law of unintended consequences, and the print medium was no exception.

The print Bible was by no means the unmixed blessing that its inventor and many of its promoters had envisioned. It effected historical developments *ad bonam et ad malam partem*. On one level, the rapid dissemination of the vernacular print Bible raised literacy to a level never before seen in Europe; it created a steadily growing readership and encouraged further vernacular translations. Moreover, general accessibility to the Bible posed a challenge to authoritarian control over the Bible, and fostered democratic instincts about ownership and content of the Bible. On a different level, however, "the infallibility of the printed word as opposed to the 'instability of script' was recognized even by contemporaries as a fiction."[71] The serious malaise that was affecting the print business, Newman observed, was of a twofold kind: "First: printers were hasty and negligent in the practice of their trade. Second: they were concerned above all with the pursuit of profits."[72] Luther himself was increasingly disturbed that "his" printed Bible had been pirated to the point where ever more printed texts of ever poorer

69. The citation is from Luther's *Tischreden* written down by Nikolaus Medler 1532 and cited by Giesecke, *Der Buchdruck in der frühen Neuzeit*, 163 and 727, n. 167: "*Typographia postremum est donum et idem maximum, per eam enim Deus toti terrarum orbi voluit negotium verae religionis in fine mundi innotescere ac in omnes linguas transfundi. Ultima sana flamma mundi inextinguibilis.*"

70. Eisenstein, *Printing Press*, I, 367–68, n. 225.

71. Newman, "Word Made Print," 101.

72. Ibid., 102.

quality were in circulation: "I do not recognize my own books . . . here there is something left out, there something set incorrectly, there forged, there not proofread."[73] In other words, the very medium that was capable of standardizing the text had set into motion a process of accelerated reproduction that resulted in textual inaccuracies. But in the mechanical medium, textual errors were likely to be multiplied a hundredfold and a thousandfold. One is bound to ask: did the new medium recapitulate, perhaps even aggravate, textual pluriformity, the very condition it had set out to overcome?

The globalizing tendencies inherent in typography were making themselves felt not only in the rapid dissemination of textual variants but in conflicting interpretations of the Bible as well. Notwithstanding its typographical orderliness, the ever more widely publicized content of the Bible became a bone of fierce contention. Among a steadily growing readership, the biblical texts were exposed to unprecedented scrutiny. Inevitably, scriptural discrepancies came to light. But whereas in chirographic culture theological controversies remained confined to a small circle of theological experts, in print culture disputes were publicized across regional and national boundaries. In this way, the new medium marketed dissension and deepened disagreements.

Last but not least, vernacular Bibles became the rallying points for national aspirations, demarcating linguistic and ethnic boundaries and contributing toward the rise of nation states. "It is no accident that nationalism and mass literacy have developed together."[74] While the new medium thus gave momentum to national languages and identities, it also helped draw new lines of religious and national division, and strongly exacerbated Catholic-Protestant polemics. Eisenstein articulated the provocative theory of typography's unintended implication in the dissolution of Latin Christianity and the fragmentation of Christian unity, asserting that "Gutenberg's invention probably contributed more to destroying Christian concord and inflaming religious warfare than any of the so-called arts of war ever did."[75]

AFTERTHOUGHT

The preceding reflections oblige us to extend, however sketchily, our survey of the history of the closure of biblical texts into modernity and early postmodernism. Closed-model thinking asserted itself in a variety of seemingly unrelated phenomena, many of them of significant consequence in

73. Ibid., 110.

74. Eisenstein, *Printing Press*, I, 363.

75. Ibid., 319.

the intellectual history and biblical scholarship of the West. Affinities with the print medium are not directly transparent, but always present at least as a subliminal influence. No doubt, closed-model thinking was effectively countered by quantum theory, relativity theory, evolutionary thinking, a revival in rhetoric and receptionist theory, and lately by the electronic medium. But the point here is to trace connections between print and closed-model thinking.

"Perhaps the most tight-fisted pre-Cartesian proponent of the closed system was the French philosopher and educational reformer Pierre de la Ramée or Petrus Ramus," writes Ong.[76] Thanks to Ong's historically and philosophically masterful study of the thought of Pierre de la Ramée, we are now well informed about changes in the sixteenth- and seventeenth-century educational system in France and across Europe. Ramus' intellectual bent approached knowledge by way of definitions and divisions, leading to still further definitions and more divisions, until every last particle of information was dissected, categorized, and located in a closed system. Ong has dramatically described Ramism as "a quantification system which is almost certainly the most reckless applied one that the world has ever seen."[77] Ramus' quantified epistemology, soon to be adopted by thousands of his followers across Europe, drove him to view all intellectual activities in spatial clusters and corpuscular units, in dichotomized charts and binary tables. "Insofar as a strong stress on closed-system thinking marks the beginning of the modern era," argues Ong, "Ramus, rather than Descartes, stands at the beginning."[78] To some degree, this quantifying drive and binary logic grew out of certain aspects of medieval logic, especially nominalism, but there also exists a relationship, however subliminal, between the rapidly growing technology of letterpress printing and the relentless spatialization and diagrammatization of knowledge. Ong has seen this clearly: "The diagrammatic tidiness which printing was imparting to the realm of ideas was part of a large-scale operation freeing the book from the world of discourse and making it over into an object, a box with surface and 'content' like an Agricolan locus or a Ramist argument or a Cartesian or Lockean idea."[79] Whereas in oral communication words are without borders, and in the ancient scribal, oral, memorial culture boundaries are only beginning to be drawn, it was, again, the printed page that created the illusion that knowledge was an autosemantic world within firmly drawn borders, fully

76. Ong, "Voice and the Opening of Closed Systems," 330–31.

77. Ong, *Ramus*, 203.

78. Ong, "Voice and the Opening of Closed Systems," 331.

79. Ong, *Ramus*, 311.

captured on visual surfaces, spatialized, linearized, hence subject to spatial, diagrammatic scrutiny.

Ramism, interacting with Humanism and Protestantism,[80] and fed by the forces of typography, provided the cultural matrix for the rise of modernity's historical, critical scholarship of the Bible. It was a generally post-Gutenberg and specifically humanistic, Ramist, and Protestant intellectualism that laid the groundwork for the philological and historical examination of the Bible, namely the print Bible.

Among key features that typify the rising philological paradigm of biblical scholarship, the following four may be cited. One, print was the medium from which the text critical, philological approach to the Bible received formative methodological habits and intellectual tools. Owing to the duplicating powers of the print medium, humanistic scholars were awash in print materials—a situation that was conducive to imagining tradition on the logic of strictly textual dynamics. By and large, intertextuality was now considered a root condition of all biblical texts. Two, biblical interpretation increasingly privileged the *sensus literalis sive historicus*, freezing the meaning of texts in their assumed historical matrix. Rather than finding the texts' rationale in their oral explication, memorization, and reception, scholars tied interpretation to the historical locus behind the texts. Three, the use of the stemmatic method locked textual versions in a tight, genealogically conceived textual diagram. Performativity was now replaced by stemmatics. Four, humanistic editors faced textual pluriformity by seeking to secure the "original" text, even though the reconstructed archetype as a rule was more often than not a virtual text that did not correspond to any historically attested textual form. It is worth speculating that the fidelity to the putative stability of the textual archetype was driven by the desire to transcend the hazards of temporality that were endemic to textual pluriformity.

These essential components of the historical, philological paradigm came to influence, indeed to define modern biblical scholarship. It is within this paradigm that most of us in academia—Jews and Catholics and Protestants alike—have been raised and educated, a paradigm, moreover, that has kept us largely uninformed about the life of biblical texts in the ancient, orally-scribally and memorially empowered tradition.

Turning to more recent developments, what comes to mind is the narrative criticism of biblical stories that got underway in the late 1960s and has

80. Pierre de la Ramée 1515–72 CE, a Huguenot convert from Catholicism, was murdered in the St. Bartholomew's Day Massacre. Joseph Julius Scaliger 1540–1609 CE, French classical scholar, eminent text critic and philologist, and one of the founding figures of the historical, critical paradigm, likewise converted to Protestantism. On Scaliger, see Grafton, *Joseph Scaliger*.

flourished ever since.[81] For many of us who had a hand in it, the exploration of the narrative nature of biblical stories was an exhilarating experience. We understood the application of narrative criticism to the Bible as liberation from a long history of ideational and historical referentiality. The old dichotomies of faith versus history, theology versus narrative, history versus fiction, and kerygma versus myth, we realized (slowly but surely), were inadequate and indeed outdated as a result of the discovery of narrative logic and narrative causalities.

However, in shifting the interpretive model from meaning-as-reference to meaning-as-narrative, biblical interpreters were inclined to adopt features of the so-called New Criticism, the very method that had prevailed roughly from the 1930s to the 1950s in Anglo-American literary criticism. In one of the best books on the literary criticism of the gospels, Stephen Moore correctly observed New Critical undercurrents in the narrative criticism of the Bible, pointing out the irony that biblical critics had embraced the creed of the holistic nature of story at a time when literary critics generally had long abandoned it.[82]

In some quarters the tendency of narrative criticism to view biblical narratives as stable, self-referential worlds came to be regarded as evidence of a self-absorbed bourgeois mentality.[83] Historically more to the point is the attempt to trace the New Criticism back to Coleridge and Kantian aesthetics. But there is a media dimension to this twentieth-century phenomenon as well. Ong has observed that the closed-model thinking characteristic of (one form of) narrative criticism was flourishing at a time in Western cultural history when the technologizing, objectivizing impact of printing had reached its peak: "nothing shows more strikingly the close, mostly unconscious, alliance between the Romantic Movement and technology."[84] Centuries of interiorization of print had made it artistically desirable and academically acceptable to view texts, including narrative texts, as autonomous object-worlds.

81. Kelber, *Mark's Story of Jesus*; Polzin, *Moses and the Deuteronomist*; Polzin, *David and the Deuteronomist*; Rhoads et al., *Mark as Story*.

82. Moore, *Literary Criticism of the Gospels*, 3–68.

83. Hawkes, *Structuralism and Semiotics*, 154–55.

84. Ong, *Orality and Literacy*, 161.

BIBLIOGRAPHY

Achtemeier, Paul. "*Omne verbum sonat*: The New Testament and the Oral Environment of Late Western Antiquity." *Journal of Biblical Literature* 109 (1990) 3–27.

Adams, Marilyn McCord. *William of Ockham*. 2 vols. Notre Dame, IN: University of Notre Dame Press, 1987.

Alexander, Elizabeth Shanks. *Transmitting Mishnah: The Shaping Influence of Oral Tradition*. Cambridge: Cambridge University Press, 2006.

Assmann, Jan. *Das kulturelle Gedächtnis. Schrift, Erinnerung und politische Identität in frühen Hochkulturen*. Munich: Beck, 1992. Translated by David Henry Wilson. *Cultural Memory and Early Civilization: Writing, Remembrance, and Political Imagination*. New York: Cambridge University Press, 2011.

Augustine. *On Christian Doctrine*. Translated by D. W. Robertson Jr. New York: Macmillan, 1958.

Barr, James. *Holy Scripture: Canon, Authority, Criticism*. Philadelphia: Westminster, 1983.

Brown, Peter. *Augustine of Hippo: A Biography*. Berkeley: University of California Press, 1967.

Burrows, Millar. *The Dead Sea Scrolls*. New York: Viking, 1955.

Carr, David M. *Writing on the Tablet of the Heart: Origins of Scripture and Literature*. Oxford: Oxford University Press, 2005.

Carruthers, Mary J. *The Book of Memory: A Study of Memory in Medieval Culture*. Cambridge Studies in Medieval Literature 10. Cambridge: Cambridge University Press, 1990.

Duffy, Eamon. *Marking the Hours: English People and their Prayers, 1240–1570*. New Haven: Yale University Press, 2006.

Eco, Umberto. *The Name of the Rose*. Translated by William Weaver. San Diego: Harcourt Brace Jovanovich, 1983.

Eisenstein, Elizabeth L. *The Printing Press as an Agent of Change*. 2 vols. Cambridge: Cambridge University Press, 1979.

Fraade, Steven D. *From Tradition to Commentary: Torah and Its Interpretation in the Madras Sifre to Deuteronomy*. SUNY Series in Judaica. Albany: State University of New York Press, 1991.

Gamble, Harry Y. *The New Testament Canon: Its Making and Meaning*. Guides to Biblical Scholarship. Philadelphia: Fortress, 1985.

Giesecke, Michael. *Der Buchdruck in der frühen Neuzeit: Eine historische Fallstudie über die Durchsetzung neuer Informations- und Kommunikationstechnologien*. Frankfurt: Suhrkamp, 1991.

Gilliard, Frank D. "More Silent Reading in Antiquity: *Non omne verbum sonat*." *Journal of Biblical Literature* 112 (1993) 689–94.

Grafton, Anthony. *Joseph Scaliger: A Study in the History of Classical Scholarship*. Oxford-Warburg Studies. 2 vols. New York: Oxford University Press, 1983–93.

Grafton, Anthony, and Megan Williams. *Christianity and the Transformation of the Book: Origen, Eusebius, and the Library of Caesarea*. Cambridge: Harvard University Press, 2006.

Hallberg, Robert von, ed. *Canons*. Chicago: University of Chicago Press, 1983.

Havelock, Eric A. *The Literate Revolution in Greece and Its Cultural Consequences*. Princeton: Princeton University Press, 1982.

Hawkes, Terence. *Structuralism and Semiotics*. New Accents. Berkeley: University of California Press, 1977.

Jaffee, Martin S. *Torah in the Mouth: Writing and Oral Tradition in Palestinian Judaism, 200 BCE–400 CE*. Oxford: Oxford University Press, 2001.

Kapr, Albert. *Johannes Gutenberg: The Man and His Invention*. Translated by Douglas Martin. Brookfield, VT: Scolar, 1996.

Kelber, Werner H. *Mark's Story of Jesus*. Philadelphia: Fortress, 1979.

Kirk, Alan. "Manuscript Tradition as *Tertium Quid*: Orality and Memory in Scribal Practices." In *Jesus, the Voice, and the Text*, edited by Tom Thatcher, 215–34. Waco, TX: Baylor University Press, 2008.

Kümmel, Werner Georg. *Introduction to the New Testament*. 14th ed. Revised and translated by A. J. Mattill. Nashville: Abingdon, 1965.

Leff, Gordon. *William of Ockham: The Metamorphosis of Scholastic Discourse*. Manchester: Manchester University Press, 1975.

Leipoldt, Johannes. *Geschichte des Neutestamentlichen Kanons*. Leipzig: Hinrichs, 1907.

Lord, Albert B. *The Singer of Tales*. Harvard Studies in Comparative Literature 24. 2nd ed. Cambridge: Harvard University Press, 2000.

Lubac, Henri de. *Exégèse médiévale: Les quatres sens de l'écriture*. 4 vols. Paris: Aubier, 1959–64.

Moore, Stephen D. *Literary Criticism of the Gospels: The Theoretical Challenge*. New Haven: Yale University Press, 1980.

Newman, Jane O. "The Word Made Print: Luther's 1522 New Testament in an Age of Mechanical Reproduction." *Representations* 11 (1985) 95–133.

Nordenfalk, Carl. *Die Spätantiken Kanontafeln*. 2 vols. Göteborg: Isacson, 1938.

Ong, Walter J. *Orality and Literacy: The Technologizing of the Word*. London: Methuen, 1982.

———. *Ramus, Method, and the Decay of Dialogue: From the Art of Discourse to the Art of Reason*. Cambridge: Harvard University Press, 1958.

———. "Technology Outside Us and Inside Us." In *Faith and Contexts*, edited by Thomas J. Farrell and Paul A. Soukup, 1:189–208. 4 vols. South Florida-Rochester-Saint Louis Studies on Religion and the Social Order 1. Atlanta: Scholars, 1992.

———. "Voice and the Opening of Closed Systems." In *Interfaces of the Word: Studies in the Evolution of Consciousness and Culture*, 305–41. Ithaca, NY: Cornell University Press, 1977.

Orr, H. Allen. Review of Philip Kitcher, *Living with Darwin: Evolution, Design, and the Future of Faith*. *New York Review of Books*, August 16, 2007, pp. 33–35.

Parker, David C. *The Living Text of the Gospels*. Cambridge: Cambridge University Press, 1997.

Polzin, Robert. *David and the Deuteronomist: 2 Samuel*. Indiana Studies in Biblical Literature. Bloomington: Indiana University Press, 1993.

———. *Moses and the Deuteronomist: A Literary Study of the Deuteronomic History*. New York: Seabury, 1980.

Rhoads, David, et al. *Mark as Story: An Introduction to the Narrative of a Gospel*. 2nd ed. Minneapolis: Fortress, 1999.

Ruppel, Aloys. *Johannes Gutenberg: sein Leben und sein Werk*. Berlin: Mann, 1939.

Saenger, Paul. "Silent Reading: Its Impact on Late Medieval Script and Society." *Viator* 13 (1982) 367–414.

Simpson, James. *Burning to Read: English Fundamentalism and Its Reformation Opponents*. Cambridge: Harvard University Press, 2007.

Stock, Brian. *The Implications of Literacy: Written Language and Models of Interpretation in the Eleventh and Twelfth Centuries*. Princeton: Princeton University Press, 1983.

Troll, Denise A. "The Illiterate Mode of Written Communication: The Work of the Medieval Scribe." In *Oral and Written Communication: Historical Approaches*, edited by Richard Leo Enos, 96–125. Written Communication Annual 4. Newbury Park, CA: Sage, 1990.

Ulrich, Eugene. *The Dead Sea Scrolls and the Origins of the Bible*. Studies in the Dead Sea Scrolls and Related Literature. Grand Rapids: Eerdmans, 1999.

Yates, Frances A. *The Art of Memory*. Chicago: University of Chicago Press, 1966.

Zahn, Theodor. *Geschichte des Neutestamentlichen Kanons*. 2 vols. Erlangen: Deichert, 1888–92.

Zumthor, Paul. *Oral Poetry: An Introduction*. Translated by Kathryn Murphy-Judy. Theory and History of Literature 70. Minneapolis: University of Minnesota Press, 1990.

8

Two Faces of the Qur'an

Qur'ān and Muṣḥaf

Angelika Neuwirth

INTRODUCTION: QUR'ĀN AND RHETORIC, *BALĀGHA*

Every prophet is given a sign that testifies to his rank as a messenger. Moses, who was sent to the Egyptians, had to convince addressees with magic. To eclipse them he had to perform a miracle, changing a rod into a snake and changing the snake back into the rod. Jesus made his appearance in an age when the most prestigious discipline was medicine; he therefore had to work a medical miracle: resurrecting the dead. Coming still later, Muhammad was sent to a people who would no longer be won by physical miracles, but—being particularly committed to rhetoric, *balāgha*—demanded a more sublime prophetic sign. Muhammad, therefore, had to present a linguistic and stylistic miracle to convince them. He presented a scripture, the *Qur'ān*.[1] This review of the prophetic missions, often evoked since the time of its first transmitter, the eighth- and ninth-century polymath al-Jāḥiẓ, seems to hit an important point in the perception of the kind of scripture the Qur'an constitutes. Although one might object to the classification of the two great messengers preceding Muhammad as professionals in magic and medicine,

1. Paraphrase of Al-Jāḥiẓ, "Hujaj an-nubuwwa." See also the summary in Pellat, *Arabische Geisteswelt*, 80.

the classification of Muhammad and the Qur'an as closely related to linguistics and rhetoric is certainly pertinent. His communication of the message is in fact the central part of his mission, unlike Moses and Jesus whose significance relies on both deeds and words. Not only by virtue of Muhammad's addressing a linguistically demanding audience should the Qur'an be acknowledged as particularly closely related to *balāgha*, but also for another reason about which the authors of the above-quoted classification were arguably less conscious. I am referring to the peculiar *iunctim* of speech and meta-speech in the Qur'an. Unframed by any narrative scenario, the entire Qur'an is speech as such. Qur'anic speech, moreover, is not limited to the oral communication of a message to listeners, but is often a metadiscourse, a speech about speech, a comment on the Qur'anic message itself, or on the speech of others. The Qur'an—so one might summarize the classifications of prophets related above—was sent down not in an age where amazement could be aroused by extraordinary deeds, but where a speaker successfully confronted and vanquished another, eclipsing the argument of the other in what in Islamic theology would later term *iʿjāz,* meaning to "render the other rhetorically impotent." That age was neither an age of magic, nor of science, but an age of exegesis. The Qur'an accordingly presents itself as a highly rhetorical and often metatextual document that reflects an ongoing debate.

In light of these considerations, the problem underlying the present crisis in Western Qur'anic scholarship—the seemingly unbridgeable divide between a traditional position that regards the Qur'an as the literary outcome of a prophetic mission in Mecca and Medina during the first half of the seventh century CE, and a skeptical position that ascribes its compilation to a later syncretistic Mesopotamian community[2]—appears to reflect a mistaken premise, very much like the problem that tormented the customs inspector in the famous Tijuana anecdote:

> Every day for thirty years a man drove a wheelbarrow full of sand over the Tijuana border crossing. The customs inspector dug through the sand each morning but could not discover any contraband. He remained, of course, convinced that he was dealing with a smuggler. On the day of his retirement from the service, he asked the smuggler to reveal what it was that he was smuggling and how he had been doing so. "Wheelbarrows; I've been smuggling wheelbarrows, of course."[3]

2. For the state of Qur'anic studies, see Neuwirth, Marx, et al., *The Qur'ān in Context.*

3. Boyarin, *Border Lines*, 1.

I mention this humorous anecdote to argue that what Qur'anic scholars should be looking for is not the whereabouts of a literary compilation called "Qur'ān," let alone asking "What the Qur'an really says," but should instead be looking at the Qur'anic text as a "medium of transport," triggering and reflecting a communication. The Qur'an in its emergent phase is not a pre-meditated, fixed compilation, a reified literary artifact, but a still-mobile text reflecting an oral theological-philosophical debate between diverse interlocutors of various late antique denominations. It is a text that first of all demands to be read as a drama involving multiple protagonists. What is demanded is a change in focus from the exclusive perception of a reified codex to a still-fluid pre-canonical text that can provide a solution to the historical problems that Qur'anic scholarship addresses.

To understand this perspective, we need to remember that the Qur'anic age roughly coincides with the epoch when the great exegetical corpora of monotheist tradition were edited and published, such as the two *Talmudim* in Judaism and the patristic writings in Christianity. These writings, not the Bible, as is often held, are the literary counterparts of the Qur'an. Daniel Boyarin repeatedly stresses that the Talmud is—no less than the writings of the Church fathers—imbued with Hellenistic rhetoric.[4] Indeed, the Qur'an should be understood first and foremost as exegetical, that is, polemical-apologetical, and thus highly rhetorical. The Qur'an is communicated to listeners whose education already comprises biblical and post-biblical lore, whose nascent scripture therefore should provide answers to the questions raised in biblical exegesis—a scripture providing commentary on a vast amount of earlier theological legacies.

This thesis contradicts the dominant views in present Qur'anic scholarship. More often than not, the Qur'an is considered as a text preconceived, so to speak, by an author, identified in Western scholarship with Muhammad, or anonymous compilers, a text that was fixed and canonized somewhat later to constitute a liturgical manual and a religious guide for the Muslim community. This view reflects Islamic tradition, which equally regards the Qur'an as an auctorial text. Islamic tradition, however, does distinguish between the (divinely) "authored Book," labeled *al-muṣḥaf,* as the canonical codex, and the Qur'anic communication process, labeled *al-qur'ān.* Yet the hermeneutical predominance of the Qur'an's perception as *muṣḥaf* in Islamic tradition is hard to deny. The shift from the "original," that is, intra-Qur'anic concept of *qur'ān,* to the post-Muhammadan concept of *muṣḥaf* is, of course, due to the event of canonization, which reconfigured the text from a historical document into a timeless symbol. Aziz al-Azmeh has shown that texts become detemporalized through canonization, their

4. Ibid.

single units being considered indiscriminate in terms of chronology;[5] instead—so we have to add—they become amalgamated with myth, turning into testimonies of the foundational myth of their communities.

The core of this paper will focus on the Qur'an not as the fixed corpus it became after the death of the Prophet, *al-muṣḥaf*, but as a chain of oral communications conveyed to the Meccan and the Medinan community, whose expectations and religious background are reflected in the Qur'anic texts. Following Daniel Madigan,[6] I claim that the oral character of the communication during the Prophet's lifetime was never substituted by a written text—not because the ongoing revelation process stood in the way of codification but rather because the emerging conviction was that the Word of God is not accessible to humans except through oral communication. To highlight the notion of *qur'ān* in the sense of "oral communication," I first will briefly survey the hermeneutical implications of a Qur'anic reading as either *muṣḥaf* or *qur'ān*. Then I will vindicate the claim that orality in the Qur'an is not limited to its function as a mediality but successively acquires the dimension of a theologumenon (that is, a conviction shared by the speaker and his audience). This will be demonstrated by tracing the strategies that the Qur'an applies to justify its essentially oral character as a legitimate scriptural manifestation and to challenge the rival concept of codified scripture. The third part focuses on literary devices that serve as markers of Qur'anic orality. Finally, I will analyze an example of the Qur'anic "rereading" of earlier monotheistic traditions as an oral and public procedure.

QUR'ĀN VERSUS MUṢḤAF

The study of the Qur'an as a post-canonical, closed text (that is, the text established after the death of the prophet, which was codified a few decades later and acknowledged as unchangeable), accessible only through the lens of traditional Islamic exegesis, is a legitimate task for elucidating the community's understanding of the Qur'an. It is an anachronistic approach, however, when it is applied—as it tacitly often is—to investigate the formation of the Qur'anic message, that is, the dynamics of its textual growth and diverse changes in orientation during the oral communication phase of the Qur'an. To evaluate the Qur'an historically one has to be aware of

5. Al-Azmeh, "Chronophagous Discourse." Although in exegesis a rough grid ascribing the texts to particular "situations of revelation" (*asbāb al-nuzūl*) has been laid over the text whose single units are more generally divided into Meccan and Medinan, this does not prevent readers from applying a purely synchronic approach when explaining texts through others.

6. Madigan, *The Qur'ān's Self-image*.

the reconfiguration that the prophetic communication underwent in its redaction and canonization: whereas the single units (suras) collected in the *muṣḥaf* are juxtaposed, constituting a sort of anthology, the oral communications build dynamically on each other, later ones often rethinking earlier ones, sometimes even inscribing themselves into earlier texts. Thus there is ample intertextuality to be observed between suras absent from the *muṣḥaf*, where the chronological order of the suras is no longer evident and the tension produced by dialectic interactions between texts is extinguished.[7] But Qur'anic texts viewed as communications also refer to extratextual evidence, to unspoken intertexts, so to speak, drawing on the discourses that were debated in the listeners' circles. These fell silent once the text was turned from a dramatic polyphonic communication into a monolithic divine account. The oral Qur'an (to use a loose expression) may be compared to a telephone conversation where the speech of only one party is audible, yet the unheard speech of the other is roughly deducible from the audible one. Indeed, the social concerns and theological questions of the listeners are widely reflected in the Qur'an text pronounced by the Prophet's voice. To approach the text as a historical document thus would demand the researcher to investigate Muhammad's growing and changing public, listeners who belonged to a late antique urban milieu, many of whom must have been aware of and perhaps involved in the theological debates among Jews, Christians, and others in the seventh century.

When studying the Qur'an from a literary perspective, it is even more perilous to use the two manifestations of the text indistinctly. In view of their generic differences, both would require different methodologies: the communication process comes closest to a drama, whereas the *muṣḥaf* presents itself as a divine monologue, in generic terms, a kind of a hagiographic account. The theory of drama that distinguishes between an exterior and an interior "level of communication" best illustrates the relation between canonized text and the communication process.[8] On the exterior level, which in literary texts is occupied by the author of the printed dramatic text and his readers, the *muṣḥaf* authored by God addresses the readers of the written Qur'an. Against that, on the interior level—in literary texts occupied by the performers of the drama who are observed acting—the speaker, Muhammad, and his listeners are interacting. This scenario demands that a number of extra-semantic signs, such as rhetoric and structure, be taken into consideration.[9] The divine voice here acts as a further protagonist speaking continuously to the Prophet, seldom directly to the listeners, but

7. Neuwirth, "Erzählen als kanonischer Prozess."

8. Pfister, *Das Drama*.

9. Neuwirth, "Zur Struktur der Yusuf-Sure."

the voice permanently stages the various scenarios of the prophet-listeners-interaction through speaking about the listeners, thus acting as a kind of invisible stage director or as a sort of reporter. Looking back once again to the exterior level, the *muṣḥaf*, the divine voice has merged with that of the Prophet to become the narrator, whereas the interacting audience has disappeared from the stage completely, to become mere objects of the sole speaker's speech. These two scenarios of the Qur'an—as a communication process and as a scriptural codex—are thus essentially different and consequently demand methodologies of their own.

STRATEGIES OF VINDICATING SCRIPTURAL ORALITY

Returning to the thesis that the orality of the Qur'anic message, rather than being a pragmatic medial option, amounts to no less than a basic theologumenon, let us look at the Qur'anic strategies of vindicating scriptural orality as an appropriate manifestation of the divine word. The Qur'an, not unlike the other Scriptures, originated from a vast body of heterogeneous traditions current in its geographical context, a selection of which, answering to the needs of an emerging community, crystallized into a Scripture in its own right. What is characteristic of the Qur'an, however, is its emergence from a milieu in which the phenomenon of Scripture, materialized in written codices, was already familiar. As Nicolai Sinai has lucidly demonstrated, it is in confrontation with the Judeo-Christian notions of scripturality that the developing Qur'an had to stake its own claim to authority.[10] What is striking here is that the Qur'an did not subscribe to the concept of a written manifestation of scripture but established a new image, that of an "oral scripture"; in William Graham's words, "The Qur'an has always been pre-eminently an oral, not a written text."[11] Daniel Madigan justly claims that "nothing about the *Qur'ān* suggests that it conceives of itself as identical with the *kitāb* (the celestial book),"[12] that is to say the Qur'an in no phase of its development strove to become a closed scriptural corpus. This claim to "an ontological difference between the recitations and their transcendent source,"[13] however, presupposes that two conditions be fulfilled, and these can only be traced through diachronic investigations that Madigan has avoided. First, it requires an awareness of the essentially oral character of the emerging Qur'an

10. Sinai, "Qur'ānic Self-Referentiality."
11. Graham, "Orality," 584.
12. Cited in Sinai, "Qur'ānic Self-Referentiality," 115.
13. Sinai, "Qur'ānic Self-Referentiality," 109.

as its entelechy, irrespective of the occasional employment of writing for its memorization. Second, it requires a set of arguments to justify the striking absence from the Qur'an of the conventional paraphernalia surrounding the revealed Word of God in the neighboring religions.

Sinai has observed that in the earliest suras the divine origins, let alone the scriptural source of the Qur'anic recitations, are not indicated. Obviously it took some time before the claim to revelation that is implicit in the use of the prophetic address "you" was translated into a consistent rhetoric of divine address, so as to raise the problem of its relationship to written models.[14] In view of the Qur'anic beginnings this is no surprise. The early suras on closer examination reveal themselves as rereadings of the Psalms.[15] They clearly reflect the language of the Psalms not only in terms of the poetical form (short poetic verses), but equally in terms of their imagery and the liturgical attitude of their speaker. This thesis is unaffected by the absence of early translations of the Psalms into Arabic, since the Psalm corpus, contrary to the other biblical books, was used primarily in liturgy, being recited by heart so that complete or at least partial texts rendered in a more or less verbal form thus may have been current through oral transmission. Though the early suras cannot be considered faithful paraphrases of individual Psalms, early suras and Psalms alike are unique in expressing the mood of their speaker articulated in close communication with the divine Other.

The step toward establishing an agency of authority in the texts was taken only at a later stage, although still in early Mecca, arguably in response to a challenge from outside. This is evident from verses like Q 69:41–42:[16]

> *Wa-mā huwa bi-qawli shā'irin—qalīlan mā tu'minūn*
> *wa-lā bi-qawli kāhinin qulīlan mā tadhakkarūn*
>
> It is the speech of a noble messenger, it is not the speech of a poet—little do you believe.
> Nor the speech of a soothsayer—little do you remember.

A perceived misinterpretation of the recitations' literary genre involving a particular mode of inspiration is corrected through appeal to their divine origin (Q 69:43):[17]

14. Ibid.

15. Neuwirth, "Psalmen."

16. Arberry, trans., *The Koran Interpreted*, ii, 298. See further the discussion in Sinai, "Qur'ānic Self-Referentiality," 111.

17. Arberry, trans., *The Koran Interpreted*, ii, 298.

tanzīlun min rabbi l-'ālamīn

A sending down from the Lord of all being

Sinai in his attempt to explain the Qur'an's contrasting of poetry/soothsaying with "revelation" focuses on the issue of literary genre:[18]

> The recitations' literary novelty . . . engendered different attempts at categorization among their audience not so much out of sheer curiosity, but rather because assigning them to a textual genre was a pre-condition for grasping their communicative intent. Muhammad's recitations in defining themselves as *tadhkira*—"reminder"—or *dhikr*—"warning"—or as *tanzīl*—"revelation"—take up a discussion which had initially been conducted outside the Qur'ān. The meta-level debate is thus interiorized, as it were.

Although the salient point in my view here is the need to reject a particular—inferior—source of inspiration rather than a non-pertinent literary genre, it is certainly true that "Qur'ānic self-referentiality must accordingly be understood as gradually emerging from a process of discussion with an audience, the expectations and convictions of which had to be convincingly addressed" (*idem*). The recitations' engagement with their audience is of course evident from the strikingly dialectical structure of many early suras, as noted by Jane McAuliffe:[19]

> The often argumentative or polemical tone of the Qur'ān strikes even the most casual readers . . . The operative voice in any given pericope, whether it be that of God or Muhammad or of another protagonist, regularly addresses actual or implicit antagonists.

The importance of such interactions as a formative factor in the emergence of the Qur'an's form and content is evident.

Let us now turn to the Qur'anic engagement with the problem of its non-written form and, moreover, the missing scriptural paraphernalia. As Madigan observes, the basic challenge for any interpretation of the term *kitāb* consists in the fact that the Qur'an claims to be "of a piece with carefully guarded, lavishly appointed, and scrupulously copied sacred codices and scrolls, while itself remaining open-ended, unwritten, and at the mercy of frail human memory."[20] This tension, according to Sinai, can be explained

18. Sinai, "Qur'ānic Self-Referentiality," 111.

19. McAuliffe, "Debate," 163.

20. Madigan, *The Qur'ān's Self-image*, 45, cited in Sinai, "Qur'ānic Self-Referentiality," 113.

as resulting "from a need to balance the obvious situatedness of Muhammad's recitation with a strategic interest in imparting to them the glow of scripturality that was felt, by his audience, to be an indispensable concomitant of genuine revelation."[21] Equally the appeal to an archetypal celestial book—an issue that I will turn to presently—may have been propelled by polemics.

As often quoted, the most explicit reproach made by Muhammad's opponents is the question posed in Q 25:32: "Why was the Qur'an not sent down to him as a single complete pronouncement—*jumlatan wāḥidatan*?"[22] The incompleteness and situatedness of the communications obviously were viewed by the audience as a deficiency that set them apart from conventional manifestations of the Word of God and thus needed to be compensated by additional credentials more in line with the familiar models. These of course had to be related to writing, since revelation in Jewish and Christian contexts was bound to the concept of a written scripture.

Should the fact that some early suras of the Qur'anic revelations are credited with an indirect participation in literacy be related to this expectation of the listeners? There is a cluster of early suras that establish a relation to the celestial book. Thus in Q 80:11–16 the Qur'anic communications are presented as being emanations, or excerpts, from the celestial ur-text:

kallā innahu tadhkirah
fa-man shā'a dhakarah
fī ṣuḥufin mukarramah
marfūʿatin muṭahharah
bi-aydī safarah
kirāmin bararah[23]

No indeed; it is a reminder
—And who so wills, shall remember it—
Upon pages high-honored,
Uplifted, purified,
By the hands of scribes, noble, pious.

The heavenly source of the Qur'anic communication is elsewhere labeled "tablet" (Q 85:22)—a reference to the Book of Jubilees—and somewhat

21. Sinai, "Qur'ānic Self-Referentiality," 114.

22. Unless otherwise noted, all translations are by the author.

23. Cf. Q 85:21–22: *bal huwa qur'ānun majīd fī lawḥin maḥfuẓ* and Q 56:77–80: *innahu la-qur'ānun karīm fī kitābin maknūn lā yamassuhu illā l-muṭahharūn tanzīlun min rabbi l-ʿālamīn.*

later, in Middle Mecca, even "mother of the book," *umm al-kitāb* (Q 43:4). Sinai justly claims that these verses "posit a transcendent source document, participation in which is supposed to invest Muhammad's recitations with a mediated kind of scripturality." He comments:[24]

> The manoeuvre clearly serves to accommodate both the Qur'ān's orality and situatedness, which could not very well be denied, and the prevailing assumption that when God addresses man, writing somehow has to come into play. Yet contrary to audience expectations, the *kitāb* is placed out of human reach, and is said to be accessible only in the shape of the oral recitations delivered to Muhammad. To a certain extent then pre-existing assumptions of the audience are embraced, yet at the same time are subjected to a profound reconfiguration.

Although I share his conviction regarding the continuous impact of the audience on the configuration of the emerging Qur'an, I would like to attribute some of the driving force behind the foregrounding of the transcendent Scripture to the important role played by the Book of Jubilees in the thinking of the community. That apocryphal text[25] had retained a strong influence on Judeo-Christianity and was in no way absent from the scenario of late antique theological debate. It is reflected in several early suras and can plausibly be considered a source of inspiration in the Qur'anic relocation of the written Word of God exclusively in the transcendent sphere. Still, the ongoing debate with opponents cannot be overestimated. And it is this debate that should have propelled the promotion of the factual orality of the Qur'anic communications to become a Qur'anic theologumenon.

Once more back to *al-kitāb*: what is the relation between the performed *qur'ān* and the celestial *kitāb*? Post-canonical thinking, of course, holds that both are identical. It is, however, striking to observe that in some middle and late Meccan texts *kitāb* and *qur'ān* are carefully kept distinct. A few remarks concerning the background may be in place here. It is in middle and late Mecca that the earlier undetermined sura structures develop into a structurally distinct shape: the tripartite sura. This composition—analogous to the structure of ecclesiastical and synagogal services—presents a biblical story as its core part, framing it by more dialogical initial and final parts, entailing polemics/apologetics, or else hymns and affirmations of the rank of the communication as a revelation.[26] These suras attest to a new *Sitz im Leben*, a new social-liturgical function. It is here that the reference to *al-kitāb* is

24. Sinai, "Qur'ānic Self-Referentiality," 114.

25. Cf. Najman, "Jubilees."

26. Neuwirth, "Vom Rezitationstext über die Liturgie zum Kanon."

reserved for the biblical accounts in particular, figuring in the center of the triad. Later the dichotomy between (biblical) recollections from the *kitāb* and other kinds of Qur'anic communications is loosened: *al-kitāb* becomes the designation of a celestial mode of storage, whereas *qur'ān* points to its earthly performance. Yet in terms of form both are never deemed identical: the excerpts from the *kitāb* are not received by the Prophet unaltered but have in the course of the transmission process been adapted to the specific needs of the recipients. Sinai emphasizes the importance of this difference that the Qur'an itself recognizes as a peculiarity, conceiving it as a hermeneutical code, so to speak; it even receives a technical designation: *tafṣīl*.[27] The *locus classicus* for this perception is Q 41:2f.:

> *tanzīlun min al-raḥmāni r-raḥīm*
> *kitābun fuṣṣilat āyātuhu qurʾānan ʿarabiyyan li-qawmin yaʿlamūn.*
>
> A sending down from the Merciful, the Compassionate
> A book whose signs have been distinguished [or "adapted"] as an Arabic Koran, for a people having knowledge.[28]

The heavenly *kitāb* is coded as an Arabic recitation—not implying, however, that it was necessarily composed in Arabic from eternity on.[29] This means that even biblical stories that are ascribed to *al-kitāb* do not involve the claim to verbal quotations from the celestial source, but *de facto* constitute a kind of paraphrase adapted to the listeners' scope. This observation equally throws light on the fact—often considered irritating—that in the Qur'an individual stories are told more than once and presented in different versions. In the light of the hermeneutics of *tafṣīl* these are to be considered as subsequent renderings of a particular *kitāb*-pericope, repeatedly rephrased and adapted to the changing communal situation. Sinai concludes:

> From the Qur'ānic perspective, therefore, the celestial scripture cannot be given to man in any other shape than *mufaṣṣalan* Q 6:114. The *kitāb* is partially accessible, but never available, it can

27. Sinai, "Qur'ānic Self-Referentiality," 121.

28. Arberry, trans., *The Koran Interpreted*, ii, 185.

29. Sinai, "Qur'ānic Self-Referentiality," 121, explains, "Elsewhere, in Q 10.37 too, this *qur'ān* is qualified as *tafṣīl al-kitāb*, a sequence of excerpts or interpretative renderings from the celestial book. In a number of passages from Mecca II and III the *kitāb* and *qur'ān* are clearly distinguished. The transformation process leading from one entity to the other being labeled as *tafṣīl*." Sinai stresses that "a *tafṣīl* of something must always target a specific audience in a specific situation. Q 41.44 *wa-law ja'alnāhu qur'ānan a'jamiyyan la-qālū law lā fuṣṣilat āyātuhu* provides additional evidence for this. If the recitations had not been in Arabic, they would not have been properly adapted to their intended audience."

> be tapped via divine revelation, but due to the need to tailor such revelations to a specific target audience, the *kitāb* as such is at no one's disposal, not even in the form of literal excerpts.[30]

At this stage, orality has acquired the dimension of a Qur'anic theologumenon.

MARKERS OF ORALITY

Proportions

Having discussed the development of orality as a Qur'anic theologumenon, let us now turn to some of the textual characteristics that strikingly point to the oral composition of the text. The most technically evident of these are quantitative regularities between verse groups that often amount to clear and certainly intended proportions.[31]

Since the sensational hypothesis presented by David Heinrich Müller claiming a strophic composition for the suras was dismissed without further scrutiny by subsequent scholarship,[32] the possibility that "a firm hand was in full control" of the composition and structure of individual suras has been virtually excluded. Against this view, structures do become clearly discernible beneath the surface through micro-structural analysis.[33] These structures mirror a historical development. Particularly in the early short suras, distinctive verse groups can be isolated that often form part of clear-cut patterns of proportions. Thus, Q 75 is built on the following balanced verse groups: 6 + 6 + 6 + 6 + 5 + 5 + 5; Q 70 is made up of 6 + 7+ 7 + 7 + 7 + 9; Q 79 entails two groups of nine verses, its proportions being strikingly balanced 5 + 9 / 6 + 6 + 6 / 9 + 5; Q 51 is made up of groups of 9 + 14 + 14 + 9 + 7 + 7 verses. Similar cases are found in many of those early Meccan suras that exceed some ten verses, proportions being obviously a mnemonic device required when memorization without written support was demanded from the listeners.

Clausulas[34]

At a certain stage of the Middle Meccan period, verses that have become longer, exceeding two-sentence structures, cease to be marked by expressive

30. Sinai, "Qur'ānic Self-Referentiality," 126.
31. Neuwirth, *Studien zur Komposition der mekkanischen Suren.*
32. Müller, *Die Propheten in ihrer ursprünglichen Form.*
33. Neuwirth, *Studien zur Komposition der mekkanischen Suren.*
34. See further Neuwirth, *Studien zur Komposition der mekkanischen Suren.*

and frequently changing rhyme formulas. Verses now start to display a more simple rhyme, mostly following the stereotypical -*ūn*, -*īn*-pattern that would hardly suffice to fulfill the listeners' anticipation of a resounding end to the verse. A new mnemonic-technical device is utilized to solve the problem. This device is the rhymed phrase, a syntactically stereotyped colon that is distinguished from its context insomuch as it does not partake in the main strain of the discourse but presents a kind of moral comment on it, such as in the case of Joseph's brothers' plea, "Give us full measure and be charitable with us," which is commented on with the statement "Truly God will repay the charitable" (*Fa-awfi lanā l-kayla wa-taṣaddaq ʿalaynā inna llāha yajzī l-mutaṣaddiqin.* Q 12:88). Or else the clausula refers to divine omnipotence and providence, such as in the case of Muhammad's night journey: *Subḥāna lladhī asrā bi-ʿabdihi laylan* [. . .] *li-nuriyahu min āyātinā innahu huwa l-samīʿu l-baṣīr.* Q 17:1, "Glory be to Him who carried His servant by night . . . that we might show him some of our signs," which is commented on with the clausula: "He is the All-hearing, the All-seeing." An elaborate classification of the rhymed phrases has shown that the clausulas display a large number of divine predicates. Although it is true that not all multipartite verses bear such formulaic endings but occasionally contain ordinary short sentences in the position of the last colon, clausula verses still may be considered a characteristic developed in the late Meccan period and present in later verses. Clausulas serve to turn the often-narrative discourse of the extended suras into paraenetic appeals, thus immediately supporting the communication of their theological message. In this manner they betray a novel narrative pact between the speaker and his audience, the consciousness that there is a basic consensus on human moral behavior as well as on the image of God as a powerful agent in human interaction, a consciousness that has of course been reached only after an extended process of the community's education.

THE EXEGETICAL QUR'AN: *SŪRAT AL-IKHLĀṢ* AS AN EXAMPLE

Let us finally turn to an example of the Qur'anic absorption of earlier traditions that were orally transmitted in its milieu and—appropriated by the Qur'anic community—emerged in a new shape that however still re-sounds their pre-Qur'anic acoustic and rhetorical shape. One of the core texts of the Qur'an, the creed articulated in *sūrat al-ikhlāṣ* (112), the "pure belief," is celebrated in Islam as a textual, visual, and acoustic icon of unity (Arberry, trans.):

Qul huwa llāhu aḥad / Allāhu ṣ-ṣamad / lam yalid wa-lam yūlad / wa-lam yakun lahu kufuwan aḥad.

Say: He is God, one / God the absolute / He did not beget, nor is He begotten / And there is none like Him.

The short text unit, made up of succinct verses with a proper end-rhyme, would, on first sight, fit into the pattern of the neatly constructed poetical early Meccan suras were it not for the introductory "*qul*," "say," that is characteristic of later—more discursive—texts. Indeed, upon closer examination, the text is not as monolithic as it appears. It is hard to ignore the way verse 1—"Say, God is One"; *qul huwa llāhu aḥad*—echoes the Jewish credo "Hear Israel, the Lord, our God, is One"; *Shema' Yisrā'ēl, adōnay ēlōhēnū adōnay eḥad.* It is striking that the Jewish text remains audible in the Qur'anic version, which—against grammatical norms—adopts the Hebrew-sounding noun *aḥad* instead of the more pertinent adjective *wāḥid* for the rhyme. This "ungrammaticality" should not go unnoticed. I refer here to Michael Riffaterre, who coined the notion of the "ungrammaticality," meaning the awkwardness of a textual moment that semiotically points to another text which provides a key to its decoding. The particular kind of ungrammaticality that is operating in our text can be identified with Riffaterre's "dual sign." To quote Riffaterre:[35]

> The dual sign works like a pun . . . It is first apprehended as a mere ungrammaticality, until the discovery is made that there is another text in which the word is grammatical; the moment the other text is identified, the dual sign becomes significant purely because of its shape, which alone alludes to that other code.

The Jewish text, as we saw, remains audible in the Qur'anic version. Why? This striking translingual quotation is certainly not without function. It is part of a negotiation strategy: to appropriate the Jewish credo by making it universal and thus acceptable to a non-Jewish audience by underscoring that difference, addressing not Israel but any believer. This kind of exegetical correction is a modification that the Qur'an applies to numerous earlier traditions. Yet the audible resonance of the earlier text seems to be a clear oral address to Jewish listeners in particular; the text might thus additionally entail a strategy to bridge the gap between the Qur'anic and the Jewish communities.

But, as the following table shows, the sura refers to more than one earlier credo:

35. Riffaterre, *Semiotics of Poetry*, 92.

Nicano-Constantinopolitanum		Deuteronomium 6,4		Qur'an, Sura 112 (al-Ikhlāṣ)	
We believe in one God,	Πιστεύομεν εἰς ἕνα Θεὸν	Hear, Israel, the Lord is our God, the Lord is One.	שְׁמַע יִשְׂרָאֵל: יְהוָה אֱלֹהֵינוּ, יְהוָה אֶחָד	Say: He is God, one,	قُلْ هُوَ اللّٰهُ أَحَدٌ
the Father **Almighty**, Maker of heaven and earth, and of all things visible and invisible	Πατέρα παντοκράτορα ποιητὴν οὐρανοῦ καὶ γῆς ὁρατῶν τε πάντων καὶ ἀοράτων			God, the absolute,	اللّٰهُ الصَّمَدُ
And in one Lord Jesus Christ, **the only-begotten Son of God, begotten of the Father** before all worlds (aeons), Light of Light, very God of very God, **begotten not made**	καὶ εἰς ἕνα Κύριον Ἰησοῦν Χριστὸν τὸν υἱὸν τοῦ Θεοῦ τὸν Μονογενῆ, τὸν ἐκ τοῦ Πατρὸς γεννηθέντα πρὸ πάντων τῶν αἰώνων, Φῶς ἐκ Φωτός, Θεὸν ἀληθινὸν ἐκ Θεοῦ ἀληθινοῦ, γεννηθέντα οὐ ποιηθέντα,			**He did not beget, nor is He begotten,**	لَمْ يَلِدْ وَلَمْ يُولَدْ
being of one substance with the Father;	ὁμοούσιον τῷ Πατρί,			**And there is none like Him.**	وَلَمْ يَكُن لَّهُ كُفُوًا أَحَدٌ

Verse 3—"He did not beget nor is he begotten"; *lam yalid wa-lam yūlad*—is a reverse echo of the Nicene creed; it rejects the emphatic affirmation of Christ's sonship—begotten, not made; *gennêthenta, ou poiêthenta*—by a no less emphatic double negation. A negative theology is established through the inversion of a locally familiar religious text. This negative theology is summed up in verse 4—"And there is none like Him"; *wa-lam yakun lahu kufuwan aḥad.* The verse that introduces a Qur'anic *hapax legomenon*, *kufuwun*, "equal in rank," to render the core concept of *homoousios*, not only inverts the Nicene formula of Christ's being of one substance with God—*homoousios to patri*—but also forbids thinking of any being as equal in substance with God, let alone a son.[36]

Although these verses negate the essential statement of the Nicene creed, they nevertheless "translate" the Greek/Syriac intertext, adopting its rhetorical strategy of *intensification*. The Nicene wording first emphatically denies Christ's being made, "begotten, not made," and then goes on to top that verdict by proclaiming his equality in nature with the Father, *homoousios to patri*, "being of one substance with the Father." In the Qur'an, the no less emphatic *exclusion* of the idea of sonship and fatherhood alike—*lam yalid wa-lam yūlad*, "he did not beget, nor is he begotten"—is likewise "topped" by a universal negation stating that there is no way to think of a being equal with God: *wa-lam yakun lahu kufuwan aḥad.* Again the pre-text is audible in the final version.

Rhetorically, again, this text echoes the earlier Christian wording. Verses 3 and 4 are certainly not primarily a polemic address to Christians, but, raising more general claims, have become part of an integral new text, a universalist monotheistic creed. That text is a composite counter-text to two powerful earlier texts, the creeds of both the Jews and the Christians, that can both still be "heard" re-sounding through the new Arabic rhetorical shape. A cultural translation has taken place, brought about most immediately by oral communication and continuing to rely for its effectiveness on the still-audible rhetorical matrix of both the Jewish and the Christian tradition. What for Islamic tradition has become an icon of unity reveals itself in the pre-canonical Qur'an as living speech—a suggestive example of the Qur'an's oral and at the same time exegetical nature.

36. I am making use of Greek quotations here for the sake of simplicity, Greek being more familiar to present readers than Syriac. I am of course aware that the creed may have been current in the Syriac language.

BIBLIOGRAPHY

Arberry, Arthur J. *The Koran Interpreted: A Translation*. London: Oxford University Press, 1964.

al-Azmeh, Aziz. "Chronophagous Discourse: A Study of Clerico-Legal Appropriation of the World in an Islamic Tradition." In *Religion and Practical Reason: New Essays in the Comparative Philosophy of Religions*, edited by Frank E. Reynolds and David Tracy, 163–211. Albany: State University of New York Press, 1994.

Boyarin, Daniel. *Border Lines: The Partition of Judaeo-Christianity*. Philadelphia: University of Pennsylvania Press, 2004.

Graham, William A. "Orality." In *The Encyclopedia of the Qur'ān*, edited by Jane D. McAuliffe, 3:584–87. Leiden: Brill, 2003.

Al-Jāḥiẓ. "Hujaj an-nubuwwa." In *Rasā'il Al-Jāḥiẓ*, edited by 'Abd al-Salām Muḥammad Hārūn, 3:221–81. Cairo, 1979.

Madigan, Daniel A. *The Qur'ān's Self-image: Writing and Authority in Islam's Scripture*. Princeton: Princeton University Press, 2001.

McAuliffe, Jane D. "'Debate with Them in a Better Way': The Construction of a Qur'anic Commonplace." In *Myths, Historical Archetypes, and Symbolic Figures in Arabic Literature: Towards a New Hermeneutic Approach*, edited by Angelika Neuwirth et al., 163–88. Beiruter Texte und Studien 64. Stuttgart: Steiner, 1999.

Müller, David Henrich. *Die Propheten in ihrer ursprünglichen Form: Die Grundgesetze der ursemitischen Poesie, erschlossen und nachgewiesen in Bibel, Keilschriften und Koran und in ihren Wirkungen erkannt in den Chören der griechischen Tragiker*. 2 vols. Vienna: Hölder, 1896.

Najman, Hindy. "Interpretation as Primordial Writing: Jubilees and its Authority Conferring Strategies." *Journal for the Study of Judaism* 30 (1999) 179–210.

Neuwirth, Angelika. "Erzählen als kanonischer Prozess: Die Mose-Erzählung im Wandel der koranischen Geschichte." In *Islamstudien ohne Ende: Festschrift für Werner Ende zum 65. Geburtstag*, edited by Rainer Brunner et al., 323–44. Abhandlungen für die Kunde des Morgenlandes 54. Würzburg: Ergon, 2002.

———. "Psalmen—im Koran neu gelesen (Ps 104 und 136)." In "*Im vollen Licht der Geschichte*"*: Die Wissenschaft des Judentums und die Anfänge der kritischen Koranforschung*, edited by Dirk Hartwig et al., 157–90. Ex oriente lux 8. Würzburg: Ergon, 2008.

———. *Studien zur Komposition der mekkanischen Suren. Die literarische Form des Koran—ein Zeugnis seiner Historizität?* 2nd ed. Studien zur Geschichte und Kultur des islamischen Orients 10. Berlin: de Gruyter, 2007.

———. "Vom Rezitationstext über die Liturgie zum Kanon: Zu Entstehung und Wiederauflösung der Surenkomposition im Verlauf der Entwicklung eines islamischen Kultus." In *The Qur'an as Text*, edited by Stefan Wild, 69–106. Islamic Philosophy, Theology, and Science 27. Leiden: Brill, 1996.

———. "Zur Struktur der Yusuf-Sure." In *Studien aus Arabistik und Semitistik: Anton Spitaler zum 70. Geburtstag von seinen Schülern überreicht*, edited by Werner Diem and Stefan Wild, 123–52. Wiesbaden: Harrassowitz, 1980.

Pellat, Charles. *Arabische Geisteswelt: Ausgewählte und übersetzte Texte von Al-Gahiz (777–869)*. Translated by Walter W. Müller. Die Bibliothek des Morgenlandes 12. Zurich: Artemis, 1967.

Pfister, Manfred. *Das Drama. Theorie und Analyse*. 8th ed. Information und Synthese 3. Munich: Fink, 1994.

Riffaterre, Michael. *Semiotics of Poetry*. Advances in Semiotics. Bloomington: Indiana University Press, 1978.

Sinai, Nicolai. "Qur'ānic Self-Referentiality as a Strategy of Self-Authorization." In *Self-Referentiality in the Qur'ān*, edited by Stefan Wild, 103–34. Diskurse der Arabistik 11. Wiesbaden: Harrassowitz, 2006.

Sinai, Nicolai, and Angelika Neuwirth. "Introduction." In *The Qur'ān in Context: Historical and Literary Investigations into the Qur'ānic Milieu*, edited by Angelika Neuwirth et al., 1–26. Texts and Studies on the Qur'ān 6. Leiden: Brill, 2010.

9

Biblical Performance Criticism

Performance as Research

David Rhoads

Traditionally, scholars have studied the writings of the New Testament by reading them silently and in private. For centuries, we scholars have been treating these scriptures as "writings"—written to be studied and interpreted as manuscripts, written to be broken up into episodes and verses for scholarly analysis. We have been dealing with them as if they originated as part of a *print* culture. But this is not at all how the early Christians of the first century experienced the writings in the context of the oral cultures of the ancient Mediterranean world. It is the thesis of this paper that the contents of the writings that comprise the New Testament were originally composed and experienced orally. As such, the New Testament writings ought to be treated as remnants of *oral events*. That is, we need to study the writings of the New Testament as (trans)scripts of performances in an oral culture.

THE NEW TESTAMENT AS ORAL LITERATURE

Treating the New Testament writings as oral literature is a "paradigm shift" that has enormous implications for the entire field of New Testament studies.[1] These collected writings did not arise as scripture on inked pages as we

1. Kuhn, *Scientific Revolutions*.

have experienced them in book form since the sixteenth century. Rather, the contents of the New Testament originated as oral stories and spoken, epic-like tales and rhetorical orations and oral-letters and theater-like performances. These traditions were most likely composed orally and then handwritten on scrolls of papyrus paper. The scripts of these oral events served the oral performances. The oral compositions preserved in the later manuscripts of the New Testament were not originally read privately or silently but were performed in social settings before gatherings of people. The compositions were most likely originally performed by memory, although they may also have been read aloud. And they were likely presented in their entirety, not broken up into smaller sections.

In order to gain an appropriate understanding of these New Testament writings as oral literature, we should study them in the same oral medium in which they originated. We need to imagine originating performance events in the context of the oral cultures of first-century Christianity. To do this, we need to revise our traditional disciplines of study and develop new methodological tools of analysis. And we can use contemporary performance as a way to help bridge the media gap between the written and the oral.

On what grounds do we assert that that the New Testament writings are remnants of oral events, namely, that they were composed orally, that they were probably performed from memory, and that they were most likely presented in their entirety? Here are some considerations to support these points.

1. Oral Cultures

First and most obvious is the fact that the first-century world of the New Testament was comprised of oral cultures.[2] Orality studies are teaching us a great deal about the societies of the ancient Mediterranean world as oral cultures. It is likely that only about three to ten percent of the people—mostly wealthy elites—were able to read and/or write.[3] In ancient societies, where there was no middle class, ninety percent or more of the people were non-literate peasants, urban dwellers, and expendables who experienced all language aurally. Everything they learned and knew, they knew by word of mouth. People had little or no direct contact with written language.

2. Havelock, *Preface to Plato*; Lord, *Singer of Tales*; Niditch, *Oral World and Written Word*; Draper, *Orality, Literacy, and Colonialism*; Achtemeier, "*Omne verbum sonat*."

3. Gamble, *Books and Readers*; Harris, *Ancient Literacy*; Bar-Ilan, "Illiteracy"; Hezser, *Jewish Literacy*.

Predominantly oral cultures tend to be collectivist cultures. There was no individualism in the first century as we know it today. The identity of individuals came as part of their collective identity. In the collectivist cultures of the first century, there was little opportunity for privacy for most people. People lived together as large nuclear or extended families. Houses were open to neighbors, and marketplaces were centers of social interaction. Life was communal life. The point is that people were with other people virtually all the time, and what one person knew everyone knew. Knowledge was commonly-held social knowledge, because everyone in a village or a network talked with everyone else. Memory was social memory.[4] In an oral culture, all expressions of language—information and instruction and wisdom and proverbs and stories—were embodied; that is, for almost everyone there was little or no experience of impersonal writing on a scroll unassociated with a person. Life was relational and social—face to face. Even those few who could write and/or read were steeped in orality.

Oral tradition-telling was, therefore, the common mode of communication in early Christianity. This came as informal gossip in the marketplaces or as teaching in the homes or as storytelling in ordinary conversation when recalling these traditions.[5] There were also formal opportunities in marketplaces and open spaces between villages and assembly halls and house churches and synagogues and other gathering places for people to recount/perform lengthier oral pieces, the vestiges of which now comprise the writings in the New Testament.

2. Capacity for Remembering Was Extensive

In such an oral culture, people were accustomed and trained to remember what they heard. This does not mean that people recalled verbatim what they heard. Indeed performers in some venues were expected to tell the traditions in their own distinctive way. At the same time, others, such as actors and rhetors and also some rabbis, were trained to memorize faithfully. People who had a knack for oral communication and people with "audiophonic" memories came to the fore, including non-literate peasants. Many were able to recall with unusual faithfulness lengthy compositions by hearing, even if they did not know how to read or write. In general, the capacity to recall well what one heard was an integral part of oral culture.

4. Kirk and Thatcher, *Memory, Tradition, and Text.*

5. Hearon, *Mary Magdalene Tradition*; Hearon, "Storytelling World and the Gospels"; Dewey, "Storytelling to Written Text"; Wire, *Holy Lives, Holy Deaths.*

People remembered in part because storytellers and orators composed speech so that it would be memorable.[6] People thought about how they talked, so that what they said could be easily remembered—with proverbs and parables and words that had a ring to them, and stories and teachings that were made to sound right and good, and that had a great deal of repetition. Also, in an oral culture, words were memorable because they were understood to have power. When you think about traditions in the early church, many of them were performative sayings—words that had power to effect a healing or exorcise a demon or pronounce a blessing. Words were actions that had an impact meant to change people, change the way people thought or related or acted or imagined the world. Such words were memorable words.

3. Composing Was Done by Ear

In an oral culture, composing is almost exclusively done with sound in mind, by oral expression or perhaps in the head, but certainly not in the process of writing. Similar to performances by modern stand-up comedians, stories and speeches were composed in speech, even lengthy ones, for the ear. Then at some point they were transcribed on a scroll, either as dictation or as an exercise in memory. The composer of Mark, for example, may have performed the Gospel of Mark orally, and then it was transcribed at some point in its performance life. The Gospel of John, with its series of lengthy scenes, may have originated the same way. The revisions and expansions that the authors of Matthew and Luke made to Mark may also be explained, in part, as oral re-compositions. The reconstructed Q may never have been written down. Paul no doubt composed his letters orally for sound and emotional effect and then dictated them to an amanuensis to be returned to orality when they were presented before an assembly of recipients.[7] The same would have been true for other letters as well. There is uncertainty and controversy about how much the work of scribes and the presence of handwritten scrolls influenced the dynamics of composition,[8] but an ethos of orality predominated.

6. Ong, *Orality and Literacy*, 31–79.

7. Botha, "Letter Writing and Oral Communication"; Dewey, "Textuality in Oral Tradition."

8. Kelber, *Oral and Written Gospel*.

4. Handwritten Scrolls Served Orality

In the oral cultures of the first century, writing was present but rare, and reading was limited. The leisure time, the training, and the financial resources necessary to learn how to make letter characters were available almost exclusively to the 5 percent plus of elites (and to their slaves and retainers who may have written or read manuscripts for them). Even some who knew how to read may not have known how to write. And some scribes probably could copy letters without knowing what they meant.

Elites used writing primarily to keep accounts for the government, promote the accomplishments of the government, and carry out business dealings.[9] Philosophers, rhetoricians, historians, playwrights, and others employed writing to preserve and distribute their work. Among elites, there may have been a manuscript culture of sorts.[10] But for them and for all others the oral ethos predominated. In this context, handwritten scrolls almost exclusively served orality. Scrolls were a handwritten depository for oral compositions. They assisted composers in producing a script of an oral composition. They served public readers in oral presentations to an audience. They assisted performers in practicing recall in preparation for performances. They enabled the compositions-for-performance to go from one location to another, although oral compositions also circulated orally from performance to performance without the aid of scrolls. The overwhelming experience of early Christian traditions was in terms of oral performances in communal settings. Scrolls may have been present to authenticate the composer of a letter or to be a symbol of the sender's authority. They may or may not have been consulted by the performer. They would have been indecipherable to the audience. First-century Christians would have thought of the gospels and letters not as scrolls but as performances they had heard and experienced.

5. Scrolls Were Peripheral to Performance

A scroll was sometimes present when the gospel stories were told and letters were read. But it seems unlikely that they were consulted. The scrolls and the writing on them do not appear to have been structured so as to facilitate public reading. The typical features that we count on to facilitate

9. Draper, *Orality, Literacy, and Colonialism*; Bowman and Woolf, *Literacy and Power*; Koester, "Writings and the Spirit."

10. Robbins, "Oral, Rhetorical, and Literary Cultures."

reading were not there.[11] On the scrolls, the letters were placed one after another without punctuation and without spaces between words. The letters were only upper case letters with no breaks to mark the beginning and ending of sentences or proper nouns or paragraphs. The size and shape of the letters were not uniform within a scroll or from scroll to scroll, as one experiences them in print. There were no accents to assist with pronunciation. Furthermore, consider the following conditions for reading: the scrolls were cumbersome and awkward to handle; it was difficult to find one's place, especially if the scroll was lengthy; and the lighting may have been quite poor depending on the location of the reading (inside) and the time of day. Furthermore, there were no desks or podia available on which to place a scroll. For reading, the scroll may have been held open on the lap or held by two people, one on either side of the reader.

Some scholars argue that these factors were not insurmountable, saying that people learned to read the handwritten continuous script and would have found ways to handle the scrolls.[12] Indeed, there are descriptions of people who could read with facility. No doubt some did, but it would have been rare. Just as musicians learn to read complex musical compositions with facility, so also some people would be accustomed to the conditions for reading. I think this occasionally occurred. Others think that to read with facility, in any case, one needed to pretty well have the text memorized. Given the oral society, all who could not read with facility probably depended on memory. In fact, those who were trained to read with facility would also have been specially trained to memorize with facility.[13] Furthermore, most people struggling to read would not have been able to read with meaningful inflection and certainly not with hands free to act out the stories or express the passions of a composition with gestures or movements. Having a gospel or letter in memory would have greatly enhanced the meaningfulness and power of the presentation. Simply reading the text aloud does not do it; this merely replicates in public the act of reading aloud in private. With reading there is no immediacy, no liveliness, and no interactive relationship with the audience. The whole job of a performer was to keep the audience listening. This is what storytellers and orators in any culture do. Lively engagement was what audiences expected. Audiences may not otherwise have tolerated it.

Hence, I would argue that even so-called "readings" would have been more of a performance than a reading. And the one presenting would likely

11. Hezser, *Jewish Literacy* .

12. Shiell, *Reading Acts*; Botha, "Letter Writing and Oral Communication."

13. Small, *Wax Tablets of the Mind.*

not have depended on the scroll for that performance. A performer may have consulted a scroll in order to do memory work in preparation for a performance; yet even here performers would read it aloud or have someone read it for them. Again, sound was primary and the handwritten scrolls were peripheral.

6. Scrolls Were Limited in Number

Writing was done on scrolls made of papyrus reeds pressed together. The scrolls and the writing implements were expensive. As such, scrolls were limited in the culture. Early Christianity was predominantly a movement of the peasant class and the urban poor with the presence of some elites (again, there was no middle class in ancient pre-industrial societies). Most communities probably had limited access to producing or using scrolls. The early Christians were not people of the book. There was no book yet. There were only scrolls, few and far between. This was true of writings considered scripture by the Judean people—there were few copies of the Torah and even fewer of other writings, seldom consulted directly, with mainly symbolic value as a venerated object.[14] Some Christian communities who gathered at synagogues may have had a scroll of the Torah, but probably not. Most first-century Christian communities in the Hellenistic world would likely have had no scrolls related to the Judean scriptures or traditions. Early Christian writings did not first appear until around the mid-century, first Paul's letters and then others. Mark was written down around 70 CE, the other gospels not until the last two decades of the first century. Because Christians expected Jesus to return soon, authors did not compose nor did scribes copy to preserve for posterity. In the first century, gospels likely circulated orally with and without the aid of a scroll. Paul's letters were meant for specific communities and would not likely have been immediately copied for use elsewhere. Indeed, some were so idiosyncratic as not even to be relevant to other communities. Later letters of the first century, such as James and I Peter (and Revelation), were designed to be circulated, but they may have been presented by an oral performer going from community to community without the scrolls themselves being widely copied.

We sometimes have the image that early Christians had access to the New Testament writings as we do. The likelihood is that individual communities would have had access at most to only one or two scrolls of the early Christian movement, if any at all. In this first century, Christianity was an overwhelmingly oral movement, even when some scrolls were present.

14. Hezser, *Jewish Literacy*.

7. The Content of the Scrolls Reflects Performance

Reinforcing the notion that gospels and letters were performed is an awareness that the writings themselves are geared to lively expression. The written gospels and the letters may be seen as records or scripts of/for oral performances. Dennis Dewey has likened the print in the Bible to fossil remains.[15] Just as a fossil is a trace record of what was once a living creature, so the New Testament writings are trace records of live performances in the first century. In this regard, the writings themselves bear witness to the dynamics of performance. That is to say, we get clues to the live performances from the written remains. For example, the gospels and letters contain language that reflects features of oral storytelling and memorable speech. In addition, the texts reflect the performer's use of voice when, for example, the text says that someone "shouted." They reflect gestures used in performance when the writings depict, say, the laying on of hands. The texts may imply facial expressions when there is irony or amazement. They also suggest movement for the performer as characters go from place to place in the story. These features may serve as stage directions for performance. They may also be in the text not so much because they give directions to the performer but because they record the manner in which the performer told the story, say by gesture or movement, in performing it. To a limited extent, then, we may be able to infer from the "fossil writings" something of what an original live performance may have been like.

8. Not Scripture

Another very important factor supporting the primary orality of the New Testament compositions is that they were not originally conceived of as scripture. They were in the mode of storytelling and orations and public letters and wisdom (James) and prophecies (Revelation), genres to be presented orally. The letters were just that, letters orally shared with communities. And it appears as if letters bear the marks of the oral compositions of Greco-Roman rhetoric. Some narrative compositions bear the marks of drama, such as the Gospel of John and Revelation. All these compositions were initially experienced in oral venues such as houses and marketplaces and public buildings. Even if first presented in synagogue gatherings, they would have been seen as lively performances in the genre of storytelling and letters. Hence, until well into the second and even third century, these

15. From a conversation with Dewey in 2004 at the Network of Biblical Storytellers conference, Atlanta, GA.

writings would not have been treated as *written* documents in the way scribes and rabbis treated some of their written traditions of the Hebrew Bible and the Greek Septuagint. Hence, when we study the New Testament writings in their original first-century context, we are not studying them as scripture, but as oral compositions of a variety of genres. This insight is critical for the whole enterprise of performance criticism.

9. Performed as a Whole

Because the early Christian compositions did not initially bear the aura associated with the Judean writings of scripture, they would not have been broken up for reading in houses of worship (a later practice of Judaism and Christianity). Rather, they would have been oral compositions expected to be heard as a whole. Besides, apart from Romans and I and II Corinthians, none of Paul's letters, even the pseudepigraphic ones, takes more than twenty to thirty minutes to present. Apart from Hebrews, the same is true for the rest of the New Testament letters. The composer of I Peter even apologizes that his letter is so brief (in time to hear, not in space to read). The Gospel of Mark and the Gospel of John take less than two hours to perform, Revelation an hour and a half. That is not a significant amount of time considering the interest in the matters and the cultural experience with storytelling and theater presentations on the part of audiences. The Gospel of Matthew and the Gospel of Luke and the Acts of the Apostles take longer, but even three or so hours is not prohibitive for a lively, engaging, and profound story. Film and theater productions (including one-person shows) of three hours in length are common today as well.

10. First Audiences

It is worth pointing out that especially first audiences of a New Testament composition would likely have heard each performed as a whole. I cannot imagine the Galatians community gathering to hear Paul's letter for the first time and not hearing the whole letter. The same can be said for all other letters. As the emissary with Revelation went from city to city, can you imagine the performer of Revelation halting that gripping apocalypse in the middle and telling people to come back the next week to hear the rest? The same is true with Mark. When I perform only part of Mark, the overwhelming response is: Don't stop now! The drama and the suspense in Mark's story hold an audience. And what ancient community receiving a letter from any of the "apostles" would have stood for hearing only a part of it?

Besides, an analysis of the rhetoric of gospels and letters shows that each was meant to have an impact *as a whole*. The desired transformation would not occur if the audience heard it in sections. The composition would be misunderstood if an audience heard only part of it. We scholars have so fragmented our treatment of these writings that we have lost the sense of the progressive rhetorical impact of a composition as it develops from beginning to end. The New Testament writings were meant to be presented and experienced in their entirety.

Furthermore, there would have been multiple first audiences, each time the composition was performed in a new place. It would have taken some years for each of Paul's letters to circulate widely; and they would have been experienced as a whole by each new audience. Other letters and the apocalypse that were meant to be circulated would have been presented to many communities for the first time, and thus heard as a whole. The same would be true of the Gospels. Furthermore, the same audiences hearing a gospel or letter for a second and third time more probably would also have heard it as a whole.

Conclusion

After about twenty centuries, we are beginning to recover something that has been lost, eclipsed from our experience—namely, the experience of telling and hearing the New Testament compositions from memory as a whole. Just as Hans Frei bemoaned the "eclipse of biblical narrative,"[16] so we lament the related "eclipse of biblical performance." So, is the Bible what we have in print? Or is it the stories and speeches that were performed, of which our Bible contains the remnants?

However we may configure it, the writings we have in the New Testament are examples of "performance literature," that is, literature that was meant for performance—no less than music, no less than theater, no less than oral interpretation of literature. Can we imagine a musicologist spending years sitting in libraries looking at scores but never hearing the music performed?[17] Can we imagine theater critics studying scripts of ancient drama but never seeing the performance of a play? Can we imagine how we biblical scholars have studied this performance literature for centuries without hearing these writings performed orally as stories and speeches? Can we now imagine biblical scholars themselves listening to and even performing these writings? The meaning of a text comes to bear at the point where it is

16. Frei, *Eclipse of Biblical Narrative*.

17. Small, *Musicking*.

performed.[18] Performers are figuring out the range of meanings for these texts and seeking to embody them. That is what we scholars are challenged to do. The act of performance is the very reason why the scripts came into existence in the first place!

A NEW APPROACH: PERFORMANCE CRITICISM

åThus there is a gap in New Testament studies. There is something missing in our study of early Christianity, namely the oral/aural events in which early Christian writings were performed before a communal audience in an oral culture. Very little research in the history of our discipline focuses on the performance event. There may be good reasons why there has been such a lacuna in New Testament studies. Such a thing as an oral performance is ethereal. It is forever gone from our experience. How can we even begin to imagine what performances may have been like for performer or audience? How can we imagine that we can use orality as a means to interpret the writings in the New Testament? Fortunately, such questions have not daunted us in the past from seeking to recover portraits of the elusive historical Jesus or from constructing the nature and dynamics of long-gone, early Christian communities. So also we can approach this challenge carefully and thoughtfully, aware of pitfalls and misdirection along the way. It will require a reorientation of our methodologies and a good measure of pioneering efforts, but addressing this gap in New Testament studies will, I believe, be well worth the effort.

And, in fact, there are many studies now emerging to help fill this gap. It seems appropriate to designate the emerging biblical discipline as "performance criticism."[19] Biblical performance criticism is not just one more methodology added on to other methodologies. Rather, it represents a paradigm shift in the interpretation of texts from print medium to oral medium that has implications for the entire enterprise of New Testament studies.[20] New methodologies and the transformation of traditional methodologies are needed to address this media shift in the biblical writings. Biblical scholars may need to retool and embrace new disciplines.

How might we formulate performance criticism? What methods might be developed that would lead to an understanding of the phenomenon of

18. Maclean, *Narrative as Performance*.

19. Rhoads, "Performance Criticism"; Doan and Giles, *Prophets, Performance, and Power*; Giles and Doan, *Twice Used Songs*.

20. Boomershine, "Biblical Megatrends"; Loubser, *Oral and Manuscript Culture*; Fowler, "Why Everything We Know About the Bible Is Wrong."

performance in early Christianity as a basis for interpreting the New Testament writings? I would like to suggest three strategies. 1) One approach is to construct in imagination performative scenarios for each writing and then study the writing as an oral performance with those scenarios in mind. 2) The second approach is to reorient traditional methods by which we study the New Testament in light of the oral dimensions of the writings. These methods will contribute to performance criticism and at the same time be transformed by the shift in medium. And new methods will be needed to address the full implications of treating the New Testament as performance literature. 3) The third approach is to do performances of these texts in our primary languages as means to get in touch with the performative dimensions of these writings in their original contexts. I will look at each of these approaches in turn, treating the first two in cursory fashion and then spending the bulk of this essay on the third approach.

1. Imagining Ancient Performance Events

I am focusing here primarily on public performances of an entire gospel or letter for gathered groups, rather than on informal storytelling of brief traditions. The performance event includes the oral/written composition, the act of performing, the performer, the audience, the location, the cultural/historical circumstances, and the rhetorical impact on the audience. To construct such performance events, we need to investigate ancient art and literature for depictions and descriptions of ancient performances done by artists and rhetoricians and storytellers and dramatists. We need to look at each writing to discover clues in the writing itself as to how such performances may have been enacted.[21] The question is: how do these factors add to or limit the range of possible meanings and the possible rhetorical impacts of the New Testament compositions in their own time?

The Oral/Written Composition

The composition will reflect style typical of communication in an oral culture. It will have certain content and order designed to be engaging and transformative to a listening audience. It will have memorable and powerful language. The sounds themselves will contribute to the meaning and impact of the composition. A composition may contain implicit stage directions for the performer.

21. Shiner, *Proclaiming the Gospel*; Shiell, *Reading Acts*.

The Act of Performing

The event of a performance includes intonation, movements, gestures, pace, facial expressions, postures, the spatial relationships of the imagined characters, the temporal development of the story in progressive events displayed on a stage area, as well as the sheer force of the bodily presence of the performer to evoke emotions and commitments. Based on what we know of various kinds of ancient performances, we need to imagine the stories and letter-speeches as being expressive and emotional, filled with drama in voice and gesture and physical movement. As such, a performance is much more than aural hearing; it is an embodiment.

The Performer

The performer bears the potential meanings and impacts of the story upon the audience in a particular context. In the performance of a narrative, the performer is acting out the characters and events of the story. In the performance of a letter, the performer is personifying the dynamics of the argument that is being presented. The early Christians had no unembodied experiences of the stories or letters. Important was the authority of the performer with the audience, the personal integrity of the performer in relation to the material presented, and the performer's social location.

The Audience

The audience was collective, and the emotional and ideological responses to a performance were communal. The audiences of gospels and letters were likely quite involved in the performance with verbal and emotional reactions throughout.[22] Furthermore, the experience of a performance created and shaped community. Social location was a key factor in the responses of ancient audiences. What might different audiences have looked like? Mostly peasants with some or no elites? All women or all men or a mixture of both? All Gentiles or both Judeans and Gentiles? Some letters reveal the likely makeup of the recipient audience. The gospels were probably performed many times before very different audiences. We need to imagine possible audiences for performances of each of the writings. And we need to consider how a performer might have adapted a performance in light of the make-up of different audiences.

22. Shiner, *Proclaiming the Gospel*; Shiner, "Oral Performance."

The Location

Contexts raise expectations of what does and does not happen in a particular place. As such, different places foster or inhibit certain audience responses. Ancient settings for performance included a village marketplace, an ancient theater, a house, synagogues, public forums, open spaces between villages. What does venue contribute to the meaning and impact of a performance?

The Sociohistorical Circumstances

We need to imagine different audiences hearing a composition-in-performance under divergent circumstance—persecution, conflict, oppression, war, social unrest, poverty, prosperity, and so on. Imagining specific sociohistorical circumstances in the context of an imagined performance event transforms our understanding of "reception." To do so is to speak in fresh ways about a "politics of performance."[23] For example, how might different factions in an audience react to a letter and to each other as a result of the reception of a letter?

Rhetorical Effect/Impact

The final factor in the dynamics of the performance event is the potential rhetorical impacts upon an audience. By rhetoric, I mean the potential impacts of the entire composition-as-performance on an audience—subversion of cultural values, transformation of worldview, impulse to action, change of behavior, emotional catharsis, ethical commitment, intellectual insight, change of political perspective, reformation of community, or the generation of a new world. Of course, there will not be just one audience reaction to a performance. What response the composition implies may be different from what actually may have occurred. Again, social location would be crucial to audience reaction.

From these elements of the performance event, we can develop distinct "audience scenarios" as a basis for interpreting each writing in the New Testament. The question for performance criticism is this: how can we find ways to analyze all these elements of the performance event together so as to transform the ways we interpret the written texts as oral performances?

23. Ward, "Paul and the Politics of Performance."

2. Reorienting New Testament Methods

The second approach of performance criticism is to reorient our methods of study in light of the oral nature of the culture and oral dynamics of the texts of the New Testament. As we have said, recognizing the orality of the New Testament writings is a paradigm shift; in principle, it impacts all methods. The key to this reorientation is to focus on the performative event as a context to reconceptualize other methodologies.

In a sense, as we have said, performance criticism is not just one more criticism added to others. Rather, because the shift to performance is a shift in medium, it affects virtually all disciplines, traditional as well as recent. At the same time, performance criticism is multifaceted; that is, many disciplines can contribute to the study of performance. In turn, these same disciplines are themselves impacted and changed by the study of the New Testament in a different medium. What follows is a thumbnail sketch of many disciplines that can contribute to and are impacted by performance criticism.

Traditional Historical-Critical Methods

Historical criticism

Historical criticism can contribute to performance criticism by investigating what we can know about diverse performers (rhapsodes, rhetors, storytellers, rabbinic tradents, orators, and so on), performances, venues for performances, and audiences.[24] In turn, historical criticism can be renewed by seeing the oral ethos of first-century cultures as an integral dimension of the entire enterprise of historical reconstruction.

Textual criticism

Scholars are rethinking textual criticism by explaining the fluidity of the earliest manuscript traditions in light of the fluidity of oral performances and by attending to the role of "memory variants" by scribes.[25] Textual critics can also take greater account of the dimensions of sound in assessing the "manuscript" tradition.

24. Scobie, "Storytellers, Storytelling, and the Novel"; Hargis, "Rhapsode"; Hearon, "Storytelling World and the Gospels"; Wire, *Holy Lives, Holy Deaths*.

25. Parker, *Living Text*; Carr, *Tablet of the Heart*; Person, "Scribe as Performer."

Source criticism

Scholars are now rethinking the "literary" solutions to the synoptic problem by taking into account multiple oral origins for the sayings of Jesus, the development of traditions as oral recompositions, and the force of oral speech as a factor in recollection. And the idea that the gospels may have been performed orally in their entirety changes significantly our assessment of the impact of orality on the gospel traditions.

Form and genre criticism

These disciplines can be reoriented from print analysis to ask how forms and genres such as parable, gospel, apocalypse, epistle, wisdom tradition, and ethical exhortation function to raise, subvert, and confirm expectations in the temporal medium of oral performance.

Recently Developed Methods

Rhetorical criticism

Scholars think many New Testament letters were oral compositions shaped by the canons of ancient rhetoric, but they are only beginning to deal with the oral dimensions of the letters as speeches.

Narrative criticism

Scholars are beginning to reassess the oral dynamics of ancient narrative so as to replace the implied author and the implied reader with the idea of an actual performer and an actual audience in an ancient performance event. A similar reorientation transforms individual reader-response criticism to communal audience-response criticism.

Discourse analysis.

This discipline seeks to show the order and flow of a composition by identifying such linguistic features as chiastic patterns, chain sentences, parallelism, word order, foregrounding and backgrounding, emphasis, elision, transitions, verbal threads, onomatopoeia, hook words, mnemonic devices, and many forms of repetition.[26] Recently, practitioners have begun to inquire about the sound of these features. We can also reflect on the impact of sound itself upon a hearer, such as we find in the use of guttural sounds, alliteration, assonance, and other phonic repetition.[27]

Orality criticism

This discipline seeks to apply knowledge gained from the study of many cultures as means to assess the orality of the New Testament period. Orality critics seek to understand the ethos of orality, the impact of writing in different cultures, the nature of performance, the responsibilities and practices of tradents, the dynamics of social memory, the power dimensions of oral/written communication, and the gender dimensions of orality. This criticism is obviously foundational to performance criticism.

Ideological criticism

These multiple approaches (feminist, womanist, liberation, postcolonial, among others) can make explicit the power dynamics of relationships in oral cultures, especially in relation to performance events, by revealing whose interests in an audience are served by the composition and whose interests are violated, denigrated, and neglected.[28]

New Methods in Biblical Studies

Speech-act theory

This approach works well with the biblical understanding that words are actions that generate and change reality.[29]

Theater studies and performance studies

New Testament research has much to learn about the drama of the biblical narratives and about performative dynamics of the New Testament texts.[30]

26. Davis, *Oral Biblical Criticism*; Harvey, *Listening to the Text.*
27. Dean, "Grammar of Sound"; Lee and Scott, *Sound Mapping.*
28. Dewey, "Competing Gospels."
29. Briggs, *Words in Action.*
30. Levy, *Bible as Theatre*; Brandt, *Dialogue and Drama.*

The art and practice of translation

This is also a fruitful area for reorientation as scholars translate from orality to orality, seeking to discern the original oral dimensions of the biblical writings and to preserve them in dynamic translations for performance in contemporary oral cultures.[31]

Performance criticism may be seen as a discipline in its own right because of its focus on the event of performance. At the same time, performance criticism also incorporates traditional and recent disciplines in its endeavor to understand fully the dynamics of oral performance.

3. Performing as a Research Method of Interpretation

In recent decades people have been performing biblical selections, including whole gospels, letters, and Revelation. And many of us have been teaching our students to learn and perform stories and other traditions from the Bible. These experiences have been an important part of our efforts to interpret the New Testament writings in their ancient contexts. As a biblical scholar, the experience of translating, memorizing, and performing a biblical text has become my own foundational method of research into the meaning and rhetoric of New Testament writings in their original first-century context. Here is the point: if we are making a medium shift to orality, why not study the New Testament compositions in the medium in which they originated? Does it not make sense to study the New Testament texts in the oral medium in which they were composed and first experienced? Does it not seem appropriate to experience performance literature as performances? Might that not get us in touch with dynamics of these oral compositions that otherwise might be lost or distorted? Whitney Shiner has remarked that "to understand performances and performers, one has to perform."[32] I would propose, therefore, that we explore acts of performing as a methodological tool for interpreting New Testament writings in their ancient context.

Let me be clear. We can never recover a first-century performative event. We can seek to construct scenarios and imagine dynamics of first-century performance, but we can never know what a performance might have been like. Based on historical investigation, we can know a lot about how they might have been done, but in fact they are lost to us. However, if the goal of interpretation is to understand a New Testament writing in its

31. Maxey, *From Orality to Orality*.

32. Cited from a private conversation.

ancient context, contemporary performing can perhaps open us exegetes to dynamics of the text that we might otherwise ignore or misunderstand. What have we been missing by studying them solely in the medium as print? What might we learn from experiencing them in an oral medium? Both hearing and performing are new media for biblical scholarship. *Hearing* the New Testament places the interpreter in a different medium relationship with the text from the traditional print medium. *Performing* the text goes further, enabling the interpreter to become the "voice" and "embodiment" of the narrative or letter.

Hence, I propose that we can experiment with twenty-first-century performances as a way to explore the first-century performance event. Here are some reasons to employ performance as a tool of research.

- Performance may help us to investigate the range of meaning potential for a given composition.
- Performance may help us to explore the potential rhetorical impacts upon ancient audiences.
- Performance may help us to recover oral features of the text and performance dynamics to which we might not otherwise have access.
- Performance may help us to restore the emotive dimensions to the text.

The remainder of this article is devoted to an in-depth exploration of ways in which performing the New Testament compositions may help in our understanding of these documents in the context of the first century.

PERFORMANCE AS A METHOD OF RESEARCH

For thirty years I have been translating, memorizing, and performing different New Testament writings, first the Gospel of Mark, then Galatians, Philemon, the Sermon on the Mount, selections from Luke, scenes from John, and, more recently, James, 1 Peter, and Revelation. These experiences have been an important part of my hermeneutical efforts to interpret the New Testament writings. As a scholar, I have found that performing a New Testament composition is a very different experience from reading it silently and leads to distinctive ways of understanding this literature.[33]

33. Roloff, *Perception and Evocation*; Pelias, *Performance Studies*; Lee and Galati, *Oral Interpretation*; Issacharoff and Jones, *Performing Texts*.

As I have argued, the New Testament texts compare to drama and music as performance pieces. Performance is integral to interpretation in fields of both drama and music. So also in New Testament studies, interpretation takes place at the site of performance, both for the performer and for the audience.[34] This performance approach involves a major shift in our traditional methodologies of studying these writings. We need new methods to assist with interpretation in the role of being an audience and in the role of being a performer.

First, the exegete can interpret from the position of being part of an audience. Taking on the role of an audience and taking in the experience of a performance can be an integral part of the process of interpretation. Many biblical scholars have told me that their experience of hearing a performance of Galatians or Revelation or 1 Peter has fundamentally changed their way of thinking about this literature. I myself have learned much about I Thessalonians and Philippians as letters of Paul by hearing my students perform them.

As such, experiencing a New Testament writing as a performance provides a significantly fresh medium through which to encounter the text and to address interpretive issues. Exegetes have likely never heard all of James or 1 Peter or Revelation on one occasion as a way to understand the rhetorical impact of those writings. When hearing the text, the critic cannot stop and reflect and look back, as one can do when reading. The story keeps moving, and one gets caught up in it and carried forward by it. The critic can take it all in and decide whether it makes sense or whether one or another thing could or should have been translated or performed a different way. In these ways, exegetes-as-audience can work to expand the range (in some cases) and to narrow the range (in other cases) of plausible interpretations of meaning and rhetoric.

To learn how to be an audience, exegetes will need to develop new methods. We will need to learn listening skills as we have traditionally learned reading skills—becoming empathetically involved, identifying with characters, being aware of our own emotions and reactions, discerning the cognitive challenges of a narrative, suspending judgment, and then afterward evaluating performances critically and constructively.[35] The experience of multiple performances of the same text will prevent one from judging the value of this procedure based on one performance only. For example, it would be interesting to hear the Gospel of Mark performed as a narrative that ultimately rejects the disciples and then as a narrative that ultimately accepts the disciples—and then assess the audience responses.

34. Maclean, *Narrative as Performance.*

35. Pelias, *Performance Studies.*

Second, the exegete can interpret by taking on the role of a performer. In music and drama, we do not usually think that the exegete/critic will be the performing artist. The role of the exegete is seen as recipient, as one who sees and hears as a means to interpret and assess. The role of performer is reserved for the artist. But what if we take this model a step further? What if we combine the two roles, so that the exegete learns not only from hearing/seeing a performance but also from the act of performing? Performing the text transforms the way of relating to the text. Becoming the "voice" and the "embodiment" of a narrative or letter places the exegete in a relationship with the text that is quite distinctive from hearing a performance. It represents a different medium. By combining the two roles of critic and performer, both the process of interpreting and the tests of interpretation are explored and worked out in artistic acts of performing.

The act of performing can be an integral part of the process of interpretation. Again, the exegete will need to learn new tools and methods. In order to perform, the interpreter/performer must make judgments about the potential meanings and the possible rhetorical impacts of a New Testament composition—taking on the roles of the characters, moving in imagination from place to place, interacting between one character and another, recounting the narrative world from the narrator's perspective and standards of judgment, and so on. I regularly discover new meanings of a line or an episode or a point of argumentation in the course of preparing for a performance and in the act of performing itself. In this way, performances can confirm certain interpretations, can expand interpretive possibilities, and can set parameters on viable interpretations. If the goal of interpretation is to understand a New Testament writing in its ancient context, contemporary performing can open us exegetes to fresh dynamics of the text that will have an impact on our interpretations.

THE PERFORMER AS ARTIST

Scholars have recently come to appreciate the aesthetic expression of the gospels as narratives and the logical force of the letters as rhetorical arguments. In commenting on the New Testament as documents, scholars have noted the straightforward but sophisticated storytelling in Mark, the powerful means that Luke uses to weave episodes and parables, the way in which a letter of Paul, even such a brief one as Philemon, may be a rhetorical tour de force, and how vivid is the imagery in Revelation. Now we need to appreciate also the artistry of the New Testament writings through experiencing them in performance. In so doing, we move the medium to orality and deal with these very same words as oral compositions. Seeing the aesthetics of a text *as* oral performance has to do with what anthropologists refer to as "verbal arts"—the arts of language that serve the effectiveness of oral expression and its impact.

In this essay, we are looking at verbal arts in terms of the way a composition is presented orally. The *language* in orality is itself an expression of verbal arts, but the *manner of presenting* the language is also an expression of verbal art in performance.[36] We need to appreciate the ways in which skilled performers can bring the performance features of these writings to life, and we need to appreciate the benefits of such performing arts in the service of interpretation.

The performer is viewed as an artist. That was certainly true of the performers and orators of the ancient world. Storytellers were popular, especially among the lower classes, and often renowned because of their skill at engaging and holding an audience. Rhapsodes were well-regarded among elites as orators who gave performances of Homer and other poetry. They were hired to entertain at banquets and festivals. Such performers were judged at competitions as part of the Olympian Games. Theater too was highly popular as an art form. Orators of rhetoric were well-known. Large crowds gathered to hear outstanding orators at funerals and in the courtroom and in public forums. The ancient world valued performance at the popular and at the elite levels alike. There is every reason to think that performances of the New Testament compositions in the early church would have been treated in similar ways—not as scripture readings of short passages in worship but as storytelling and poetic-like performances and orations.

Today, the performer is also an artist, and the performance is an artistic expression,[37] even if, as in my case, the performer is clearly not trained. If we are speaking of performance art, we are talking about such matters as stage presence, the knack for entertaining and engaging an audience, a skilled use of voice, the capacity to bring different characters to life, the art of conveying irony and humor, the enlivening use of body language, the means to evoke emotions, the ability to project suspense and develop a plot, and so on. The craft of performance involves being authentic and convincing, being natural in a way that does not draw attention to oneself, bringing alive the story and the rhetoric without distraction, heightening the senses and the imagination.[38] All these represent the means for a performer to enthrall and move an audience, to transport them into another world and, potentially, to work a transformation. In this aesthetic model, both performer

36. Bauman, *Verbal Art as Performance*; Bauman, *Story, Performance, Event.*

37. Bozarth, *Word's Body.*

38. Pelias, *Performance Studies,* 18.

and audience-as-critics are interpreters of contemporary renditions and of the faithfulness of their presentations. The artist interprets by performing, and the critic interprets by reception and commentary on the performance.

Hence, for the exegete-as-performer the act of performing is not simply an end in itself. The performer gets in touch with the artistic dynamics of performing and becomes familiar with the verbal arts of performing. To be sure, this is an indirect relationship with the performances of the New Testament compositions in antiquity. Nevertheless, the advancement comes with the fact that we are interpreting them in the same oral medium in which they were originally composed and first experienced.

As such, the whole process of translation, memorization (or composing/revising in performance), preparation, performance, interaction with audiences, and post-performance reflection are methods of exploring the meaning and rhetoric of the text. Just as some New Testament scholars have learned and adapted the disciplines of narrative analysis and rhetorical analysis and cultural anthropology, so now some scholars can be engaged in learning and training in oral interpretation of literature and performance studies. These become critical methods for analyzing texts.[39]

Certainly not all scholars will be engaged in performing, but a critical mass can bring this approach into vital dialogue within biblical studies (www.biblicalperformancecriticism.org). And it may not be as daunting to engage in performing as it may seem at first blush. Many of my students memorize and perform much more easily than they had thought possible. The more I learn and memorize, the easier it becomes. In this sense, all scholars and students can appreciate the approach by learning and telling a few brief stories to test interpretations or by becoming a sophisticated audience for performances. Others can be more ambitious and learn whole texts. Reading the text aloud does not engage an audience. To experience the text in the medium of a performer, it is necessary to learn a composition by memory and tell it to others—over and over.

THE PERFORMER'S APPROACH

The contemporary performer of these ancient scripts has to make some basic decisions about her or his approach. In general, the performer needs to distinguish between then and now. This involves several key choices.

One choice has to do with language, to perform either in Greek or in one's contemporary native language. I think it is very important to hear and do performances in Greek. Some biblical scholars today know how to

39. Ibid., 39.

speak and listen to ancient Greek well enough to understand the language in the oral medium and appreciate the oral impact of the verbal arts and the sound of Greek. I think we need greater training for the future exploration of performance criticism.

I prefer to perform in my own language, English, because it places me in an actual performance event with an audience. I find it most helpful to do my own translations and then to refine them through performance. I have followed this procedure, for example, with the Gospel of Mark, the Sermon on the Mount, and scenes from John, Philemon, and James. In some cases I have adapted for performance the translations of others, for example, Hans Dieter Betz's translation of Galatians and George Caird's rendition of Revelation.[40] In translating, I have sought to retain aspects of the verbal art of the composition. Through translating for performance, I have become sensitive to the effectiveness of word choice, word order, repetition, the sounds of words, the length of words and sentences, additions and omissions, and many other aspects of the communication event. I am unaware of any translations of the New Testament currently available that reflect the orality of the first century or that are specifically designed for oral performance.[41]

The performer also needs to decide whether to do an abbreviated version of the writing, as some performers of biblical texts do, or to perform the entire piece. Apart from performances of the Sermon on the Mount, selections on wealth and poverty from Luke, and stories from John, I have chosen to do entire texts. Mark takes almost two and one-half hours with a break. Revelation takes about an hour and forty-five minutes without a break. Others that I perform—Galatians, James, and 1 Peter—take about thirty minutes. Philemon is quite brief. The performance of any smaller rhetorical unit can be helpful, along with abbreviated versions. However, I myself do not find it possible to understand or convey the full meaning or the overall rhetorical impact of a text without performing it in its entirety. Besides, as I have argued, performing them in their entirety is the original manner in which they were experienced by the earliest Christian communities.

The performer also needs to decide whether to do a text-based performance (absolute memory) or a fluid performance in which one composes and recomposes in performance. Fluid compositions are important to give us a sense of how some ancient tellers composed as they performed and performed. Based on studies of ancient manuscripts and contemporary oral cultures, scholars think most performers were creative in their own right

40. Betz, *Galatians*; George Caird, *Commentary on Revelation*.

41. Maxey, *From Orality to Orality*.

and recomposed (at least to some extent) by putting their individual stamp on the performance and in response to the situation and the audience.[42] Some think that the performers of Paul's letters would have expanded on various points as they presented. However, we also have reason to think that actors of ancient drama, some rhapsodes, and some bearers of rabbinic traditions stayed quite close in memory to a script.[43] I prefer to do memorized performances, although I am aware of making mistakes in memory and making some minor adaptations based on audience and context. I prefer memorization because each of the New Testament writings is the closest thing we have to an actual composition of at least one occasion of an ancient performance, and I am eager to use contemporary performance as a way to understand the biblical composition in its ancient context.

Also, the interpreter/performer must choose either to seek to replicate the style of an ancient performance or to express a contemporary style of performance—at the same time seeking to do so in the service of being faithful to the composition. As I have suggested, there is no way to replicate an ancient performance, although there are some indications of the style in which these presentations may have been carried out and some information about conventional gestures that may have accompanied certain expressions. There is good reason to believe the performances were lively and emotional and interactive with the audience.[44]

In any case, I prefer to work with a contemporary style of performing for a contemporary audience. I think of this practice as being faithful to the original performances in this way: as the original performances were in the style of the populace, so we can do presentations in the popular style of performance today. I proceed in this way because it gives real-time experiences of a performance event as a performer trying to engage and move an audience and as a performer in interaction with an audience that can understand, participate, and react. From such contemporary performing, we can learn much about ancient performances—in part because performances in general, ancient and modern, share many dynamics in common.

These are my preferences, but I am convinced that we need to experience different styles of performance and diverse interpretations—with various audiences, material settings, and social locations. In what follows, I will share some dynamics of performing that I have found helpful in an effort to comprehend the meaning and rhetoric of New Testament writings—presenting the whole world of the text, altered states of consciousness, acting out

42. Foley, *Singer of Tales in Performance*; Foley, *How to Read an Oral Poem*.

43. Pelias, *Performance Studies*, 31.

44. Shiner, *Proclaiming the Gospel*, 143–91.

the "script," personification of characters, onstage/offstage focus, nonverbal communication, emotions, humor, temporal experience, and rhetoric.

THE WORLD OF THE COMPOSITION IN IMAGINATION

The very acts of memorizing and performing enable the exegete to know the text in detail and to know it thoroughly. When you memorize, it is not easy to screen out details or to consider them inconsequential. When you perform a composition many times, different details come to the fore. I have performed the Gospel of Mark more than three hundred times, and I become aware of new dimensions of the story almost every time I perform. Also, by knowing the whole text, the performer knows not only everything that is in the text but also what is *not* in the text. As such, there is a clear sense when interpreting Mark not to consider what might be in other Gospels or when interpreting Galatians not to consider what might be in other letters of Paul. Such a thorough grasp of the text leads the performer to decide anew what in the text might be emphasized with each performance.

However, the real benefit to memorization and performance is not a matter of knowing details, but of experiencing the world of the narrative or letter *as a whole*. When I learn a narrative, I am eager to get "inside" this world. I set out my translations as a short story or speech, without the fragmentation of chapters and verses. After I learn the words, can recount them with facility, and am able to act them out, some significant shifts occur. The first shift is that I am no longer thinking about words as I see them on the page. Rather, I hear the sounds of the words as I anticipate them in my head. The text is off the page and into the world of sound. Then, the next shift is that I am no longer thinking of the sounds of the words. Rather, I am imagining the scene I am recounting, and I am telling you what I am "seeing." The story or letter becomes three-dimensional. It is the difference between seeing something on a flat surface and viewing a hologram. This is the breakthrough that enables the performer to live "inside the world of the story" in imagination.

But the experience in performance of the entire composition goes even further. Traditionally, we have tended toward a fragmented approach to a narrative or letter, thinking in terms of individual episodes or portions of a letter. A performance of the whole composition opens out into a world that compares to the world of a film or the experience of a theater production, which creates a holistic world that is not simply a sequence of events but an entire story with beginning, middle, and end. The whole story or letter is a world. Movie-goers and theater-goers speak of being drawn into the world of a film or of a dramatic performance. Readers of novels talk about getting lost in the world of the story. In this case of performing, however, a performer is even more involved than a viewer. As a performer, I imagine the world from the perspective of the narrator/speaker, and I myself am part of that world. Even when, as the overall narrator, I am not a character in the story, I am nevertheless a participant in the performance.

As such, the act of memorizing the whole text and performing it enlivens the imagination of the exegete to be aware of the "story world" or "letter world" created by the composition. Narrative criticism has taught us about the narrative world of the text. The references in the story do not in the first instance refer to historical events but to the story world—character, events, settings as depicted in the story. The narrator has distinct ideological takes on this world. Each letter and the apocalypse also has a distinctive narrative world.

This world becomes even more distinctive in performance. The performer brings the story to life on the "staging area" as characters, places, and events are portrayed for the imagination of the audience. The exegete becomes immersed in this world of a gospel or of a letter, imagining its characters and settings, experiencing events as a movement in time, with its past and future, its cosmology of space and time, its cultural dynamics, and its sociopolitical realities—all from the standards and beliefs of the narrator's perspective. When I perform the whole text, the entire narrative world of a gospel or a letter comes to have an integrity of its own, again, much as one experiences the world of a film or drama.

To imagine the world of the narrative, the exegete-performer uses all the tools of the New Testament trade to inform her or his imagination—geography, archaeology, studies of daily life, historical information, and cultural anthropology. Of course, there are many ways to imagine the world of a story. The point I am making, however, is that in the process of performing I discern coherence in the levels of a gospel or a letter that I would not otherwise have seen (and also become aware of gaps and breaks in the story-line). Entering this world is like walking through an imaginary door (on stage, so to speak) into a different reality or imaginatively crossing a border into another culture. I never cease being who I am as a person, even as I take on this role of performer, but the performance enables me to grasp and imagine this world more clearly as a whole.

I cannot emphasize enough how much this experience of the world of the text has changed my approach to interpretation. This experience of the narrative world as an integrated whole provides the frame for the interpretation of specific parts of a story or letter. Every specific thing is interpreted in relation to everything else and the whole in time. By such an immersion into the text and its sequence of events and its pattern of argumentation, the performer interprets each sequential line in the context of the gradual unfolding of the composition as a whole. The characters are all evaluated according to values embedded in the narrative. The actions and events are possible within the parameters allowed by the cosmology. The settings provide the conditions for conflicts. The flow of the narrative as movement in time becomes clearer—just what the hearers know and when they learn it. And so on.

WORLD AND AUDIENCE

Performing a whole story makes it absolutely clear to the performer-exegete that the text is a rhetorical act of communication designed to change/transform an audience. In performing, the exegete becomes acutely conscious that every performance of every line in sequence is a speech-act designed to have a rhetorical impact. There is no escaping the choices one needs to make both to understand and to present the story/letter to an audience. In so doing, the performer is both inside this world and outside of it, interacting with the audience. The performer wants the audience to see what the performer sees and experience what the performer shows. The performer seeks to engage the audience, present the world of the composition, draw the audience into that world and lead them through it, persuade the audience to overcome its resistance to the narrator's way of seeing the world, and thereby lead the audience to embrace the values of the performer/composition and accept the composition's way of seeing the world. The performer does not just tell about a world; rather the performance *is* a world.

There are two dynamics to this interaction between performance and audience. One dynamic is that the audience experiences their own real world reflected in the composition. Orality critics tell us that memory works when the audience of a performance interprets the narrative or epistolary world of the composition within the political, social, and religious structures and traditions with which they are already enculturated. Richard Horsley has argued, for example, that the Gospel of Mark is presented from a peasant perspective and to a peasant audience in such a way that they will hear the Gospel within the frames of the "little traditions" of Israel that inform their world.[45] Obviously, this synchronicity in framework between composition and audience has to be true to a significant extent or the composition will not make sense.

45. Horsley, *Hearing the Whole Story*.

Yet there is another dynamic at work in performing these writings of the New Testament. These compositions were also seeking to present a new world, a world that could not be adequately understood within the contemporary traditions of the audience. The compositions are pushing audiences to new and different understandings of their world. The writings are virtually apocalyptic in their efforts to accomplish this goal, because the composers believed a *new* kingdom or a *new* creation had dawned in their midst. In fact, it has seemed to me at times that the rhetorical function of some writings like Mark or Galatians or Revelation was to enculturate the audience into a new way of being in the world. For example, Mark has Jesus announce that "the empire of *God* has arrived" (Mark 1:15) and then proceeds to display this world in the healings and exorcisms that follow. The Markan Jesus even warns people not to "put new wine into old wineskins" (Mark 2:22). Matthew claims that a scribe of the kingdom brings out of his treasure both "what is new and what is old" (Matthew 13:51), and his gospel has this thematic ring of connection to the past and the dawning of something new. Also, Paul announces in Galatians that God has acted in Jesus to "snatch us out of this present evil age" (Galatians 1:4) and that the only thing that really matters is their participation in "new creation" (Galatians 6:15). The rhetorical force of his letter seems to be accomplishing the replication of that very act.

The composition-in-performance of many New Testament writings, therefore, functions almost with an apocalyptic force that means to lead the audience to end their previous way of being in the world and to enter a new way of seeing and being in the world—beliefs and ethical standards and relationships and hopes and new realities. In some sense, one can be in touch with this dynamic through the act of performing to contemporary audiences, even when contemporary audiences would not be aware of it. Although the cultural frames of contemporary audiences are vastly different from those of ancient audiences, a performer can still sometimes sense where the composer seems to be taking something for granted with the audience and where the composer is seeking to subvert and change the cultural assumptions of an audience.

ALTERED STATES OF CONSCIOUSNESS

There is another feature at play in performing the world of the story or letter. Anthropologists of theater regularly point out that the experience of a play places an audience in a liminal space, a space in which our ordinary world of daily life is somehow suspended while we enter the world of the drama being played out before us.[46] The audience is drawn into the suspension of disbelief and invited to entertain the world being acted out before them. This world may be similar to their world or it may be quite fantastic. In either case, there is a temporary loss of immediate awareness of one's own world and the absorption into another time and place. This altered state of consciousness may occur when one is reading a novel or short story. Unfortunately, because we do not read most biblical writings in their entirety, this experience seldom happens for us. However, performance shifts the understanding of a composition from the knowledge conveyed by the composition to an "experience" of it. Hence, when the biblical materials are put to performance, the possibility of experiencing an altered state of consciousness becomes more likely.

Here is the point. People are changed and transformed by encountering and entering an imaginary world. Many people will talk about the stories that have transformed them or about the "movie that changed my life." People talk about being changed by visiting or living in another culture. When we experience a different world, our views of things may change, our values may be shifted, our emotions may be transformed, our relationships may be altered, and we may be empowered to live different lives. We enter a world, are changed by the experience, and then emerge to be different people or—as in the case of the New Testament writings—to be different communities. Our research into the meaning and rhetoric of the New Testament writings may take a new turn if we can come to understand this performance dynamic and how it led people to embrace and be loyal to fresh, alternative ways of living.

Yet there is more to the idea of altered states of consciousness. On occasion, I as a performer have gone into a kind of "zone" in the telling. I invest myself so much in a gospel or letter that I get "lost in the performing." Even beyond engaging another world, I attain a kind of oneness with the telling and a oneness with the audience. At times, I have had people tell me that they were mesmerized by a performance at various points or that they were caught up in a way that transcended their ordinary experience. On occasion, people tell me that you could have heard a pin drop and that the audience was rapt by the story. I have had a few people tell me that they made some life-changing decisions as a result of their encounter with a biblical work in performance. I attribute these experiences to the nature of the composition I am telling and to the dynamics of performance, not to my capacity as a performer. In light of these experiences, I am convinced that performance events lend themselves to evoking altered states of consciousness.[47]

46. Turner, *Ritual Process*.

47. Pelias, *Performance Studies*, 18.

These quite limited reflections on the mystical-like experiences of performers and audiences have led me to reflect on descriptions of some audience responses to speeches in the New Testament—the speaking in tongues/baptism in the Holy Spirit at Pentecost in response to Peter's preaching (Acts 2:37–47) or Paul's description of people experiencing the Spirit in response to his proclamation (Galatians 3:15; 1 Thessalonians 1:2–10) or John's expectation that hearers of his story will move from death into "life." In these examples, the altered states of consciousness were communal experiences. In the ancient world, altered experiences were rarely individualistic. In my experiences, many modern audiences, particularly European-American audiences, tend to respond silently and privately, even as individuals within the audience. Sometimes an audience responds collectively with laughter, or some people may weep at a particularly poignant scene. People may indeed be transformed, but more likely in a personal way.

By contrast, ancient audiences would have been much more communal and vocal in their responses in a performance event. Whitney Shiner has shown the involvement of ancient audiences in performances.[48] They participated actively in the event throughout. Utter amazement at hearing the story about the healing of a blind man, or wails at seeing Jesus's last moments depicted before them, or joy and surprise at the narrative of Jesus's appearance from the grave—these responses may have spread through an audience like wildfire in a way that caught the whole group up in a transformative experience. These reactions would have been especially likely when the performance was closely related to the audience's own life world.

The study of performance events as altered states of consciousness may help us to explain better how Christianity came to be such a powerful force that spread so rapidly in the ancient world and captivated people's allegiance even in the face of persecution. Reading the New Testament in print may bring such experiences to our attention, but performance can bring them to life.

ACTING OUT THE COMPOSITION AS "SCRIPT"

As I have experienced it, the role of the performer is not merely to memorize and repeat the text. The performer acts it out. It is important to note that the contrast between reading a text in private and performing it in public is more than the difference between written and oral communication. It is not as if the audience has sound alone as a basis for interpretation, as if one were listening to a tape recording. A performance is *embodied* in the performer

48. Shiner, *Proclaiming the Gospel*, 143–90.

and the audience. The performer is present in body with voice, sounds, movements, gestures, proximity, appearance, and context. The audience is present and experiencing all of these dimensions along with the reactions of others in the audience. Performance is word-become-flesh in an event of embodied immediacy.[49]

To do a faithful interpretation, the performer needs to bring out or fill in what is missing in the composition as a written "transcription" of the oral performance. She or he needs to add sounds, gestures, facial expressions, glances, pace, pauses, pitch, volume, movement, posture, body language, proximity to audience, and so on. As mentioned earlier, the text may be seen as the fossil remains of a living performance. Scientists infer from a fossil what the living creature looked like. Similarly, we can infer from the transcription something of what the living performance may have been like. Our knowledge here is limited. However, there is some evidence from descriptions of storytellers, and there are guidelines in rhetorical handbooks indicating that stories such as we encounter in the gospels and orations such as we experience in the letters were animated and emotional. In doing a contemporary-style performance, while eager to be animated and engaging, we are not trying to replicate ancient performances, but rather to get in touch indirectly with the dynamics of orality. In order to succeed in this effort, we need to see the text as a "script" for performance. In some cases, the directions for these elements of performance are explicit in the text. In some cases, they are implied by the text. In other cases, the performer has to supply what the performer thinks will make the best sense of the text in context.

Trained storyteller Pam Faro has pointed out that just as punctuation needs to be supplied to a Greek manuscript and vowels need to be provided for a Hebrew manuscript as a basis for determining interpretation,[50] so in similar manner the performer needs to supply what performance dimensions are suggested or absent from the written transcription. To make this point, we note the title of an article by Bobby Loubser, "How Do You Report What Was Said with a Smile—Can We Overcome the Loss of Meaning When Oral-Manuscripts are Represented in Modern Print Media?"[51] The performer seeks to restore what is missing from the written script we have before us, which can be a significant amount. Consider the oft-quoted statistic from various studies claiming that communication is 80% body lan-

49. Bozarth, *Word's Body*.

50. From a conversation with Faro in 2004 at the Network of Biblical Storytellers conference, Atlanta, Georgia.

51. Loubser, "How Do You Report Something That Was Said with a Smile?"

guage, 10% tone, and 10% content—although, of course, these studies were based on ordinary language in a print culture.

As noted earlier, my first step in working with a text is to do the memorization, to get the words down. This is simply a matter of rote memory work that involves seemingly endless repetition of one line after another. Often I will practice such memory work by repeating the text as quickly as I am able to speak. This way, I get control over the words so that they flow easily. Once I have learned the words well, I can begin the process of exploring the text—playing, testing, choosing, presenting, changing the pace and tempo, trying out gestures, moving around, working with inflection and timing, experimenting with pitch and volume, listening for sound and silence—all as means to explore the potential meaning and impact of the text.[52] In this process I begin to engage my whole psychosomatic self in the embodiment of the text, not only to *tell* the story or *speak out* the letter but also to *show* the story or the letter to an audience.

Note that this practice is a reversal of the ancient process. For the most part, early tellers composed and performed orally and then the text as transcription was put in writing. By an inverse process, the contemporary performer is seeking to recover the performance by starting with the transcription. To be sure, I am a contemporary performer with another language and style of performing. In this reverse process, I am looking for all kinds of clues in the text itself about how I can faithfully bring the fossil text to life.

As I have indicated, the text itself is like a script that offers possible "stage directions" for voice, movement, body language, and emotions. As the story is told, directions for performance are suggested. These "suggestions" occur in virtually every episode of the gospel stories and are present everywhere in the letters and Revelation. Here are a very few representative examples:

> "He cried in a loud cry . . ." (*voice volume of what follows*)
>
> "They were astonished . . ." (*tone, facial expression*)
>
> "He sighed deeply in his spirit . . ." (*sound, body posture*)
>
> "He stretched out his hand and touched him . . ." (*gesture, pace*)
>
> "He withdrew with his disciples to the sea" (*movement*)
>
> "He looked up to heaven . . ." (*head gesture, facial expression*)
>
> ". . . gave to me and to Barnabas the right hand of partnership" (*hand gesture*)

52. Pelias, *Performance Studies*.

"The sixth angel poured his bowl over . . ." (*gesture, emotional expression*)

". . . and in his mouth it tasted bitter" (*facial movement and expression*)

No stage direction is carried out in a wooden or mechanical way. It must be a natural part of the performance, not something simply illustrative or added on. These aspects are part of the composition-in-performance. The performer makes judgments about how they can be expressed—sometimes in obvious and at other times in merely suggestive ways.

The composition also implies other performance features by virtue of grammar, syntax, word order, position of subordinate clauses, various forms of parallelism, length of sentences, choices of words, and devices of discourse, such as irony and innuendo, questions, depictions of characters by word and action, and descriptions of movement. The text may suggest onomatopoetic sounds or sounds other than words, such as ripping or sighing or weeping or beating the breast. It may suggest the use of props (real or imaginary), such as a trumpet or a bowl to demonstrate series of seven in Revelation, for example. Revelation depicts, in addition to sights and sounds, a period of silence, sweet and bitter tastes, as well as the odor of sacrifices. The performer seeks to recount the episodes so that audiences can imagine, indeed experience these aspects. All these dimensions give fullness to the text and make it alive for an audience with appeals to all the senses and with many emotions.

In addition, the text suggests occasions when the performer is to show the audience connections with episodes that occur one after another or that are spread across the narrative. For example, the performer might show the connections between the episodes in a series of three in the Gospel of Mark by performing them at the same spot on the stage and/or with the same tone, perhaps in a tone of secrecy or in a whisper. In other cases, it may be necessary for the performer to fill in gaps in a narrative or in an argument with performance features that seem to make good sense of the text—making connections of causation and consequence, of similarity and continuity. These connections might forecast what is to follow or echo what has already been said or done. Many of these features of a text may also be noted by narrative critics and discourse analysts; yet the experience of performing heightens their significance, enlivens their presence, and shows how they work orally. Often, in narrative, connections are implicit and not explicit, due to assumptions the composer makes of the hearer or to the paratactic nature of oral narration. The performer needs to be aware of these gaps and to know where it is appropriate to fill them in order to make sense of the narrative—not by adding words to the text but by discerning what seems to be implied for performance. What is so in narrative is also true of the connections between a series of arguments or examples or teachings in a letter.

As with most exegesis, this procedure of filling gaps is somewhat circular. You hypothesize/infer certain ways to fill the oral/performing gaps, and then you use these inferences in performance to see if that interpretation makes sense of and illuminates the story/speech in the telling. For example, the episode of Jesus healing the man with the withered hand (Mark 3:1) suggests that the Pharisees were not able to bring charges against Jesus because Jesus did not touch the man when he healed him and therefore did not do work on the Sabbath. When I perform this story, I cannot add this information verbally, but I can suggest that Jesus was about to touch him and then hesitates and does not touch him. By acting out "missing" information, a performer may clarify through interpretation the possible meaning of a composition and perhaps resolve some gaps and fissures with tone and nonverbal expressions. Indeed, by voice and body language and staging, the performer may serve to embody the coherence of the composition.

PERSONIFICATION OF CHARACTERS

When acting out a narrative, the performer takes on the role of the narrator. Although the narrator is not a character in the story, the narrator has a definite persona, for example, in manner, tone, intensity, and sense of humor. In this role the narrator is the storyteller addressing the audience. At the same time, the narrator as performer is also reacting to the story while telling it, with emotions and attitudes expressed in voice and body. For example, when a healing is recounted, the narrator-performer may express a tone of amazement both when recounting the outcome of the healing and when describing the response of onlookers. In all, it is important for the performer in the role of narrator to find a voice appropriate to the story and to express a tone that engenders trust in the audience. Knowing the text well, exploring the characters, and understanding the plot all help to determine how one line or the next might be delivered in ways appropriate to the narrative.

As the narrator "acts out" the story, the performer brings the characters to life—each with his or her own attitudes, emotions, physical manner, and vocal traits.[53] The narrator takes on the distinct role of each of the characters as each speaks and acts in the narrative—by personifying them through voice, tone, pace, posture, facial expressions, and so on. We get the idea from listening to almost any book on tape. With his voice alone

53. Lee and Galati, *Oral Interpretations*, 319.

on tape, the actor Jim Dale has brought more than two hundred characters to life in the tapes of the *Harry Potter* books. The live performer also uses posture, facial expressions, gestures, and movement to distinguish between characters, most often simply by suggesting these features of a character. The Gospel of Mark has more than fifty different speaking voices and many more characters. Personification helps the audience to see the distinct points of view of the different characters: "an almost imperceptible change of angle, combined with the other changes in posture, muscle tone, facial expression, and voice characteristics, will make it clear that another character is speaking."[54] Personifying the characters also enhances entertainment as a means to engage and hold an audience. The importance of engaging an audience was especially crucial in antiquity.

More than that, personification is a form of interpretation. The dynamic of personification leads performers to put themselves in the place of the character, to think about what drives that character, what each character is looking for, what their "desires" are, what their manner of relating is, what their beliefs and values are, and what they are willing to do to accomplish their goals—as an interpretation of the way in which the composition has portrayed them.[55] There is a form of embodiment here in which the performer puts himself or herself into the place of the character and takes his or her role in the story, whether the character happens to be an opponent or a sympathizer of Jesus.

It is important for the performer to "get into" every character. Each character can easily get lost in the overarching voice of the narrator. When this blurring happens, the drives, goals, beliefs, standards, style of speaking, and relationships of each character do not come across to the audience. The characters may become so stereotyped as to lose the realistic nature of the narrative. I do an exercise that helps me screen out other points of view and focus on one character at a time. For example, when working with Mark I retell an episode from the point of view of one or other of the characters, simply by changing the pronouns and the tone. So in one of the conflict stories with Jesus, I will recount the episode word for word from the point of view of the opponents, changing only the pronouns. In this way I get into their righteous anger and frustration at Jesus's offensive action. Or I will retell a healing story from the point of view of the suppliant and thereby experience in new ways the joy of being brought to health. Retelling the same episode from the point of view of the crowd will get me in touch with the wonder and delight of the healings of Jesus. When I tell a story from

54. Ibid., 380.

55. Pelias, *Performance Studies*, 88–89.

the point of view of Jesus, I get in touch with the forcefulness of his authority, the mission that drives his determination, and the focused attention he gives to the characters whom he encounters. All these fill out/fill in the story that the narrator of Mark is telling. Then, when I return to recount an episode from the narrator's point of view, I can move quickly in portraying one character after another, seeking to retain the emotions, attitudes, inflections, and affect I have discovered with each character. This exercise helps me not only to invest in each character but also to see the conflicts, the contrasts, and the relationships between characters much more clearly. This exercise also lays bare how the narrator leads the reader to identify with some characters and to resist others.

Such personification makes it clear that characters are not simply stereotypes, nor are they reducible to mere plot functions. They come to life in performance, however briefly. They become three-dimensional. It is the role of the performer to make the characters memorable, even the minor ones. Through the process of personification, the performer's acute awareness of such diverse points of view in characterization leads the interpreter-performer to understand more sharply the developing plot, what is at stake in the conflicts, the diverse points of view encompassed by the overarching point of view of the narrator, and the power dynamics of the text. For the benefit of the audience, all efforts to "show" each character and to "see" each character in imagination through the eyes of the narrator or other characters enliven the imagination and engagement of the audience—with the result that they are better able to experience what you portray, to see what you see.

In performing a letter or an apocalypse, the performer becomes aware of certain dynamics by seeking to personify the senders—their personal appeals (Galatians and Philemon), self-descriptions (2 Corinthians), depictions of the audience and other characters (Philippians), along with descriptions of events and emotions (Revelation). As "commissioned agent" of the sender/letter-writer, the performer "becomes" the sender in the act of presenting the letter. Since the performer is portraying just one persona (the sender of the letter) throughout the whole letter, the performer may go through many changes in emotion and appeal. The presentation of a letter-sender involves a more sustained and complex personification, a personification that also includes changes in the relationship with the audience as the letter progresses.

ONSTAGE/OFFSTAGE FOCUS

The issue of the performer's focus in addressing an audience directly gets us in touch with the relationship between performer and audience and how the audience figures in the story being told. In most stage productions, the actors never address the audience. They address each other. When there is direct address to an audience, such as may be the case in a one-person show, contemporary oral interpretation distinguishes an onstage focus from an offstage focus. When one is telling a story, the performer directly addresses the audience in front offstage. In a theater production, when an actor has been interacting with other characters onstage and then suddenly turns and addresses the audience directly, this is referred to as "breaking the fourth wall"—that is, the "fourth wall" of the stage area, the imaginary wall that separates the performers from the audience.

The performer of a story is primarily engaged in speaking through this fourth wall directly to the audience offstage. When, however, in the course of telling, the performer personifies a character and speaks as that character, the performer addresses another imaginary character onstage as if inside the world of the story, with the audience "overhearing" and "overseeing" what is being said and done "onstage"—much as an audience would observe one character in a play addressing another character onstage. In a narrative like Mark, the audience is first addressed offstage and then the narrator portrays characters onstage as they come to act and speak. This onstage/offstage focus moves back and forth rapidly and frequently as the narrator weaves the story. Making such a distinction helps to clarify for the audience when the narrator is speaking as the narrator and when the narrator is portraying a character. Thus, the narrator uses personification in onstage/offstage focus as a means to keep the narrator distinct from the characters and thereby be able to lead the audience to identify with some characters and distance themselves from others.

The onstage/offstage distinction helps the performer to bring out the conflicts more clearly for the audience, distinguish the points of view of different characters, show the contrasts between characters, and clarify the developing plot. In so doing, it manifests fully the personification process that the narrator uses to get into the roles of different characters and express their drives and strategies. Onstage/offstage focus also tends to make it more obvious to the audience which characters the narrator is promoting and which characters and actions the narrator is seeking to discourage the audience from identifying with.

In contrast to an approach that uses both onstage and offstage focus, Tom Boomershine has argued that, in ancient performances, the performer always addressed the audience offstage and made distinctions between characters without using any onstage focus at all.[56] The difference is significant. In this latter scenario the audience is always addressed directly, even when the characters speak. Hence, for example, when Jesus condemns the Pharisees, the narrator-as-Jesus addresses the audience directly—and thereby the audience "becomes" part of the drama by playing the Pharisees for Jesus. When Jesus teaches/corrects the disciples, the audience becomes the disciples being addressed. When the narrator-as-Pharisees addresses Jesus, the audience "becomes" Jesus. In this way, then, the audience is led to identify with all the characters at one time or another. Such a dynamic leads to a distinctively different rhetorical impact on the audience. For example, as Boomershine argues, this approach may have worked to undercut anti-Judaism in a composition like the Gospel of John—since the audience is led to identify at one point or another with all the characters, including the Jewish opponents of Jesus.

Yet the matter may be more complex yet. The impact of this kind of audience identification may be obviated somewhat by other strategies that the narrator has used to lead an audience in the process of identification—the positive and negative descriptions of characters, the promotion of certain standards that lead the audience to judge the characters positively and negatively, the development of protagonists and antagonists, and so on. For example, even when Jesus is speaking to the audience-as-opponents, the audience may still identify with the pathos or passion of the protagonist Jesus rather than with the opponents being addressed. Nevertheless, in general, the composition-in-performance will mean something different and have a different impact for an audience when the audience is always addressed as the different characters in the story.

Therefore we need to tell and to hear the biblical narratives both with and without the onstage/offstage focus, as a means to understand better the dynamics of the story and its potential rhetoric—"playing" with the text to discern its boundaries and possibilities. This issue is also interesting when applied to letters, in which the performance collapses the onstage/offstage dichotomy—in that the audience becomes a major character (the recipients of the letter) throughout the entire presentation. Different hearers experience different things. When performing a letter, I have found it helpful to assign students as the audience to assume roles from diverse ancient social locations (including those referred to in the letter)—slave, householder, soldier, male/female, outsider, wealthy/poor, and so on—as a way to help us see the differing impact a letter may potentially have had within an

56. Boomershine, "Jesus' Voice in John."

audience. Conversations with students in these assumed roles have been quite illuminating.

A performer is aware of the performer's relationship with the audience that persists throughout a performance as well as the relationships the performer displays between the characters in the story—and their impact on an audience. Experiencing these relationships in performance, either as performer or as audience, will help us to understand better the dynamics of rhetorical impact.

SUBTEXT

Perhaps the most generative feature of performance for research is that of the "subtext." The subtext refers to the message and impact that the performer conveys in the way a line is delivered. In performance, whether ancient or modern, the subtext represents a layer of meaning that is present in every line. Subtext is a level of exegesis largely unexplored in biblical studies, because silent reading in print does not require one to address the issue of subtext. Yet all performers have to decide what they will convey by *how* they say each line. Consider Jesus's manner of relating to the disciples in Mark. Take, for example, the line "Don't you understand yet?" in which Jesus addresses the disciples (Mark 8:17). Does the question imply inquiry, patience, impatience, sarcasm, disappointment, disdain, resignation? This is an obvious example, even to readers, but *every line* requires this kind of reflection. Listen to two different performances of the same passages and experience how differing inflections change the meaning and impact of the text.

A performer must seek to infer the subtext from the context and then try different subtexts to determine which approaches work best. There is no way to do a performance without conveying a subtext message with every line, no matter how badly done or ill-informed it is. Subtext can be conveyed both by voice and by physical expression (see below). For the most part, however, subtext is conveyed primarily through the voice—what tone to convey, where to put the emphasis, what pace to say it, whether there should be a pause, how loud it should be, and so on. It is a common exercise in oral interpretation to take a simple line and attempt to say the same line in as many different ways as possible. Or take any episode in Mark or a passage in a letter of Paul and try each line with different subtexts to see what works and how it works. This is an exercise well worth doing, if only to see how important the subtexts are and what a difference they can make.

The subtext is not an add-on. Rather, it is integral to and determinative of the meaning and rhetoric of a text. In performance, the subtext is an implicit part of the "text." There are many clues in a script that suggest how a line can be delivered, and the immediate clues are assessed in relation to the composition as a whole. To look for clues in the text that suggest appropriate subtexts for every line is to see a dimension of the text that may otherwise not even be part of the interpretation.

NONVERBAL COMMUNICATION

Nonverbal expressions can also convey the subtext.[57] Again, both the presence of subtext and embodiment are constitutive of the composition-in-performance. Physical expression or the lack thereof will contribute to the subtext. Nonverbal communication includes gestures, posture, bodily movement, "winks" to the audience, walking or moving around, as well as facial expressions such as a smile, frown, raised eyebrow, grimace, look of surprise or amazement, and so on. In the context of performing a story, these bodily expressions seem to be myriad. Any and all movement—lips, eyes, cocking the head, crossing arms, even the lack of movement—are part of the nonverbal communication. Obviously some movements are more important and integral to meaning than other movements. However, the very em-body-ment of the composition-in-performance means that physical movement (or the restraint of it) is unavoidable at all times. These represent the body language, the kinesthetic dimensions of performance.[58]

In some cases, the body language is clearly suggested by the text. When you perform any text, it is amazing how many physical gestures are described or implied in the world of the text—touch, lay on hands, shake, kneel, fall at one's feet, put arms around, run, look up, look around, weep, wash hands, eat, and so on. And it is surprising how much movement from place to place (on the "stage-area") is suggested in every text, particularly from one episode to another. In other less explicit matters, nonverbal expressions may be inferred from the text and used to convey the subtext to a line. Often these gestures can be conveyed with the slightest movement.

Take the example used above of Jesus saying to his disciples, "Don't you understand yet?" The subtext of the line can be expressed with hands reaching forward to appeal for understanding or with arms crossed or a hand on the forehead to indicate frustration or eyes rolling to express disgust or with hands thrown up in the air to reinforce the denseness of the disciples. Again, the nonverbal expressions will be there. What are they conveying?

57. Botha, "Exploring Gesture."

58. Lee and Galati, *Oral Interpretation*, 66–67.

And how does this help us to amplify or narrow interpretive possibilities? The performer's body, even when fairly stationary, conveys something.

The key is this: nonverbal communications do not just reinforce or illustrate verbal communication; rather, they are an integral part of the verbal communication itself, and they often determine its meaning. When I scowl or laugh or scratch my head or show impatience with my body or look puzzled or shrug my shoulders or throw up my hands, I am conveying the potential meanings of a line just as much as the tone and pitch and volume of the words convey it. How, for example, do we use our bodies to show that a line is ironic or humorous or derisive? Again, these nonverbal expressions do not just accompany the composition. They are an integral and indispensable means by which the potential meanings of the words are determined and by which the impact of the rhetoric is conveyed. As with the use of the voice in performance, nonverbal communication becomes an integral part of the composition.

EMOTIONS

The experience of performing recovers the emotive dimensions of a text and makes it clear that emotions are a significant form of persuasion—conveyed by the words of the text, the subtext, and nonverbal communication. Sound itself as a medium is a primary means of conveying and evoking emotion. A common response by audiences to performances of New Testament texts is the surprising realization that these texts express and evoke strong emotions. Many, if not most, of these emotions are explicitly referred to in the text or are strongly implied by the rhetoric. The range of emotions expressed and described in Mark and Revelation, for example, is so extensive as to be astounding—fear, amazement, awe, horror, puzzlement, anguish, grief, frustration, determination, anger, joy, love, and much more. In addition to the voice, via its volume, pitch, pace, and intensity, these emotions may be conveyed by shaking the head, gritting the teeth, laughing, cringing, weeping, employing various facial expressions, and so on. The issue is this: how does the performer express these emotions in such a way as to evoke an emotional response also in the audience? We do not know a great deal about the nature of emotions in antiquity. Nor do we know much about what bodily expressions showed or triggered emotions. Nevertheless, performing the text does serve to engage us with the emotive dimensions of the text and enables us to understand the part emotions played in the meaning and rhetoric of the composition.

Ancient rhetoricians agree that the power of emotion is more persuasive than logical argumentation in oration. The rhetorical "proof" of ethos—the appeal to emotions as a means of persuasion—is pervasive in New Testament letters. Emotions can be implied everywhere in a text. Galatians expresses Paul's love for the Galatians, his anger at their abandonment of the gospel he preached, his disdain for the opponents, his emotional appeal to the experience of the Spirit, the affection of his personal relationship with the Galatians as his children, and his intense desire to bring them back to grace. I used to think some passages in Galatians were personal and others were impersonal arguments. After performing it over and over, I have come to realize that every line—whether it be ethos, pathos, or logos—represents a personal, indeed emotional, appeal in which Paul considers the stakes to be extremely high. The emotions may vary in type and intensity in the ebb and flow of the letter, but they are always present.

Performance can bring to the fore the emotive dimensions of a text as an integral and indispensable means of conveying its meaning and persuasive power. We exegetes are challenged to cultivate critical thinking that will allow us to assess what are the appropriate emotions expressed by and evoked by the composition.

HUMOR

There is humor in texts that performers can bring out in the act of performing. We may infer the potential for humor in the text based on such features as fractured grammar, unusual syntax, irony, contrasts, inconsistencies, plays on words, misunderstandings, and revealing insights into human nature. We recover this humor as part of the meaning and rhetoric of the text. As we explore the text, we should not assume that what may be humorous to us will have been humorous to original audiences. Conversely, there may have been things humorous to ancient communities of particular social locations that are not so humorous to us. I am convinced that Jesus's punch lines in the controversies with elites—in which Jesus eludes their efforts to charge him or punctures their pretentions—would have brought howls of delight and expressions of applause from peasant audiences.

Humor is more pervasive in the New Testament than we have judged to be the case. And performing the text brings it out. I have on occasion gotten "on a roll" with humor in the Gospel of Mark that has the audience laughing repeatedly. At such times, I find myself in response to the audience saying lines humorously that I did not previously think were funny, but which suddenly became occasions for great laughter. The series of failures of the disciples in Mark can be tragic and quite humorous at the same time. The "punning" dialogues of misunderstanding between Jesus and other characters in the Gospel of John can be hilarious when seen as a sort of Abbott and Costello repartee about "Who's on first?" with characters speaking past each other. Such irony can express wry humor that is conveyed with great subtlety. Or it can reflect an absurdity that is acted out through exaggeration. Consider the line to Philemon in Paul's request on behalf of Onesimus, when he says, "Not to mention that you do owe me your life!" (Philemon 19). Consider Paul's comment in Galatians wishing that the opponents who favor circumcision would "cut it all off" (Galatians 5:12). The conversation between body parts in 1 Corinthians 12 can be quite amusing—and the humor significantly enhances the power of Paul's point, as well as its chances of being remembered and repeated!

Humor is a significant part of performing. Again, humor is integral to both meaning and rhetoric. Humor entertains, engages an audience, gives insight, establishes a bond between performer and audience, creates community among those who understand the humor, and is an effective means of persuasion—and also enhances memory. Reading silently may not bring out the humor. By contrast, playing with inflection and pace and body language in performance can enable us to see in what ways passages may be using humor and to what effect.

TEMPORAL DIMENSIONS

Performing a text from beginning to end enables performer and audience to experience the text in a temporal way. We are used to thinking of the text as a spatial display on the page and to identifying texts by chapters and verses (again, a spatial display). In so doing, we have lost the sense of time that is such an integral part of the performance of a text. In interpreting a written text, we often collect references across a text without regard to sequence. We can stop and reread and go back and forth in our own time with little regard for order. When you perform or hear a text, you become aware of the unstoppable nature of the movement. You also become aware of the temporal sequence of what the hearers know and when they know it, when something new is introduced, how an earlier part prepares the hearers for a later event, and how a later part clarifies and elaborates an earlier event. You become aware, for example, that episodes in a gospel are usually not interchangeable; their location in the sequence of the story is appropriate and often critical to the developing plot and integral to the meaning and impact of episodes that precede and follow.[59]

59. Rhoads, *Reading Mark*, 63–94.

Furthermore, one becomes aware of the potential ebbs and flows of a narrative or a letter. There are fluctuations in intensity, variations in emotion, ranges of intimacy and distance, flows in action and description. In the plot, there may be a rise or fall in the action, transitions, shifts and breakthroughs, moments of climax. Things speed up and slow down. The possibilities of the paces and rhythms of a text become apparent in the act of performing. Being in relation to an audience and experiencing its responses as the narrative or letter moves along in time helps the performer to judge the most effective pace, where an emphasis belongs, and where a high moment occurs. Standing up, sitting down, moving closer or further from the audience, raising and lowering the volume, along with a variety of gestures, can bring this flow of the narrative to have the greatest impact on the audience. Such experiences may help us to see how the rhetoric of a performance may have worked its magic on ancient audiences.

In addition, there is a distinctive process of persuasion to a story or a letter or an apocalypse that is difficult to understand without performing the composition—an inner logic (deeper than hook words, connections, and transitions) that enables the performer to recall what comes next in the narrative or in the course of an argument. Interestingly, I have found that this temporal coherence of a text may often be found not in the text itself, but in a particular sequence of implied impacts on an audience as they experience the temporal movement of the composition—like the steps in a combination lock as the sequential drops of the tumbler prepare for a final "unlocking." First, the hearers must know "x" before they are prepared to experience "y," which in turn enables the audience to accept what comes next, and then leads them to the ultimate place the performer wants them to be.

In Mark the hearers will not be prepared to accept Jesus as a rejected messiah until they become convinced that Jesus is the messiah through his healings, exorcisms, and nature miracles. In experiencing Galatians, the audience must go through a sequence of affirmations, appeals, and arguments that Paul must make before that moment comes in the performance when Paul is "confident that you will take no other view" (Galatians 5:10). He moves from his own story to their story to God's story, weaving these together until he comes to that clarion call, "For freedom Christ has set us free" (Galatians 5:1). Paul assumes (rightly or wrongly) that the audience begins at a certain place with certain assumptions and allegiances and attachments. He has to take the hearer from one position or point of view to another, so that the audience is at a different place at the end than they were at the outset. In other words, there is a temporal sequence to the rhetoric of the letter; the arguments have an inner logic and cannot be dealt with in just any order. And they have an accumulative impact on the audience.

A similar sequence takes place in the experience of the hearers of Revelation. The hearers must first know what Jesus expects and that he can see into their hearts (the letters); then they must know the evil nature of Rome (the beast and the whore) before they are prepared to reject Rome; then, they must grieve their own loss of Rome and detach from it before they can embrace the New Jerusalem. The expressions of worship throughout Revelation prepare them to be attached to the New Jerusalem when it comes and thereby enable them to withdraw from Rome now and be willing to die in allegiance to the God of a new heaven and earth. Returning to the image of the combination lock, the narrator of Revelation leads the hearers to the point when the tumblers have fallen and the lock is ready to be opened. In other words, there is a dynamic to the cognitive and emotional catharsis the hearers are being led through from beginning to end—a rhetorical dynamic that gives continuity to a text located in successive responses of the audience, a dynamic that is difficult to discern without the experience of doing a performance. Comprehending the sequential developments of a composition in terms of their impact on hearers adds a fresh perspective to the work of interpreters.

RHETORIC AND AUDIENCE

I keep coming back to the rhetorical impact of the New Testament compositions because my experience has been that performance enables one to be especially aware of the significance of audience and context. We exegetes often talk about ancient audiences and imagine their reactions. Often our constructions of these contexts are vague or general. To perform a text is to become aware of the audience and its impact upon performance in a very specific and immediate way. The setting of the audience matters. To perform in a university or in a church or in a prison or on the street corner or at a homeless shelter leads the performer to perform texts differently. The same must have been true for the ancient world—synagogue or marketplace or private home or public building. Also, social location of the audience matters. A text takes on different meanings spoken by and to people in different social locations. People identify with different characters, connect with different sayings, desire differing outcomes for the plot, and so on. The sociopolitical context matters. What is going on in people's lives and in the larger world at the time brings issues and resonances to the experience of the performance.

In my opinion there is no better way to be in touch with the rhetorical impact upon an audience than to perform before a live audience. Simple reading may eclipse the rhetorical impact. Reading-exegetes tend to focus on what the text *means* and neglect what the text *does* in performance. Even those who study the rhetoric of letters tend to focus on the organizational dynamics of the text and the identification of ethos and pathos rather than on the experience of an audience. Clearly the text is more powerful in performance than in reading; thus performing offers a better chance to be in touch with the rhetorical dynamics. As we have suggested, the performer is seeking to draw the audience into the world of the composition and to persuade the audience to take on the point of view presented in the text.

But more than this, the experience of performing has convinced me that we need to expand our idea of the various kinds of impact a narrative or letter may have had on hearers. Persuading an audience to embrace a certain viewpoint or persuading an audience to take a certain action are only some of the effects that may result from a performance. For example, Mark does not just give people the reasons not to be paralyzed by fear; rather, the rhetorical dynamic of the gospel also seeks to evoke in the audience the actual capacity to be faithful in the face of threat. The composer of Matthew does not just condemn hypocrisy; his sayings serve to expose/reveal it in the audience. The creator of John does not just talk about eternal life; he seeks to create the experience of it in the audience. In Philemon, Paul does not just want Philemon to take a certain action; the letter seeks to effect a transformation of relationships from hierarchy to mutuality in the whole community. The author of James does not just promote a certain viewpoint to a disengaged reader; he wants to generate in the hearers the capacity to be wise in their context. Our challenge as exegetes is to ask what the composition-in-performance is doing and how it does it.

Furthermore, performance generates transformation not primarily for individuals but for communities. Performances in a communal setting create and solidify community. The shared event gives the audience an experience of solidarity. The community has experienced the performance together; the event becomes part of their social memory. The performer seeks to create or strengthen the communal dimensions of the audience through inside information, irony, humor, drama, the evocation of emotions, and much more. In addition, New Testament compositions addressed such communal issues as factions, lethargy, fear of persecution, apostasy, and misunderstandings; and they sought to bring to the community unity, inspiration, corporate courage, loyalty, and clarity. Reading that focuses on the text may overlook the kinds of immediate responses we can imagine as a direct result of the communal responses to a performance. Of course, intentionally or unintentionally, a performance can also exacerbate the dueling forces within the community or generate conflict between the community and those outside.

Finally, in generating a new way of being in the world, the composition/performer seeks to lead a community to see itself as an alternative way of thinking about the world and to experience itself as a counter-cultural community. The performance is nothing less than an attempt to create a world. In all these instances, how did the compositions-in-performance do that? And how might we imagine that communal audiences actually responded to such performances?

I have found that the post-performance conversations I have with an audience have given me an opportunity to reflect on all these factors and to reinforce them. Each performance is an expression of that particular performer's interpretation of the text in that context with that particular audience. Even if the words spoken are exactly the same, the text is still fluid in its diverse performative incarnations. Even the same performer will enact or embody the text in different ways on different occasions with different audiences in different places. Other performers will interpret the text differently and will defend their interpretations. The point is that the exegete as performer gets in touch with the fact that there are rhetorical dimensions to every line in the developing composition, all of which contribute to the overall impact of each performance. Conversations with audiences about their experiences have helped me to grasp these rhetorical dimensions more clearly.

PERFORMANCE AS TEST OF INTERPRETATION

Finally, I have written about the way in which performance can expand the range of interpretations and also reveal the limits of interpretation. How can performance be a test of interpretations? We often give interpretations of the text without ever asking: could the lines be performed in such a way that the hearer would understand the meaning you are giving to it? Can the subtext stretch to accommodate an interpretation such that the audience can "get it"? I am not here writing about the fact that modern hearers would have to know certain cultural information to understand a line. Rather, I am asking whether the line can even be said at all in such a way as to express a certain interpretation. For example, some Markan scholars understand Jesus's words about the poor widow in the temple (Mark 12:41–44) to be a criticism of the widow for contributing to a corrupt temple that is doomed to destruction. However, I cannot figure out a way to perform that line—in which Jesus lifts her up as a model (12:43–44)—so as to convey a negative meaning to it. Or could one convey Jesus's cry of abandonment on the cross (Mark 15:34 from Psalm 22:2) so as to express hopefulness? We can see the response of the centurion (Mark 15:39) as affirmation or confession, but can the centurion's line work in performance as sarcasm?

For example, take your interpretation of something and test it by saying the lines in such a way that you actually bring across to an imaginary audience, ancient or modern, that particular interpretation of the text. Of course, the text has a range of possible meanings and a range of possible performances. Through performances, we may be able to identify which interpretations have a consensus, which interpretations are controversial but permitted, and which interpretations constitute a fundamental misconstrual of the possibilities of the text.[60] In this way, performance may be an important way to test the limits of viable interpretations and provide criteria for making critical judgments in adjudications over interpretation.

CONCLUSION

All these performance choices together comprise an interpretation—not as a commentary, not as a monograph, not as a lecture about the text, but as a performance of the text. This is an incarnation, an embodiment, of the text. In a sense, the performer becomes the text. Yet in an even larger sense the Bible becomes embodied in the community in the performance event—by performance, by response, by memory. Rather than a book, the performer and audience become the medium. Just as a reader interprets the words on the page, so the audience interprets what the performer has presented. Experiencing the performance—a performer in community—places interpretation in a public and communal arena. Such efforts to recover the original medium of the biblical traditions, including all the facets of performance articulated here, may provide many new dimensions to the Bible and its interpretation. Interpretation lies at the site of performance.

BIBLIOGRAPHY

Achtemeier, Paul J. "*Omne verbum sonat*: The New Testament and the Oral Environment of Late Western Antiquity." *Journal of Biblical Literature* 109 (1990) 3–27.

Bar-Ilan, Meir. "Illiteracy in the Land of Israel in the First Centuries C.E." In *Essays in the Social Scientific Study of Judaism and Jewish Society*, edited by Simcha Fishbane et al., 46–61. 2nd ed. Hoboken, NY: Ktav.

Bauman, Richard. *Story, Performance, Event: Contextual Studies of Oral Narrative*. Cambridge Studies in Oral and Literate Culture 10. Cambridge: Cambridge University Press, 1986.

———. *Verbal Art as Performance*. Rowley, MA: Newbury House, 1977.

60. Pelias, *Performance Studies*, 159.

Betz, Hans Dieter. *Galatians: A Commentary on Paul's Letter to the Churches of Galatia.* Hermeneia. Philadelphia: Fortress, 1979.

Boomershine, Thomas E. "Biblical Megatrends: Towards a Paradigm for the Interpretation of the Bible in the Electronic Age." In *Society of Biblical Literature Seminar Papers* 28, edited by Kent Richards, 144–57. Atlanta: Scholars, 1989.

———. "Jesus' Voice in John." In *Preaching John's Gospel: The World It Imagines*, edited by David Fleer et al., 145–56. St. Louis: Chalice, 2008.

Botha, J. Eugene. "Exploring Gesture and Nonverbal Communication in the Ancient World: Some Basic Concepts." *Neotestamentica* 30 (1996) 253–66.

Botha, Pieter J. J. "Letter Writing and Oral Communication in Antiquity: Suggested Implications for the Interpretation of Paul's Letter to the Galatians." *Scriptura* 42 (1992) 17–34. Reprinted in *Orality and Literacy in Early Christianity*, 193–211. Biblical Performance Criticism Series 5. Eugene, OR: Cascade Books, 2012.

Bowman, Alan K., and Gref Woolf, eds. *Literacy and Power in the Ancient World.* Cambridge: Cambridge University Press, 1994.

Bozarth, Alla Renee. *The Word's Body: An Incarnational Aesthetic of Interpretation.* Lanham, MD: University Press of America, 1997.

Brandt, Jo-Ann A. *Dialogue and Drama: Elements of Greek Tragedy in the Fourth Gospel.* Peabody, MA: Hendrickson, 2004.

Briggs, Richard S. *Words in Action: Speech-Act Theory and Biblical Interpretation.* Edinburgh: T. & T. Clark, 2001.

Caird, George B. *A Commentary on the Revelation of Saint John the Divine.* San Francisco: Harper & Row, 1966.

Carr, David M. *Writing on the Tablet of the Heart: Origins of Scripture and Literature.* Oxford: Oxford University Press, 2005.

Davis, Casey Wayne. *Oral Biblical Criticism: The Influence of the Principles of Orality on the Literary Structures of Paul's Epistle to the Philippians.* Journal for the Study of the New Testament Supplements 172. Sheffield: Sheffield Academic, 1999.

Dean, Margaret E. "The Grammar of Sound in Greek Texts: Towards a Method of Mapping the Echoes of Speech in Writing." *Australian Biblical Review* 44 (1996) 53–70.

Dewey, Arthur J. "Competing Gospels: Imperial Echoes, A Dissident Voice." In *The Bible in Ancient and Modern Media: Story and Performance*, edited by Holly E. Hearon and Philip Ruge-Jones, 64–82. Biblical Performance Criticism Series 1. Eugene, OR: Cascade Books, 2009.

Dewey, Joanna. "From Storytelling to Written Text: The Loss of Early Christian Women's Voices." *Biblical Theology Bulletin* 26 (1996) 71–78. Reprinted in *The Oral Ethos of the Early Church: Speaking, Writing, and the Gospel of Mark*, 131–44. Biblical Performance Criticism Series 1. Eugene, OR: Cascade Books, 2013.

———. "Textuality in Oral Tradition: A Survey of the Pauline Tradition." *Semeia* 65 (1995) 37–65.

Doan, William, and Terry Giles. *Prophets, Performance, and Power: Performance Criticism of the Hebrew Bible.* New York: T. & T. Clark, 2005.

Draper, Jonathan A., ed. *Orality, Literacy, and Colonialism in Antiquity.* Semeia Studies 47. Atlanta: Society of Biblical Literature, 2004.

Foley, John Miles. *How to Read an Oral Poem.* Urbana: University of Illinois Press, 2002.

———. *The Singer of Tales in Performance.* Voices in Performance and Text. Bloomington: Indiana University Press, 1995.

Fowler, Robert M. "Why Everything We Know about the Bible Is Wrong: Lessons from the Media History of the Bible." In *The Bible in Ancient and Modern Media: Story and Performance*, edited by Holly E. Hearon and Philip Ruge-Jones, 3–20. Biblical Performance Criticism Series 1. Eugene, OR: Cascade Books, 2009.

Frei, Hans W. *The Eclipse of Biblical Narrative: A Study in Eighteenth and Nineteenth Century Hermeneutics*. New Haven: Yale University Press, 1984.

Gamble, Harry Y. *Books and Readers in the Early Church: A History of Early Christian Texts*. New Haven: Yale University Press, 1995.

Giles, Terry, and William J. Doan. *Twice Used Songs: Performance Criticism of the Songs of Ancient Israel*. Peabody, MA: Hendrickson, 2009.

Haines-Eitzen, Kim. *Guardians of Letters: Literacy, Power, and the Transmitters of Early Christian Literature*. Oxford: Oxford University Press, 2000.

Hargis, Donald E. "The Rhapsode." *Quarterly Journal of Speech* 56 (1970) 388–97.

Harris, William V. *Ancient Literacy*. Cambridge: Harvard University Press, 1986.

Harvey, John D. *Listening to the Text: Oral Patterning in Paul's Letters*. Grand Rapids: Baker, 1988.

Havelock, Eric. *Preface to Plato*. Cambridge: Harvard University Press, 1963.

Hearon, Holly E. *The Mary Magdalene Tradition: Witness and Counter-Witness in Early Christian Communities*. Collegeville, MN: Liturgical, 2004.

———. "The Storytelling World of the First Century and the Gospels." In *The Bible in Ancient and Modern Media: Story and Performance*, edited by Holly E. Hearon and Philip Ruge-Jones, 21–35. Biblical Performance Criticism Series 1. Eugene, OR: Cascade Books, 2009.

Hezser, Catherine. *Jewish Literacy in Roman Palestine*. Texts and Studies in Ancient Judaism 81. Tübingen: Mohr/Siebeck, 2001.

Horsley, Richard A. *Hearing the Whole Story: The Politics of Plot in Mark's Story*. Louisville: Westminster John Knox, 2001.

Issacharoff, Michael, and Robin F. Jones, eds. *Performing Texts*. Philadelphia: University of Pennsylvania Press, 1988.

Kelber, Werner H. *The Oral and the Written Gospel: The Hermeneutics of Speaking and Writing in the Synoptic Tradition, Mark, Paul, and Q*. Philadelphia: Fortress, 1983.

Kirk, Alan, and Tom Thatcher, eds. *Memory, Tradition, and Text: Uses of the Past in Early Christianity*. Semeia Studies 52. Atlanta: Society of Biblical Literature, 2005.

Koester, Helmut. "Writings and the Spirit: Authority and Politics in Ancient Christianity." *Harvard Theological Review* 84 (1991) 353–72.

Kuhn, Thomas S. *The Structure of Scientific Revolutions*. 3rd ed. Chicago: University of Chicago Press, 1996.

Lee, Charlotte I., and Frank Galati. *Oral Interpretation*. 5th ed. Boston: Houghton Mifflin, 1977.

Lee, Margaret Ellen, and Bernard Brandon Scott. *Sound Mapping the New Testament*. Salem, OR: Polebridge, 2009.

Levy, Shimon. *The Bible as Theatre*. Brighton: Sussex Academic, 2002.

Lord, Albert B. *The Singer of Tales*. Cambridge: Harvard University Press, 1960.

Loubser, J. A. (Bobby). "How Do You Report Something That Was Said with a Smile?—Can We Overcome the Loss of Meaning When Oral-Manuscript Texts of the Bible Are Represented in Modern Printed Media?" *Scriptura* 87 (2004) 296–314.

———. *Oral and Manuscript Culture in the Bible: Studies on the Media Texture of the New Testament*. 2007. 2nd ed. with new Foreword by Werner H. Kelber. Biblical Performance Criticism 7. Eugene, OR: Cascade Books, 2013.

Maclean, Marie. *The Baudelairean Experiment*. New York: Routledge, 1988.

Maxey, James A. *From Orality to Orality: A New Paradigm for Contextual Translation of the Bible*. Biblical Performance Criticism Series 2. Eugene, OR: Cascade Books, 2009.

Niditch, Susan. *Oral World and Written Word: Ancient Israelite Literature*. Library of Ancient Israel. Louisville: Westminster John Knox, 1996.

Ong, Walter J. *Orality and Literacy: The Technologizing of the Word*. New Accents. London: Routledge, 1988.

Parker, D. C. *The Living Text of the Gospels*. Cambridge: Cambridge University Press, 1997.

Pelias, Ronald J. *Performance Studies: The Interpretation of Aesthetic Texts*. New York: St. Martin's, 1992.

Person, Raymond F., Jr. "The Ancient Israelite Scribe as Performer." *Journal of Biblical Literature* 117 (1998) 601–9.

Rhoads, David. "Performance Criticism: An Emerging Methodology in Second Testament Studies, Part 1." *Biblical Theology Bulletin* 36 (2006) 1–16.

———. "Performance Criticism: An Emerging Methodology in Second Testament Studies, Part 2." *Biblical Theology Bulletin* 36 (2006) 164–84.

———. *Reading Mark, Engaging the Gospel*. Minneapolis: Fortress, 2004.

Robbins, Vernon K. "Oral, Rhetorical, and Literary Cultures." In *Orality and Textuality in Early Christian Literature*, *Semeia* 65 (1994) 75–91.

Roloff, Leland H. *The Perception and Evocation of Literature*. Glenview, IL: Foresman, 1973.

Scobie, Alex. "Storytellers, Storytelling, and the Novel in Greco-Roman Antiquity." *Rheinisches Museum für Philologie* 122 (1997) 229–59.

Shiell, William David. *Reading Acts: The Lector and Early Christianity*. Biblical Interpretation Series 70. Boston: Brill Academic, 2004.

Shiner, Whitney. "Oral Performance in the New Testament World." In *The Bible in Ancient and Modern Media: Story and Performance*, edited by Holly E. Hearon and Philip Ruge-Jones, 49–63. Biblical Performance Criticism Series 1. Eugene, OR: Cascade Books, 2009.

———. *Proclaiming the Gospel: First-Century Performance of Mark*. Harrisburg, PA: Trinity, 2003.

Small, Christopher. *Musicking: The Meanings of Performing and Listening*. Middleton, CT: Wesleyan University Press, 1998.

Small, Jocelyn Penny. *Wax Tablets of the Mind: Cognitive Studies of Memory and Literacy in Classical Antiquity*. New York: Routledge, 1997.

Turner, Victor. *The Ritual Process: Structure and Anti-Structure*. Ithaca, NY: Cornell University Press, 1969.

Ward, Richard Finley. "Paul and the Politics of Performance at Corinth: A Study of 2 Corinthians 10–13." PhD diss., Northwestern University, 1987.

Wire, Antoinette Clark. *Holy Lives, Holy Deaths: A Close Hearing of Early Jewish Storytellers*. Studies in Biblical Literature 1. Atlanta: Scholars, 2002.

10

The Constitution of the Qur'an as a Codified Work

Paradigm for Codifying Hadith and the Islamic Sciences?

Gregor Schoeler

The Qur'an[1] was already a book during the life of the Prophet—although only as an objective or an idea, not in reality.[2] It wasn't until 20–25 years after the death of the Prophet that it became an actual book. The codification process progressed from occasional notes to deliberate collections to an edited and published book.

Hadith (the tradition, singular), that is, the transmitted reports (traditions or hadiths, plural)[3] on the words and deeds of the prophet Muham-

1. For the codification of the Qur'an, see Nöldeke, *Geschichte des Qorāns*, iii; Neuwirth, "Koran," 101–110; Motzki, *Ḥadīth*; and Schoeler, *Ecrire et transmettre*, 31–41 (= Schoeler, *The Genesis*, 30–34.).

2. The fact that, in the text of the Qur'an, the term *al-qurʾān* ("recitation") was in the course of time more and more replaced by *al-kitāb* ("book") as the term for the revelation as a whole clearly demonstrates that the ideal of an actual book came more and more into focus.

3. For the hadith in general, see Sezgin, *Geschichte*, i, 53–84; Motzki, *Ḥadīth*, esp. xiii–liii and Introduction; Goldziher, "Ueber die Entwickelung des Ḥadīth"; Juynboll, *Muslim Tradition*. For the codification of the hadith, see Goldziher, "Ueber die Entwickelung des Ḥadīth," 194ff.; Sezgin, *Geschichte*, i, 55–58; Schoeler, *Ecrire et transmettre*, 43–56 (= Schoeler, *The Genesis*, 40–50); and Schoeler, *Oral and Written in Early Islam*, 111–129.

mad, were originally to have been taught and passed on purely orally and not in writing. Some hadith scholars (also called traditionists) nonetheless occasionally made notes from the beginning; later (from about 680 CE on) they compiled collections, and, as of the middle of the eighth century, systematic collections subdivided into chapters according to content-relevant criteria.[4] After about another 100 years, hadith was in existence in (more or less) codified works, the most important of which, the canonical collections of al-Bukhārī (d. 870) and Muslim ibn al-Ḥajjāj (d. 875), almost equal the Qur'an in importance for the religion of Islam.

Based on observations that the codification process of both Qur'an and hadith exhibits considerable similarities and that the codification of many Arabic-Islamic sciences proceeds analogously to that of hadith, the following will examine whether the codification of the holy book of Islam was *paradigmatic* for the codification process of hadith and the other Arabic-Islamic sciences. "Paradigm" here is understood not as a "mystical" prefiguration, but as a pattern of development that repeats itself two or more times because the same or similar prerequisites elicit the same or similar effects. The question as to whether such a pattern exists can demand a certain interest: if a positive answer can be arrived at, it would be possible to demonstrate a regularity according to which the development from speech to writing took place in Islam.

THE QUR'AN

Initially, when the revelations were still short, there was possibly no need to write them down. This situation changed, however, when they became longer and more frequent. It is most probable that Muhammad began to have revelations put into writing early on, during the so-called second Meccan period (615–20).[5] Islamic tradition provides numerous details regarding this process of writing, including the names of the various individuals to whom Muhammad dictated Qur'anic passages. Suffice it to mention here the most important "scribe of the revelation" (*kātib al-waḥy*), Zayd ibn Thābit (d. ca. 666). These writings were, however, nothing more than mnemonic aids to help the faithful in their recitation.

We do not know precisely when the project of producing a "book," a veritable "scripture," became a priority. The fact, however, that within the

4. These are the first six chapters of al-Bukhārī's *aṣ-Ṣaḥīḥ* (see below): 1. The beginning of the revelation, 2. faith, 3. knowledge, 4. the ablution before prayer, 5. the major ritual ablution, 6. menstruation.

5. Nöldeke, *Geschichte des Qorāns*, i, 45ff. and ii, 1ff.; Watt, *Bell's Introduction to the Qur'ān*, 37 and 136; Bellamy, "Mysterious Letters," 271; Neuwirth, "Koran," 102.

Qur'an itself the term *kitāb* ("scripture," "book") began to be used in increasing measure to describe the sum total of the revelation, effectively replacing the term *qur'ān* (Qur'an, "recitation"), shows that the idea of a scripture, in book form, like those possessed by the "people of the book" (Christians and Jews), namely a lectionary,[6] gained more and more prominence.

Yet no "scripture" or compiled "book" existed at the time of Muhammad's death—Muslim tradition and the majority of modern scholars are in agreement on this point.[7] According to Muslim tradition, all that existed at the time, besides oral tradition, were scattered writings on various materials, such as fragments of parchment and papyrus, slates, pieces of leather, shoulder blades, palm stalks, and *ṣuḥuf*, sheets, "containing the Book" (*fīhi al-kitāb*).[8]

According to the dominant opinion in Muslim tradition, the first collection of the Qur'an was ordered by Abū Bakr on ʿUmar's advice, a task then undertaken by Zayd ibn Thābit, the most important "scribe of the revelation": this resulted in the compilation of a copy on leaves of the same shape and dimension. A book "between two covers" (*bayna l-lawḥayn*), an actual codex, thus came into existence. This collection, called *ṣuḥuf* ("leaves") in the sources, was a personal copy that the caliph wanted to have available for his private use. When ʿUmar died, it was inherited by his daughter Ḥafṣa.

Yet the caliph and his family were not the only ones to have in their possession a copy of the Qur'an for their private use. According to Muslim tradition, there also existed other collections, initiated by various individuals who were contemporary with the Abū Bakr/ʿUmar collection. Tradition credits numerous prominent individuals with copies, the most well-known of whom are Ubayy ibn Kaʿb (d. 640 or later) and ʿAbdallāh ibn Masʿūd (d. 653 or later), who are said to have had in their possession complete copies based on their own collections.

In the absence of an official "edition," however, marked variants became the object of disputes about the "correct" form of the sacred text. When disputes even arose in the army, threatening the sense of Muslim unity, the Caliph ʿUthmān (ruled 644–56) decided to commission an official edition of the Qur'anic text. That recension came to be known as the ʿUthmānī codex (*muṣḥaf*).

The task of collecting and editing the revelations fell once again to Zayd ibn Thābit, this time with the help of an advisory commission (three members of noble Meccan families). On this point, Muslim tradition is to a

6. Neuwirth, "Koran," 102–104.

7. Wansbrough, *Quranic Studies* and Burton, *Collection of the Qur'ān*, whose theories contradict one another, are exceptions in this regard.

8. Ibn Abī Dāwūd, in Jeffery, *Materials*, 24 [Arabic].

large extent unanimous. The majority of accounts agree that Zayd and those who assisted him based themselves on the collection (*ṣuḥuf*) in the possession of Ḥafṣa, ʿUmar's daughter. ʿUthmān gave the edition he had commissioned official status by ordering that copies be sent to all the provincial capitals of the empire, where they were to serve as authoritative exemplars. In addition, he ordered that all collections not conforming to the new official edition be destroyed.

The Qur'an had now become in reality what it had only been in theory at the time of the Prophet: a book of (almost) definitive form and configuration, a codex (*muṣḥaf*). What is more, it was, in the minds of the central authority, a "published book," the text of which was binding on every single Muslim. It was "published" in the sense that exemplar copies had been sent to the provincial capitals. "With the ʿUthmānic recension, the main emphasis in Qur'anic transmission shifted toward the written book."[9]

The oral transmission of the Qur'an proceeded from the start alongside written transmission and was carried primarily by the "caste" of Qur'an "readers" (or rather reciters). Before the ʿUthmānic recension, their recitation was the only way of dissemination and "publication" of the text. Afterwards this "caste" lost part of its importance because it was now no longer the sole custodian of the text of the Holy Book. This is why the Qur'an readers also appear to have been vehemently opposed to the undertaking. Their opposition is clearly visible in the charge later leveled against ʿUthmān by numerous rebels: "The Qur'an was (many) books; you have discarded them except for one."[10] The Qur'an readers were nonetheless able—with limitations—to maintain their importance even after the editing; in view of the fact that the ʿUthmānic text was an undotted and unvocalized consonantal text (*rasm*),[11] that is, unable to be read correctly without the guidance of experts, the Qur'an reciters still had enough to do. From now on, however, they were obliged to take the ʿUthmānic consonantal text as the basis for their recitations.

THE HADITH

Unlike the Qur'an, hadith was originally intended to be taught and transmitted purely orally. This surely did not rule out that already in early

9. Nöldeke, *Geschichte des Qorāns*, iii, 119.

10. aṭ-Ṭabarī, *Taʾrīkh*, i, 2952.

11. Initially, only consonants were written, and even these were not adequately distinguished from one another, since the same written shape may sometimes indicate two or even more consonants.

times many companions of the Prophet had made notes as a supplement to memory. We have ample testimony of this practice. Some companions are reported to have had *ṣuḥuf* (notebooks). Ibn ʿAbbās, the cousin of the Prophet and purported founder of Qur'an exegesis, is said to have been seen carrying "tablets" (*alwāḥ*) "upon which he wrote something of the doings of the Messenger of God."[12] All of this recording, however, was the result of sporadic, unsystematic efforts.

This approach didn't change until the first generation of the "followers," who, roughly estimated, were active in the last quarter of the seventh century and in the first quarter of the eighth century and themselves had no direct experience of Muhammad. Some of them pointedly began to make inquiries with different persons about the life and words of the Prophet, namely with the companions who were still alive. They compiled these reports, the hadiths, one way or another. It is immediately seen that the compilers, before launching their report, generally named their informants; later transmitters proceeded in like manner so that chains of transmitters arose that were placed before the respective texts (so-called *isnād*s; for example, "A said, B told [or transmitted to] me from C"). This procedure was to become obligatory later on; in this way, each hadith consists of two parts: a chain of transmitters (*isnād*) and the text proper (*matn*).

The most important scholar of the first generation of followers is ʿUrwa ibn az-Zubayr (ca. 643–ca. 712), the son of a cousin of the Prophet and the nephew of his favorite wife, ʿĀʾisha.[13] On the one hand he collected numerous juristic traditions and on the other historical reports on Muhammad's life, which formed the matrix of the later *Sīra* (that is, the Biography of Muhammad) books. Named most frequently as his informant is his aunt, ʿĀʾisha. The sources expressly mention that he had written documents in his possession for his juristic hadiths. He customarily recited them arranged content-wise in chapters—indeed a precursor of *taṣnīf* that became common practice only at a later date (see below). Thus, he used to begin with the chapter on divorce (*ṭalāq*), then treated divorce requested by the wife (*khulʿ*), then the pilgrimage (*ḥajj*), and so on.[14] ʿUrwa and his contemporaries disseminated their collected traditions orally through public instruction. The imparting of knowledge in this way, in which transmission and instruction were one, and in which the lecturer referred to an informant, or a series of informants (*isnād*), became determinant from that point on

12. Ibn Saʿd, *Kitāb aṭ-Ṭabaqāt al-kabīr*, ii, 2, 123.

13. For ʿUrwa see Schoeler, *Ecrire et transmettre*, 45–49 (= Schoeler, *The Genesis*, 41–44); Gibb, Kramers, et al.; Bearman, Bianquis, et al. 1960–2005:x, 910–13, s.v. ʿUrwa ibn al-Zubayr (G. Schoeler). = Encyclopaedia of Islam

14. al-Fasawī, *Kitāb al-Maʿrifa wa-t-taʾrīkh*, i, 551.

in many Arabic-Islamic sciences. We speak of the "methodology" of the traditionists.

It is possible that ʿUrwa initially received the stimulus towards his occupation with the life of the Prophet from the court of the caliph. The caliph, ʿAbd al-Malik (685–705), sent him letters with questions about events in Muhammad's life, and these he answered by means of letters. The content of these epistles was transmitted further by ʿUrwa in his lectures; the letters survive in this transmitted form and represent the oldest extant written testimony on the life of Muhammad. The first large-scale collections of juristic hadith are also supposed to have been launched by the initiative of the court, namely the Umayyad caliphs ʿUmar II (717–20) and Hishām (724–43). They are, however, no longer extant.[15]

Two generations later—around the middle of the eighth century—a more systematic method for presenting the transmitted material emerged: *taṣnīf*, that is, arrangement according to chapter content.[16] The relevant works are called *muṣannafāt* (singular, *muṣannaf*). The most famous example of a *muṣannaf* collection of juristic hadiths and doctrines is Mālik b. Anas's (d. 795) *Muwaṭṭaʾ*; and the most famous Prophet-vita compiled this way in this time is Ibn Isḥāq's (d. 767) "Book of Campaigns." This movement continued for a century and beyond; the canonical collections of al-Bukhārī and Muslim are *muṣannafāt*. The oldest compilations of this type made in the eighth century were still little more than ordered leaves (or other mnemonic aids) that were the basis of oral lectures; from the ninth century on, however, the canonical works had more or less fixed texts. By "more or less fixed texts," I mean that all of these hadith collections, even the canonical, exist in multiple recensions and manuscripts, exhibiting differences in chapter arrangement and text structure. Of the *Ṣaḥīḥ* of al-Bukhārī, something akin to a "critical edition" appeared only in the thirteenth century.[17] It is nonetheless certain that some of the ninth-century compilers penned their works with a reading public in mind; the *Ṣaḥīḥ* of Muslim b. al-Ḥajjāj demonstrates this clearly: his canonical collection is the only one with an Introduction addressed to the readership—the unmistakable mark of a "proper" book.[18]

15. Goldziher, "Ueber die Entwickelung des Ḥadīth," 208ff.; Sezgin, *Geschichte*, i, 55–58; Schoeler, *Oral and Written*, 123ff.

16. Goldziher, "Ueber die Entwickelung des Ḥadīth," 226ff. [213ff. on Mālik's *al-Muwaṭṭaʾ*]; Sezgin, *Geschichte*, i, 55ff.; Schoeler, *Ecrire et transmettre*, 71–89 (= Schoeler, *The Genesis*, 68–81). A precursor of *taṣnīf* was ʿUrwa's method for presenting his collections of legal hadiths; see note 21 below.

17. Fück, "Beiträge," 79ff.

18. Muslim, *Ṣaḥīḥ Muslim bi-sharḥ an-Nawawī*.

The entire codification process of hadiths—until the canonical works came into being in the ninth century—was accompanied by a vehement discussion between traditionists about whether it was allowed at all to write down hadiths.[19] One faction of the hadith scholars took the position that the traditions should be transmitted only orally and that only the Qur'an was entitled to exist in writing. From the point of view of these scholars, the Qur'an was the only book of Islam and should remain so. Many scholars thus lectured their collected traditions from memory, leaving their notes (which, in spite of everything, they almost always had) at home or hidden. They forbade their pupils to write down the hadiths they heard in class. Whereas in Iraq, in the centers of Basra and Kufa, the postulate of strict oral transmission was upheld well into the ninth century, it was already abandoned from the middle of the eighth century in the centers of Mecca and Medina. One of the first *Fiqh* works that has come down to us (not in its original form, but in versions transmitted by students) is the previously mentioned *Muwaṭṭa*ʾ of Mālik b. Anas (d. 795). The texts of the different recensions of this work, however, still differ substantially.

As time passed the orality of hadith gradually became mere postulation; in practice, there was more and more copying of written texts. When the codification processes of Qur'an and hadith are compared, we see that in both cases three phases can be discerned. These were already recognized by indigenous scholarship and, in the case of hadith, provided with a terminology.[20]

Codification of the Qur'an proceeded as follows:

1. Unsystematic writing of the revealed texts on disparate materials (fragments of parchment and papyrus, pieces of leather, sheets, palm stalks, shoulder blades, and so forth) during the life of the Prophet Muhammad (up to his death in 632).
2. Deliberate collections on sheets of equal size (*ṣuḥuf*) very soon after Muhammad's death. Examples are the Qur'an copies of ʿUmar, Ibn Masʿūd, and Ubayy.
3. Definitive official recension under ʿUthmān (around 650). Production of a *rasm* (that is, undotted and unvocalized consonantal text) *ne varietur* (*muṣḥaf*). Dissemination by depositing samples in the big cities, later through copying manuscripts.

Codification of the hadith:

19. Schoeler, *Oral and Written*, 111–41; Cook, "Opponents."

20. For the Qur'an, see Nöldeke, *Geschichte des Qorāns*, ii, 11ff. and 47ff.; for the hadith, see Sezgin, *Geschichte*, i, 55–58.

1. Unsystematic notes (*kitāba*) at the time of the companions of the Prophet Muhammad and earliest followers (632–80) on tablets and sheets and in notebooks.
2. Deliberate collections (*tadwīn*) of scattered material in the last quarter of the first and first quarter of the second century AH (ca. 680–740 CE).
3. Production of compilations arranged systematically according to chapter content (*taṣnīf*), as of around 125 AH / 740 CE into the ninth century and beyond; since the ninth century more or less final, redacted compositions.

Alongside the conformities,[21] there are also differences to be noticed between the codification processes of Qur'an and hadith. It is important to keep in mind that while the Qur'an got its final form (at least with respect to *rasm*, the undotted and unvocalized consonantal text) already approximately 25 years after Muhammad's death, that is, around 650, the first hadith works with more or less fixed texts did not emerge until about 250 years afterwards, in the ninth century. Nonetheless, the conformities in the codification processes of both of Islam's most important literary phenomena are still conspicuous and in need of an explanation.

WHY WERE ONLY LOOSE NOTES MADE IN THE FIRST PHASE OF CODIFICATION FOR QUR'AN AND HADITH?

Qur'an

The pre- and early-Islamic Arabs had only vague ideas of a "real," that is, a complete and edited, book. Aside from the Torah scrolls of the Jews, which were not to be seen at all outside the Jewish places of teaching, the only edited books known were lectionaries, liturgical books used by Syriac- or Arabic-speaking Christian clerics. Hence when the Qur'an terms itself a book, it is certainly a lectionary that is meant. During the lifetime of the Prophet, however, the Qur'an could not be edited because the revelation

21. In reality, the three stages were not quite as schematic as the above exposition implies. Indeed, for the official recension of the Qur'an an organizing principle was implemented that had already been developed and applied to the first deliberate Qur'an collections, namely the decreasing length of the suras under arrangement. And for the deliberate collections of hadith, as we have seen, at least one was already a compilation systematically arranged by content: ʿUrwa's collection of legal traditions.

was ongoing and because juristic stipulations were occasionally modified (abrogated).[22] There was also no need whatsoever to edit the text of the Qur'an, because, as a lectionary, or liturgical book, only individual sections were recited at a time. The "secretaries of the revelation" and Qur'an readers thus did not have occasion during the lifetime of the Prophet to produce an edited book. Notes for bolstering the memory were sufficient.

Hadith

As we have seen,[23] the Qur'an, even before receiving its definitive form, was "the book" *par excellence* in Islam, even if initially only as an objective, or an idea. All the more must the following notion have imposed itself subsequent to the definitive recension: edited book equals book of God. Although not all traditionists shared this view—from the mid-eighth century on there were also proponents of writing—for a long time this notion hampered, even prevented, the emergence of books beside the Qur'an. This situation explains the resistance to putting the hadiths into writing. This aversion is even reflected in hadith itself; for example, Muhammad is to have said, when someone wanted to write down his words: "Do you want a book other than the book of God?"[24] and a "follower" (or successor; that is, a member of the generation that followed the companions of Muhammad): "Do you wish to adopt it as copies of the Qur'an?" And another notion coalesced with this one, namely that the "people of the book" (*ahl al-kitāb*), the Jews and Christians, had corrupted their religions by accepting additional books that were not revealed. Muhammad is reported to have said: "The peoples before you were led into error by those very books that they wrote in addition to the book of God." (The concern here is in great measure with the oral doctrine of the Jews [Mishnah and Talmud] that likewise was originally not supposed to be written down.) This is why hadith (and the other Arabic-Islamic sciences as well) are taught and transmitted only orally by means of lectures in scholarly assemblies. However, notes and mnemonic devices (later on even comprehensive compilations, arranged according to chapter content) proved to be ever more necessary and were able—despite objections—to assert themselves in increasing measure.

22. This is why Burton's theory that the Prophet himself had already edited the Qur'an is highly improbable! See his *Collection of the Qur'ān*.

23. See note 2 above.

24. al-Khaṭīb al-Baghdādī, *Taqyīd al-ʿilm*, 33ff., 36ff.

HOW DID THE DELIBERATE COLLECTIONS COME ABOUT?

Qur'an

With the death of the Prophet, revelation came to a standstill. The proclamations could now be viewed as a self-contained corpus. Many of the companions, in particular of course the successors of Muhammad, the caliphs, now wanted to have private copies at their disposal. So they produced deliberate collections. We hear nothing of any opposition to these initiatives.

Hadith

Deliberate collections of Muhammad's words and reports about his deeds emerged in the time that the generation of Muhammad's contemporaries was dying out. In the meantime, the idea of the exemplary character of Muhammad's way of life began to form among the legal scholars, or at any rate among a section of them;[25] the reports about his words and deeds that were expressed in the hadiths, and until then had been transmitted unchecked, should be preserved and compiled and made available. We repeatedly hear about such projects initiated by the court. Here is where the aspect of bias comes into its own; we hear that the caliphs intended, through their inquiries (for example, with ʿUrwa) and by means of the collections they commissioned, to get access to material suitable to themselves.[26] Unlike the case of the Qur'an, during this second phase of committing hadiths to writing, considerable and enduring controversies arose. Throughout the eighth century and beyond, the traditionists discussed whether it was allowed to write traditions down, and the court-commissioned deliberate collections, in particular, were sharply criticized.

HOW WERE THE QUR'AN AND LATER COLLECTIONS OF TRADITIONS REDACTED?

Qur'an

The readers of the Qur'an had become accustomed to transmitting and publishing the Qur'an through oral recitation, which was surely based for the

25. Juynboll, *Muslim Tradition*, 30f.

26. Schoeler, *Charakter und Authentie*, 150 (= Schoeler, *The Biography*, 104); Schoeler, *Oral and Written*, 123–29; Petersen, "ʿAlī-Muʿāwiya-Conflict," 102ff.

most part on their written notes. In this regard it was of no matter to them whether their texts were identical or not. Each took the position that he was in possession of the best text. For the reigning powers, on the other hand, the different forms in which "the Book" existed in writing and in speech was a problem, particularly since disputes had arisen in this regard, even in the army. Thus it became necessary to produce a definitive, uniform, and binding text for what, in the meantime, had become a huge empire. This text was the ʿUthmānic recension. The first written vouchers we have of this recension (Qur'an specimens from Sanaa) date from the reign of the caliph al-Walīd (705–15);[27] the ʿUthmānic recension must therefore already have been in widespread circulation at this time.[28] Opposition to the undertaking seems to have arisen from the Qur'an readers, who feared the loss of their monopoly.

Hadith

Indigenous transmission connects the emergence in the middle of the eighth century of the *taṣnīf* movement with the spread of scholars into the provincial towns and the rise of the heretical movements: "This was at the time when scholars had spread out to the large cities and when heretical . . . innovations had became more numerous."[29] That could be understood to mean that comprehensive compilations were deemed necessary at that point in time when the scholars, who were in part no longer in Medina, the home of the *sunna*, but in other centers, had to deal with more numerous traditions, authentic and inauthentic alike, and which they now had to subject to inspection. This is indeed also the time when hadith critique came into being.[30] Large collections, however, in order to be usable, needed a system; an arrangement according to chapter content was particularly convenient (*taṣnīf*), but a bit later another one came into use, that is, arrangement according to the earliest transmitters (*musnad*).[31] It took at least another century for these works to attain a more or less fixed form.[32]

27. Von Bothmer et al., "Neue Wege der Koranforschung," 46. For the oldest (non-ʿUthmānic) manuscripts of the Qur'an see now Sadeghi and Bergmann, "The Codex of a Companion" and Déroche, *La transmission écrite*.

28. With this, Wansbrough's theory (*Quranic Studies*), according to which the Qur'an did not receive its definitive form until the beginning of the ninth century, must be deemed refuted.

29. Ibn Ḥajar, *Fatḥ al-bārī*, 5.

30. Juynboll, *Muslim Tradition*, 134ff.

31. Sezgin, *Geschichte*, i, 55; Juynboll, *Muslim Tradition*, 22.

32. The sequence of (unsystematic) note-taking, deliberate collection of scattered

Now let us return to the question posed at the outset: does the codification of the Qur'an represent a paradigm for the codification of hadith and the other Arabic-Islamic sciences? A detailed examination of the single stages in the codification of Qur'an and hadith, and of the respective underlying reasons and backgrounds, has shown that it was only in part the same motives that led to the same or similar results. If we divide the motives that promoted or hampered progress in codification (for a certain period of time) into "practical" and "ideological," several points can be ascertained.

First, it was on practical grounds that the first writing-down of both Qur'an and hadith was undertaken. Script served in both cases to bolster memory. In this first phase of codification there were no ideological reasons opposing the undertaking. Second, there were practical grounds for the deliberate collections of Qur'an and hadith (second phase of codification): individuals, above all ruler and courtiers, wanted to have copies of the Qur'an and collections of hadith at their disposal for private use. While there was no reason to oppose a non-official codification of copies of the Qur'an for private use, strong ideological reservations arose against codification of the hadiths. It was precisely the existence of the now-codified Qur'an that

material, content-wise arrangement of collections (more or less redacted) also holds for the biography of the Prophet (Sezgin, *Geschichte*, i, 237–56, 251–56, and 275–302; Schoeler, *Ecrire et transmettre*, 45–49, 56 and 71–72 [= Schoeler, *The Genesis*, 41–44, 49, 71–72] and Schoeler, *Charakter und Authentie*, 39ff. [= Schoeler, *The Biography*, 26ff.]), Qur'an reading (as a genre of systematic writing) (Nöldeke, *Geschichte des Qorāns*, ii; Sezgin, *Geschichte*, i, 3–18; Schoeler, *Oral and Written*, 78–82), Qur'an exegesis (Sezgin, *Geschichte*, i, 19–49; Schoeler, *Ecrire et transmettre*, 49–52, 79 [= Schoeler, *The Genesis*, 45–47, 73]), history (Sezgin, *Geschichte*, i, 237–56 and 257–74; Schoeler, *Ecrire et transmettre*, 79–81 [= Schoeler, *The Genesis*, 74–75], philology, especially compilation of poetry (Sezgin, *Geschichte*, ii, 24–33; Schoeler, *Ecrire et transmettre*, 18–26 and 115–19 [= Schoeler, *The Genesis*, 18–24, 113–15]; Schoeler, *Oral and Written*, 65–72); and lexicography (Sezgin, *Geschichte*, viii, 7ff.; Versteegh, *Arabic Grammar and Qur'ānic Exegesis*; Schoeler, *Ecrire et transmettre*, 91–107 and 100–102 [= Schoeler, *The Genesis*, 85–96, 94–96]). The similarity is explained in that the scholars of all of these sciences followed the methodology of the hadith scholars (imparting knowledge through lectures in a way in which instruction and transmission were one; adducing chains of transmitters, and so on). In addition to that, for the biography of the Prophet, the borders to hadith are blurred.

Like biography of the Prophet, Qur'an exegesis has much in common with hadith though exegetical traditions are never traced back to the Prophet. Found in al-Bukhārī's hadith collection are chapters with traditions treating the biography of the Prophet (*Kitāb al-Mabʿath*, "Book of the mission [of Muhammad]"; *Kitāb al-Maghâzī*, "Book of the campaigns") as well as a chapter containing exegetical traditions (*Kitāb at-Tafsīr*, "Book of the commentary [on the Qur'an]"). The historical traditions spanning the time of the first caliphs and the great conquests are nothing other than the temporal continuation of the Prophet-biographical traditions. And philology emerged in intimate contact with Qur'an exegesis (Versteegh, *Arabic Grammar and Qur'ānic Exegesis*, 1ff. and passim).

hindered for a long time the development of a second prospectively codified body of religious texts. There were additional reasons: in particular, the apprehension that the compilers, or their commissioners, would sneak erroneous, uncertain, and tendentious traditions into their collections and so make such dubious texts binding for all time.

The final, official recension of the Qur'anic text, and the systematic collection and definitive redaction of the hadiths (third phase of codification), also had practical grounds: in both instances one wanted to produce uniform and authentic texts (note the name *aṣ-Ṣaḥīḥ*, "the correct, authentic [collection]," for al-Bukhārī's and Muslim's canonical works.). Both undertakings ran into ideologically grounded opposition. In the case of the Qur'an it was from the professional interests of the Qur'an readers who appeared to lose their monopoly as the sole custodians of the Holy Book; in the case of the hadith there were continued misgivings about placing similar text corpora alongside the Qur'an, the spreading of uncertain and tendentious traditions, and so forth.

Hence, while the motives for the codification of Qur'an and hadith were the same or similar, the reasons for obstructing codification were completely different. Notably, the Qur'an was *the* redacted book of Islam for centuries and demonstrably prevented the definitive codification of hadith. Regularity can be seen only to the extent that groups of experts who transmit large bodies of texts tend—with the availability of writing and for practical reasons—to redact this corpus in writing. "Ideological" objections can forestall this process for a long period of time. Examples of this from other cultures are the extremely delayed codifications of the Vedas and Avesta,[33] which took some 1000 years (or more) to become codified.[34]

BIBLIOGRAPHY

Bellamy, James A. "The Mysterious Letters of the Koran: Old Abbreviations of the Basmalah." *Journal of the American Oriental Society* 93 (1973) 267–85.

al-Bukhārī, Muḥammad ibn Ismāʿīl. *Ṣaḥīḥ al-Bukhārī*. 7 vols. Edited by M. D. al-Bughā. Beirut: Dār Ibn Kathīr, 1990.

Burton, John. *The Collection of the Qur'ān*. Cambridge: Cambridge University Press, 1977.

Cook, Michael. "The Opponents of the Writing of Tradition in Early Islam." *Arabica* 44 (1997) 437–530.

33. von Hinüber, *Der Beginn der Schrift*; Hoffmann and Narten, *Der sasanidische Archetypus*.

34. I would like to thank Dr. G. Bertram Thompson for his excellent English translation.

Déroche, François, *La Transmission écrite du Coran dans les débuts de l'islam. Le codex Parisino-petropolitanus*. Leiden: Brill, 2009.
al-Fasawī, Yaʿqūb ibn Sufyān. *Kitāb al-Maʿrifa wa-t-ta'rīkh*. 2nd ed., 3 vols. Edited by A. D. al-ʿUmarī. Beirut: Muʾassasat ar-Risāla, 1981.
Fück, Johann. "Beiträge zur Überlieferungsgeschichte von Buḫārī's Traditionssammlung." *Zeitschrift der Deutschen Morgenländischen Gesellschaft* 92 (1938) 60–87.
Gibb, H. A. R., Kramers, J. H. et al., ed. *The Encylopedia of Islam*. 2nd ed., 12 vols. Leiden: Brill, 1960–2005.
Goldziher, Ignaz. "Ueber die Entwickelung des Hadith." In *Muhammedanische Studien*, vol. 2, 1–274. Halle: Max Niemeyer, 1890.
Hoffman, Karl, and Narten, Johanna. *Der sasanidische Archetypus*. Wiesbaden: L. Reichert, 1989.
Jeffery, Arthur. *Materials for the History of the Text of the Qur'ān. The Old Codices. The Kitāb al-Maṣāḥif of Ibn Abī Dāwūd*. Leiden: Brill, 1937.
Ibn Ḥajar al-ʿAsqalānī, Aḥmad b. ʿAlī. *Fatḥ al-bārī: Sharḥ Ṣaḥīḥ al-Bukhārī. Muqaddima* (Introduction) and 28 vols. Edited by T. ʿA. Saʿd and M. M. al-Hawārī. Cairo: Maktabat al-Kulliyyāt al-Azhariyya, 1978.
Ibn Saʿd, Muḥammad. *Kitāb aṭ-Ṭabaqāt al-kabīr*. 9 vols. Edited by E. Sachau et al. Leiden: Brill, 1904–28.
Juynboll, Gautier H. A. Muslim *Tradition: Studies in Chronology, Provenance, and Authorship of Early Ḥadīth*. Cambridge: Cambridge University Press, 1983.
al-Khaṭīb al-Baghdādī, Aḥmad ibn ʿAlī. *Taqyīd al-ʿilm*. 2nd ed. Edited by Y. al-ʿIshsh. N.p., 1975.
Motzki, Harald. "The Collection of the Qur'ān: A Reconsideration of Western Views in Light of Recent Methodological Developments." *Der Islam* 78 (2001) 1–34.
———, ed. *Ḥadīth: Origins and Developments*. Aldershot, UK: Ashgate, 2004.
Muslim b. al-Hajjāj, *Ṣaḥīḥ Muslim bi-sharḥ an-Nawawī*. 2nd ed., 18 parts in 9 vols. Beirut: Dār Iḥyāʾ at-Turāth al-ʿArabī, 1972.
Neuwirth, Angelika. "Koran." In *Grundriss der arabischen Philologie*, vol. 2, *Literaturwissenschaft*, edited by Helmut Gätje, 96–135. Wiesbaden: L. Reichert, 1987.
Nöldeke, Theodor. *Geschichte des Qorāns*. 3 vols. Edited by Friedrich Schwally et al. Reprinted, Hildesheim: Olms, 1981.
Petersen, Erling Ladewig. "Studies on the Historiography of the ʿAlī-Muʿāwiya-Conflict." *Acta Orientalia*, 27 (1963) 83–118.
Sadeghi, Behnam and Bergmann, Uwe. "The Codex of a Companion of the Prophet and the Qurʾān of the Prophet." *Arabica* 57 (2010) 343–436.
Schoeler, Gregor. *Charakter und Authentie der muslimischen Überlieferung über das Leben Mohammeds*. Berlin: de Gruyter, 1996. Translated by Uwe Vagelpohl as *The Biography of Muḥammad. Nature and Authenticity*. Edited by James E. Montgomery. New York and London: Routledge, 2011.
———. *Ecrire et transmettre dans les débuts de l'islam*. Paris: Presses Universitaires de France, 2002. Translated by Shawkat M. Toorawa as *The Genesis of Literature in Islam. From the Aural to the Read*. Edinburgh University Press, 2009.
———. *The Oral and the Written in Early Islam*. Edited by James E. Montgomery. Translated by Uwe Vagelpohl. New York: Routledge, 2006.
Sezgin, Fuat. *Geschichte des arabischen Schrifttums*. 9 vols. Leiden: Brill, 1967–84.
Sezgin, Ursula. Abū Miḫnaf. *Ein Beitrag zur Historiographie der umaiyadischen Zeit*. Leiden: Brill, 1971.

aṭ-Ṭabarī, Muḥammad ibn Jarīr. *Ta'rīkh ar-rusul wal-mulūk* (*Annales*). 15 vols. Edited by M. J. de Goeje et al. Leiden: Brill, 1879–1901.

Versteegh, Cornelius H. M. (Kees). *Arabic Grammar and Qur'ānic Exegesis in Early Islam*. Leiden: Brill, 1993.

von Bothmer, Hans-Caspar Graf, et al. "Neue Wege der Koranforschung." *Magazin Forschung*, Universität des Saarlandes 1 (1991) 33–46.

von Hinüber, Oskar. *Der Beginn der Schrift und frühe Schriftlichkeit in Indien*. Stuttgart: Franz Steiner, 1990.

Wansbrough, John. *Quranic Studies: Sources and Methods of Scriptural Interpretation*. Oxford: Oxford University Press, 1977.

Watt, William Montgomery, ed. *Bell's Introduction to the Qur'ān*. Edinburgh: Edinburgh University Press, 1977.

11

From *Jāhiliyyah* to *Badīʿiyyah*

Orality, Literacy, and the Transformations of Rhetoric in Arabic Poetry

Suzanne Pinckney Stetkevych

INTRODUCTION

This essay[1] offers a speculative exploration of the transformations in the form and function of rhetorical styles and devices at three distinctive points of Arabic literary history. It takes as its starting point the mnemonic imperative governing the use of rhetoric in pre- and early Islamic oral poetry and proposes that in the later literary periods rhetorical devices, now free of their mnemonic obligation, took on further communicative or expressive functions. It then turns to the effect of literacy on the "retooling" of the no longer mnemonically bound rhetorical devices to serve as what I term the "linguistic correlative" of Islamic hegemony as witnessed in the High Abbasid caliphal panegyrics of the rhetorically complex *badīʿ* style. Finally, it attempts to interpret what seems to modern sensibilities the rhetorical excess of the post-classical genre of *badīʿiyyah* (a poem to the Prophet Muhammad

1. An earlier version of this paper was presented under the title "Orality, Literacy, and the Semiotics of Rhetoric in Arabic Poetry" at the Orality and Literacy VII Conference at Rice University, Houston, Texas, April 12–14, 2008. I wish to thank Werner Kelber and Paula Sanders for their invitation, hospitality, and organizational work for the conference. All translations from the Arabic in this essay are my own.

in which each line must exhibit a particular rhetorical device) as a memorial structure typical of the medieval manuscript (as opposed to modern print) tradition.

RHETORIC AS RITUAL IN THE EARLY ARABIC *QAṢĪDAH*

The Arab-Islamic literary tradition is rooted in the pagan era that preceded the advent of Islam, termed the *Jāhiliyyah*, the Age of "Ignorance" or "Impetuousness." The preeminent literary form was the *qaṣīdah*, the formal mono-rhymed and mono-metered polythematic ode of praise, boast, invective, or elegy, as practiced by the warrior aristocracy of tribal Arabia and in the courts of the Arab client-kings to the Byzantine and Sasanian empires. Dating from around 500–620 CE, these odes, as the tradition tells us, were orally composed and transmitted, and were not put into writing until the massive *tadwīn* movement of collection and compilation of the second and third Islamic centuries—ca. 750–800 CE—based on the oral transmission of Bedouin informants. The oral-formulaic nature of these poems in terms of the Parry-Lord theory was definitively demonstrated by James Monroe.[2] Although Monroe is concerned primarily with identifying and quantifying verbal formulae rather than with issues of mnemonics as they affect transmission, he also addresses the need to modify elements of the Parry-Lord theory, especially in regard to the composition and memorization of the short lyrical, and therefore more textually stable, Arabic ode. The pre-Islamic Arabic *qaṣīdah* situation is not, as Monroe well realized, one of poets merely re-creating in performance a single "epic." He realized that a shorter lyric[-heroic] form like the Arabic ode may well have been memorized in a way that oral epic is not. As he notes, the role of the *rāwī* or "transmitter" of poetry, that is, a younger, usually would-be poet who memorizes the poems of his mentor, often in the service of his own poetic apprenticeship, certainly points to the idea of a poet having distinct poems each with its own individual identity; and to individual poets and tribes (or families of poets) sharing certain stylistic features.[3]

My own work,[4] in which I have sought to establish the ritual structure and function of the Arabic ode in the pre-Islamic and Islamic periods, has accepted Monroe's conclusions and made some initial attempts to integrate

2. Monroe, "Oral Composition."

3. Ibid., 39–41.

4. Stetkevych, *Mute Immortals Speak*; Stetkevych, "Poetics of Redemption"; Stetkevych, *Poetics of Islamic Legitimacy*.

further work on orality and literacy theory, notably the work of Walter J. Ong and Eric Havelock,[5] into the discussion of Arabic poetry.

I recapitulate here some of my earlier work, with a shift in emphasis from the ritual aspects of the structure of the pre-Islamic *qaṣīdah* to the ritual dimension of its rhetorical devices. I take as my starting point Havelock's conclusion that virtually all the linguistic features that we classify as "poetic"[6]—rhyme, meter, assonance, alliteration, antithesis, parallelism, "poetic diction"—and in particular those figures of speech that we term "rhetorical devices"—metaphor, simile, metonymy, antithesis—are originally and essentially mnemonic devices that serve to stabilize and preserve the oral "text."[7] And, at the same time, I accept that the main features of oral poetries that Ong enumerates apply quite precisely to pre-Islamic and early Arabic poetry,[8] which we now generally accept as primarily oral in its composition and transmission up until around the second Islamic century.

What I would like to propose in particular in the present essay is the idea that within the oral context abstract concepts can be expressed only by means of metaphor or simile (or other rhetorical devices). Metaphors and similes are not intended to convey merely sensory similitude—that is, they are not primarily descriptive—but serve to convey an underlying semantic relationship, what I will term "the conceptual correlative." Nowhere is this clearer than in the rhetorical play between blood and food, killing and eating, that pervades the poetry of blood-vengeance and battle, and conveys the concept that to kill the enemy is to revitalize or nourish one's own kin and vice-versa. Thus, as I have argued, slaying the enemy in battle is the conceptual correlative of blood sacrifice.[9] This concept is conveyed in many rhetorical forms: Using a simile, Zayd ibn Bishr al-Taghlibī boasts of killing his enemy:[10]

> On the day the ironclad warriors leapt around ʿUmayr
> Like vultures hopping 'round the slaughter-camel.

In terms of the poetics of orality, what makes this simile effective is the graphic sensory comparison of the two scenes, but in the context of tribal warfare the essential message is the identification of the desecration of the

5. Ong, *Orality and Literacy*; Havelock, *Literate Revolution*; Havelock, *Muse Learns to Write*.

6. Havelock, *Literate Revolution*, 116–17.

7. Stetkevych, *Mute Immortals Speak*, chs. 5, 6.

8. Ong, *Orality and Literacy*, ch. 3, see below.

9. Stetkevych, *Mute Immortals Speak*, 55–83.

10. Ibid., 81; al-Jāḥiẓ, *Al-Ḥayawān*, vi, 331.

enemy with the revitalization of the kin. In the Muʿallaqah of ʿAntarah we find a metaphor whereby the slaying of an enemy who becomes carrion for scavengers is again equated with its conceptual correlative or its ritual inversion: the slaughtering of a beast to feed one's kin:[11]

> Then I left him slaughtered for the wild beasts
> To tear at him from head to wrist.

Another example of a compelling visual image that conveys an underlying ritual meaning is al-Aʿshā's metaphor describing the opening of a wine skin:[12]

> And when it runs low we raise our wineskin
> Open up its neck-vein, and it bleeds.

Clearly the shared sacrificial nature of wine and animal sacrifice is essential to the message the poet wishes to convey.

By rhetoric as ritual, then, I mean that if we follow Walter Burkert in defining ritual as "a behavioral pattern that has lost its primary function—present in its unritualized model—but which persists in a new function, that of communication,"[13] and if we understand "communication" in an oral society to include transmission and preservation, then we see that rhetorical devices are ritual. For example, in oral-mnemonic terms—what I am calling "ritual"—the point of a simile or metaphor is not to physically describe an object, but to imprint its conceptual correlative in the memory. It is not descriptive but rhetorical. This is why it is not the technical precision of a simile that makes it effective, but rather its affective and sensory (that is, rhetorical) aspects. In a pre-Islamic elegy for ʿAmr Dhū Kalb, his sister Rayṭah concludes with a jolting simile to convey, through her description of the scavengers, the *Schadenfreude* of his slayers, with the rhetorical goal of stirring her kinsmen to take vengeance:[14]

> The vultures walk upon him in delight
> Frolicking like virgins clad in smocks.

I do not want to dwell here on the fairly well-established poetics of orality, but rather to offer these few examples and to make the point that in the context of oral poetry, the abstraction involved in the conceptual correlative can be successfully conveyed and preserved only through the use of

11. al-Anbārī, *Sharḥ al-Qaṣāʾid al-Sabʿ*, 347, v. 52.

12. al-Maʿarrī, *Risālat al-Ghufrān*, 174.

13. Burkert, *Homo Necans*, 23.

14. Stetkevych, *Mute Immortals Speak*, 189; al-Baghdādī, *Khizānat al-Adab*, x, 391.

palpable, sensory, and emotionally charged images. In effect, then, in addition to rhyme, meter, poetic diction, rhetorical figures, and so on, Ong's list of "further characteristics of orally based thought and expression" (that is, in addition to oral-formulaic composition) are not, in an oral context, aesthetic choices, but rather requirements for successful performance, transmission, and preservation.[15] In the context of rhetorical devices, the points of interest to us, clearly in evidence in the poetry cited above, are these five characteristics from Ong's list: (4) conservative or traditionalist; (5) close to the human lifeworld; (6) agonistically toned; (7) emphatic and participatory rather than objectively distanced; (9) situational rather than abstract.

The question that remains before us is, why are these mnemonic structures—poetry, and the Arabic *qaṣīdah* in particular—maintained even after the advent of writing? I would venture that the answer is twofold. First, in oral poetry, the mnemonic is also the rhetorical: the same elements that make poetry memorable and memorizable are precisely those that make it moving and effective: it is the most emotionally charged and sensory-based form of language. Therefore, even though the advent of writing makes the mnemonic aspects of oral poetry technically redundant, their rhetorical function remains in force. Second, its ritual, or communicative, functions remain operative even when its purely mnemonic functions are rendered obsolete. In brief, then, the very elements that make oral poetry memorable and memorizable are those that make it emotionally effective, which is precisely what we mean when we define rhetoric as the "art of persuasion" and understand ritual as essentially communicative.

RHETORIC OF/AS ISLAMIC HEGEMONY IN THE CLASSICAL ABBASID PANEGYRIC

With the establishment and consolidation of literacy in Umayyad and Abbasid times, we find in Arab cultural history much of the same sorts of shifts that Havelock describes as the result of the transition from orality to literacy in Greek culture. He writes that "all possible discourse became translatable into script, and that simultaneously the burden of memorization was lifted from the mind . . . the alphabet therewith made possible the production of novel or unexpected statement, previously unfamiliar and even 'unthought.'"[16] The spirit of cultural ferment of the second and third Islamic centuries (eighth and ninth centuries CE) and its concomitant

15. Ong, *Orality and Literacy*, ch. 3 passim.

16. Havelock, *Literate Revolution*, 88.

linguistic inventions is captured in a passage quoted by al-Jāḥiẓ in *Al-Bayān wa-al-Tabyīn*:[17]

> For the Mutakallimūn [speculative theologians] selected expressions for their concepts, deriving terminology for things for which the Arab language had no word. In doing so they have set the precedent in this for all who came after them and the model for all who follow. Thus they say accident (*ʿaraḍ*) and essence (*jawhar*); to be (*aysa*) and not to be (*laysa*). They distinguish between nullity (*buṭlān*) and nihility (*talāshin*) and they use the terms "thisness" (*hādhiyyah*), identity (*huwiyyah*), and quiddity (*māhiyyah*). In the same way, al-Khalīl ibn Aḥmad assigned names to the meters of the *qaṣīdahs* . . . whereas the [Bedouin] Arabs had not known the meters by those names. Similarly, the grammarians named and referred to the circumstantial accusative (*ḥāl*), the adverbial accusatives (*ẓurūf*), and such things. . . . Likewise, the mathematicians draw upon names which they have designated as signs in order to understand one another. . . . Someone preaching in the heart of the Caliph's palace said, "God brought him out of the door of non-being (*laysiyyah*) and let him enter the door of being (*aysiyyah*)." These expressions are permissible in the art of Kalām when existing words lack the requisite range of meaning. The expressions of the Mutakallimūn are also befitting to poetry . . .

Above all, and quite broadly speaking, the establishment of writing frees literary composition from the mnemonic imperative and exigencies of oral preservation. It allows for the gathering, compilation, and stable setting forth of extensive materials that can then be systematically compared, analyzed, categorized, and so forth.

What most concerns us here is that at this period *language* itself, now "nailed down" through writing, is subjected to this very process of classification, analysis, and systematization. The linguistic sciences are born and flourish: syntax and morphology, lexicography and etymology. In brief, the code of language is cracked. For Arab Islamic culture, in which the creation of language was perceived as being as much a divine prerogative as the creation of the world and of mankind, this linguistic breakthrough was on a par with, for us, Einstein's discovery of relativity and the smashing of the atom, the discovery of the double helix, or our current cracking of the human genetic code in the Human Genome Project. And in the Abbasid case as well as ours, conservatives accused those who dared to act upon this newfound knowledge/power of "playing God."

17. al-Jāḥiẓ, *Al-Bayān wa-al-Tabyīn*, i, 138–41; Stetkevych, *Abū Tammām*, 16–17.

The Arabs' sudden and astounding political, military, scientific, and cultural hegemony in the High Abbasid period is expressed in what I have termed an ideology of "Islamic Manifest Destiny,"[18] which was formulated and propagated above all by the master panegyrists of the caliphal courts. It is my argument in the present essay that the rhetorically ornate and conceptually complex style of panegyric ode of the High Abbasid caliphal court, termed *badīʿ* ("new," "innovative"), that appeared in the third/ninth century is nothing other than the exercise of the poet's newfound power to generate new words and linguistic structures, never seen before.[19] This power derives from the cracking of the "linguistic code" through the newly developed linguistic sciences of syntax, morphology, and, especially, *ishtiqāq* (morphological derivation), and the crucial point in the context of the present essay is that this code could never have been cracked without the establishment of literacy, as explained above. Once this code was cracked, the poet could generate new words and new constructions, never experienced before.

But why would he want to do this? Here, I would like to connect the two sides of my argument, that is, to see them as closely related aspects of the establishment of Islamic imperial hegemony. First, the rise of Islam and the Islamic states entailed astounding political, military, cultural, and scientific growth, of which the establishment of literacy and the concomitant flourishing of analytical sciences was an organic part. With this vast and vertiginous accrual of imperial hegemony in all its aspects came an irresistible sense of power and mission: an "Islamic Manifest Destiny." Second, the job of formulating and propagating a new ideology of Arab Islamic hegemony fell to the court panegyrists. The power of their poetry had to match the might and dominion of their patron. In other words, just as the caliph exercised a God-given might and dominion far beyond that of the kinglets and tribal lords of the *Jāhiliyyah*, so were the court poets required to come up with a poetic idiom that could express this previously unimagined and God-given might.

The transition from orality to literacy had several related consequences for the classical Abbasid panegyrist. First, now that poems could be written down, compiled, and compared, there was increased pressure for originality and, related to this, more likelihood of accusations of plagiarism. Second, relieved of mnemonic imperatives, in terms of both composition and preservation, poets were free to abandon the oral formulae and to experiment in order to create expressions and images that, although they use largely the

18. Stetkevych, *Poetics of Islamic Legitimacy*, 145, 152, 169–70.

19. It is worth noting here that the derivatives of this same root *b-d-ʿ* ("to originate, to invent, to do something new, for the first time") include *al-Bādiʿ* ("the Creator"), one of the names of Allāh, and *bidʿah* ("heresy"), see Stetkevych, *Abū Tammām*, 5.

same "poetic diction," were too convoluted or abstract for oral composition and transmission.[20] Third, not only were poets liberated from the oral formulae of the poetic metalanguage, but they were empowered through the new linguistic sciences to derive new words and structures. In terms of rhetorical elements in particular, we find, as I have written elsewhere, that the Abbasid poet has "re-tooled" them to create expressions that are—instead of affective and sensory—conceptually abstract and complex.[21] The final step in this argument is that the expression, by which I mean both formulation and propagation, of caliphal power became the goal to which this newfound linguistic might was directed. Along this line of argumentation, I would like to conclude, then, by proposing that *badīʿ* poetry, whatever its roots in the lighter amorous, jocular, or even obscene verse of the age of Hārūn al-Rashīd (r. 170–193/786–809), came to function, certainly in the hands of the panegyrists of al-Muʿtaṣim (r. 218–227/833–842), as the "linguistic correlative" of caliphal power.

At this point, we can perceive quite clearly that the dramatic stylistic changes that appeared in the late Umayyad and the Abbasid period can be linked directly to the transformation of Arabic culture from primary orality to literacy. Reading al-Marzūqī's (d. 431/1030) formulation of the traditional aesthetics termed *ʿamūd al-shiʿr* ("the pillar of poetry") that characterize what is *maṭbūʿ* ("natural") as opposed to *maṣnūʿ* ("artificial," "contrived"), and traditional as opposed to modern, we can now discern that this distinction is between the affective and sensory poetics rooted in the pre-Islamic oral tradition and the intellectual and conceptual poetics that literacy made possible. Al-Marzūqī writes in his introduction to Abū Tammām's *Ḥamāsah*:[22]

> It is necessary to clarify what the well-known *ʿamūd al-shiʿr* is among the Arabs, in order to distinguish inherited artistry from the new, and the ancient method of composing poetry from the modern . . . and to know the difference between *maṣnūʿ* ("artificial") and *maṭbūʿ* ("natural"), and the superiority of the easy and compliant to the difficult and intractable. Thus we say . . . that they were striving for nobility and soundness of meaning, for purity and correctness of expression, and for accuracy of description . . . for closeness of simile, for cohesion of the parts of the poem, and the suitable choice of a pleasing meter for them, for the appropriateness of the two terms of the metaphor, for

20. See Monroe, "Oral Composition," 37; Stetkevych, *Abū Tammām*, 18–19.
21. Stetkevych, *Abū Tammām*, 33–38.
22. Al-Marzūqī, *Sharḥ Dīwān al-Ḥamāsah*, i, 8–9; Stetkevych, *Abū Tammām*, 260.

the conformity of expression to meaning, and the strength of their demand for the rhyme-letter until there is no discrepancy between them.

The second-third/eighth-ninth century blossoming of the high classical rhetorical style, termed *badīʿ*, of such Abbasid masters as Bashshār ibn Burd, Muslim ibn al-Walīd, al-Buḥturī, and, above all, Abū Tammām, is celebrated, by both its supporters and detractors, as innovative and original in the dramatic intensity of its use of rhetorical devices such as *istiʿārah* (metaphor), *tashbīh* (simile), *jinās* (paronomasia, root-play), *ṭibāq* (antithesis), *radd al-ʿajuz ʿalá al-ṣadr* (repetition of an early word in a line in the rhyme-word), and especially *al-madhhab al-kalāmī* ("the manner of Kalām," that is, abstruse logical constructions, conceits that are abstract, conceptual, or far-fetched, in the manner of the speculative theologians [the Mutakallimūn], in other words, what in its High Abbasid heyday constituted bold, even scandalous, innovation). The sciences and the analytical methods they involve give their practitioner a sense of control and mastery over his scientific domain. For the poet, for example, the sciences of *ishtiqāq*, *naḥw*, and *ṣarf* (derivation, syntax, and morphology) allow him to invent new words and constructs never before imagined.

Thus, much to the horror of conservative critics such as al-Āmidī (d. 370/981) in his *Al-Muwāzanah*, we see Abū Tammām (d. 231 or 232/845 or 846), the most celebrated (or notorious) proponent of *badīʿ* poetry, coin new words, such as *tafarʿana* ("to be despotic"), which he derived from *firʿawn* ("pharaoh"):[23]

> You appeared and death bared a brazen cheek,
> And death's appointed time was pharaonic (*tafarʿana*) in its deeds.

He also devised, through a process of grammatical analogy to such Kalām postulates about the Divine as *huwa huwa* ("He is He"), unheard-of constructions such as *lā anta anta* ("you are not you"):[24]

> You are not you, the abodes are not abodes,
> Passion has faded, destinations have changed.

It is worth noting, too, that the conservative critic al-Āmidī consistently takes Abū Tammām to task for constructions that, upon analysis, are metaphors or personifications involving concepts, particularly of time

23. Stetkevych, *Abū Tammām*, 66; al-Āmidī, *Al-Muwāzanah*, i, 238–39.

24. Stetkevych, *Abū Tammām*, 36, 82, 144; al-Āmidī, *Al-Muwāzanah*, i, 511–12.

or fate, and that therefore require a process of abstraction and analysis to decipher:[25]

> By you the sides of our days are polished
> And our nights are all the break of day.

Again:[26]

> Then you clothed yourselves in the disgrace of a time
> Whose nights were, among the nights, menstruating.

We also find Abū Tammām's personification of time itself as "perishing"—a reflection perhaps of the disputes of the Mutakallimūn over whether time is finite or infinite—now subordinated to the poet's panegyric purpose of praise for his longtime friend and patron, the general Abū Saʿīd Muḥammad ibn Yūsuf al-Thaghrī:[27]

> When your fated time comes, you will not perish,
> But time, that has destroyed [others] like you, will perish.

This period was the apex of Abbasid politico-cultural hegemony and military might, and, I argue, the *badīʿ* style evolved to express, celebrate, and immortalize that hegemony and that might. In other words, the transformation of Arab civilization in the first three centuries of Islam and the astounding political dominion and cultural florescence of the High Abbasid Age demanded that the expressive capabilities of the Arabic language, and its poetic metalanguage in particular, be expanded to convey ideas and experiences hitherto unknown. More simply, the *badīʿ* style in practice is precisely the dominant mode of expression of the High Abbasid court panegyric, a body of poetry that celebrates Arab-Islamic political and cultural hegemony, military might, and religious authority as vested in the caliph himself or, in a subordinate manner, in lesser patrons of the court. The *badīʿ* style became inseparable or indistinguishable from the ideology of Arab-Islamic hegemony and triumphalism. By this, I do not mean merely that the subject of particular lines and poems is caliphal power—although this is a, maybe *the*, major theme of such poems, but rather that this very style of poetry became in and of itself a projection or analogue of that power. Again, the *badīʿ* style is what I term the "linguistic correlative" of caliphal might and Islamic hegemony, an ideology of "Islamic Manifest Destiny."

25. Stetkevych, *Abū Tammām*, 75; al-Āmidī, *Al-Muwāzanah*, i, 270.
26. Stetkevych, *Abū Tammām*, 76; al-Āmidī, *Al-Muwāzanah*, i, 264.
27. Stetkevych, *Abū Tammām*, 24; Ibn al-Muʿtazz, *Kitāb al-Badīʿ*, 23.

Above all, in the context of the transition from orality to literacy, this "retooling" of rhetoric to perform breathtaking feats of verbal "derring-do" is possible only because the establishment of literacy has, to a large degree, freed rhetoric of mnemonic exigencies or obligations. The successful Abbasid panegyrist, while adhering to the conventional generic dictates of the *qaṣīdah*, had to navigate between the requirement of originality and the lure of *badīʿ* on the one hand, and, on the other, the pull of a traditional, conservative aesthetic (*ʿamūd al-shiʿr*) still grounded in what we can now understand as the pragmatic exigencies of orality. In critical terms, this took the form of classifying poets who inclined toward abstract and conceptual formulations as *maṣnūʿ* ("contrived," "artificial"), whereas those whose poetry was more in line with the traditional *ʿamūd al-shiʿr* were termed *maṭbūʿ* ("naturally gifted," that is, spontaneous).

In this respect, al-Āmidī's judgment in *Al-Muwāzanah* between Abū Tammām and al-Buḥturī (in favor of the latter) is a case in point, and this conservative critic's distaste for the rhetorical manipulation of abstractions and generative manipulation of syntax and morphology[28]—which we are considering here to be the essence of *badīʿ* as the linguistic correlative of (God-like) caliphal power—is merely symptomatic of the conservative critic clinging to poetic techniques rendered obsolete by a new technology—writing. Nevertheless, in our zeal for the new and technologically advanced style of poetry, we must not forget that certain necessary requirements of oral poetry have an essential aesthetic component that goes beyond their oral-mnemonic functionality: images that are sensorily derived and emotionally charged have an "affective" pull that is, as al-Āmidī realized, however different his framework of reference and terminology, altogether distinct from the "mental" or "intellectual" appeal of *badīʿ*.

It is noteworthy in the context of the present essay that the formulation of the doctrine of the miraculous inimitability of the Qur'an (*iʿjāz al-qurʾān*), consisting above all of its unmatchable rhetorical power, took place between the third and fifth Islamic centuries (750–1000 CE).[29] I would like to propose that this development is no accident, but rather, that only after the *badīʿ* poets achieved their astounding heights of rhetorical power—in a way that very explicitly related rhetorical power to divine power through its employ in formulating and propagating the concept of a divinely appointed caliphate (that is, they expressly joined the notions of rhetorical beauty and Islamic might)—was the concept ratcheted up to the divine level: if rhetorical beauty equals power, then absolute rhetorical beauty equals absolute

28. Stetkevych, *Abū Tammām*, 49–89.

29. von Grunebaum, "Iʿdjāz."

power. In more down-to-earth terms, this is the proposition arrived at by the scholars of *iʿjāz al-qurʾān*, such as ʿAlī ibn ʿĪsá al-Rummānī (d. 384/994) and ʿAbd al-Qāhir al-Jurjānī (d. 470/1078), that true faith can be achieved only through the thorough study of rhetoric: that is, that the truth of Muhammad's prophecy is the divine nature of the Qur'an, which resides in its unmatchable rhetorical beauty. Therefore, the believer who does not understand rhetoric cannot truly grasp the miraculousness of the Qur'an, and the truth of Muhammad's prophethood (*ṣiḥḥat al-nubuwwah*) (see below).

RHETORIC OF/AS DEVOTIONAL EXERCISE: THE *BADĪʿIYYAH* AND MANUSCRIPT AND MEMORY IN THE POST-CLASSICAL PERIOD

It is, I think, useful and reasonable to apply the terms Post-Classical and Medieval to the period of Arab-Islamic poetry and literature from about the sixth-thirteenth Islamic centuries (1100–1850 CE). The classical poetic tradition of the *qaṣīdah* reached its pinnacle in the unrivaled high heroics and high rhetorics of Aḥmad Abū al-Ṭayyib al-Mutanabbī (d. 354/965), who, as his sobriquet "the would-be prophet" indicates, cast a pall of unmatchable poetic genius over all the poets who succeeded him, in a manner suggestive of the miraculous inimitability of the Qur'an. This sense is nowhere better captured than in Abū al-ʿAlāʾ al-Maʿarrī's (d. 449/1058) title for his commentary on al-Mutanabbī's *dīwān*: *Muʿjiz Aḥmad* ("the Miracle of Aḥmad")—an evident pun on the "miracle of Muhammad," that is, the Qur'an. Al-Maʿarrī himself is a pivotal figure who exemplifies in the trajectory from his first *dīwān*,[30] the *qaṣīdah*-based *Saqṭ al-Zand*, to his second, the programmatic double-rhymed alphabetized series of epigrams of the *Luzūmiyyāt*, the transition from Classical to Post-Classical poetics and aesthetics.

Among the Arab critics and literary historians of the nineteenth and twentieth centuries (the *Nahḍah* or Arab Renaissance and the Modern periods, comprising the Neo-Classical, Romantic, and Modern/Free Verse schools of poetry), the period between 1100 and about 1850 is normally referred to as the Age of Decline (*ʿAṣr al-Inḥiṭāṭ*). On the one hand this was the age of great commentators, compendiarists, and lexicographers whom we can credit with the formulation of a classical period, that is, who conferred on their forebears the authority of classics. Yet on the other hand, in the twentieth century, among the Neo-Classicists, Romantics, and Modernists alike, the poetry of this period was largely dismissed as derivative

30. Smoor, "al-Maʿarrī."

and characterized by excessive rhetorical artifice and artificiality.[31] The Neo-Classical poets and critics of the Nahḍah used this period as a foil—an Age of Decline from the High Abbasid Age whose master *badīʿ* poets the Neo-Classicists took as their models and whose political and cultural hegemony they hoped to revive. The Romantics and Moderns, by contrast, dismissed the entire Classical and Post-Classical *qaṣīdah* tradition as sclerotic, artificial, and obsolete. All schools, however, shared the disdain for the Post-Classical period as one of particular artificiality and lack of originality. Within this context, the *badīʿiyyah* was singled out for special vilification as the prime example of "decline"—of artifice run amok coupled with the paralysis of the creative impulse.

However, as we shall see, the creators and practitioners of the *badīʿiyyah* did not see it this way. What I propose to do here, using the *badīʿiyyah* as my prime example, is to explore the aesthetics and poetics of the Post-Classical age to see how they differ from those of the pre-Islamic and High Abbasid ages respectively, and how the *badīʿiyyah* is the consummate, and perhaps inevitable, poetic expression of the Post-Classical aesthetic. Just as the exigencies and opportunities of orality and literacy have allowed us to understand some aspects of the aesthetics of the *Jāhiliyyah* and the High Abbasid age, and the differences between them, so too the exigencies and possibilities of the manuscript-memorial culture of the Middle Ages, especially as magisterially formulated by Mary Carruthers for the Christian Middle Ages,[32] will help us arrive at a new aesthetic and an appreciation of the new role of rhetoric in this period.

GENESIS OF THE *BADĪʿIYYAH*

The *badīʿiyyah* is a curiously hybrid poetic form that first appears in the eighth/fourteenth century. The *badīʿiyyah*-proper is a subgenre of *madīḥ nabawī* (praise poem to the Prophet Muhammad) that consists of a *muʿāraḍah* (an imitation or contrafaction in the same rhyme and meter) of the preeminent medieval praise poem to the Prophet, Abū ʿAbd Allāh Muḥammad Ibn Saʿīd al-Būṣīrī's (d. 694–96/1294–97) celebrated Burdah (Mantle Ode),[33] with the added requirement that each line exhibit a particular rhetorical device.[34] The poet most often credited with producing the

31. See Cachia, "Sound to Echo," 219–20.

32. Carruthers, *Memory*.

33. See Stetkevych, "Text to Talisman"; Stetkevych, "*Sīrah* to *Qaṣīdah*"; Stetkevych, *Mantle Odes*.

34. There is some variation in definition, but this, to my mind, is the strictest and

first such poem, Ṣafī al-Dīn al-Ḥillī (d. 749/1348 or 750/1349),[35] offers an anecdote about its composition that is a key to its essential hybridity: having originally intended to compose a prose treatise on the figures of rhetoric and *badīʿ*, al-Ḥillī tells us:[36]

> I collected everything that I found in the books of the scholars and added to this other figures that I extracted from the poetry of the ancients, with the intention of composing a book that would cover most of them, since there was no way to cover them all. Then I was afflicted with a severe and protracted illness and it so happened that I saw in a dream a message from the Prophet (the greatest blessings and peace be upon him) demanding that I compose a praise poem to him and promising that I would be cured thereby of my ailment. So I turned from compiling the treatise to composing a *qaṣīdah* that gathered the various types of *badīʿ* and was embroidered with the praise of [the Prophet's] glory. So I composed 154 lines in the meter *basīṭ* containing 151 types of devices . . . and I made each verse an example illustrating a particular type.

The most striking feature of this anecdote to anyone familiar with the medieval Arabic tradition is that it is a clear reference to, or variation upon, the renowned story of al-Būṣīrī's Burdah, which he is said to have composed when afflicted with semi-paralysis, recited in a dream to the Prophet, only to awake the next day cured of his malady. By this means al-Ḥillī establishes a "mythic concordance," to use Paul Connerton's term,[37] a sort of spiritual as well as literary identification with the Master of the Burdah. This seems to serve as sufficient reference to al-Būṣīrī and the Burdah, and al-Ḥillī feels no need to mention explicitly that his new poem is a contrafaction (*muʿāraḍah*) of al-Būṣīrī's—since it would have been immediately recognized from the opening line. Of further note is that the contractual obligation between poet and patron that the *qaṣīdah* entails is explicitly stated here: poem for cure. It

most accurate. Many scholars, although they mention the distinctive features of al-Būṣīrī's Burdah, that is, the meter *basīṭ* (- - ˇ - / - ˇ -) and the rhyme in the letter "m" that the *badīʿiyyah* must exhibit, do not explicitly mention al-Būṣīrī's Burdah (although they must be well aware of the relationship). For an overview and discussion of this issue, see Abū Zayd, *Al-Badīʿiyyāt*, 40–51 and al-Jawharī, *Kitāb Ṭirāz al-Ḥullah*, 26–34. An attempt to treat the aesthetic issues of the *badīʿiyyah* is made by Pierre Cachia in his work on ʿAbd al-Ghanī al-Nabulusī's (d. 1143/1731) *badīʿiyyah* (see Cachia, "Sound to Echo," and Cachia, *Arch Rhetorician*, Introduction.

35. Heinrichs, "Ṣafī al-Dīn al-Ḥillī."

36. al-Ḥillī, *Sharḥ*, 54–55.

37. Connerton, *How Societies Remember*, 43.

is the same as al-Būṣīrī's contract, but with a twist: this time the contractual relation is initiated by the Prophet rather than the poet.

Further, we should note that, far from seeing his poetry as constrained or artificial, al-Ḥillī makes the claim, however curiously phrased, that he was striving for a fluid, limpid style, which he describes entirely along the lines of the Classical *ʿamūd al-shiʿr* (*idem*):

> And *I compelled myself in composing it to avoid constraint and forced language* but to follow what my soul led me to of delicacy and ease of expression, strength and soundness of meaning [emphasis mine] .

Another key element in al-Ḥillī's sense of accomplishment is that his *badīʿiyyah* is a condensed yet comprehensive rhetorical work based on seventy books (which he lists at the end of his commentary) of rhetoric, so that he concludes his introduction as follows (55):

> So, look, o littérateur-critic and wise scholar, at this rich collection that is delightful to the ear, for indeed it is the product of seventy books of which I did not skip a single chapter. So with it you can dispense with the excess stuffing of lengthy books and the arduousness of repetitive speech.

And finally, in what is to us an astounding claim for originality, he quotes a famous line by al-Mutanabbī (56):

> Leave off every voice but my voice, for I
> Am the voice that speaks, the others are [mere] echoes.

In this sense then, the title *Al-Kāfiyah* (the Sufficient) indicates that al-Ḥillī's *badīʿiyyah* provides so sufficient an account of the rhetorical figures that the other seventy books are rendered superfluous. It is in terms of mnemonic technique what the iPod is to digital technology.

What is the logic behind the formal combination of rhetorical handbook and praise poem to the Prophet? That is, how and why do these two components of the *badīʿiyyah* fit together? I would like to suggest the following: as I have argued in my recent studies of al-Būṣīrī, the Burdah—and the *badīʿiyyah*s, which for the most part follow closely its thematic structure, motifs, and style—is essentially structured along the lines of a classical Arabic panegyric of the supplicatory type. What is distinctive is that the patron, the *mamdūḥ* (the one praised and supplicated), is now the Prophet Muhammad and—this is essential—the object of supplication is, first and foremost, the intercession of the Prophet on the Day of Judgment (= salvation). That is, its performative role is a ritual exchange of the poet's praise for the Prophet's intercession. In this it embodies, or enacts, the essence of medieval Islamic belief: the guarantee that the Prophet will lead his Ummah to salvation on Judgment Day. The praise of the Prophet in this sense is not merely praise, but, as with all Arabic panegyric, the effectuation of a contractual obligation between poet and patron, an exchange of praise (self-abasement, submission, recognition of the Prophet's authority) for *shafāʿah*, the intercession of the Prophet on the Day of Judgment and inclusion in his Ummah, which he will conduct to salvation under his banner. The *badīʿiyyah* is in this respect a spiritual exercise, the performance of which is understood to produce a spiritual result or to confer a spiritual benefit.

This, then, brings us to rhetoric. The miraculously inimitable rhetorical beauty of the Qur'an is not merely an article of faith but the essence of Islam, which, in the highly polemical religious atmosphere of the medieval period, distinguishes it from its main contenders of the time, Christianity and Judaism. Therefore, the Muslim has no true understanding of his faith until he understands rhetoric and can grasp for himself the unsurpassable beauty of the Qur'an. Following the scholars of *iʿjāz al-qurʾān*, such as al-Rummānī or ʿAbd al-Qāhir al-Jurjānī, al-Ḥillī opens his introduction to *Sharḥ al-Kāfiyah* by stating:[38]

> The science most deserving of precedence and most worthy of being learned and taught, after the knowledge of God Almighty, is the knowledge of the verities of His Noble Speech [the Qur'an] and the understanding of what He sent down in the Wise Remembrance [the Qur'an], so that they might be safeguarded from the calamity of doubt and delusion . . . And there is no way to [acquire this knowledge] except through the knowledge of the science of rhetoric, including the figures of *badīʿ*, through which the meaning of the inimitability of the Qur'an and the veracity of the prophethood of Muhammad (peace and blessings of God upon him) is known by evidence and proof.

To grasp through the study of rhetoric the unsurpassable beauty of the Qur'an is to experience firsthand the evidentiary miracle of Muhammad's prophethood. It is as if you witnessed *with your own eyes* Moses turning his rod into a serpent or Jesus raising Lazarus from the dead or Muhammad splitting the moon in half—this is what *iʿjāz* scholars mean when they say that the Qur'an is a permanent miracle, whereas Moses's or Jesus's are merely passing, ephemeral miracles. In this respect, then, to combine in a single poem a contractual guarantee of the Prophet's intercession on Judgment

38. al-Ḥillī, *Sharḥ*, 51–52.

Day with the rhetorical knowledge requisite for witnessing the miracle of the Qur'an and the truth of Muhammad's prophethood is to consummate the Islamic faith.

The masters of the *badīʿiyyah*, as we see from al-Ḥillī's statement, do not see themselves as derivative epigones of an irretrievable Golden Age, but rather as poets of originality and genius who have produced the consummate poetic, rhetorical, and religious devotional work. This serves as further explanation of the title that al-Ḥillī has given his *badīʿiyyah*, that is, *Al-Kāfiyah*, "the Sufficient."

It should be noted, however, that al-Ḥillī's *badīʿiyyah* as a poetic text is not entirely self-sufficient; it exemplifies the rhetorical and *badīʿ* figures, but does not label or explain them (see Appendix: I). Thus, in the *Dīwān* printing, each verse requires a label to indicate which rhetorical figure it exemplifies.[39] It is rather in his commentary upon it, *Sharḥ al-Kāfiyah*, where al-Ḥillī presents the poem together with his commentary—which typically offers an identification and definition of the figure treated, concise information on other scholars' opinions and definitions, plus a few examples from the Qur'an and then from poetry—that the project is complete. It is as though the two together form a whole in which there is a symbiotic relationship between the poetic text and its commentary.

At this point we can introduce the idea that the *badīʿiyyah* itself, as a poem exhibiting the eminently mnemonic characteristics associated with poetry, could serve as a memorial framework to which the scholarly material on the science of rhetoric is appended. We are no longer dealing with the primary orality of the *Jāhiliyyah*, but rather with the "memorial" culture of the medieval manuscript tradition, in which a written base text with marked mnemonic features (poetry, the Qur'an, didactic poems such as the *Alfiyyah* of Ibn Malik) serves as a memorial framework for less memory-friendly material (rules and examples of grammar, philology, rhetoric, and so on). The "memorial" text, inasmuch as it does not need the radical mnemonics of the primary orality of the *Jāhiliyyah*, exhibits the poetics and aesthetics of the literary Abbasid period and provides a written base text that the "student" can memorize by rote and against which he can check his memory.

Thus al-Ḥillī's *badīʿiyyah* itself provides such a memorial framework, admirably fulfilling through its *qaṣīdah* or specifically *madīḥ nabawī* (praise poem to the Prophet Muhammad) the genre characteristics of Carruthers's prescriptions for "memorization" and "recollection."[40] That is to say, for the medieval Muslim, the *madīḥ nabawī* is deeply felt and emotionally intense.

39. al-Ḥillī, *Dīwān*, 685–702.

40. Carruthers, *Memory*.

Not only does it express intimately felt love for and devotion to the Prophet, but, in its supplicatory form, so successful in al-Būṣīrī's hands, a spiritual drama of sin and repentance unfolds. The emotions of passion, regret, hope, and fear dominate the affective landscape and the psychological trajectory of the poem. Thus both the ritual-poetic structure and the emotionally intense spiritual transformation that it entails render the *madīḥ nabawī* an effective memorial framework admirably suited to Carruthers's requirements. She summarizes the chief features of a "memory image" as follows:[41]

> Most importantly, it is "affective" in nature—that is, it is sensorily derived and emotionally charged . . . Successful memory schemes all acknowledge the importance of tagging material emotionally as well as schematically, making each memory as much as possible into a personal occasion by imprinting emotional associations like desire and fear, pleasure or discomfort.

A second point that she emphasizes for successful memorization or recollection is that one must "use a set order with a clearly established beginning" (61), which, of course, is an apt description of the *qaṣīdah*-form in general, and the *madīḥ nabawī* in particular.

Although much of what Carruthers discusses is "memorial structures" devised by the memorizer to commit material to memory, my argument here is that the poetic work itself serves as a memorial structure, and further, perhaps more precisely, can be understood in terms of the medieval *catena*, or "chain," as she describes Thomas Aquinas's compilation in around 1263 of patristic texts on the Bible, the *Catena Aurea*:[42]

> The authorities are chained, or hooked, together by a Biblical phrase. Thus the commentary entirely follows the sequence of the main text, each chapter division of the Gospel book forming a division of the *Catena* and each verse . . . quoted separately with a string of relevant comments following it.

Of course, it seems to me the *madīḥ nabawī* as a *qaṣīdah* with mono-rhyme and mono-meter resembles a chain and its links more closely than the Biblical text.

We should not, however, let the purely scholarly and devotional aspects of the *badīʿiyyah* genre divert us from the highly charged competitive atmosphere in which it was spawned and spread. It is clear from his introduction to his commentary, *Sharḥ al-Kāfiyah*, that al-Ḥillī sees himself in competition with his predecessors in identifying and classifying rhetorical

41. Ibid., 59–60.

42. Ibid., 6.

figures, chief among them Ibn Abī al-Iṣbaʿ (d. 654 H.). In this respect the "inspiration" to combine a rhetorical handbook with a *madīḥ nabawī* imitating al-Būṣīrī's Burdah is an attempt to trump his competition, both among scholars of rhetoric and among poets (remember, he was above all renowned as a poet of vast and varied oeuvre)—to kill two birds with one stone.

In terms of the history of rhetoric and *badīʿ*, it is important to note that since the High Abbasid period with its radically innovative linguistic and rhetorical developments, which in our argument we have linked to the establishment of literacy, there has occurred, under the influence of the third/ninth-century critic ʿAbd Allāh Ibn al-Muʿtazz's *Kitāb al-Badīʿ*,[43] a homogenization of rhetorical figures to the point where the term *maḥāsin al-badīʿ* (adornments of *badīʿ*) includes any figure or stylistic trait that "adorns" language or poetry. The traditional oral-mnemonic-derived aesthetics of *ʿamūd al-shiʿr* (pillar of poetry) have been merged with even the most contrived and complicated rhetorical devices that a literacy-based poetry could produce. Further, we see that even these later have been identified in the Qur'anic text. This produces a curious situation in which, at least as it seems to the modern reader, the proof of the Qur'an's miraculousness is that it exhibits far-fetched rhetorical devices that no one thought up until centuries later.

Another noteworthy feature of al-Ḥillī's commentary, a phenomenon also apparent in al-Būṣīrī's Burdah, as I have demonstrated, but perhaps more obvious when given rhetorical labels, is that what I term the "ritual core" parts of the poem—the deeply spiritually affective sections expressing repentance, self-abasement, supplication, and pleas for intercession. These contain rhetorical "figures" that we associate with the smooth and harmonious *ʿamūd al-shiʿr* aesthetic, whereas the martial-heroic passages of the Prophet's raids and military expeditions exhibit the highly complex and jarring *badīʿ* figures of Abbasid panegyric.[44]

Al-Ḥillī's *badīʿiyyah* spawned many imitators, or rather competitors, seeking to outdo him. We should remark that within the Arabic poetic tradition, the very composition of a *muʿāraḍah* (contrafaction), as both the Arabic and English terms etymologically indicate, constituted *nolens volens* a challenge or contest. Here we will look at just a few examples of the competitive spirit that drove later practitioners of the *badīʿiyyah*. The first such case is ʿIzz al-Dīn al-Mawṣilī (d. 789/1387).[45] Dispensing with the

43. See Stetkevych, *Abū Tammām*, 19–37.

44. Stetkevych, "*Sīrah* to *Qaṣīdah*."

45. al-Ḥamawīet al., *Al-Badīʿiyyāt al-Khams*, 15–22; Abū Zayd, *Al-Badīʿiyyāt*,

necessity of a commentary to identify and define the figure exemplified in each line, he took it upon himself to compose a *badīʿiyyah* in which each line not only exemplified a device, but included its name (most often in the form of a pun) in the line itself (see Appendix: II). This then produces a freestanding independent poem in which the technical term and example of each device are fully fused in a fashion that is eminently mnemonic itself within a self-contained poem of prophetic praise. For al-Mawṣilī this was the consummate poetic work.

This, of course, did not preclude his composing a commentary, and, although it appears that he did not give his *badīʿiyyah* a title, it is commonly known by the quite perceptive title of its commentary: *Al-Tawaṣṣul bi-al-Badīʿ ilá al-Tawassul bi-al-Shafīʿ*.[46] This title, however charming, is not empty rhetoric. Through its wordplay it conveys the total fusion of *badīʿ* into *madīḥ nabawī* that al-Mawṣilī has achieved. It means something like "achieving by means of *badīʿ* supplication to [Muhammad] the Intercessor." Inasmuch as the rite of supplication has at its heart a ritual exchange—praise for prize, or here praise for intercession—the rhetorical figures of the *badīʿiyyah* are not mere rhetorical examples, but rather they constitute the very gift that the poet is giving. Following through on this logic, *badīʿ*, because it is the means to acquiring the Prophet's intercession on Judgment Day, is therefore the means to salvation. This logic then comes full circle, because the understanding of *badīʿ*/rhetoric, as we saw above, is also the consummation of the Islamic faith, for it is equated with witnessing the miracle of the Qur'an and, *ipso facto*, the truth of Muhammad's prophethood. In addition, al-Mawṣilī's poem, as a memorial structure, is self-contained, not relying upon a commentary to name or explain the rhetorical figures it employs. The poem as a devotional exercise assumes as well an unusual performative quality. To compose, memorize, and/or recite the poem is to achieve, or make one's own, through its words and tropes, that very knowledge of rhetoric that constitutes witnessing Muhammad's miracle (the Qur'an) and, at the same time, to present those rhetorical "gems" as gifts of praise in a ritual of exchange and supplication for the Prophet's intercession on Judgment Day.

Finally, we will look at a further development that exemplifies the complex interplay of factors associated with both orality and literacy in medieval memorial culture, Abū Bakr Ibn Ḥijjah al-Ḥamawī's (d. 837/1434) *Khizānat al-Adab wa-Ghāyat al-Arab* ("The Treasury of Literature and the

79–80. All the lines of al-Mawṣilī's *badīʿiyyah* are also included in the commentary of al-Ḥamawī, *Khizānat al-Adab*, see below.

46. Abū Zayd, *Al-Badīʿiyyāt*, 77.

Utmost Aim").[47] It is his "commentary," composed in 826/1433 on his most celebrated poem, his *badīʿiyyah*. In his brief introduction, al-Ḥamawī clearly establishes his intent to outdo two of his predecessors in the *badīʿiyyah* genre, Ṣafī al-Dīn al-Ḥillī and ʿIzz al-Dīn al-Mawṣilī, by combining the limpid style of the former with the word play on the rhetorical terms of the latter (see Appendix: III). In addition, he points out that he has taken the opportunity to settle a religious score. Since his two predecessors, both Shiʿites, as it appears, did not mention the precedence of Abū Bakr, the first Orthodox caliph, in their *badīʿiyyah*s, he titles his *Taqdīm Abī Bakr* ("The Precedence of [the caliph] Abū Bakr" [over ʿAlī]), but equally the superiority of his [Abū Bakr al-Ḥamawī's] *badīʿiyyah* over theirs.[48]

But al-Ḥamawī does not leave his poem as a freestanding entity. Here I would like to suggest that, in general, in the classical and medieval periods, poems, especially of the pre-Islamic and early Islamic period, at least in the realm of *paideia* or *adab* as cultural formation, had come to exist not so much as freestanding texts, but had begun to function as memorial structures—harking back to all the oral-mnemonic features of pre-Islamic poetry—from which, as in the medieval Christian *catena*, vast amounts of learning (grammatical, philological, cultural, rhetorical, and so on) were suspended. Take for example such classics as al-Anbārī's commentary on the *Mufaḍḍaliyyāt*, al-Tibrīzī's or al-Zawzanī's commentaries on the *Muʿallaqāt*, or al-Tibrīzī's commentary on Abū Tammām's *Ḥamāsah*. Following Carruthers's general line of thinking, we can note that 1) the commentator authorizes and authenticates the base text as a "classic" worthy of commentary; 2) the commentator not only explains the base text, but uses his commentary as a compendium of various sorts of information; and 3) in this respect, the base text becomes a memorial structure to which non-mnemonically formatted (that is, prose) information is appended.

In this light, the semiotics of al-Ḥamawī's title *Khizānat al-Adab wa-Ghāyat al-Arab* ("The Treasury of Literature and the Utmost Aim") is of interest. For the first part, Carruthers has noted that a storehouse or treasury is a common metaphor for the memory.[49] For the second, we are to understand that this work has achieved the utmost aim or desire, presumably of human knowledge. By appending a storehouse or treasury of *adab/paideia* knowledge to his own composition of *madīḥ nabawī*, al-Ḥamawī's first of all validating and authorizing his own poem as a "foundational text"—a

47. al-Ḥamawī, *Khizānat al-Adab*.

48. Brockelmann, "Ibn Ḥidjdja al-Ḥamawī," notes that al-Ḥamawī further strove to establish his superiority over al-Ḥillī and al-Mawṣilī in a work entitled *Thubūt al-Ḥujjah ʿalá al-Mawṣilī wa-al-Ḥillī li-Ibn Ḥijjah* (ms. Berlin).

49. Carruthers, *Memory*, 34–35.

classic. In doing so, praise of the Prophet, of however recent vintage, displaces the pagan classics as the conceptual framework on which all *adab* learning "depends." I believe that this is indicative of a huge cultural shift from the classical to the medieval period. Some such idea appears belatedly in Yūsuf ibn Ismāʿīl al-Nabhānī's (d. 1350/1921) introduction to his renowned compendium of *madīḥ nabawī*,[50] in which he declares that praise of the Prophet is the highest form of poetry and expresses his perplexity at the vexed issue as to why the master poets of the classical (Umayyad and especially Abbasid) periods (the so-called *fuḥūl*, or "stallions," of the poets) did not compose in this genre.

As his title suggests, al-Ḥamawī goes far beyond the straightforward explanation of rhetorical figures such as we find in al-Ḥillī to produce an all-inclusive compendium of *adab*, including, for example, an entire *maqāmah* of al-Ḥarīrī.[51] This (re)configuration of *adab* around an eminently religious and medieval text, his *badīʿiyyah*, and furthermore around rhetorical figures embedded in a supplicatory ritual, should then be considered the consummate medieval or post-classical work. It embodies in its structure as well as contents the essential beliefs and the epistemological hierarchy of the medieval Muslim literary scholar.[52]

BIBLIOGRAPHY

Abū Zayd, ʿAlī. *Al-Badīʿiyyāt fī al-Adab al-ʿArabī: Nashʾatuhā—Taṭawwuruhā—Atharuhā*. Beirut: ʿĀlam al-Kutub, 1983.

al-Āmidī, Abū al-Qāsim al-Ḥasan ibn Bishr. *Al-Muwāzanah bayn Shiʿr Abī Tammām wa-al-Buḥturī*. 2 vols. Edited by Aḥmad Saqr. Cairo: Dār al-Maʿārif, 1972.

al-Anbārī, Abū Bakr Muḥammad ibn al-Qāsim. *Sharḥ al-Qaṣāʾid al-Sabʿ al-Ṭiwāl al-Jāhiliyyāt*. Edited by ʿAbd al-Salām Muḥammad Hārūn. Cairo: Dār al-Maʿārif, 1969.

al-Baghdādī, ʿAbd al-Qādir ibn ʿUmar. *Khizānat al-Adab wa-Lubb Lubāb Lisān al-ʿArab*. 2nd ed., 13 vols. Edited by ʿAbd al-Salām Hārūn. Cairo: Maktabat al-Khānjī, 1984.

50. Nabhānī, *Al-Majmūʿah al-Nabhāniyyah*, i, 33–34.

51. al-Ḥamawī, *Khizānat al-Adab*, ii, 478–81.

52. It is entirely indicative of the transfer from the manuscript to the print tradition, and likewise from a religious to a secular approach to rhetorical knowledge, that Pierre Cachia, *Arch Rhetorician*, has extracted and translated a handlist of rhetorical figures, definitions, and examples from ʿAbd al-Ghanī al-Nābulusī's (d. 1143 H.) commentary on his own *badīʿiyyah*, entitled *Nafaḥāt al-Azhār ʿalá Nasamāt al-Asḥār*, while eliminating and/or dismantling the *badīʿiyyah* itself that forms the structure of the original Arabic work.

Brockelmann, C. "Ibn Ḥidjdja, Abū Bakr Taḳī al-Dīn al-Ḥamawī." In *The Encyclopaedia of Islam*, new ed., edited by H. A. R. Gibb et al., 3:799–800. 12 vols. and index. Leiden: Brill, 1960–2009.

Burkert, Walter. *Homo Necans: The Anthropology of Ancient Greek Ritual and Myth*. Translated by Peter Bing. Berkeley: University of California Press, 1983.

Cachia, Pierre. *The Arch Rhetorician or The Schemer's Skimmer: A Handbook of Late Arabic badīʿ drawn from ʿAbd al-Ghānī an-Nābulsī's* Nafaḥāt al-Azhār ʿalā Nasamāt al-Asḥār *Summarized and Systematized by Pierre Cachia*. Wiesbaden: Harrassowitz, 1998.

———. "From Sound to Echo in Late *Badīʿ* Literature." *Journal of the American Oriental Society* 108 (1988) 219–25.

Carruthers, Mary J. *The Book of Memory: A Study of Memory in Medieval Culture*. Cambridge Studies in Medieval Literature 10. Cambridge: Cambridge University Press, 1990.

Connerton, Paul. *How Societies Remember*. Themes in the Social Sciences. Cambridge: Cambridge University Press, 1989.

al-Ḥamawī, Abū Bakr Muḥammad ibn ʿAlī Ibn Ḥujjah. *Khizānat al-Adab wa-Ghāyat al-Arab*. 2 vols. Edited by Ṣalāḥ al-Dīn al-Hawwārī. Beirut: al-Maktabah al-ʿAṣriyyah, 2006.

al-Ḥamawī, Taqī al-Dīn Ibn Ḥijjah, et al. *Al-Badīʿiyyāt al-Khams fī Madḥ al-Nabī wa-al-Ṣaḥābah al-Kirām*. Cairo: Maṭbaʿat al-Maʿārif, 1897.

Havelock, Eric A. *The Literate Revolution in Greece and Its Cultural Consequences*. Princeton: Princeton University Press, 1982.

———. *The Muse Learns to Write: Reflections on Orality and Literacy from Antiquity to the Present*. New Haven: Yale University Press, 1986.

Heinrichs, W. P. "Ṣafī al-Dīn ʿAbd al-ʿAzīz b. Sarāyā al-Ḥillī al-Ṭāʾī al-Sinbisī, Abu ʾl-Maḥāsin." In *The Encyclopaedia of Islam*, new ed., 12 vols. and index, edited by H. A. R. Gibb et al., 8:801–5. Leiden: Brill, 1960–2009.

al-Ḥillī, Ṣafī al-Dīn. *Dīwān*. Beirut: Dār Ṣādir/Dār Bayrūt, 1962.

———. *Sharḥ al-Kāfiyah al-Badīʿiyyah fī ʿUlūm al-Balāghah wa-Maḥāsin al-Badīʿ*. Edited by Nasīb Nashāwī. Damascus: Maṭbūʿāt Majmaʿ al-Lughah al-ʿArabiyyah bi-Dimashq, 1982.

Ibn al-Muʿtazz, ʿAbd Allāh. *Kitāb al-Badīʿ*. Edited by Ignatius Kratchkovsky. London: Luzac, 1935.

al-Jāḥiẓ, Abū ʿUthmān ʿAmr ibn Baḥr. *Al-Bayān wa-al-Tabyīn*. 4 vols. Edited by ʿAbd al-Salām Hārūn. Cairo: Maktabat al-Khānjī, 1968.

———. *Al-Ḥayawān*. 8 vols. Edited by ʿAbd al-Salām Muḥammad Hārūn. Cairo: Muṣṭafá al-Bābī al-Ḥalabī, 1965–69.

al-Jawharī, Rajāʾ al-Sayyid, ed. *Kitāb Ṭirāz al-Ḥullah wa-Shifāʾ al-Ghullah lil-Imām Jaʿfar Shihāb al-Dīn ... al-Gharnāṭī*. Alexandria: Muʾassasat al-Thaqāfah al-Jāmiʿiyyah, 1990.

al-Maʿarrī, Abū al-ʿAlāʾ. *Risālat al-Ghufrān*. 7th ed. Edited by ʿĀʾishah ʿAbd al-Raḥmān. Cairo: Dār al-Maʿārif, 1981.

al-Marzūqī, Aḥmad ibn Muḥammad. *Sharḥ Dīwān al-Ḥamāsah*. 2nd ed., 4 vols. Edited by Aḥmad Amīn and ʿAbd al-Salām Hārūn. Cairo: Maṭbaʿat Lajnat al-Taʾlīf wa-al-Tarjamah wa-al-Nashr, 1967.

Monroe, James T. "Oral Composition in Pre-Islamic Poetry." *Journal of Arabic Literature* 3 (1972) 1–50.

al-Nabhānī, Yūsuf ibn Ismāʿīl. *Al-Majmūʿah al-Nabhāniyyah fī al-Madāʾiḥ al-Nabawiyyah*. 4 vols. Beirut: Dār al-Kutub al-ʿIlmiyyah, 1996.

Ong, Walter J. *Orality and Literacy: The Technologizing of the Word*. New Accents. London: Methuen, 1982.

Smoor, P. "al-Maʿarrī, Abu 'l-ʿAlāʾ Aḥmad b. ʿAbd Allāh b. Sulaymān." In *The Encyclopaedia of Islam*, new ed., 12 vols. and index, edited by H. A. R. Gibb et al., 5:927–35. Leiden: Brill, 1960–2009.

Stetkevych, Suzanne Pinckney. *Abū Tammām and the Poetics of the ʿAbbasid Age*. Leiden: Brill, 1991.

———. "From *Sīrah* to *Qaṣīdah*: Poetics and Polemics in al-Būṣīrī's *Qaṣīdat al-Burdah* (*Mantle Ode*)." *Journal of Arabic Literature* 38 (2007) 1–52.

———. "From Text to Talisman: al-Būṣīrī's *Qaṣīdat al-Burdah* (*Mantle Ode*) and the Supplicatory Ode." *Journal of Arabic Literature* 37 (2006) 145–89.

———. *The Mantle Odes: Arabic Praise Poems to the Prophet Muhammad*. Bloomington: Indiana University Press, 2010.

———. *The Mute Immortals Speak: Pre-Islamic Poetry and the Poetics of Ritual*. Ithaca, NY: Cornell University Press, 1993.

———. *The Poetics of Islamic Legitimacy: Myth, Gender, and Ceremony in the Classical Arabic Ode*. Bloomington: Indiana University Press, 2002.

———. "Pre-Islamic Poetry and the Poetics of Redemption: *Mufaḍḍaliyyah 119* of ʿAlqamah and *Bānat Suʿād* of Kaʿb ibn Zuhayr." In *Reorientations: Arabic and Persian Poetry*, edited by Suzanne Pinckney Stetkevych, 1–57. Bloomington: Indiana University Press, 1994.

von Grunebaum, G. E. "Iʿdjāz." In *The Encyclopaedia of Islam*, new ed., 12 vols. and index, edited by H. A. R. Gibb et al., 3:1018–20. Leiden: Brill, 1960–2009.

Appendix of *Badīʿiyyah* Examples

(Underline = rhetorical device; **bold** = play on rhetorical term)

I: Ṣafī al-Dīn al-Ḥillī (1982:57, v. 1; 1962:685, v. 1)

> *in ji'ta Salʿan fa-salʿan jīrati l-ʿAlami*
> *w-aqrā l-salāma ʿalá ʿurbin bi-Dhī Salami*
>
> If you come to Salʿ then ask about the neighbors of ʿAlam,
> And recite a greeting to the Bedouin of Dhū Salam.

1. *barāʿat al-maṭlaʿ* (masterful opening): smooth, clear, and delicate
2. *jinās murakkab* (compound root-play): *Salʿan . . . salʿan*
3. *jinās muṭlaq* (pure root-play): *salām . . . Salam*

II: ʿIzz al-Dīn al-Mawṣilī (al-Ḥamawī, al-Mawṣilī et al. 1897:15, v. 1)

> *fa-ḥayyi Salmá wa-sal mā* ***rakkabat*** *bi-shadhan*
> *qad* ***aṭlaqat****hu amāma al-ḥayyi ʿan amami*
>
> Then greet Salmá and ask what has she mixed with the musk
> That she has released before the tribe from nearby.

1. *jinās* ***murakkab****: Salmá . . . sal mā*
2. *jinās* ***muṭlaq****: amāma . . . amami*

III: Ibn Ḥijjah al-Ḥamawī (al-Ḥamawī 2006:i, 57, v. 2)

> *bi-Llahi sir bī fa-sirbī* ***ṭallaqū*** *waṭanī*
> *wa-****rakkabū*** *fī ḍulūʿī* ***muṭlaqa*** *l-saqami*
>
> By God, take me away, for my people deserted my homeland,
> And have fixed in my heart an endless pain.

1. *jinās* ***murakkab****: sir bī . . . sirbī*
2. *jinās* ***muṭlaq****: ṭallaqū . . . / muṭlaqa*

12

Response from an Africanist Scholar

Ruth Finnegan

This response comes from the position of a nonspecialist on the scriptures of Judaism, Christianity, and Islam. My own background lies mainly in comparative work on orality, literacy, and communication media, with a focus on oral literature and performance, especially though not exclusively in Africa. Like other conference participants I too have been tussling with the "written text" paradigm, but begin from relative ignorance of the specialist fields covered here.

Because of this unfamiliarity I found the papers all the more fascinating, not only as a wonderful introduction to a substantial body of interrelated work but because certain themes seemed to emerge so clearly. These struck me as having interesting parallels with developments in oral literary studies in Africa, something that I have recently spent some time tracing.[1] I will take this overlap as the starting point for my remarks.[2]

1. Finnegan, *Oral and Beyond*; Finnegan, "Studying the Oral Literatures of Africa in the 1960s and Today."

2. My brief was to respond to papers on the first day, but since all had been circulated in advance I ventured to include occasional references to later papers also. Given that this is a personal response rather than a substantive paper, I have been sparing with references (recent bibliographies on oral and written expression in Africa can be found in Barber, *Anthropology of Texts, Persons and Publics*, and Finnegan, *Oral and Beyond*).

FROM UNIFORMITY TO MULTIPLICITY

Recent work on oral and written expression in Africa has seen a move away from the broad sweeps once typical of much conventional wisdom. In earlier decades it seemed self-evident that Africa was the home of tribal allegiances and undifferentiated "oral tradition." Its pervasive "oral culture" would in due course be swept away by that of literacy, just as would primitiveness by civilization, tradition by modernity. These were patterns that scholars could confidently chart in general terms, a recognized framework for their studies. Today the emphasis is more often on cultural-historical specifics. Scholars now incline less towards the uniformities than the diversities, seeing not a generalized African "response" to external intrusion or some impersonal advance forward out of the syndrome of "orality," but human actions, multiple voices, and many diverse parties in play. Recent studies have been uncovering successive and variegated struggles for control, whether over schools, access to political power, or the right to foreground particular formulations and cultural artifacts. Strikingly similar approaches emerge in many of the papers here. Rather than broad statements about orality and its contrasts with written text, or even about the narrower concept of "oral–scribal dimensions," the authors bring out the actions of particular parties and the competitions for control over ideas or texts. Within Islam Gregor Schoeler points to Muhammad's companions and later caliphs wanting private copies and collections, with material suitable to themselves. We hear of Caliph Uthman commissioning an official edition of Qur'anic text as part of his political project, sending out exemplar copies to provincial capitals and ordering other collections to be destroyed, countering the power of Qur'anic reciters as the holders of tradition. Nor, it seems, were contests for authority over the text confined to that period, for we hear too of the contending positions of different regions or groups in later centuries over the vocalization of the Qur'anic text, or, from Suzanne Pinckney Stetkevych, of highly charged competition among scholars and poets in post-classical Arabic-Islamic devotional poetry. Again, Talya Fishman describes the contests over rabbinic powers and over who should vet the chain of tradition and define the boundaries of the canon, with disparate political contests at different historical moments. Similarly, David Nelson[3] depicts how early rabbis in the aftermath of the Temple destruction reshaped theological concepts and ritual, refashioning a particular ideology of the orality of their textual tradition to suit their specific views, while Catherine Hezser shows individual rabbis attempting to monopolize the communications network in the late

3. This presentation from the Rice conference is not included in the present volume.

Roman "culture of mobility" that led to the collection and fixing of rabbinic traditions and, eventually, the written documents. Holly Hearon speaks of the polemics in the early Christian period, not least those over the status of individual speakers and interpreters, and of the competing groups involved. Battles have also long raged over the precise delimitation of the Christian scriptural canon, and both before and after the Council of Trent, of which Kelber properly reminds us, divisive definitions continued. What becomes clear in the way these accounts are presented is that the establishment of authoritative written texts is not being envisaged as some predestined oral-to-literate trajectory, but in each case a historically specific process, shaped by many diverse actors and contests within particular situations—and might indeed have turned out otherwise.

That multiple voices are in play, some still audible, some unheard or at least unheeded, has similarly become a theme in recent studies in Africa, widening the scope of those that can and should be attended to, and complicating any simple story of uniformity. For long it had been presumed that on the one hand it was the analyses of Western scholars that held authority and should be listened to, on the other that the material to be investigated essentially comprised the collective tribal tradition of "authentic," "age-old," and isolated Africa before the unsettling intrusion of external forces. The trend now, however, is to include local scholars and competing interpretations within the realm of knowledge. At the same time it is no longer just "traditional," rural, and quintessentially "oral" practices that are considered worthy of account but also, and increasingly, urban experiences, written forms, and popular media,[4] and, amidst all this, the presence of differing and divisive voices. It has been interesting to note the similar pressure towards widening the scope of study here, like Richard Horsley's emphasis on popular movements (not just the cultural elite) and Holly Hearon's on the input (and challenges) from a range of "ordinary," not necessarily intellectual and literate, voices—and her pertinent question of whose voices were heard, whose silenced.

An increasing awareness of a host of multiple actors also comes from another angle. Many recent studies of African oral literature engage with issues of performance and, alongside that, portray audiences as co-creators, directing attention to a wider range of diverse voices than just composers or front performers—or, indeed, just authors or scribes. A parallel inclusiveness runs through several papers here, similarly interacting with current transdisciplinary interests in performance and in processual studies

4. See for example, Barber, *Readings in African Popular Culture;* Barber, *Anthropology of Texts, Persons and Publics;* Ricard and Swanepoel, *Oral–Written Interface;* further references in Finnegan, *Oral and Beyond,* 2–3, 179ff.

of textuality.[5] This recurrent perspective comes through, for example, in Angelika Neuwirth's elucidation of the dialogic processes in early Koranic performances and John Miles Foley's perceptive unwrapping of the multiple creators in "distributed authorship."

I find these parallels in approach both informative and reassuring. They certainly reinforce my appreciation of the fruitfulness of moving away from generalized assertions to more focused insights into multiple historical and culturally specific diversities, and the active interaction—and contests—of many participants whose presence has sometimes in the past, and for a variety of reasons, been brushed aside.

THE ELUSIVENESS OF "ORALITY"

African studies today are at the same time characterized by a more carefully nuanced approach to "the oral" than in earlier years. Certainly there are debates and differing viewpoints, but by and large there is a trend towards questioning whether terms like oralism, orality, oral culture, oral biosphere, and so on can readily direct us to some uniform range of properties. Rather, as also emerges in the papers here, it is acknowledged that there are many different ways of being "oral," and diverse relations and overlaps between oral and written.

This variety comes through in part from the many different ways words are described as being delivered: read, recited, sung, cantillated, chanted, declaimed, multimodally performed, communicated through audio recordings or the web, experienced in the sonic memory. They can be individually or collectively enacted, informal or liturgical, public or private, announcements by one person or dialectical engagement. Hearon's account takes us vividly through a variety of oral communication in the first century CE: speeches declaimed, crowds addressed by public officials, teaching delivered, issues debated, messages proclaimed, stories told, news passed on and discussed, written matter read aloud, and much else. We hear of a plethora of channels and settings, each with its own specificities, for which generalized characterization would be naïve. Just saying "oral" is no longer sufficient.

5. Notably by such scholars as John Miles Foley, Lauri Honko, Richard Bauman, Richard Schechner, and the influential *Oral Tradition* journal, all twenty-five years of which are now available online at http://journal.oraltradition.org (further references in Finnegan, *Oral and Beyond*, 189ff.; Barber, *Anthropology of Texts, Persons and Publics*, 137ff.).

Similarly, both in Africa and here attention is drawn to the many twists in the forms of transmission. Just what it is that is "transmitted" is not always the same: exact words; gist; paraphrase; sound; recognized cultural traditions; repertoires . . . Diversities emerge too over the processes of memorization (a number of them interestingly illustrated in David Carr's paper) as well as the purposes of transmission and how these are acknowledged and organized (systematically, informally, in schools, learned through a master, through some formal transmission chain). There are differences as well in how an accredited original source is conceptualized: sometimes as oral communication direct from God or prophet, sometimes as the knowledge and creation of expert authorities, or just as a matter of general knowledge. Whatever the precise channel and its evaluation, its characteristics cannot, it emerges, be predicted from some label of "oral" but must, as the papers here demonstrate, be uncovered with a careful eye to the specificities.

In the current approaches, oral and written are no longer automatically viewed as antagonistic or mutually exclusive. Written textuality is now commonly presented in its engagement with aural/oral modes and performances (and vice versa), and not just as an interaction of separate modes but also as merging, overlapping, or mutually working together as different sides of the same coin. Kelber speaks of oral/written "interpenetration," Hearon of the "intersection" of spoken and written words, Nelson of "oral–literary dynamics" and the "oral-circulatory conceptualization of Rabbinic textual evidence."[6] Hearon aptly quotes Quintilian on the inseparable connection of writing, reading, and speaking. This intertwining, it appears, takes many forms. A written text can be a transcript capturing (more or less) some spoken performance; written from dictation; related to oral delivery whether as *aide-mémoire* (notes, paraphrase, text, unofficial jottings), or as a full text (locally defined as such, that is) for enunciation in some approved manner and recognized situation. Rendering a written text aloud—in variously designated settings and for more, or less, restricted audiences—is one common pattern, as in the lector chanting from written text for public display. And then there is Neuwirth's nuanced analysis of the intertextuality and dramatic polyphony of oral dialectic, constrained in different ways when captured into a fixed order in the written Qur'an. "Reading" too is an elusive and varied term. We hear of differing degrees of scope for readers and reciters of the Qur'an, for example, and varying conceptualizations of the relation of written text and reader. The *ḥadīth* is described as not disseminated for word-for-word reading but for oral lectures, and early

6. This presentation from the Rice conference is not included in the present volume.

rabbinic texts as used less for linear reading than as provisional script for future oral performances. We hear too of the material codex or hard copy book as essentially for display or symbol rather than for reading as such (as in Priscilla Soucek's account of the veneration of the Qur'an as sacred object[7]), and varying views on the significance of spoken interpretations and performances.

The term "oral," which at one time seemed so clear, emerges not as some single quality but as overlapping or intermingled in varying ways with other modes (visual, acoustic, tactile, material, olfactory). Liturgical contexts provide good illustrations, while the multisensory potential of live delivery also comes out in David Nelson's account of recitations of the Exodus narrative as multi-dimensional ritual process rather than purely textual undertaking, and was vividly demonstrated in David Rhoads' performance during the conference showing how oral enactment might (or on occasion might not) involve not just words but gestures, stances, modulations, material props, or dramatization. Nor does it stop with the fleeting flows of the verbal, for this dimension in turn can interweave with calligraphic, pictorial, and material images (colorfully illustrated in Soucek's paper), the more profoundly meaningful for their religious connotations.

Once again the approach is no longer in terms of some apparently uniform "orality" or of the "mystique of the oral" that John Miles Foley warns us against. Rather we learn of the multiple—and fascinating—ways in which humans have made use of vocalized and verbal media in varying combinations with other media, in differing cultural contexts and to differing purposes.

FADING INFLUENCE OF TELEOLOGICAL MODELS?

Alongside the written-text model that is already so much in question and perhaps equally far-reaching, stand the teleological and evolutionary paradigms that have for many years run across much humanistic study. By this terminology I refer in part to the widespread impulse to argue back from hindsight, but also to that linked set of assumptions that picture some natural line of development, as from oral to written, primitive to civilized, sometimes linked to the impact of successively developing technologies. There have undoubtedly been variant forms of these assumptions, but underlying many of them is—to put it succinctly—a vision of historical developments as predestined and one-way. Perhaps nowhere has this framework been more

7. This presentation from the Rice conference is not included in the present volume.

influential than in the interpretation of Africa and its expressive arts, with the vision of the West leading "traditional" and "oral" Africa upward toward a foreordained literate fulfillment, above all the pinnacle of alphabetic print attained by European civilization.

The cruder versions of such paradigms are now of course under widespread attack both for their West-centered ethnocentricity and their oversimplifications. Within African studies the "grand story" is no longer universally accepted as either inevitable or accurate. Teleological interpretations retain a powerful attraction, however, whether for Africa or more comparatively, at times still implicitly linked into the grander evolutionary timescales. They are perhaps especially resonant in the religious sphere, where it seems particularly apt, in the words of the much-loved Christian hymn, to envisage God "working his purpose out as year succeeds to year." It has seemed natural to bring a similar perspective to the canonizing of sacred texts, the more so given the pervading influence of philological textual models in the study of the monotheistic religions. We picture the "early" or "formative" incipient forms foreshadowing the final outcome: first oral precursors, then perhaps partial or unsystematic written versions, then onward to the final apotheosis into writing. In the apparently inevitable Western path toward literacy, the fulfillment can readily be envisaged as that of fully written and authorized text, the standard and correct canon, by now above the battle.

It is a seductive set of images, the more persuasive for their religious associations and, in a sense, celebratory overtones. So it is striking to see so many papers emphasizing the dangers of hindsight, of teleological thinking, and of the anachronisms of reading back later developments or defining earlier formulations in the terms of more recent canons or modern, print-dominated definitions. The canonization of many sacred texts in the form they now circulate (or are supposed by some authorities to circulate) was not after all, it now seems, a predetermined result; nor indeed are the canons as undisputed as some earlier accounts might imply. Certainly there have been points at which sacred texts apparently became more definitively fixed—among certain powerful parties and for certain purposes, that is—and this textual stabilization and the influence of print are indeed features of great significance. But, tempting as it may seem to view it this way, history did not then, as it were, come to a full stop. Diversities and textual instabilities in one or another respect continue. As Foley points out these supposedly "final" versions have often been in practice inaccessible to the majority, and there are still disagreements over what counts as the canon and who has authority. Scriptural texts are defined and handled in different ways by different groups and on different occasions.

One notable aspect is the continuing *oral* presence of sacred words, a presence too often obscured in evolutionist paradigms. As Foley rightly emphasizes, oral expression remains important, with variegated oral–written interactions a pervasive feature of the contemporary world. Thus we *can* present the Bible or other sacred text as comprehensive finalized written text, a model that may indeed be reflected (at least in part) in the practices of theologians, academics, and religious specialists; such a concept also undoubtedly carries far-reaching symbolic connotations. But for most people an equally important medium, perhaps the principal one, is oral/aural: hearing or reading aloud among gathered congregations or listening to broadcast or recorded performances, supplemented by repeatedly vocalized passages and phrases in sermons, prayers, liturgy, and hymns. Werner Kelber well describes the centuries-long recognition of the Bible as oral authority—proclaimed, expounded, listened to, internalized. The same pattern is not totally absent today. Biblical text circulates orally in both religious and non-religious contexts through quotations and allusions in conversation, popular song, and widespread biblical imagery. The scriptures can be said to exist not just in formalized verbal text between hard covers, the dimension on which print-based scholars naturally fix their eyes, but also in an oral mode. Though different in detail, something of the same might be said for Islamic sacred text. I vividly recall my first encounter with Islam: hearing a group of young boys chanting around an evening fire during fieldwork in up-country Sierra Leone. There was no way they were *reading* the text, nor were they likely ever to do so (nor probably their teacher either): for them their engagement with the sacred text was an oral one. As was brought out in William Graham's illuminating *Beyond the Written Word* (1987) as in more recent papers, the Qur'an has long had an oral as well as written dimension, its acoustic substance existent in people's sonic memories as much as, perhaps more than, in visual text.

And even for written scripture there remain diversities and changing practices, with boundaries constantly contested. As Kelber points out, the establishment of print did not prevent plural versions or contending interpretations, indeed in some ways encouraged them. Many are the translations too, especially of biblical text, with their own wordings and emphases (I think of the fraught choice in my own church of which translation to adopt for the pulpit bible—the differences mattered!). The crystallization of sacred text may indeed be one notable dimension of the three "religions of the book," but it is by no means a smooth one-way pathway leading to the establishment of some true and timeless text, but rather a history of recurrent adaptation, of contests, of repressions, and of struggles for authority.

The complexities and contests evident in the contemporary world, whether African or European, can, perhaps, facilitate a clearer view of earlier periods. They warn of the dangers both of too ready an acceptance of certain teleological stories (not least, we might suggest, those associated with a theologically resonating textual paradigm?), and of reading back not only from more recent times but also, equally misleadingly, from a partial view of the present and how it has come about.

EPISTEMOLOGIES OF ORAL AND WRITTEN

In what does the existence of verbal formulations lie? The question seems inescapable both in the papers here and in current issues within African studies. For textually trained scholars it has seemed obvious to approach all verbal practices through a "textual ideology" (as Foley terms it). Kelber equally aptly speaks of the "typographical captivity" that tends to dominate our thinking. Certainly that was the paradigm from which I, and many others, first engaged in the study of oral literary forms in Africa. Writing was, surely, the way to pin down these forms, transcribed into one-line text on a page. That indeed seemed the fundamental mode in which they unquestionably had their "real" substance.

That powerful model has not totally gone away. But new technologies, not least electronic, are unsettling our idea of stable, finalized, and closed text, and as Foley so well explains we now have new ways of capturing and disseminating verbal forms, giving us a new take on their ontology. Equally important, the rise of what could summarily be referred to as "performance studies" has radically altered how many scholars now regard such forms. From this perspective, well exemplified in Rhoads' description and performance during the conference, the substance is found not on the textualized page but in multimodal performance—embodied, situational, and dialogic. Current interests in usage and practice raise similar questions about where the essential reality lies. So what, I now ask myself, did I ultimately encounter when I heard those young boys recite in that far-off Sierra Leone village, and for whom—the "original" Qur'anic text? The direct words of Allah? The ephemeral sounds and understandings of performance? The terms in which they and/or their teacher conceptualized or experienced them? All of these? We now raise questions that before seemed closed off about the varying ways in which verbal formulations are conceived and hierarchized, by whom, in what situations, and to whose interest(s).

The papers here finely demonstrate the point of tackling such issues. We hear of the disputes surrounding the arguably dual reality of the Qur'an as both oral and written, of the resistance to committing the *ḥadīth* to writing, and, in Neuwirth's comments, of the relation between the situatedness of Muhammad's recitation and the vision of transcendent celestial book with its "glow of scripturality." Among the issues around the Torah was the "epistemological hierarchy" of talmudic texts, with disputes over the status of the "oral Torah" and whether authority lay in the text or in the active practice of the tradition, once again with interested parties taking different positions. Along the same lines too are the differing views over the status and role of writing: as necessary evil; as paramount or at least as possessing preeminent symbolic force; or as merely mnemonic aid for the "real" thing, recitation.

The differing viewpoints have become not just debates among ourselves but part of our subject matter. Fishman charts epistemological rivalries within Judaism and how rabbinic valorizing of oral expression worked out in different periods and for differing purposes, with specific views about how "oral matters" were to be distinguished from "written matters" and how treated. Nelson similarly depicts early rabbis constructing a particular ideology about the orality of their textual tradition, privileging the elaborate ideological myth of the "Torah in the Mouth." Schoeler's account reveals the arguments about the relative importance of orally transmitted teachings and written text as in part a contest over epistemology, while Hearon comments on the authority of governmental or scriptural written forms, and how they worked as symbols.

Clearly there have been diverse viewpoints in differing historical periods, cultural settings, and, no doubt, specific interest groups with their contending claims; nor, significantly, have the practices always been in accord with the overtly dominating ideologies. As Hearon pertinently remarks, the fact that something is written says little; we must also understand how the particular written word is viewed and engaged. As so well illustrated in the papers, the varying and sometimes clashing ideologies are often enough loaded and highly emotive, entangled as they are with issues of authority and control. These culturally and historically specific epistemologies are both fascinating in themselves and now recognized as part of the subject of study.

MULTI-LITERACIES AND MULTI-ORALITIES?

The conference organizers raised the question of whether the philological-textual paradigm that has in the past proved such a rich intellectual matrix for approaching the monotheistic religions can now be supplemented by new challenges and insights from the viewpoint of orality and literacy studies. Is a new paradigm emerging?

My conclusion was in one sense no. Certainly contributors seemed to agree in querying, even explicitly rejecting, a "written-text" paradigm as *the* universal and somehow natural model for all verbalized formulations. This could be called a negative position, then, rather than some new paradigm. But like other critical rethinking of powerfully tenacious assumptions, that shared approach is by no means worthless. It has given rise to much valuable work and, whether regarded as newly emergent or already established, is a welcome feature of the conference papers.

And perhaps it is more than just a negative. For it interacts positively with developments in other fields, in particular the burgeoning field of literacy studies with their deconstruction of the seemingly transparent concept of "writing": not just something neutral and obvious, after all, but something to be analyzed and studied in its variegated social settings. In contrast to the generalized polarities of traditional "Great Divide" theories, comparative scholarship both in Africa and elsewhere is now focusing on the *diverse* usages and evaluations of writing, its differing forms, purposes, settings, clashing definitions, interactions with other media, and entanglements with the hierarchies and ideologies of the social order. One trend now is to speak not of "literacy" but of "literacies" and "multi-literacies"—shorthand terms to sum up a critical approach rooted in detailed close studies illuminated by a hopefully non-ethnocentric perspective.[8] A similar approach seems evident in the conference papers (witness, for one, Soucek's analysis of differing modes of writing in Islamic manuscripts and architecture). More than mere negative reaction against print-dominated interpretations, it constitutes a positive endeavor to reach more critical and nuanced understandings of detailed cases informed by crosscultural and transhistorical perspective.

Can we perhaps speak equally of "multi-oralities"? It seems to me that this is also what these articles are about. And from this collection we are the more aware of the multifaceted range of possibilities along which multi-literacies and multi-oralities have been brought to intersect. The papers treat not just the variegated ways that people—multitudes of people—have used, interpreted, deployed, and capitalized on verbalized media, but also how these have so often been reciprocally engaged together and in interaction with yet other media again. And part of the subject matter has been not so much how *we*, as twenty-first century scholars, conceptualize oral and written expression—though we must indeed be sensitive to our own

8. For example, Collins and Blot, *Literacy and Literacies*; Cope and Kalantzis, *Multiliteracies*; Street, *Cross-Cultural Approaches to Literacy*.

assumptions—as how the differing ideologies and practices around these notions have been not only organized but also debated, manipulated, and struggled over throughout the centuries. These are issues that, I believe, have been finely articulated and taken forward within shared sensibilities in the conference papers.

BIBLIOGRAPHY

Barber, Karin. *The Anthropology of Texts, Persons and Publics: Oral and Written Culture in Africa and Beyond.* New Departures in Anthropology. Cambridge: Cambridge University Press, 2007.

———, ed. *Readings in African Popular Culture.* Oxford: James Currey, 1997.

Bauman, Richard. *Verbal Art as Performance.* Rowley, MA: Newbury House, 1977.

Bauman, Richard, and Charles L. Briggs. *Voices of Modernity: Language Ideologies and the Politics of Inequality.* Studies in the Social and Cultural Foundations of Language 21. Cambridge: Cambridge University Press, 2003.

Collins, James, and Richard K. Blot. *Literacy and Literacies: Texts, Power, and Identity.* Studies in the Social and Cultural Foundations of Language 22. Cambridge: Cambridge University Press, 2003.

Cope, Bill, and Mary Kalantzis. *Multiliteracies: Literacy Learning and the Design of Social Futures.* London: Routledge, 2000.

Finnegan, Ruth. *The Oral and Beyond: Doing Things with Words in Africa.* Oxford: James Currey, 2007.

———. "Studying the Oral Literatures of Africa in the 1960s and Today." *Journal des africanistes* 80 (2010) 15–28.

Foley, John Miles. *How to Read an Oral Poem.* Urbana: University of Illinois Press, 2002.

———. *The Singer of Tales in Performance.* Voices in Performance and Text. Bloomington: Indiana University Press, 1995.

Graham, William A. *Beyond the Written Word: Oral Aspects of Scripture in the History of Religion.* Cambridge: Cambridge University Press, 1987.

Honko, Lauri, ed. *Textualization of Oral Epics.* Berlin: de Gruyter, 2000.

Ricard, Alain, and C. F. Swanepoel, eds. *The Oral–Written Interface.* Special issue of *Research in African Literatures* 28 (1997).

Schechner, Richard. *Performance Studies: An Introduction.* London: Routledge, 2002.

Street, Brian V., ed. *Cross-Cultural Approaches to Literacy.* Cambridge Studies in Oral and Literate Culture 23. Cambridge: Cambridge University Press, 1993.

13

Summation

William A. Graham

I want to preface my remarks with a word of thanks to both Paula Sanders and Werner Kelber, as well as Rice University, for hosting this conference so generously and well. I was asked by our two conveners to offer, at the end of our work these past two days, some reflections on what has transpired among us. Let me begin by noting that, for me, the key to any successful conference—and I have attended several unsuccessful conferences and a smaller number of successful ones over the past four decades with which to compare this one—is the degree of interaction and interchange, the frequency of give and take, the ease of asking and learning, and the minimum of demonstrations of cleverness or willingness to upstage or diminish the work of other scholars. By these criteria, I am happy to say that this has been an unusually fruitful and successful consultation, for it has been marked, so far as I can tell, by a genuine colloquy among a thoughtfully assembled group of scholars who have been not only willing but genuinely interested in engaging one another concerning issues to which we all have devoted time and about which we care, albeit in often very different ways and from differing perspectives. In my opinion, the give and take, even when differing positions were being presented and differing conclusions were being drawn, have been exemplary, and I want to thank all of my colleagues and our two hosts again in particular for their parts in what has proven to be a most valuable and productive interchange.

As we conclude, I would like to identify five issues in particular among those that have been in play, all of which seem to me especially worth holding up for our shared, concluding reflection. All of these are, I think, worthy also of continued or new consideration.

The first issue is the possibility that the reciprocity, interdependence, and overlap of the oral and the written is in most contexts more important than the undeniable contrast, opposition, or competition between these two modes of expression and communication. Ruth Finnegan, in her response to the first day's papers, emphasized much the same notion in her discussions of "uniformity to multiplicity" and "the elusiveness of orality." David Carr writes specifically in his paper of the "interplay of textuality, orality, and memory in the emergence of literary textuality," noting that his own work has proven to him that the "bible was formed and used in an *oral–written* context." I might note also here Talya Fishman's emphasis, like that of both Werner Kelber and Gregor Schoeler, on the changing balance of oral and written emphases on the sacred texts that she, like Kelber and Schoeler, studies, and the various motivations for these changes over time.

David Nelson's[1] assessment that "early rabbinic textuality was comprised of both oral and literary processes" and his nuanced presentation of evidence for this go nicely with Catherine Hezser's remarks on the various complementary and sometimes overlapping roles of written and oral messages in Jewish and Christian contexts in the Roman period. Examples include Josephus' reports that express the need for personal oral confirmation to establish the reliability of a written message; the importance of the oral reading of written letters, as in the early Christian churches in the time of Paul and later apostles; the significant but differing roles of both oral preaching and written documents in the growth and consolidation of the Christian community; and the importance of both personal contact and oral communication, as well as letters, among early rabbis after the fall of the temple. Hezser also notes the ambivalence in many of these cases toward the use of written communications to supplement oral letters or face-to-face meeting. (Here I might point out the comparable elements in the phenomenon in classical Islamic religious learning of preferring to hear oral reports transmitted from the Prophet and Companions over, though not excluding, simple transmission of physical, written documents).

Holly Hearon's paper joins Catherine Hezser's in showing the strong reciprocity of the spoken and the written word and their interplay in the words of the varied writers, from the Synoptics to Paul (Hearon notes, for example, that "the interchange between written and spoken word was

1. This presentation from the Rice conference is not included in the present volume.

pervasive and exhibited itself in variety of ways" in the early Christian world). Similarly, Werner Kelber's discussion of performative-chirographic dynamics "imbedded in an oral biosphere" speaks eloquently to the same close relationship of oral and written communications in the early Christian world. Here I would note also Dick Horsley's characterization of "written texts as copies of oral instructions," and his characterization of canonical texts as both written and oral, as important support for this general phenomenon of overlap and interdependence of the written and oral.

In a similar vein, Angelika Neuwirth's stress on strong oral–written interchange and the "communication process" as the scenario for the development and codification of the Qur'an in interchange with Jewish and Christian traditions reminds us of the close relationship between the written and the oral that persisted into later Islamic times. She does, however, rightly stress the overriding importance of the oral Qur'an as unframed or mediated Word: "Unframed by any narrative scenario the entire Qur'an is speech as such." Or, to put it another way, "The Qur'an . . . should be acknowledged as a highly rhetorical, frequently meta-textual document reflecting the situation of an ongoing debate." Her paper reminds us forcefully of the precedence in the Islamic case of oral communication of the Word in what she aptly calls the "Qur'anic theologumenon" over the codified text of the later written *muṣḥaf*—though it is an oral Word that is also an exegetical reality.

Suzanne Stetkevych's acute remarks on the memorial culture of the medieval manuscript tradition provide yet other testimony from Islamic tradition to the oral dimensions of textual study and transmission. Finally, Priscilla Soucek's exploration of "functional and aesthetic dialogue"[2] between oral and written versions of the Qur'an is an especially suggestive and creative way to think about the interplay of Muslims' historical engagement with the recited, the calligraphed, and the visually embellished chirographic word of God, of which they have always seen their community as guardians or trustees for succeeding generations.

It may not make much difference in the end whether one uses oral or written terminology in speaking about sacred texts in particular, since both media were clearly in play in the Near Eastern world to which all of the aforementioned papers are addressed. My own work has stressed the oral dimensions of written texts, and, conversely, it is clear that many oral texts function demonstrably in, and are then taken from, written versions once literacy is sufficiently in place to allow for this. Consequently, oral texts

2. The presentation, entitled "The Interaction of Speech and Calligraphy in Manuscripts of the Qur'an," does not appear in the current volume. An abstract of the presentation is at http://www.voicestexts.rice.edu/papers.html.

can become written ones and have a powerful impact as such, just as easily as written texts can be used and received, often primarily so, through oral communication (recitation, reading, chanting, paranetic citation and allusion, and so on). We need to take these seemingly simple, even simplistic, facts more seriously, as obvious as they may seem to be, since much previous work on orality and literacy has proceeded from the firm but false assumption that the two are opposites, mutually exclusive, or in every important way tied to entirely different spheres of activity, consciousness, sophistication, or civilization.

The second issue I would point to is the importance of the sociopolitical and socioeconomic location of textual practices and uses. Ruth Finnegan again pointed to this issue when she spoke about the "multiplicity" of orality and especially the "competitions for control over ideas or texts." Dick Horsley's association of oral textuality with low-literacy or non-literate majorities and the association of writing with small but powerful elites of a very different level of sociopolitical power is a striking instance of this. I think that John Miles Foley's delineation in his keynote address of "democratic" agoras present us with another instance of the socially and economically differential effects of any vehicle of communication and a very productive way of contemplating and evaluating this fact. This is most persuasive in the case of his eAgora, since the oAgora and tAgora in overlap exhibit often sharp class differences. Gregor Schoeler's remarks on the role of the specialized Qur'an reciters (*qurrāʾ*) in political dimensions of writing is also relevant to this issue of where in a society we should look for contexts that encourage one kind of textuality or another, differing one. Here I would note also David Carr's work on "long-duration literature seen in the Bible" as linked to the "education and socialization of leading elites." He goes on to make clear that with "elites" he means not only scribal professionals, but also "priestly, governmental, high-level military, bureaucratic and other elites as part of larger-scale city-states, empires, and similar formations."

We also need to pay attention to Priscilla Soucek's remarks about the importance of the intervention of prestigious early Islamic leaders such as ʿUthmān or al-Ḥajjāj b. Yūsuf in the preservation and codification of the Qur'anic text in its written or epigraphic forms especially. Also important are her remarks about the difference that liturgical and devotional practices in the early community made in creating the so-called "defective" and "complete" scripts used in the earliest Qur'an copies that we have today. Her comments indicate vividly that different contexts of religious usage (as evidenced, for example, in the inscriptions of the Dome of the Rock in Jerusalem or the very different, huge "display" copies of the Qur'an that have survived at least partially from the early period) also have affected the forms of textual preservation and the relationship of the text's oral recitation to its physical, visible inscription. She makes clear that different Qur'anic versions or inscriptions were conceived and executed variously because they were aimed at users who differed markedly in their needs, intentions, and capacities.

Especially important with regard to the social context of oral and written forms of scriptural usage are Holly Hearon's comments on the social functions and hierarchies of speech in early Christian contexts where power, status, and access intersected in teaching and other settings of scriptural usage (such as claiming scriptural tradition as a communal identity marker). Her closing questions about social implications, in particular of the New Testament evidence, are especially suggestive of her argument that evidence of developments in the early Christian world can be found in the oral–written tensions and contrasts. Catherine Hezser's remarks on issues of networking and social power or prestige for particular rabbis and of the political impact of letter writing in early Christianity (in the control of ideology) are very much to the point here as well.

Suzanne Stetkevych imaginatively links Abbasid power and the *badīʿ poetry* movement (as well as emphasizing the role of eloquence, or *balāgha*). She does this by identifying what she calls the "retooling" of formerly mnemonic rhetorical devices into the "linguistic correlative" devices of high caliphal panegyrics closely linked with Abbasid hegemony. And Angelika Neuwirth's argument for seeing "the Qur'an in the phase of its emergence" as "not a pre-meditated fixed compilation, a reified literary artifact, but a still mobile text reflecting an oral theological-philosophical debate between diverse interlocutors of various late antique denominations" points us as well to the historical context of the early Islamic period for a clearer sense of the Muslim scripture's development as an organic part of the wider development of an increasingly complex religious as well as socio-political world. Her deft linking of the development of the Qur'an to the developments in the overlapping contemporary Jewish and Christian worlds is especially suggestive for the issue of context in understanding the creation and interpretation of scriptures.

Jeff Opland's remarks,[3] as well as those of many others around the table, have also emphasized the issue of power in the history of textual function. Why move to a canon? How to justify political control? How to bolster economic and social elites' power? Scriptures have long been linked to power, from the successful inculturation of Indo-European Vedic culture in the Subcontinent of the second millennium BCE, to the Han Chinese fixation

3. This response is not included in the present volume.

on the "classics/ scriptures" (*ching*) of authoritative ethics and worldview, to the institutionalization of Buddhist texts and norms in Buddhist kingdoms of South and Southeast Asia. One can also add many other examples, from Egypt and the Ancient Near East to colonial regimes and cultures established in South America, Africa, and India. Culturally powerful texts are not neutral matters, nor merely material objects, nor only piously recited texts.

The third thing I would point to is the recurring issue or theme of mnemonic, recitative, liturgical, or performative dimensions of the religious texts of the communities that the scholars gathered here have studied and interpreted for us. This is certainly a theme that might bear serious scrutiny and study in all historical traditions. A number of comments about this dimension of religious texts in the course of our discussions could be taken as ratification of the persuasive and important conclusion of Leipoldt and Morenz in their now classical work of 1953, *Heilige Schriften*—namely, that the universal trait of scriptural texts in the Near Eastern world, to which they addressed themselves in their study, was their liturgical use.

We know that liturgical reading, recitation, cantillation, and/or performance are crucial in virtually every religious community, not simply those in the Near East. However, we could benefit from much closer study of these active and oral functions of texts in religious communal traditions. Talya Fishman points out that the writings that the rabbis excluded from the emerging biblical canon after 70 CE, even if they were venerated by others as inspired, "were not to be liturgically performed." Liturgical readings were reserved for "canonical" writings, not anything else, and this was not least a distinction that served the rabbi's efforts "to authorize and advertise the Scriptural canon as defined by the rabbis."

David Nelson's paper reminds us forcefully of the crucial importance in the Passover Seder of ritual recitation and oral rehearsal of the Exodus to Rabbinic biblical interpretation. He does this by examining "how oral-performative and literary dynamics enabled early Rabbinic 'hermeneutics of the Exodus' to produce meaning in response to Jewish theological dissonance and concern for historical continuity/discontinuity." With regard to early Christian communities, David Rhoads says that the New Testament was "performance literature" and argues that in communicating scripture, "frequently, perhaps more often than not, no written text was present. . . . Or a manuscript was present as a symbol of authority but not consulted. Performance was the way early Christians experienced the New Testament traditions."

Compare here also Werner Kelber's discussion of the importance of the phenomena of memory, *aides-mémoires*, and "re-oralization of textual compositions" out of the "oral-performative tradition" when the balance of oral and written texts started shifting in the medieval world. Particularly important here is his depiction of Second-Temple biblical textuality involving "multiple scriptural versions finding their hermeneutical rationale in recitation, oral explication, and memorization," in which context he wants us to think of "the early Jesus tradition as an insistently pluriform phenomenon" involving performative or rhetorical oral textuality as well as multiple chirographic forms, and where there likely never existed an "original" text of Jesus' words but "a plurality of originals."

One observation that seems to be borne out by several of the papers we have shared is that any focus on the oral dimensions of the sacred texts we study, especially in the earliest, but also in all later periods of their existence, reveals that it is difficult to reconstruct adequately the functions of those texts in actual living usage. David Rhoads reminds us, for example, how little we know of the historical "oral performance" of our texts, as important as we know oral transmission to be. Nor do we really have sufficient understanding of what memorization does to our relationship to a text (in this regard, note Catherine Hezser's remarks on Rabbinic reliance on memory for the transmission of traditions in the first and second centuries CE). Similarly, we know little of the historical oral "performance" of our texts, as Rhoads indicates clearly. Dick Horsley's focus on the performative aspects of Mark and Matthew give further voice to the need to work on a better understanding of the living uses and functions of sacred texts that we study. This harks back also to John Miles Foley's attention to the "iconic" uses of written texts along with their oral uses.

And, of course, the liturgical and emblematic or symbolic treatment of the physical book, scroll, or written words of sacred texts should not be overlooked. Priscilla Soucek's nuanced paper is a salient reminder of this fact, especially where she points us to the lavish, monumental Qur'an copies that have survived the centuries, or to the importance of copying the scriptural word by hand as a religious act, or to the widespread and lavish use of inscriptions from scripture on buildings in the Islamic world. Certainly the work of those assembled here points to openings for work on the concomitants of orality in literate as well as nonliterate contexts—concomitants that typically determine our relation to texts in a given place/time much more than do physical texts of paper and ink.

A fourth issue arising from the papers we have heard is that of the clearly shared background of our texts. With few exceptions, we have dealt with texts and traditions broadly or narrowly derived from and characteristic of the Near Eastern world of the Mediterranean basin and adjoining territories, whether Europe or West Asia. This means that the texts, traditions, and cultures we have considered and mined for our material share in large part a common vocabulary, and even, in many ways, a common conceptual world. Thus patterns of treatment of and attitudes toward the spoken and recited word, the written word, notions of deity and revelation, attitudes toward ritual and liturgy, human inspiration and communication, and so forth, are discernible even where two of the treated cultures or religious traditions most differ. Patterns of historical tradition and interpretation are also evident, especially those involving the shared collective history of God's dealing with humankind through prophets and scriptural revelations. Even the shared Abrahamic or Flood background of prehistorical Israelite tradition and the Semitic linguistic background of the terms and ideas of most of the religious traditions considered, as well as the histories of the great empires of Babylonia, Persia, Egypt, Greece, and Rome, are shared backdrops to most of the material we have considered here, something implicit or explicitly recognized in several of the papers, notably Neuwirth and Fishman.

This leads to what is a very simple, but I think important, observation: that it would be good on some future occasion to bring such a collection of scholars and scholarship on written and oral traditions together with a group of scholars of other great traditions of religion and culture and textual history (for example, the Indian, both Vedic and later Hindu; the Buddhist, both Mahayana and Theravada; the Chinese, including Confucian/classical, Taoist, and others; and so-called "little" or "nonliterate" traditions of Africa, the Pacific and Australasia, Central and North Asia, the Americas, and many other places). Ruth Finnegan's many allusions and comparisons to African examples of orality give a good idea of the richness of other traditions and contexts around the globe that would be fruitful to compare with those focused on in our conference. I am convinced that such additional contexts for considering the questions we have raised would both enrich the specific studies each of us has embarked upon and expand and likely change the questions we ask of our subjects and the answers we are comfortable giving to those questions.

Fifth, and finally, there was (in both the papers and our discussions) the recurring issue of the authority of textual books, especially of the physical form of a text as book, but also of the authority of oral transmission of religious texts in many instances. In many cases this may involve more than simply the contrast of written word with oral word. Further, authority seems not to reside exclusively in the inscribed book any more than in the memorized and orally transmitted word. We need to take note of the difficulty of recapturing just how a written text, especially a sacred one, was actually understood and dealt with in earlier ages.

A telling point on the side of the authority of chirographic texts is evident in Dick Horsley's comment that the "scriptures in Jerusalem" are as much or more a statement about authority as one about writtenness. At another point, he makes the relationship between the written scripture and authority for New Testament writers very clear:

> That a prophecy or a law was "written" on a scroll, especially if it was in a revered text of great antiquity, gave it an added aura of authority, for ordinary people as much as for the literate elite. In virtually all of the instances where the Gospel of Mark uses the formula "it is written," it is making an appeal to authority.

Similarly, Holly Hearon's emphasis on the "permanence" of scriptural texts is about much more than their physical form. She has a particularly interesting comment regarding the way written legal or public-record texts referred to the New Testament:

> These written texts represent public records of one kind or another that define social relationships, marking out the boundaries between them. This is true whether or not those bound by the documents can read them. In this respect, the documents serve a purpose beyond the words written; like inscribed coins and edifices, they function like a seal and imbue the written word with the power and authority of the person who issues or authorizes the document.

Another example is Talya Fishman's careful parsing of rabbinic debates about the differing ambits of authority for written scriptural texts on the one hand and rabbinic "oral matters" on the other. She offers particularly interesting commentary on the rabbis' varied use of both written and oral textuality (and the accompanying proscriptions against improper uses of both) to reinforce authority within a learned scriptural tradition. Her further suggestion is also relevant to the issue of authority of texts: namely, her idea that perhaps the regional rivalry between Palestinian and Babylonian rabbis played out in their disagreements about the uses of oral and written texts and had some roots in Muslim Abbasid-Umayyad rivalries and their religious ramifications vis-à-vis hadith inscription.

In his paper, Werner Kelber points several times to the importance of the (very late) codification of a written Biblical canon, but also of the (early and long-persisting) oral communication and treatment of scripture as authorities for Christian life. He emphasizes especially the often downplayed importance of oral scripture as authoritative through the European Middle Ages: "For centuries . . . the Bible was to a very large extent present in the lives of the people as an oral authority: proclaimed, homiletically interpreted, listened to, and internalized."

Gregor Schoeler's discussion of the redaction of the written Qur'an against the much delayed redaction of written Hadith collections points to issues of the relative authority of God's book and Muhammad's traditions as crucial to the differential treatment with regard to use of writing for each. As crucial as the oral preservation and "performance" (recitation) of the Word of God has been for Muslims, it was also the case, at least in the early centuries of Islam, that the written Qur'an, or *muṣḥaf,* carried special authority as *the* Book, something with which even the words and actions of the Prophet could not be allowed to compete.

On the use of written texts to reinforce social, political, or religious authority, I would note Catherine Hezser's emphasis on the early Christian community's "Jerusalem center" as the prime source for "official" letters sent out to guide the "diaspora" communities and thus claim authority over their "practices and beliefs." She notes that Paul's letters to diasporal communities "meant that the Jerusalem center's claim to superior authority had been broken." The center had shifted, but the written letters (probably delivered orally to largely illiterate congregations, of course) retained authority that the oral word alone did not have.

Here I want to use the prerogative of having almost the final word to essay rather cautiously—but I hope suggestively—a notion that I have on occasion entertained working out of the Islamic context. Specifically, I wonder if the Ancient Near Eastern traditions of written laws (probably symbolized most vividly and recurrently by Hammurabi's code) and of "books" of wisdom, destinies, works, or life do not finally have more to do with their imputed authority than they do with their physical form as inscribed texts. David Carr notes in his paper the roles of written texts as "numinous symbols of . . . ancient tradition" as well as "learning aids." I have wondered if there is the possibility that terms like *ha sefer, gegraptai/hai graphai,* and *kitāb* are used more with reference to the authority of the word than with reference to their written character. I might note the importance of the use of the Arabic preposition *ʿalā*, "on, over, upon," after the verb *kataba,* "to write," which renders often the idea not so much "to write (something) on" but rather to "prescribe (something, especially that which is written down) *for* (someone)"; namely, to put forth not so much a written word (although also that) as a written word that is *authoritative,* that "makes incumbent upon" or "obligates" someone *to do* or *to be* something in particular. In other words, scripture may be more about a text that is authoritative than about a text that is written down, even though the two often seem to belong together.

What I want to say with this short final digression is that what we may be dealing with is that writtenness in the traditions we have been studying carries some signification of authoritativeness for the text that is inscribed. "Book" does seem in most of the cases we have been dealing with to be something special, something a sacred text ought to have as at least a prominent form for its meanings. What we have also seen, however, is that "book" has been an oral and aural fact at the same time that it has been a written and inscribed fact. The authority of being written down takes nothing away from the authority of the living oral word that is inscribed in the heart/memory as well as on the page/tablet. Both aspects of authoritative, important, and/or sacred texts need to be given their due as of major importance to the use and meaning of texts historically. The papers here have borne eloquent testimony to the complexity of both orality and literacy, as well as their interplay in the textuality of the traditions we have considered.

Index of Scriptural Citations

HEBREW BIBLE

Genesis
5:1 83n40

Leviticus
18:12–13 41
20:21, 17 41

Deuteronomy
6:4 183, 184
6:6–9 30
7:25 41
11:18–21 30
16:18–20 41
17:5 41
22:6 41
23:2 102
26:27 74n16
31:19, 22 30
32:44–46 30
52:6 41

2 Samuel
2:1–5 120n22
5:1–5 120n22

1 Kings
8:29 40n44

2 Kings
10:10 40n44
22:3–23:24 116

2 Chronicles
9:9 40n44

Nehemiah
8 116

Psalms
22:2 235
40:9 30
41:7–8 LXX 74n16
119:26 58

Proverbs
3:3; 7:3 24n8, 30

Isaiah
6:9–10 118
8:16–18 30
29:13 118
30:9–11 30

Jeremiah
7:11 118
31:33 LXX 73
31:33–34 30

Ezekiel

2:9–3:3 30

Zechariah

13:7 118

Malachi

3:1 118

TALMUD

b. Ber. 45a 56
b. Giṭ. 66a, 73a 103
b. Šabb. 115a 60n40
b. Soferim 5, 15 60n40
b. Zebaḥ. 87a 103
b. ʿArak. 22a 103
y. Ber.
2:4, 5a 99
2:8, 5c 99
6:5, 10c 99
y. Giṭ. 46d 102
y. Ḥag. 1:8 (76d) 53
y. Meg. 4:1 (74d) 53
y. Moʿed Qaṭ. 3:1, 81c 102
y. Peʾah
2:16 (17a) 53
3:9, 17d 99
y. Qidd. 3:14, 64d 102
y. Roš. Haš. 2:8, 58b 104
y. Šubb.
2:1, 4d 99
16a 60n40
y. Sanh.
1:2, 19a 102
6:8, 23c 102
y. Taʿan. 2:2, 65c 104
y. Yebam. 12:2, 12d 104
y. ʿAbod. Zar. 2:3, 41a 99

MISHNAH

m. Kil. 6:4 98
m. Yebam. 16:7 100
m. ʿErub.
1:2 100
2:6 100

TOSEFTA

t. Demai 3:1 101
t. Maʿaś. 2:1 98
t. Šabb. 13:2 98
t. Šabb. 14 60n40
t. Sanh. 2:6 101
t. Šeb. 5:12 101
t. Soṭah 7:9 99

NEW TESTAMENT

Mark

1:1 79
1:1–13 130
1:2 75, 117
1:2–3 117, 118
1:14–15 130
1:15 216
1:16–3:35 130
1:16–20 126
1:21 130
1:21, 39 92
1:22 83
1:28 93
1:44 94n7
1:45 71, 79
2:1 130
2:1–3:6 128
2:13 83
2:22 216
2:25 77, 118
3:1 130, 222
3:13–19 126
3:19 130
3:20–35 128
4:1–34 130
4:2 83
4:9 76
4:12 118
4:35–8:21/26 130

4:35–8:26 129
4:35–41 129
5–8 126
5:1–20 129
5:20 71
5:21–24, 35–43 129
5:21–43 128
5:24–34 129
5:43 94n7
6:1–6 83
6:2 92
6:7–13 126
6:30–44 129
6:45–52 129
7:6 117
7:6–8 117
7:9–13 118, 133
7:13 81
7:24–30 129
7:31–37 129
7:36 71
8:1–10 129
8:17 227
8:22–10:52 129
8:22–26 129
8:22/27–10:52 130
9:12–13 118
10 146
10:2–45 127
10:3–5 119
10:4 72
10:17–22 118
10:25 133
11:1–13:2 130
11:10 75
11:12–25 128
11:17 118
12:1–9 133
12:10 77, 118
12:13–14 82
12:19 119
12:26 75, 77, 118
12:38–40 133
12:41–44 235
12:43–44 235
13:3–37 130
13:10 78
13:14 83
14–15 130
14:7 119
14:9 78
14:21 118
14:21, 27 118
14:27 118
14:28 120
15:34 235
15:39 236
15:52–72 128
16:1–8 130
16:7 120
18:19 79

Matthew

1:22 75–76
2:5 75–76
2:15, 17, 23 75–76
3:1 79
3:3 75
4:17 78n27
4:17, 23 79
4:23 83, 92
4:24 94
5 146
5:2 83
5:19 79
5:31 72
8:17 75
9:35 79, 92
10 146
10:5ff 94
10:7 78n27
10:27 78, 80
11:1 79
11:10 76n19
11:15 76
11:27 81
12:3, 5 77
12:17 75
13:9 76
13:51 216
13:53–58 83
13:54 92
15:3 81
16:12 82

Matthew (*continued*)

19:4 77
19:7 72
19:16 79
21:4 75
21:13 76n19
21:42 77
22:16 94
22:31 77
23:10 83
24:15 83
25:19 72
26:24, 3 76n19

Luke

1:4 80
1:63 69, 93
1:65 69
1:70 75
2:1–5 72
2:2 70
3:3 71
3:4 75
4:14 93
4:15 69
4:15–17 92
4:16–17 76, 80
4:16–18 76
4:16–20 70
4:17 92
4:17–20 74
4:18 79
4:20 83n37
4:31 71
4:44 69, 92
5:3 69
5:17 80
6:3 77
6:6 71
6:11 69
7:3 94
7:17 69
8:1 71, 78n27
8:8 76
8:39 69, 71, 79
9:1–2 94
9:2 71, 78n27
9:4 76
10:24 76
10:26 77
11:1–7 69
12:3 71, 78, 80
13:16 76
13:32 69
13:43 76
16 146
16:1–9 69
16:6, 7 70, 72
18:18 79
20:17 77
20:24 70
20:27 78
20:42 75
23:4 82
23:20 69
23:30 70
23:38 70
24:27 69
24:44 74
24:44–45 79
24:45 78
24:47 71, 78, 78n27

John

1:14 81
1:23 75
2:17, 22 83
5:39 77
7:15 93
7:16 93
7:35 82
7:40–42 77
7:52 77
10:35 81
12:15 83
15:20 83
19:20 83
20:30 74n16
20:30–31 83
21:24–25 83
21:35 74n16

Acts

1:20	75
2:4, 14	69
2:16	75
2:37–47	218
3:2	75
4:2	71
5:21, 25, 42	71
5:34	80
5:37	70
5:42	69
6:7	81
7:38	75
7:42	75
8:5	69, 71, 78n27
8:17	68, 85
8:26–35	74
8:27–28	80
8:28	77
8:28, 30, 32	77
8:30	68
8:35	78, 79
9:2	72, 94
9:42	69
10:36	78n27
11:16	83
11:26	69, 71
12:21	69, 70, 85
13:15, 27	76
13:27	80
14:3	71
14:9	80
15:20, 30	69
15:21	69, 76, 79, 80
15:23–29	94
15:26	70
15:27	95
15:30	72
15:31	76n21
15:33	95
15:35	71
15:36ff	95
17:2	69, 77
17:11	77, 80
17:13	81
17:21	69
17:23	70, 72
18:4, 19	69
18:11	71, 72
18:24–25	77
18:24–28	71
18:26	71
19:8	71
19:8, 9	69
19:19	70, 75n17
20:35	83
21:25	69
21:40	69
22:2	69
22:3	80
22:5	94
23:25, 33	69, 72
23:34	76n21
26:5	69
28:31	71

Romans

1:2	76n21
2:15	73
2:18	80
2:21	80
2:27	76n21
3:2	75
3:19	68
7:6	76n21
9:6	81
10:8, 15	79
10:14–15	78, 80
15:4	78, 79
16:1–3	72
16:7	82

1 Corinthians

1:23	78n27
10:11	79
11:17–26	81
14:36	81
15:1–8	81

2 Corinthians

1:13	76n21
3:2	73
3:6–7	76n21

2 Corinthians (*continued*)

3:7 73
3:14, 15 76

Galatians

1:4 216
3:10 74n16
3:15 218
6:15 216

Ephesians

3:4 76n21
4:14 82n34

Philippians

2:19–24 72
4:3 73

Colossians

2:14 72
2:22 82n34
4:16 76n21
5:16 77

1 Thessalonians

1:2–10 218
5:27 76n21, 77

2 Thessalonians

3:6 81

1 Timothy

1:3 82n34
1:7 80
2:12 82
4:1, 11 82n34
4:13 76, 80
6:2, 3 82n34

2 Timothy

3:15 76n21
3:16 79
4:3 82n34
4:13 75n16

Titus

1:11 82
2:3–5 82

Philemon

19 231

Hebrews

4:6 79
5:12 75, 80
8:10 73
9:19 74
10:7 74m16
10:16 73
12:23 72
13:9 82n34

1 Peter

4:11 75

2 Peter

2:1 82n34
3:16 73n14

1 John

9, 10 82n34

Jude

1:17 83

Revelation

1:2, 9 81
1:3 68, 76n21
1:7 73n13
2:14 82
2:15 82
3:3 83
3:5 73
5:1–2 73n13

6:9 81
20:4 81
20:12, 15 73
21:12 70
22:18–19 73n13

QUR'AN

10:37 180n29
12:88 182
17:1 182
25:32 178
41:2f 180
41:44 180n29
43:4 179
51 181
56:77–80 178n23
69:41–42 176
69:43 176–77
70 181
75 181
79 181
80:11–16 178
85:21–22 178n23
85:22 178
112 182–85
112:1 183
112:3 185
112:4 185

Subject Index

Specific citations to scriptures and related documents (Hebrew Bible, Qur'an, New Testament, Mishnah, Tosefta, and Talmud) are listed in the separate Index of Citations. Names beginning with al- are alphabetized under the main part of the name.

Abbasid-Umayyad rivalry and oral transmission of hadith, 62–63
R. Abbahu *b. Roš Haš*, 55n33
ʿAbd Allāh ibn al-ʿAlāʾ of Damascus, 50n3
ʿAbd al-Malik (caliph), 245
Abū Bakr (caliph), 242, 275
Abū Tammām, *Ḥamāsah*, 262–65, 275
acrostics, 29
Acts. *See* Luke-Acts; *specific citations in* Index of Citations
Aelius Theon, 68, 69
Aeschylus, *Prometheus Bound*, 24n7
Africanist perspective on orality-scribality, xvi–xvii, xxi, 280–91, 299
  elusiveness of orality as concept, 283–85
  epistemologies of the oral and the written, 288–89
  multi-literacies and multi-oralities, 281–93, 289–91, 295
  teleological and evolutionary paradigms, fading influence of, 285–88
Agoras or word-marketplaces, 2–3, 7–11, 17, 295
ʿĀʾisha (wife of Muhammad), 244
Alberti, Leon Battista, 159
Alexander, Elizabeth Shanks, 147–48
Alexander, Loveday, 80, 82, 83, 86
codex Alexandrinus, 149
Allen, Rosamund S., 36
Alster, Bendt, 37
altered states of consciousness, performance events as, 216–18
al-Āmidī, *Al-Muwāzanah*, 263, 265
ʿAmr Dhū Kalb, 258
ʿamūd al-shiʿr (pillar of poetry), 262–63, 265, 269, 273
al-Anbārī, 275
Anii, Instruction of, 36–37
Anzu epic, 40
Apocalypse. *See* Revelation
Apollos (in Acts), 71, 77, 83
Apthorp, Michael J., 35–36
R. Aqiba, 100, 101, 104
Aquila's Greek version of Bible, 151
Arabic poetry. *See* transformation of rhetoric in Arabic poetry
Arabic-Islamic sciences, paradigm for codification of, 241, 251–52
Aristophanes, 28
artists, oral performers as, 208–10
al-Aʿshā, 258
Assmann, Jan, 150

Assyrians. *See* Mesopotamia
Atrahasis epic, 40
audience
New Testament writings as record of performance before, 196–97, 200
ordinary people as audience for Gospels, 111, 118, 119–21, 215
performance of New Testament texts as research method and, 215–16, 218, 233–35
Auerbach, Erich, 114
Augustine of Hippo, 124, 154–55, 156, 157
De Doctrina Christiana, 157
authority of oral and written religious texts, 299–302
authorship, concept of, 3, 12–15
Avesta, 252
al-Azmeh, Aziz, 172–73

Babylonian Talmud. *See* Talmud; *specific citations, in* Index of Scriptural Citations
Babylonians. *See* Mesopotamia
Bacher, Wilhelm, 103
badīʿ style (of Arabic poetry), 255, 261–66, 273–74, 296
badīʿiyyah genre (of Arabic poetry), 255–56, 266–76, 279
Bajgorić, Ćamil, 18–20
Bajgorić, Halil, 13, 19–20
balāgha (rhetoric), 170–73, 296
Bartlett, Frederic, 32–33, 34, 35, 43
Remembering (1932), 32, 40n45
Bashshār ibn Burd, 263
Bašić, Ibro, 13
Baugh, Albert C., 36
Bauman, Richard, 183n5
Ben Sira, 31
Ben-david, Abba, 39
R. Berakhiah, 102
bertsolaritza (Basque oral improvisation), 10–11
Betz, Hans Dieter, 211
Bible. *See* closure of biblical texts; living voice, scripture as; *specific entries at* Hebrew Bible *and* New Testament
Biblia *pauperum*, 114
biblical performance criticism, as discipline, 198–206
biography of the Prophet books, 244, 250–51n32
Book of Hours, 154
Book of Jubilees, 178–79
Boomershine, Tom, 225–26
Botha, Pieter, J. J., 96n10, 127
breaking the fourth wall, 225
Brockelmann, C., 275n48
Brown, Peter, 154–55
Bucer, Martin, 160
Buddhist texts, 297, 299
al-Buḥturī, 263, 265
al-Bukhārī, 62, 241, 245, 251n32, 252
Burkard, Günter, 37
Burkert, Walter, 258
Burrows, Millar, 142–43
Burton, John, 248n22
al-Būṣīrī, Abū ʿAbd Allāh Muḥammad Ibn Saʿīd, Burdah (Mantle Ode), 267–68, 269, 273

Cachia, Pierre, 268n33, 276n52
Caird, George, 211
Calvin, John, 160
canon and codex, relationship between, 148–53
Carr, David M., ix, xxi, 8, 21, 138–40, 146, 284, 293, 295, 301
Writing on the Tablet of the Heart: Origins of Scripture and Literature (2005), 23, 24, 38, 138–39
Carruthers, Mary J., 267, 271–72, 275
The Book of Memory (1990), 154n48, 158n59
Celsus, 111–12
chiastic patterns, 29, 128–29

Chinese texts, 297, 299
Christianity. *See also* closure of biblical texts; *specific entries at* New Testament; *specific New Testament texts, e.g.* Mark's Gospel
appropriation of Hebrew Bible by, 53, 111
authority in, 301
communication and transmission of knowledge in early stages of, 92–96
Gospels compared to Hebrew Bible, 112
Jewish concept of Oral Torah as response to, 53
letters and letter writing in, 69, 72–73, 76n23, 77, 85, 94–96, 106, 301
literacy of early Christians, 122–24
Nicene Creed, 184, 185
pluriformity of texts in Jesus tradition, 145–47
Qur'anic age coinciding with patristic era of, 172
Qur'an's *sūrat al-ikhlāṣ* and, 184, 185
reciprocity, interdependence, and overlap of the oral and the written, 293
shared background of Jewish, Christian, and Islamic texts, 298–99
sociopolitical context, importance of, 296
viewed as renewal or fulfillment of Israel, 111, 120, 126, 129, 130, 131, 132–33
classical world. *See* Greco-Roman world
clausulas in Qur'an, 181–82
Clement of Alexandria, 122–23
closure of biblical texts, xxii, 137–66
codex and canon, relationship between, 148–53
education/enculturation paradigm and, 138–40
media technologies, human effects of, 137–38
modernity and early postmodernism, development of critical approaches to Bible in, 163–66
mouvance, concept of, 140–41, 143, 145, 146, 150, 152, 159
patristic and medieval periods, 153–57
pluriformity of texts in Jewish and Christian biblical traditions, 141–48
pluriformity of types of compilations, 149, 153–54
printing and print culture, effects of, 157–63
sola scriptura, concept of, 154, 159–60
codex and canon, relationship between, 148–53
codification of Bible (chapter and verse division), 156
codification of Qur'an and hadith, xxii, 240–52
Arabic-Islamic sciences, as paradigm for codification of, 241, 251–52
comparison of processes, 246–47
deliberate collections as second phase of, 249
hadith, historical codification process of, 243–47
loose notes as first phase of, 247–48
Qur'an, historical codification process of, 241–43, 246
recension/redaction phase, 249–50
taṣnīf movement, 244, 245, 247, 250
Coleridge, Samuel Taylor, 166
collectivism of oral cultures, 190

communication and transmission of knowledge in antiquity, xxv, 8, 89–107. *See also* letters and letter writing
in early Christianity, 92–96
Greco-Roman philosophers, networks between, 106–7
link between communication and mobility, 89–90
as network theory, xxv, 8, 105n28
in rabbinic Judaism, 96–105
rebel leaders in Josephus' *Vita*, 90–92, 293
Roman "culture of mobility" and, 104, 282
Roman road system and, 97
conceptual correlative, 257
Connerton, Paul, 268
consciousness, performance events as altered states of, 216–18
Constantine I the Great (Roman emperor), 125
Cook, Michael, 49–50, 51, 61n47, 63n59
Cooper, Jerrold, 39, 41
Council of Trent (1546 CE), 150, 282
Counter-Reformation, 157
Cranmer, Thomas, 160
Cyprian, 96n12

Dale, Jim, 223
Danzig, Nahman, 59
Darwin, Charles, 161
Dead Sea Scrolls. *See* Qumran documents and community
democracy in media, xxii, 1–20
authorship and referentiality, 3–4, 12–16
concept of democracy, 4–7
eAgora (electronic Agora), 2, 7–11, 15–16
freeing concept of scripture from print culture, xxii, 1–20
oAgora (oral Agora), 2, 7–11, 15
oligarchic nature of text, 4–7
Pathways Project and reading democratically, 3, 16–18, 19
resemblance between oAgora and eAgora, 3, 8–11, 18–20
tAgora (textual Agora), 2, 4–7, 15
textual ideology and, 2
word-marketplaces or verbal Agoras, 2–3, 7–11, 17, 295
Descartes, René, 164
Dewey, Dennis, 195
Dewey, Joanna, 127
Didachê ("The Teaching of the Twelve Apostles"), 117
discourse analysis, 203–4, 221
distributed authorship, 13–15
Doane, Alger N., 36, 38
Dome of the Rock, Jerusalem, 295
Douris cup 2285 (Berlin), 28
Duffy, Eamon, 154
Duggan, Hoyt N., 36

Eco, Umberto, *The Name of the Rose* (1983), 139–40n6
Edubba dialogue, 24n5
education/enculturation
closure of biblical texts and, 138–40
Hebrew Bible, composition and revision of, 22–23
literary-educational systems in Mesopotamia, Egypt, Greece, and Israel, 25–31
proclamation and teaching in New Testament and, 78–84, 85–86
effort/striving after meaning, 32, 33, 43
Egypt
literary-educational system, 26–27, 28, 29
manuscript evidence for memory variants, 36–37
Eisenstein, Elizabeth, 159, 161, 162, 163
R. Eleazar b. Azariah, 99
electronic revolution. *See* Internet technology

enculturation. *See* education/enculturation
Enuma Elish, 22
codex Ephraemi Rescriptus, 149
Epiphanius, 124
epistemologies of the oral and the written, 288–89
equiprimordiality, 145
Erasmus, Desiderius, 161, 162
essentialist preference for oral over written, arguments against, 2, 50
ethnography of speaking, xv
ethnopoetics, xvi
Euripides, 28
Eusebius of Caesarea, 125
 Canon Tables, 150, 152–53
 Historia Ecclesiastica, 122n29
evolutionary and teleological paradigms, fading influence of, 285–88
eWorld Link-map, 18

Faro, Pam, 219
Finnegan, Ruth, ix, xiv, xvi, xxi, 2, 280, 293, 295, 299
 Oral Literature in Africa (1970), xvii
 Oral Poetry (1977/1992), xvii
Fishman, Talya, ix, xxiii, 2, 49, 281, 289, 293, 299, 300
Fitzmyer, Joseph A., 75n18
five daily Muslim prayers, xxiv
Flavius Josephus. *See* Josephus
Foley, John Miles, ix–x, xv, xxii, 1, 121n26, 283, 285, 286, 287, 288, 295, 298
 How to Read an Oral Poem (2012), 16
 Pathways of the Mind: Oral Tradition and the Internet (2012), 16–17
 The Wedding of Mustajbey's Son Bećirbey as Performed by Halil Bajgoric (2004), 18–20
folkloristics, xvi, 128
form and genre criticism, 203
fourth wall, breaking, 225
Fox, Robin Lane, 93n5
Fraade, Steven D., 148n27
Frei, Hans, 197
fundamentalism of nineteenth and twentieth centuries, 161

R. Gamliel II, 98–99
R. Gamliel the Elder, 99, 100–101
genre and form criticism, 203
Geonim
 motives for guarding oral transmission, 53–55, 63–64
 responsa, forerunner of, 103
Giesecke, Michael, 159
Gilgamesh epic, 22, 26, 38, 40, 41
girsaot (oral formulations learned from a master), 59
gnosticism, 150
Gospels. *See specific entries at* New Testament; *specific gospel books*
Grafton, Anthony, 150–51
Graham, William A., x, 2, 110, 113, 114, 117, 175, 292
 Beyond the Written Word: Oral Aspects of Scripture in the History of Religion (1987), xvii–xviii, 287
Great Divide, xiv, xvii, xix, 23, 290
Greco-Roman world. *See also* Homer, *Iliad* and *Odyssey*
 "culture of mobility" in, 104, 282
 Judean revolts, 90–92, 133, 144
 literacy in Roman Judea, 115–17, 122, 189
 literary-educational system in Greece, 27–29
 oral culture of, 189–90
 philosophers, networks between, 106–7
 road system, 97
guarding oral transmission, xxiii, 49–64
 continued emphasis on oral transmission of hadith after official written collection, 61–64, 246, 248

disparate Jewish motives for, 51–58, 63–64
Oral Torah, concept of, 51, 53, 57
possible Jewish origins of emphasis on oral transmission of hadith, 49–50
Qur'an, resistance to codification of, 243
written-down "oral" texts in Judaism, treatment of, 58–61
Gunner, Liz, xvii
guslari (South Slavic oral epic singers), xv, 13–15
Gutenberg, Johannes, 5, 8, 158–59, 163, 165

hadith. *See also* codification of Qur'an and hadith
continued emphasis on oral transmission of, 61–64, 246, 248
defined, 240
elusiveness of concept of orality and, 285
notes, making and treatment of, 61, 241, 244, 247, 248
possible Jewish origins of emphasis on oral transmission of, 49–50
taṣnīf movement, 244, 245, 247, 250
written collections of, 62, 241, 245, 247, 249
Ḥafṣa (daughter of ʿUmar I), 242, 243
R. Hai Gaon, 55–57
Haines-Eitzen, Kim, 125
al-Ḥajjāj b. Yūsuf, 295
R. Halafta, 98-99
al-Ḥamawī, Abū Bakr Ibn Ḥijjah, *Khizānat al-Adab wa-Ghāyat al-Arab*, 274–76, 279
Hammurabi's code, 301
al-Ḥarīrī, 276
harmonization trend, 41–42
Harris, William, 27
Harry Potter books, performance of, 223
Hārūn al-Rashīd, 262
Havelock, Eric A., xxii, 257, 259
Hearon, Holly, x, xix, 67, 282, 284, 289, 293–94, 296, 300
heart, writing texts on, xviii, xx, 24, 26, 28, 30–31
Hebrew Bible. *See also* closure of biblical texts
authority of, 300
chapter and verse divisions, 156
"finding" of ancient books in, 116
Gospels compared to, 112
inclusion in Christian Bible, 53, 111
Masoretic *textus receptus*, 141–44
multiple textual traditions, 116
New Testament references to, 74–78, 115, 117–19, 235
Origen's *Hexapla*, 150–52, 153
persistent oral dimension of, 287
vernacular, Bible translated into, 162–63
Hebrew Bible, composition and revision of, 21–44
character of memorized and performed versus purely written texts, 31–35
dichotomies between orality and literacy, importance of overcoming, 23–24
education/enculturation of elites as primary context for, 22–23
expansion, tendency toward, 40, 43
harmonization trend, 41–42, 43
heart, writing texts on, xviii, xx, 24, 26, 28, 30–31
implications of, 43–44
literary-educational systems in Mesopotamia, Egypt, Greece, and Israel, 25–31

Hebrew Bible (*continued*)
manuscript evidence for oral-written transmission and revision, 39–42
material technology versus cognitive technology of, 22
memory variants, 35–38, 39–40
music, possible role of, 23–24, 28
preservation of ancient written materials, overall trend toward, 42–43
scholarly neglect of, 22
Herod Agrippa, 69, 70, 85
Herod Antipas, 76, 129, 131
Herodotus, 4
Hezser, Catherine, x, xxv, 8, 53n11, 89, 281, 293, 296, 298, 301
Hieracas (Egyptian professional copyist), 124
al-Ḥillī, Ṣafī al-Dīn, 268–69, 270–71, 272–73, 275, 276, 279
Hippolytus of Rome, 124
Hishām (caliph), 245
historical criticism, 165, 202
R. Hiyya b. Ba, 103
Homer, *Iliad* and *Odyssey*
on democracy, 4
Greek literary-educational system and, 28, 29
as long-duration literature, 22
manuscript evidence for oral transmission in, 31–36
oligarchic nature of text and literacy, 5
orality, Homeric, xv
pathway-driven power of OT in, 9
Honko, Lauri, 183n5
Horsley, Richard, x–xi, xx, xxiv, 5, 110, 215, 282, 294, 295, 298, 299–300
Hours, Book of, 154
Human Genome Project, 260
Humanism, 161, 165
humanistic scholarship, xiv, 165, 285
Hunter, Ian, 34–35
Hus, Jan, and Hussites, 115
Hymes, Dell, xvi
Hymn to the Inundation, 27
hypomnêmata versus *syngrammata*, 58–60, 61n47

Ibn ʿAbbās, 244
Ibn Abī al-Iṣbaʿ, 273
Ibn Ḥazm, 59n35
Ibn Isḥāq, "Book of Campaigns," 245
Ibn Malik, *Alfiyyah*, 271
Ibn Masʿūd, ʿAbdallāh, 242, 246
Ibn al-Muʿtazz, ʿAbd Allāh, *Kitāb al-Badīʿ*, 273
Ibn Saʿd, *Ṭabaqāt*, 50n3
Ibn Shihāb al-Zuhrī, 50n3
ideological criticism, 204
iʿjāz al-qurʾān (doctrine of miraculous inimitability of Qur'an), 265–66, 270–71
Instruction of Anii, 36–37
Instruction of Merikare, 26
Instruction of Ptah-Hotep, 22, 26, 37
Internet technology (IT)
authorship and referentiality in, 3–4, 12–16
democracy in media and eAgora, 2, 7–11
OT and IT, resemblance between, 3, 8–11, 18–20
pathway-driven power of, 8–10
Pathways Project and reading democratically, 3, 16–18
scholarly research and, xviii–xix
Islam. *See also* codification of Qur'an and hadith; guarding oral transmission; hadith; transformation of rhetoric in Arabic poetry; *specific entries at* Qur'an
Arabic-Islamic sciences, paradigm for codification of, 241, 251–52
authority in, 301
biography of the Prophet books, 244, 250–51n32
five daily Muslim prayers, xxiv

Jāhiliyyah (pre-Islamic period), 256, 261, 267
Mishnah, Muslim views on transcription of, 50
reciprocity, interdependence, and overlap of the oral and the written, 293, 294
shared background of Jewish, Christian, and Islamic texts, 298–99
sociopolitical context, importance of, 295–96
Islamic Manifest Destiny, 261, 264
Israel, ancient and late antique
cultural tradition and performances of Mark's Gospel, 126–27
literacy in Roman Judea, 115–17, 122, 189
literary-educational system in, 29–31
manuscript evidence for memory variants, 38
revolts in, 90–92, 133, 144
scribal oral tradition in, 116–17
Vita of Josephus, communication between rebel leaders in, 90–92
IT. *See* Internet technology

Jaffee, Martin, 53, 116–17, 147–48
Jāhiliyyah (pre-Islamic period), 256, 261, 267, 271
al-Jāḥiẓ, 270
Al-Bayān wa-al-Tabyīn, 260
James, epistle of
circulation of, 194
length of performance of, 211
performance as research method, 206, 207, 211
scripture, not originally regarded as, 195
Jerusalem Talmud. *See* Talmud; *specific citations, in* Index of Scriptural Citations
Jews. *See* Judaism
John's Gospel. *See also specific citations, under* Index of Scriptural Citations
composition by ear, 191
as drama, 195
length of performance of, 196
performance as research method, 206, 211, 218, 226, 231
Josephus
on communication between rebel leaders, 90–92, 293
evidence for oral-written education in, 31
Jewish Antiquities, 120
Jewish War, 120
popular movements in Galilee and, 120
scriptural materials in works of, 143
Vita, 90–92
Joubert, Annekie, xvii
Jousse, Marcel, xiv–xv
Le Style oral rhythmique et mnémotechnique chez les Verbo-moteurs (1925), xiv, xvi
Jubilees, Book of, 178–79
R. Judah the Patriarch, 60
Judaism. *See also* closure of biblical texts; Geonim; guarding oral transmission; Mishnah; performance, Jewish texts as; Pharisees; rabbinic Judaism; Talmud; Tosefta; *specific entries at* Hebrew Bible
pluriformity of texts in, 141–45, 147–48
Qur'an's *sūrat al-ikhlāṣ* and, 183, 184
reciprocity, interdependence, and overlap of the oral and the written, 293
Sadducees, 77, 118–19
shared background of Jewish, Christian, and Islamic texts, 298–99
Shema, xxiv, 183

Judaism (*continued*)
- sociopolitical context, importance of, 296

Judea. *See* Israel, ancient and late antique
al-Jurjānī, ʿAbd al-Qāhir, 266, 270
Justin Martyr, 124

Kairouan, sages of, 53–57
Kant, Immanuel, 166
Kelber, Werner H., xi, xiii, xxii, xxiv, 2, 6, 12, 76n20, 113, 130, 137, 282, 284, 287, 288, 292, 293, 297–98, 300
- *The Oral and The Written Gospel* (1983/1997), 127–28, 132

Kirk, Alan, 141n7
Kister, Menahem, 51
al-kitāb (the book), Qur'an as, 175, 177, 179–81, 240, 242
Kukuruzović, Mujo, 13

Lauterbach, Jacob, 103
lectionaries, 153, 242, 247–48
Leipoldt, Johannes, and Ludwig D. Morenz, *Heilige Schriften* (1953), 297
letters and letter writing. *See also* Paul and Pauline epistles
- in early Christianity, 69, 72–73, 76n23, 77, 85, 94–96, 106, 301
- in Josephus' *Vita*, 91–92
- in rabbinic Judaism, 100, 101–3
- of ʿUrwa ibn az-Zubayr, 245

Levine, Louis, 37
Lieberman, Saul, 58, 59
link-maps, 18
literacy
- of early Christians, 122–24
- in Roman Judea, 115–17, 122, 189
- transformation of rhetoric in Arabic poetry and, 255, 259–66
- vernacular print Bibles and, 162

little tradition, 120–21, 215
liturgical dimensions of scripture, 297–98
living voice, scripture as, xviii, xx–xxi, xxv, 298, 302
- Mark's Gospel and, 122, 124
- in medieval period, 154
- New Testament, interplay between spoken and written word in, 68, 75, 76, 78–80, 84–86
- as oral authority, 154, 287
- performance as research method and, 219
- Qur'an and, 185
- for Reformation leaders, 160
- Scripture-Bible (as living voice), xx-xxi, 75-86, 124, 154, 287

Lollards, 115
long-duration literature, concept of, xx, 21–23, 295
Lord, Albert, xv–xvi, xxii, 13, 145
Lord's Prayer, xxiv
Loubser, Bobby, "How Do You Report What Was Said with a Smile?" (2004), 219
Luke-Acts. *See also specific citations, under* Index of Scriptural Citations
- length of performance of, 196
- oral re-composition of Mark, Luke as, 191
- "orderly narrative," self-assertions about, 112
- performance as research method, 206, 211, 218
- on Roman destruction of Jerusalem as God's punishment for killing of Jesus, 133

Luther, Martin, 160, 162–63
LXX (Septuagint), 143, 151, 196

Mack, Burton, 110
Madigan, Daniel, 173, 175, 177
madīḥ nabawī (praise poem to the Prophet Muhammad), 267, 271–76
Maimonides, 60n43, 61n45, 156

Mālik b. Anas, *Muwaṭṭa*ʾ, 245
R. Mana, 102–3
manuscript technology, 156
Marcionism, 150
Mark's Gospel, 110–34. *See also specific citations, in* Index of Scriptural Citations
  Christianity viewed as renewal or fulfillment of Israel in, 111, 120, 126, 129, 130, 131, 132–33
  composition of, 115–19, 191
  date of written composition of, 194
  dependence on oral communication in Roman Judea and, 119–25
  familiarity of story to hearers, 126
  freeing concept of scripture from print culture, 113–15
  Hebrew Bible, references to, 74–78, 115, 117–19
  inclusion in Christian scriptures, 111–12
  Israelite cultural tradition and, 126–27
  length of performance of, 196, 211
  oral narrative features and devices, 127–32
  oral performance of, 79, 86, 121–22, 125–34, 191, 298
  ordinary people as audience for, 111, 118, 119–21, 215
  performance as research method, 206, 207, 211, 213, 215, 216, 221, 222, 223, 227, 229, 230, 232, 235–36
  as proclamation when read aloud, 79, 86
  resonance with hearers in context, 132–34
  whole, performance as, 196
al-Marzūqī, 262–63
Matthew's Gospel. *See also specific citations, in* Index of Scriptural Citations
  audience for, 111
  length of performance of, 196
  as oral re-composition of Mark, 191
  performance as research method, 216, 234
  performative aspects of, 298
  read as anti-Judaism, 132
  Sermon on the Mount, 127, 206, 211
al-Mawṣilī, ʿIzz al-Dīn, 274, 275, 279
al-Maʿarrī, Abū al-ʿAlāʾ, 266
McAuliffe, Jane, 177
McGuire, Martin R. P., 96n12
McKenzie, Steven, *Deuteronomic History*, 39–40n44
meaning, effort/striving after, 32, 33, 43
media. *See also* democracy in media; Internet technology; scroll technology
  codex and canon, relationship between, 148–53
  as context for orality-scribality in scripture, piety, and practice, xxii–xxv
  Ong's theory on human effects of, 137–38, 149
  socio-cultural location (of different media), 23, 28, 51–64, 82–84, 182 85
megilot setarim (sequestered scrolls), 59, 60
memory
  capacity for memorization in oral cultures, 190–91
  character of memorized and performed versus purely written texts, 31–35
  Greek literary-educational system, memory training in, 28–29
  manuscript-memorial culture of Middle Ages, 154n48, 267, 271–72, 294
  memory variants, 35–38, 39–40, 125

memory (*continued*)
mnemonic imperative, 255, 259–60, 261
in patristic and medieval periods, 154–56
performance as research method and, 210, 211–12, 213–14, 220
Menache, Sophia, 105
Merikare, Instruction of, 26
Mesopotamia
expansion, tendency toward, 40
literary-educational system, 25–26, 27, 28, 29
manuscript evidence for oral-written transmission and revision in, 39–41
memory variants from, 37–38
metaphor and simile, expression of abstract concepts in oral context through, 257–58
Mills, Margaret A., xxiv*n*12
Mishnah. *See also specific citations, in* Index of Scriptural Citations
communication and transmission of knowledge between rabbis in, 98, 99–101, 104–5
Jewish views on transcription of, 60
Muslim views on transcription of, 50
performative effects of, 148
mnemonic imperative, 255, 259–60, 261
mobility and communication. *See* communication and transmission of knowledge in early Judaism and Christianity
Monroe, James, 256
Montanism, 150
Moore, Stephen, 166
Morenz, Ludwig D., and Johannes Leipoldt, *Heilige Schriften* (1953), 297
Morić, Salko, 13
mouvance, concept of, 140–41, 143, 145, 146, 150, 152, 159
Müller, David Heinrich, 181
multi-literacies and multi-oralities, 281–93, 289–91, 295
multi-modal performance, 288
multiple textual traditions in Hebrew Bible, 116
multisensory character and function of scripture, xxi–xxii
al-muṣḥaf (codex), Qur'an as, 172–75, 242–43, 246, 294
Muslim ibn al-Ḥajjāj, 62, 241, 245, 252
Muslim ibn al-Walīd, 263
Muslims. *See* Islam
Mutakallimūn, 263, 264
al-Mutanabbī, Aḥmad Abū al-Ṭayyib, 266, 269
Muʿallaqah of ʿAntarah, 258
al-Muʿtaṣim, 262

al-Nabhānī, Yūsuf ibn Ismāʿīl, 276
al-Nabulusī, ʿAbd al-Ghanī, 268n33, 276n52
narrative criticism, 165–66, 203, 214, 221
Nechemiah of Bet Deli, 100–101
Nelson, David, 281, 284, 285, 289, 293, 297
network theory, xxv, 8, 105n28. *See also* communication and transmission of knowledge in early Judaism and Christianity
Neusner, Jacob, 101
Neuwirth, Angelika, xi, xx, xxii*n*11, xxiii, xxiv, 4, 170, 283, 284, 289, 294, 296, 299
New Criticism, 166
New Testament. *See also* closure of biblical texts; performance, New Testament writings as record of; performance of New Testament texts as research method; *specific texts, e.g.* Revelation
audience for, 111

authority of, 299–300, 301
chapter and verse divisions, 156
Hebrew Bible, references to, 74–78, 115, 117–19, 235
"orderly narrative," Luke's self-assertions about, 112
persistent oral dimension of, 287
vernacular, Bible translated into, 162–63
New Testament, interplay of written and spoken word in, 67–87
complex and porous nature of, 84–86
examples of, 68–70
Hebrew Bible, references to, 74–78
in proclamation and teaching, 78–84, 85–86
social dimensions of, 70–74
tradition, language of, 81–82
"word of God," 81
Newman, Jane O., 162
Nicene Creed, 184, 185
Njegoš, Petar Petrović, 15
nushaot (written inscriptions), 59

oligarchic nature of text and literacy, 4–6
Olsen, Alexandra Hennessy, 36
Ong, Walter J., xxii, 147, 164, 166, 257, 259
"Technology Outside Us and Inside Us" (1992), 137–38, 149
open-source software, distributed authorship of, 13
Opland, Jeff, xvii, 296
Oral Theory, xv
Oral Torah, concept of, xiii, xxiii, 51, 53, 57, 289
Oral Tradition (OT)
concept of, xv, xvi–xvii, xxiii
IT and OT, resemblance between, 3, 8–11, 18–20
in narrative, 127–30
Oral Tradition (*OT;* journal) and *eOT*, 6–7, 283n5
Oral-Formulaic Hypothesis (Parry-Lord Thesis), xv, 256
orality criticism, 204, 215
orality-scribality in scripture, piety, and practice, xiii–xxv, 292–302
Africanist perspective on, xvi–xvii, xxi, 280–91, 299 (*See also* Africanist perspective on orality-scribality)
authority of religious texts and, 299–302
closure of biblical texts, xxii, 137–66 (*See also* closure of biblical texts)
communication and transmission of knowledge, xxv, 8, 89–107 (*See also* communication and transmission of knowledge in antiquity)
democracy in media and, xxii, 1–20 (*See also* democracy in media)
elusiveness of orality as concept, 283–85
epistemologies of the oral and the written, 288–89
essentialist preference for oral over written, arguments against, 2, 50
freeing concept of scripture from print culture, 113–15
guarding oral transmission, xxiii, 49–64 (*See also* guarding oral transmission)
in Hebrew Bible, 21–44 (*See also specific entries at* Hebrew Bible)
IT evolution and, xviii–xix (*See also* Internet technology)
liturgical dimensions of scripture and, 297–98
living voice, scripture as, xviii, xx–xxi, xxv, 298, 302 (*See also* living voice, scripture as)
media context, xxii–xxv

orality-scribality (*continued*)
multi-literacies and multi-oralities, 281–93, 289–91, 295
in New Testament, 67–87, 110–34 (*See also specific entries at* New Testament; *specific texts, e.g.* Mark's Gospel)
performance, scripture as, xxii, 188–236 (*See also specific entries at* performance)
in Qur'an, 137–66 (*See also specific entries at* Qur'an)
reciprocity, interdependence, and overlap of the oral and the written, 293–95
scholarly context, xiii–xix
shared background of Jewish, Christian, and Islamic texts, 298–99
social context, importance of, 295–97
teleological and evolutionary paradigms, fading influence of, 285–88
transformation of rhetoric in Arabic poetry and, xxii, 255–79 (*See also* transformation of rhetoric in Arabic poetry)
world religions, in context of, xix–xxii
Origen, 96n12, 111–12, 124
Hexapla, 150–52, 153
Orr, Allen, 157
OT. *See* Oral Tradition
OT (*Oral Tradition;* journal) and *eOT*, 6–7, 283n5

Palestinian Talmud. *See* Talmud; *specific citations, in* Index of Scriptural Citations
Papias, bishop of Hierapolis, 122, 124
Parker, David, 125, 145–47
Parry, Milman, xiv, xv, xxii, 13, 31–32, 33, 34, 35, 37
Parry-Lord Thesis (Oral-Formulaic Hypothesis), xv, 256
pathway-driven power of OT and IT, 7–11
Pathways Project, 3, 16–18, 19
Paul and Pauline epistles, 301. *See also specific citations, in* Index of Scriptural Citations
authority of, 301
circulation of, 194, 196
communication and transmission of knowledge in, 92–96, 106
interplay of written and spoken word in, 69, 71–73, 74n15, 75, 76nn20–21, 77, 79–80, 82
length of performance of, 196
in patristic and medieval periods, 155
performance, as research method, 207, 208, 211, 212, 213, 216, 218, 224, 227, 230–34
performance, New Testament as written record of, 191, 194, 196–97
reciprocity, interdependence, and overlap of the oral and the written, 293
rhetorical nature of, xiii
specific communities, letters meant for, 194
"people of the book," 242, 248
performance, Jewish texts as
character of memorized and performed versus purely written texts, 31–35
Mishnah, performative effects of, 148
performance, New Testament writings as record of, xxii, 188–205
act of performing, 200
audiences, 196–97, 200, 225–27
biblical performance criticism as new approach to, 198–206

composition by ear in oral cultures, 191
evidence for, 188–98
imagining ancient performance events, 199–201
locations for performances, 201
Mark's Gospel, 79, 86, 121–22, 125–34, 191, 298
memory, capacity for, 190–91
in oral culture of first-century world, 189–90
oral/written composition, 199
performers, 200
reorienting New Testament critical methods toward, 202–5
rhetorical impact, 201
scripture, texts not originally viewed as, 195–96
scroll technology and, 192–95
sociohistorical circumstances, 201
whole, individual writings performed as, 196–97
performance criticism, as discipline, 198–206
performance of New Testament texts as research method, 205–36
abbreviated versus whole performances, 211, 213–14
altered states of consciousness and, 216–18
artist, performer as, 208–10
audience and, 215–16, 218, 233–35
biblical performance criticism, as genre, 205–6
emotion, conveying, 229–30
humor, conveying, 230–31
interpretation and exegesis through performance, 207–8, 235–36
language of performance, 210–11
memory and memorization, 210, 211–12, 213–14, 220
nonverbal communication, 228–29
onstage/offstage focus, 225–27
performers, 208–13
personification of characters, 222–24
post-performance conversations with audience, 235
rhetorical impact, 233–35
script, acting out composition as, 218–22
style of performance, 212
subtext issues, 227–28
temporal dimensions of text, experiencing, 231–33
text-based versus fluid performance, 211–12
world of composition, imaginative presentation of, 213–15
performance studies, as discipline, 204, 288
Person, Raymond, "The Ancient Israelite Scribe as Performer" (1998), 38
Peter
three-fold denial of Jesus by, 128, 131
"up country" dialect of, 119
1 Peter. *See also specific citations, in* Index of Scriptural Citations
circulation of, 194
length of performance of, 196, 211
performance as research method, 206, 207
Petrus Ramus (Pierre de la Ramée), 164–65
phantom texts, 58–61
Pharisees
guarding oral transmission, 53n11
interplay of written and spoken word in New Testament and, 77, 82, 94
Mark's Gospel, emergence of, 116, 118–20, 129, 131

Pharisees (*continued*)
performance as research method and, 222, 226
Philo of Alexandria, 31
philosophers, Greco-Roman, networks between, 106–7
Pirkoi ben Baboi, *Epistle*, 54–55, 60, 63, 64
Plato, *Laws*, 28
pluriformity of texts, 141–48
poetry, Arabic. *See* transformation of rhetoric in Arabic poetry
printing and print culture
print culture-typography, 113–15, 138, 157–63
Prophecy of Neferti, 27
proportions in Qur'an, 181
Protestantism
Reformation and closure of biblical text, 157, 160–63
rise of modern historical critical scholarship and, 165
Psalms, Qur'anic suras as re-readings of, 176. *See also specific citations, in* Index of Scriptural Citations
Ptah-Hotep, Instruction of, 22, 26, 37

Q (Gospel prototype), 83, 191
qaṣīdah style (of Arabic poetry), 256–59, 265, 266, 271, 272
al-Qāsim ibn Muḥammad, 50n3
Quintilian, *Institutio Oratoria*, 68, 69, 77, 80, 83n39, 84, 86, 284
Qumran documents and community
1QIsa[a], 38
1QS (Community Rule), 39, 116–17, 127
4QRP, 39, 40
4QSam[a], 38
11QT (Temple Scroll), 39, 41
closure of biblical texts and, 142–45, 148
Damascus Rule, 127
education/enculturation and, 36, 38–41
emergence of Mark's Gospel and, 116–17, 127
interplay between written and spoken word, 76n23
Qur'an, 170–85. *See also* codification of Qur'an and hadith; *specific citations, in* Index of Scriptural Citations
authority of, 301
Book of Jubilees and, 178–79
characteristics of orality in, 181–82
clausulas in, 181–82
display copies of, 295, 298
doctrine of miraculous inimitability of *(iʿjāz al-qurʾān)*, 265–66, 270–71
elusiveness of concept of orality and, 285–86
as *al-kitāb* (the book), 175, 177, 179–81, 240, 242
as lectionary, 242, 247–48
as *al-muṣḥaf* (codex), 172–75, 242–43, 246, 294
persistent oral dimension of, 287
proportions in, 181
Psalms, suras as re-readings of, 176
rasm (undotted and unvocalized consonantal text), 243, 246, 247
reciprocity, interdependence, and overlap of the oral and the written, 294
as recitation *(qurʾān)*, 172–75, 240, 242
as rhetoric *(balāgha)*, 170–73
sociopolitical context, importance of, 295–96
strategies of vindicating scriptural orality in, 175–81
as *ṣuḥuf* ("leaves"), 242, 246
sūrat al-ikhlāṣ, oral and exegetical nature of, 182–85
as theologumenon, 173, 175, 179, 181, 294
as unsystematic notes, 242, 246, 247–48

ʿUthmānic recension of, 243, 250
written transmission from time of third caliph, 49

rabbinic Judaism. *See also* guarding oral transmission
chapter and verse division of Bible and, 156
communication and transmission of knowledge in, 96–105
pluriformity of texts in, 147–48
Qur'anic age coinciding with, 172
Ramism, 164–65
rasm (undotted and unvocalized consonantal text) of Qur'an, 243, 246, 247
Rayṭah, 258
reading
as oral activity in patristic and medieval periods, 156
Pathways Project and reading democratically, 3, 16–18, 19
referentiality, concept of, 3, 15–16
Reformation, 157, 160–63
re-oralization, xxiv
research method, performance as. *See* performance of New Testament texts as research method
Resh Laqish, 53
Reuchlin, Johann, *De Rudimentis Hebraicis*, 162
Revelation. *See also specific citations, in* Index of Scriptural Citations
circulation of, 194
as drama, 195
length of performance of, 196, 211
performance as research method, 206, 207, 211, 216, 224, 229, 233
scripture, not originally regarded as, 195
whole, performance as, 196, 197
rhetoric. *See also* transformation of rhetoric in Arabic poetry
balāgha, Islamic concept of, 170–73, 296
emotion and, 229–30
Paul and Pauline epistles, rhetorical nature of, xiii
performed New Testament texts, rhetorical impact of, 201, 216, 233–35
Qur'an as, 170–73
rhetorical criticism, 203
as ritual, 256–59
Rhoads, David, xi, xx, xxi, xxii, 8, 188, 285, 288, 297, 298
Riffaterre, Michael, 183
Ringgren, Helmer, 38
ritual, rhetoric as, 256–59
Romans. *See* Greco-Roman world
Rothenberg, Jerome, xvi
Rubin, David C., 37
Ruffini, Giovanni, 105n28, 107
al-Rummānī, ʿAlī ibn ʿĪsá, 266, 270

Sadducees, 77, 118–19
Samaritan Pentateuch, 143
Sanders, Paula A., xi–xii, 2, 292
"sandwich" formations in Mark's Gospel, 128, 129
Satiric Letter II, 24n6
Scaliger, Joseph Julius, 165n80
Schechner, Richard, 183n5
Schoeler, Gregor, xii, xx, xxii, xxiii, xxiv, 5, 51, 62–63, 240, 281, 289, 293, 295, 301
scribality. *See* orality-scribality in scripture, piety, and practice
"scribe" and "scribal," in Egypt and Mesopotamia, 27
scriptura sui ipsius interpres, 160
scriptural orality, concept of, xviii, xxi, xxiii–xxiv, xxv
Scripture. *See* orality-scribality in scripture, piety, and practice; *specific scriptures*

scroll technology
codex and canon, relationship between, 148–53
limited access to, 194–95
orality served by, 192
performance and, 192–95
Second Testament. *See* New Testament
sensus literalis sive historicus, 160, 165
Septuagint (LXX), 143, 151, 196
serial reproduction, 32, 34
Sermon on the Mount, 127, 206, 211
Shema, xxiv, 183
Shepherd of Hermas, 123–24
Sherira Gaon, *Epistle*, 60
Shiner, Whitney, 110–11, 124, 132, 218
simile and metaphor, expression of abstract concepts in oral context through, 257–58
Simpson, James, 161
Sinai, Nicholai, 175–81
codex Sinaiticus, 149
Sisam, Kenneth, 36
socio-cultural location (of different media), 23, 28, 51–64, 82–84, 182–85
sola scriptura, concept of, 154, 159–60
Solomon's prayer, 40n44
Song of Moses, 30
Soucek, Priscilla, 285, 294, 295, 298
source criticism, 140, 203
speech-act theory, 204
stemmatic method, 165
Stetkevych, Suzanne Pinckney, xii, xx, xxii, 15, 255, 281, 294, 296
Stock, Brian, 5
Stowers, Stanley K., 96
striving/effort after meaning, 32, 33, 43
Ṣufyān al-Thawrī, 50n3
ṣuḥuf ("leaves") of Qur'an, 242, 246
sūrat al-ikhlāṣ (Qur'an), 182–85
Symmachus' Greek version of Bible, 151
syngrammata versus *hypomnêmata*, 58–60, 61n47

Talmud. *See also specific citations, in* Index of Scriptural Citations
communication and transmission of knowledge between rabbis in, 99, 102–3
Qur'anic age coinciding with production of, 172
R. Tanhum b. Papa, 102–3
taṣnīf movement, 244, 245, 247, 250
Tedlock, Dennis, xvi
teleological and evolutionary paradigms, fading influence of, 285–88
Tertel, Hans Jürgen, 41
textual communities, 5
textual criticism
closure of biblical text and, 142, 143–44, 146, 159, 165
concept of, 12, 202
Hebrew Bible, composition and revision of, 25, 31–32, 43
Mark's Gospel, emergence of, 125
reorientation toward performance, 202
textual ideology, 2, 288, 290
al-Thaghrī, Abū Saʿīd Muḥammad ibn Yūsuf, 264
theater studies, 204
Theissen, Gerd, 93
Theodotion's Greek version of Bible, 151
theologumenon, 173, 175, 179, 181, 294
Theon (Aelius Theon), 68, 69
Thomas Aquinas, 156
Catena Aurea, 272
three Agoras or word-marketplaces, 2–3, 7–11, 17, 295
al-Tibrīzī, 275
Tigay, Jeffrey, 38, 39, 41
Tijuana, smuggling wheelbarrows through, 171
Tosefta, communication and transmission of knowledge

between rabbis in, 98–99, 101. *See also specific citations, in* Index of Scriptural Citations
transformation of rhetoric in Arabic poetry, xxii, 255–79
adab/paideia knowledge and, 275–76
ʿamūd al-shiʿr (pillar of poetry), 262–63, 265, 269, 273
badīʿ style of High Abbasid period, 255, 261–66, 273–74, 296
badīʿiyyah genre, 255–56, 266–76, 279
iʿjāz al-qurʾān (doctrine of miraculous inimitability of Qur'an) and, 265–66, 270–71
Jāhiliyyah (pre-Islamic period), 256, 261, 267, 271
literacy, effects of, 255, 259–66
madīḥ nabawī (praise poem to the Prophet Muhammad), 267, 271–76
manuscript-memorial culture of Middle Ages and, 267, 271–72
mnemonic imperative, 255, 259–60, 261
Nahḍah period (nineteenth and twentieth centuries), 266–67
Post-Classical period (1100–1850), 266–67
qaṣīdah style, 256–59, 265, 266, 271, 272
ritual, rhetoric as, 256–59
translation studies, 205
travel and communication. *See* communication and transmission of knowledge in early Judaism and Christianity
Trent, Council of (1546 CE), 150, 282
Tyndale, William, 160

Ubayy ibn Kaʿb, 242, 246
Ulrich, Eugene, 143, 144n17
ʿUmar I (caliph), 62n50, 242, 246
ʿUmar II (caliph), 62, 245
Umayyad-Abbasid rivalry and oral transmission of hadith, 62–63
ungrammaticality, concept of, 183
ʿUrwa ibn az-Zubayr, 244–45, 249
ʿUthmānic recension of Qur'an, 243, 250, 281
ʿUthman (caliph), 242–43, 246, 295

Vannutelli, Primo, 39
Vansina, Jan, *Oral Tradition: A Study in Historical Methodology* (1961), xvi–xvii
codex Vaticanus, 149
Vedas, 35, 252, 296, 299
Veldhuis, Niek, 37–38
vernacular, Bible translated into, 162–63
via moderna, 160
Volten, Axel, 36–37
vox intexta, xxi
Vujnović, Nikola, 13
Vulgate (Latin Bible), 158–59

al-Walīd (caliph), 250
Wansbrough, John, 250n28
The Wedding of Mustajbey's Son Bećirbey as Performed by Halil Bajgoric (2004), 18–20
West, Stephanie, 35–36
wheelbarrows, smuggling, 171
Widengren, Geo, 37
Wikipedia, distributed authorship of, 13
William of Ockham, 157–58
Williams, Megan, 151
written and oral texts. *See* orality-scribality in scripture, piety, and practice

R. Yaakov ben Nissim of Kairouan, 55
Yates, Frances, *The Art of Memory* (1966), 154n48
R. Yehoshua, 98–99

R. Yehudah b. Baba, 100
Yehudah b. Tavai, 103
R. Yehudah ha-Nasi, 105
Yehudai Gaon, 54–55, 63
R. Yochanan b. Beroqah, 99
R. Yochanan b. Nazif, 98
R. Yochanan b. Zakkai, 98
R. Yose, 102–3
R. Yudan the Patriarch, 103
al-Zawzanī, 275
Zayd ibn Bishr al-Taghlibī, 257
Zayd ibn Thābit, 241, 242–43
Zedda, Paolo, 11
Zewi, Tamar, 39
Zumthor, Paul, 36, 141
Zussman, Yaakov, 59